A Student's Guide to
EQUITY AND TRUSTS

This engaging introduction explores the key principles of equity and trusts law and offers students effective learning features. By covering the essentials of each topic, it ensures students have the foundations for successful further study. The law is made relevant to current practice through chapters that define and explain key legal principles. Examples set the law in context and make the subject interesting and dynamic by showing how these rules apply in real life. Key points sections and summaries help students remember the crucial points of each topic and practical exercises offer students the opportunity to apply the law. Exploring clearly and concisely the subject's key principles, this should be every equity student's first port of call.

Judith Bray is a leader in law at the University of Buckingham. She has taught property law and family law for over twenty years, having previously qualified as a barrister. She is the author of several student texts on land law and also a short casebook on equity and trusts.

A Student's Guide to
EQUITY AND TRUSTS

Judith Bray

CAMBRIDGE
UNIVERSITY PRESS

CAMBRIDGE UNIVERSITY PRESS

Cambridge, New York, Melbourne, Madrid, Cape Town,
Singapore, São Paulo, Delhi, Tokyo, Mexico City

Cambridge University Press
The Edinburgh Building, Cambridge CB2 8RU, UK

Published in the United States of America by Cambridge University Press, New York

www.cambridge.org
Information on this title: www.cambridge.org/9780521196307

First published 2012

Printed in the United Kingdom at the University Press, Cambridge

A catalogue record for this publication is available from the British Library

Library of Congress Cataloguing in Publication data
Bray, Judith, 1954–
    A student's guide to equity and trusts / Judith Bray.
        p. cm.
    Includes index.
    ISBN 978-0-521-19630-7 (hardback) – ISBN 978-0-521-15299-0 (pbk.)
    1. Equity–England. 2. Equity–Wales. 3. Trusts and trustees–England.
    4. Trusts and trustees–Wales. I. Title.
    KD674.B73 2012
    346.42′004–dc23
    2011049742

ISBN 978-0-521-19630-7 Hardback
ISBN 978-0-521-15299-0 Paperback

CONTENTS

PREFACE

Of all the subjects studied by law students equity and trusts can seem the most opaque and impenetrable. They are intimidated by the 'fog of Chancery' described by Dickens in his introduction to *Bleak House.* I have tried to lift some of this fog by explaining the principles of trusts in simple terms and then relating those principles to practical situations which affect all our lives. I have used detailed scenarios throughout the text to illustrate the key principles. I wanted to change the popular perception that the study of trusts is remote and detached from everyday life. Trusts no longer simply affect a limited section of the public but often govern the most important assets that people own, such as the family home and rights under a pension scheme. At the heart of trusts lies the relationship between the trustee and beneficiary and the strict duties imposed upon the trustee which can be traced back to the early forms of trust. Such duties are just as relevant today in cases involving commercial relationships as in the more traditional express trust. I hope that this practical approach will bring alive the subject and its many different aspects. I know that once the main principles of equity and trusts are grasped and their practical effect is fully understood this becomes a fascinating and intriguing subject.

I would like to thank Sinead Moloney at Cambridge University Press for her encouragement and support for the idea and writing of this book, also Deepa Somasunderam for her valuable contributions in reading the text and suggestions from a student's perspective on the subject and most of all I would like to thank my husband Richard without whose support, good humour and invaluable advice this book would never have been completed.

Judith Bray
University of Buckingham
June 2011

1 Historical introduction

key points

KEY POINTS ON THE HISTORICAL BACKGROUND TO EQUITY AND TRUSTS

- equity means fairness or justice;
- equity was introduced to meet the deficiencies in common law;
- common law lacked flexibility in remedies; it failed to recognise rights such as the right of a mortgagor or of a beneficiary under a trust and the writ system was inadequate;
- equity provided a 'gloss on common law' rather than a complete system of rules and worked alongside common law;
- equity was administered initially by the king with assistance from the Chancellor who was a religious person;
- the Chancellor later took sole control of equity and the Chancery Court was established;
- equity became inflexible and unpopular and consequently there were many conflicts with the common law;
- equity and common law were fused under the Judicature Acts 1873–5; and
- equity continues to exist as a separate system of law.

1 THE INTRODUCTION OF COMMON LAW

Until the Norman Conquest, there was no single system of law in England and Wales. The legal system before 1066 mainly consisted of customs that were local to a particular area and were administered and enforced locally or by the King's Council. After 1066, a system of royal courts was introduced as well as a unified system of rules, which initially existed alongside the local rules. It was a gradual process but eventually a system of law was in place that was 'common to all' in England and became common law.

2 THE INADEQUACY OF COMMON LAW

The introduction of common law was welcomed at first but gradually litigants became dissatisfied because it had a number of limitations. There were three main ways in which the common law was inadequate.

(a) The writ system

Applications to court could only be made if the claimant had the correct *writ*. Without the correct writ no application could be made. A claimant could either use the established writ or if none covered the claim exactly then the court would issue a new writ. There was an initial flexibility in allowing new writs to be issued and many litigants were later successful and were granted a remedy. Larger property owners such as the lords and barons were often forced to make compensation payments and they felt that the law was too willing to allow claimants to come to court. As a result, after 1285, it was decreed that no new writs could be introduced. From then on the claim of any litigant had to be based on one of the existing writs and if none fitted the claim the case could not be brought to court. This caused hardship to many who were prevented from accessing the court. It had the effect of making the common law very rigid and inflexible.

(b) The limitations in the remedies provided under common law

Common law was very inflexible in the types of remedies that it could provide. Damages could be claimed 'as of right' under common law if a litigant was successful but this was often not the most appropriate remedy.

> **EXAMPLE**
>
> Silas lives next to Jude. His house is some way from the main road to the nearest town and so he uses a quicker route through Jude's garden to get to the main road. He regularly uses this route although he does not have permission from Jude. The law would regard Silas as a trespasser. Jude would be able to claim damages from Silas but he would prefer an order from the court to stop Silas from using his garden because it interferes with his own enjoyment and money does not adequately compensate him for this.
>
> In this example the appropriate remedy for Jude is an *injunction* which is an order from the court that usually prevents certain behaviour.

In other situations the claimant may wish to force the defendant to act in a particular way as shown in the example below.

> **EXAMPLE**
>
> X enters into an agreement with Y to purchase Y's house. If Y refuses to proceed with the sale, damages will not fully compensate X for the loss of this opportunity. X has looked at many houses over the past six months and he has decided that Y's house satisfies all his requirements. The most appropriate remedy in this case would be an *order for specific performance*. This order would force Y to sell to X.
>
> Such a remedy was not available initially under common law.

(c) The failure of common law to recognise certain rights

The common law was also very rigid in the type of right that it was prepared to recognise. Common law would not recognise the rights of someone who did not own the property at law but had been given rights to enjoy that property. Today we know these rights as rights of a beneficiary under *a trust*. These rights are enforceable against the owner (the trustee) at law and a remedy may be granted if the trustee will not allow the beneficiary a right but instead claims the property for himself. Common law also did not recognise the rights of a mortgagor (the borrower) under *a mortgage*. Equity recognised the rights of mortgagors and would uphold their rights to recover the property against a mortgagee (the lender) on repayment of the money borrowed.

3 THE ORIGINS AND DEVELOPMENT OF EQUITY

Equity developed as a way of responding to the many problems of the common law. Many were dissatisfied once they discovered that there was no writ to cover their claim and they were left without any right to go before the court. The last resort for these claimants was to petition the king asking that the case should be heard or that a remedy other than damages be granted or that rights under a trust or a mortgage should be recognised and a remedy could be sought. The king exercised his discretion when making any decision so cases were decided on their individual facts. Many litigants were successful and this success persuaded others to approach the king for relief. The decisions were not consistent and today they would be regarded as being made on their merits rather than following previous decisions. Of course, because many were successful these cases grew in number and eventually the king sought the assistance of the Chancellor. Initially the decisions were made in the king's name but by the end of the fifteenth century they were made in the name of the Chancellor alone. At this stage equity began to be regarded as a separate system of law supplementing the gaps and deficiencies in the common law.

4 THE ROLE OF THE LORD CHANCELLOR AND THE CHANCERY COURT

(a) The Chancellor

The Chancellor was an important figure in the fourteenth and fifteenth century both as a figure close to the king and party to major decisions and also as a religious person. He was the obvious person to assist the king in deciding the petitions made to him. The Chancellor was responsible for deciding cases in ecclesiastical law or canon law. The Chancellor's religious roots were important as they affected the basis on which he made decisions, as he would always base them on fairness or conscience. The Chancellor was described as the 'keeper of the king's conscience'. However, one of the early criticisms of equity was the breadth of discretion that was reserved at first for the king and later for the Chancellor. The extent of discretion varied with whoever was Chancellor at the time. Some had a greater sense of justice and morality than others and were more willing to intervene than others. For this reason equity was said to vary 'according to the length of the Chancellor's foot'. By the seventeenth century lawyers replaced the ecclesiastics who had held the role of Chancellor. Today, there remains an element of discretion in the areas of law where equity plays a significant part. An important example is where the court decides where the ownership of the family home lies. In these cases the court will decide the case on the basis of an implied trust and here the court continues to retain for itself significant discretion in particular when quantifying the shares of the individual parties, as shown in *Stack* v. *Dowden* [2007] UKHL 17.

(b) The Court of Chancery

The decisions of the king and Chancellor were initially heard on an ad hoc basis without any particular procedure. Gradually the decision-making became formalised and decisions were heard in the Court of Chancery. This court was once an administrative department for the king but it later grew into a separate court, which administered equity. The court had separate rules and procedures from those of the common law courts. At first the Chancellor alone could decide cases, which naturally led to inordinate delays in cases reaching final judgment. In the early part of the nineteenth century, additional judges were appointed who sat specifically in the Court of Chancery and these judges could also decide cases. The most well known was the Master of the Rolls, a role created in 1833 although the first additional judge of the court was the vice chancellor appointed in 1813. At this stage there were two separate systems of law in operation: common law and equity. Cases could be brought in both the common law courts and the Court of Chancery but costs could be incurred if an action was started in the wrong court. For example if a case claiming an injunction was brought in the common law court it could not be heard and the costs of the hearing would normally be borne by the claimant.

5 THE DEFECTS OF EQUITY

Equity's ability to resolve disputes on the basis of discretion was at first welcomed by dissatisfied litigants many of whom were able to bring actions where previously they had no right. There was always a chance that their case would be decided favourably. Gradually, with the impact of law reporting, cases were decided on the basis of past decisions rather than purely on the merits of the case before the courts and the law adopted the system of precedent which took away much of the flexibility of equity. Equity became slow and cumbersome and had none of the initial advantages but instead many of the defects that had been directed at the common law, centuries earlier, had emerged.

One of the most serious defects was the need to bring separate actions in a single dispute which was both time-consuming and wasteful.

EXAMPLE

Edgar entered into a contract with his neighbour for the supply of hay and straw for his cattle over the winter. He has paid in advance for the hay. The straw has not been delivered and the hay delivered last week is of such poor quality he has had to purchase more from another farmer. Edgar would have to bring an action in the Chancery courts for an order for specific performance of the contract to supply the straw and a separate action in the common law courts for damages for his loss over the supply of the hay. These actions would run parallel to each other and involve two separate sets of lawyers and separate costs.

Fusion of common law and equity

During the nineteenth century, several acts were passed to address the problems of the conflict between common law and equity and also of having two separate systems of law operating at the same time.

1 The Common Law Procedure Act 1854 allowed common law courts limited power to grant equitable remedies; the Chancery courts also had the power to decide questions of common law. Even trial by jury was introduced into Chancery cases.
2 The Chancery Amendment Act 1858 gave the Chancery courts the power to award damages either as an alternative to or in addition to an equitable remedy.
3 The Judicature Acts 1873–5 were the most significant pieces of legislation passed to solve the problems of having separate systems of law. The main effect of the Acts was to merge the two systems of common law and equity so there was now only one system of law and procedure in England and Wales. All the judges of the newly formed Supreme Court of Judicature had jurisdiction in cases in both equity and common law. Under the 1873 Act it was laid down that in any matter where the rules of common law and equity conflicted the rules of equity were to prevail.

Although it was assumed that after 1875 there was just one system of law operating in England and Wales and that the rules of equity and common law had fused this has since been doubted. For over five hundred years two separate systems of law operated so it was inevitable that some differences would remain. However the cases in which these differences are important are comparatively rare.

One example of an area where the distinction between common law and equity remains, lies in the process of recovery of property from someone who has wrongfully taken it, known as *tracing*. Today tracing in equity and tracing in common law are based on different rules. In equity, tracing can only take place where there is a fiduciary relationship, which is not necessary at common law. This difference was criticised by Lord Millett in *Foskett* v. *McKeown* [2001] 1 AC 102 but it remains.

6 THE EMERGENCE OF THE TRUST

The trust emerged at the time of the Crusades. Knights would leave to go abroad to fight for the Crusades and they were likely to be absent for some time, possibly many years. Therefore they would leave their property with another who was entrusted with it for safekeeping. The property would be transferred into the name of the friend to be kept for the knight's return and also for the enjoyment of the rest of his family.

The transferor was called a '*feoffor*' and involved transferring the legal estate in the land to a '*feoffee to use*' (the trustee) to hold it to the use of a '*cestui que use*' (*the beneficiary*). The right of the claimant was a right called a '*use*'. If the *feoffee to use* refused to transfer the property to the *cestui que use*, the common law courts would not recognise his right. At common law the *feoffee to use* was regarded as the owner of the property but as he had made a promise to the knight who had chosen him to care for his property it was unconscionable for him to deny the claimant beneficiary a right. Such an act would offend the conscience of the court of equity.

The emergence of the trust from the original use giving enforceable rights to the beneficiary was complex and slow and involved attempts by the Crown to argue that the beneficiary owned the property so that tax would become payable on his death whereas if he only owed a lesser interest it could be avoided.

EXAMPLE

Today a trust would arise in the following situation:

SAMI (the settlor) – – – – – – – TONY (the trustee)

(owns Blackacre Farm)

BEN (the beneficiary)

SAMI is the legal owner of Blackacre Farm. He transfers the legal title to his land to TONY who now becomes owner of the property at *law*. However if SAMI tells TONY he is not the absolute owner of this property but instead TONY is now to hold the property for BEN aged 13, who cannot own land for himself because he is too young, then the law will recognise Ben's rights; and if Tony tries to take the land for his own enjoyment, then this is perceived as a breach of trust and the court will come to the aid of BEN and enforce his rights against TONY.

7 THE MAXIMS OF EQUITY

One of the main contributions of equity was the introduction of a number of maxims which can be applied generally when cases are decided in court. Maxims are used for guidance rather than as binding principles of law. There are countless examples of cases that have been decided over the past centuries with reference to one or more of these maxims. The following are some examples of the most widely used maxims but there are many others.

(a) Equity will not suffer a wrong without a remedy

One of the main criticisms of common law was its lack of flexibility in the remedies that it was able to grant and its failure to recognise certain rights such as the rights of a beneficiary under a trust. However equity will not automatically grant a remedy in all circumstances but it will intervene to ensure a fair result.

(b) Equity will not assist a volunteer

Equity will not uphold a claim of someone who has not given consideration for the promise. Beneficiaries under a trust are volunteers but equity will enforce their rights if the formalities and other requirements necessary for the creation of a valid trust have been complied with. Where the trust is not fully constituted, the court will not enforce the trust. This is discussed further in Chapter 5 under constitution of a trust.

(c) Equity will not perfect an imperfect gift

Where a donor attempts to make a gift to a donee but fails to comply with the formalities of transfer, the court will not intervene in order to perfect the gift even where there is evidence that the donor intended a gift to be made.

(d) He who comes to equity must come with clean hands

Any claimant for a remedy in equity will be denied a right if he has not behaved in good conscience himself over the matter. Unconscionable behaviour in another sphere will not affect the claim. In *Argyll (Duchess)* v. *Argyll (Duke)* [1967] Ch 302 the Duchess of Argyll brought an action against her husband to stop him from publishing confidential material about her. He argued that she could not claim an injunction because she had committed adultery and so did not come to the court with 'clean hands'. The court ignored her adultery as it was not material in the case.

(e) Equity looks to substance and not form

This is a practical maxim which shows that equity looks at the substance of an agreement rather than the form of an agreement which means it is concerned with the desired effect rather than the form in which the agreement has been put.

(f) Equity regards that as done which ought to be done

If X is obliged to carry out an act under a contract with Y which is specifically enforceable, equity will regard X as having already carried out what he promised to do. This is because he can be compelled to do so by the court. In *Walsh* v. *Lonsdale* (1882) LR 21 Ch D 9 a contract to grant a lease was treated by the court as creating an equitable lease on exactly the same terms.

(g) Delay defeats equity

The courts of equity will not uphold the claimant's rights where he has unduly delayed in bringing the action. The discretionary nature of equity allows the court to decide what is an unreasonable delay. In *Nelson* v. *Rye* [1996] 2 All ER 186 a claim for past earnings by a musician, which he argued had been wrongfully retained by his manager was refused because he had significantly delayed in bringing a claim.

(h) Where equities are equal the first in time prevails

This principle applies where two or more claimants have equitable interests in the same piece of property but none of them holds a legal estate. The court will uphold the claim of the claimant whose equitable interest was created first.

(i) Equity follows the law

This rule reflects the early growth of equity. The rules of common law were acknowledged to be the law and equity only intervened where the common law failed. Equity did not aim to overrule the common law and accepted that where possible it should follow the law. This maxim has been adopted very recently in the context of jointly owned land. In *Stack* v. *Dowden* [2007] UKHL 17 Baroness Hale held that where there are two owners at law (always joint tenants under the Law of Property Act 1925), then usually 'equity follows the law' and they will be regarded as joint tenants in equity. On the facts of this case the maxim did not apply because Baroness Hale found exceptional circumstances which displaced it.

(j) Equity is equality

This principle is applied where two or more claimants have rights in equity in property and the court must decide how to quantify each share in equity. This is a maxim so it can be ignored if the parties have expressly declared how their interests are to be held.

(k) Equity will not allow a statute to be an instrument of fraud

A claimant may rely on the lack of formalities in the transfer of rights as a way of claiming property. An example would be where the strict requirements of the Law of Property Act 1925 have not been adhered to in the transfer of land. Equity may step in to prevent the statute being relied on in order to prevent rights arising. An example arose in the case of *Rochefoucauld* v. *Boustead* [1897] 1 Ch 196 where a court upheld a claim to land in spite of the lack of written evidence required by statute because the defendant owner of property knew that he held it under trust and it was not intended to be held by him personally. This case and the maxim on which it is based is discussed further in Chapter 6.

8 THE ROLE OF EQUITY TODAY

The role of equity and its capacity to develop the law has diminished over the centuries and it can be questioned whether it has a significant creative role today. Initially a key characteristic of equity was its creativity and ability to respond to new situations but gradually the creativity was lost.

In 1975 Lord Denning famously pronounced 'equity is not past the age of child-bearing' in *Eves* v. *Eves* [1975] 1 WLR 1338. He continued 'one of her latest progeny is a constructive trust of a new model. Lord Diplock brought it into the world [see *Gissing* v. *Gissing* [1971] AC 886] ... and we have nourished it.' The truth of this statement can be challenged since new rights to compare with the trust and the mortgage have not been introduced but it is possible to show examples of creativity over the past fifty years.

Among the best recent examples of the creativity of equity are the two new forms of injunction: the *Mareva* injunction (the freezing order) and the *Anton Pillar* order (the search order). The freezing order allows the court to make an order preventing the defendant from dissipating or removing his assets from the jurisdiction. Lord Denning described this extension of the equitable remedy as 'the greatest piece of judicial law reform in my time'. The search order allows the court to make an order allowing the claimant to enter and search premises which may prevent the defendant from destroying vital evidence. There are strict rules governing when such orders may be made.

SUMMARY

This chapter examines the growth of common law and equity. It shows that equity developed as a response to the shortcomings of the common law which were the limits of the writ system, the lack of range of remedy that could be granted by the courts and its failure to recognise certain rights. Equity was based on the exercise of discretion by the king and later the Chancellor. The Chancellor's background as a man of the church imported notions of fairness and conscience into the decision-making. Equity became inflexible and cumbersome. It was often complex and slow mainly because there were two separate systems of law (common law and equity) in existence at the same time. The Judicature Acts 1873–5 fused the two systems. Although in theory there is just one law in existence today there are examples of how equity and common law still differ. Equity has largely ceased to be creative but there are isolated examples of its continuing contribution to the development of law.

2 Equitable remedies

KEY POINTS

- historically common law remedies did not provide adequate compensation;
- common law provided one remedy which was monetary compensation;
- equity supplemented the common law by providing a broader range of remedies;
- equitable remedies include injunctions: specific performance, rescission and rectification; and
- equitable remedies are discretionary and are never awarded as of right.

key points

1 INTRODUCTION: BACKGROUND TO EQUITABLE REMEDIES

One of the main criticisms of the early common law was the lack of flexibility in the type of remedy that it was willing to award. At common law the usual remedy was the award of damages but it was not always an adequate remedy. The claimant may have wished a type of behaviour to cease or perhaps he may have wished the defendant to act in a particular way. It was only when claimants petitioned the king that remedies other than damages began to be granted. The grant of these remedies was discretionary so the claimant had no assurance that the remedy would be granted. Equitable remedies are still awarded on a discretionary basis today. Since the fusion of common law and equity all courts are able to award equitable remedies.

2 SPECIFIC PERFORMANCE

Definition: specific performance is an order from the court compelling the defendant to perform duties agreed under a contract.

Specific performance will not be awarded in all types of contracts. There are many types of contract where it will not be awarded. Further, it will not be awarded in certain circumstances. The court will also examine the behaviour of the claimant because it will not award this remedy, as with all equitable remedies, if he does not come to the court 'with clean hands', meaning that he has not behaved properly towards the defendant.

(a) The principles for the award of specific performance

(i) Lack of consideration

This remedy is granted when ordering the defendant to perform his part in a contract. The court will not grant this remedy unless consideration has been given by the claimant. The court does not consider the adequacy of the consideration but merely that it has been provided.

Although an agreement under deed is regarded as a binding contract (see Chapter 5) it will not be specifically enforceable.

The right of a third party to enforce the terms of a contract under the *Contracts (Rights of Third Parties Act) 1999* does not extend to the right to seek specific performance of the contract.

(ii) Inadequacy of damages

In many contracts damages will not be adequate compensation for failure to complete the contract. An example would be a contract for the sale of land. Land has always been regarded as unique. Likewise a sale of unique goods, such as paintings by famous artists or valuable antiques, can be specifically enforceable as is a contract for the sale of shares in a private company.

Damages may also be inappropriate in a case where the amount awarded would be nominal but there is a measurable loss. This is illustrated by *Beswick* v. *Beswick* [1967] 2 All ER where a widow claimed that damages would not be adequate when a promise by her husband's nephew to pay her a pension after his death was not honoured. The claim was brought by the widow in her capacity as executor of her deceased husband's estate rather than in her personal capacity so her measure of loss as executor was nominal. Her measure of loss as the widow was the full value of the pension. In these circumstances Lord Denning was prepared to order specific performance.

(iii) Undue hardship

Specific performance will be refused where undue hardship will be caused to either of the parties. It may also be refused where it will cause hardship to a third party.

An example of undue hardship can be seen in *Patel* v. *Ali* [1984] Ch 283 where a series of very unfortunate events affected Mr and Mrs Ali, the vendors of property after they had exchanged contracts and before completion of the sale to the purchasers Mr and Mrs Patel. The husband was adjudicated bankrupt and was sent to prison. The wife became seriously ill with cancer and had to have a leg amputated before giving birth to their third child. The wife was dependent on her neighbours to help her and in these exceptional circumstances the court did not order specific performance of the contract of sale because it would cause undue hardship for the defendants.

(iv) Mutuality

Traditionally, the court would not order specific performance if the claimant would not himself be able to fulfil such an order.

An example would be a contract against a minor. The court would not order specific performance in favour of a minor because such a contract could not be specifically enforceable if the defendant was a minor.

Today the court looks at the issue in a more pragmatic way. An order for specific performance will be made if it can be made without injustice or unfairness to the defendant according to Goff LJ in his judgment in *Price* v. *Strange* [1978] Ch 357.

In this case the claimant had carried out work on premises that he rented from the defendant on the defendant's instruction. The claimant had not completed all the repairs because the defendant had carried out some of them himself. The court ordered specific performance against the defendant although the claimant could not have carried out the remaining repairs which had been agreed under the contract.

(v) Delay

Unlike common law, equity does not regard time to be of the essence of a contract so some delay in bringing an action will not prevent a claim for specific performance. By contrast undue or excessive delay in bringing the action could affect the claimant's case.

In *Lazard Brothers & Co. Ltd* v. *Fairfield Property Co. (Mayfair) Ltd* (1977) 121 SJ 793 the claimants sought to enforce a contract for sale two years after it had been drawn up. The court held that they could not refuse to grant the remedy merely because the claimants had been guilty of some delay. The order should be made if the court felt it to be just, in the circumstances of the case, that the claimants should be granted the remedy.

(vi) Lack of clean hands

Specific performance is a discretionary remedy and the court is entitled to refuse to grant the order where the claimant has not acted properly in his dealings with the defendant.

(b) Specific contracts where specific performance may be awarded

(i) Land

Land has always been regarded as unique because the law assumes that no two pieces of land will be identical. Any contract concerning land can be the subject of an order for specific performance. The order is not limited to contracts for the sale of land or the granting of a lease.

The court was prepared to order this remedy in *Verrall* v. *Great Yarmouth Borough Council* [1981] QB 202 which concerned the grant of a contractual licence. This had been granted in favour of the claimant who was later prevented from using the premises for a party political conference by Great Yarmouth Borough Council. The Council did not support the politics of the political party and refused to allow it into the premises. The court ordered specific performance of the agreement. The agreement concerned land, albeit for an agreement for a licence, and so the court upheld it.

The contract will only be enforceable if it complies with the formalities necessary for contracts in the sale of land as laid down in s.2(1) Law of Property (Miscellaneous Provisions) Act 1989. The contract must be evidenced in writing and signed by the parties. An oral contract for the sale or disposition of an interest in land will not be specifically enforceable.

EXAMPLE

Donald is anxious to purchase a house in Norwich where he has just been offered a new job. He views Cilla's house one Saturday afternoon, which is perfect for his needs. They agree terms and on Monday morning Donald sends Cilla his half of the contract which lists all the terms they agreed and is in writing but he fails to sign it. Cilla sends him an identical contract but she also fails to sign her portion. The following week Cilla is offered more money by Evan and she refuses to sell her house to Donald.

The court will only order specific performance where the contracts comply with s.2(1) Law of Property Act 1989. Although the contracts for the sale of Cilla's house are in writing and contain all the terms they do not comply with the requirements of the 1989 Act as they are not signed by the parties.

(ii) Items of special value

Contracts for the sale of personal property will not normally be specifically enforceable because personal items can normally be replaced by a substitute which is the same or very similar and so in such cases damages will compensate the claimant. Some items will not be easily replaced because they are unique and impossible to replace and in these cases the courts will order specific performance. Specific performance may be granted if an item is not unique but difficult to replace.

In *Sky Petroleum Ltd* v. *VIP Petroleum Ltd* [1974] 1 All ER 954 the claimants claimed an injunction against the defendants preventing them from withholding supplies of petrol which they were under contract to supply during a period where there was a shortage of petrol. The defendants had tried to terminate the contract and replace it with a new contract because the original prices agreed under the fixed contract did not reflect the new higher price they were paying for petrol to their suppliers. The claimants argued successfully that they could not find another supplier and so damages in this case would not have been adequate. An injunction was ordered which would have had the same effect as an order for specific performance.

(c) Contracts where specific performance may not be awarded

Where a court makes an order in favour of the claimant it must be possible for the court to be able to supervise the order itself in order to ensure that it had been carried out. In some circumstances such supervision will not be possible or it may be the type of contract where enforcement may infringe certain basic principles in which case specific performance will not be granted.

(i) When is such an order inappropriate?

The order for specific performance would be inappropriate where the order would require constant supervision. The court has also been reluctant to order the defendant to work for the claimant or carry out any personal service for the claimant because it would be viewed as something similar to slavery.

(ii) Contracts for personal services

Equity will never enforce a contract which requires the defendant to work for the claimant because this would be viewed as an infringement of his personal liberty.

the courts are bound to be jealous, lest they should turn contracts of service into contracts of slavery.

(Fry LJ *De Francesco* v. *Barnum* (1890) 45 Ch D 430)

There are two aspects to this principle:

1 the order for specific performance of the employment contract; and
2 an order preventing the defendant from working for another person or perhaps anyone else and so indirectly forcing the defendant to work for the claimant.

Although the rule that the court will never order specific performance of an employment contract is still enforced today, occasionally there has been some relaxation of the second aspect of this rule.

In *Lumley* v. *Wagner* (1852) 1 De G.M. & G 604 an injunction was ordered against the claimant preventing her from breaking her agreement to sing only at the defendant's theatre. This had the effect of forcing her to sing for the defendant.

In *Page One Records Ltd* v. *Britton* [1967] 3 All ER 822 Stamp J. had refused to grant an injunction to enforce a contractual term in an agreement where a pop group had agreed not to work for any other manager, because in effect it would not put pressure on them to retain their manager as they could not work without a manager.

(iii) Compare

In *Hill* v. *CA Parsons & Co. Ltd* [1972] Ch 305 a court prevented an employer from dismissing an employee and so enforcing an employment contract because once dismissed, the employee's right to a full pension would have been prejudiced.

Megarry J. commented in *CH Giles & Co. Ltd* v. *Morris* [1972] 1 WLR 307 'such a rule is plainly not absolute and without exception ... the reasons why the court is reluctant to decree specific performance of a contract for personal services ... are ... more complex'. He thought it was a question of looking at the obligations in each individual contract.

(d) Contracts requiring supervision

The court is reluctant to order specific performance of a contract where there must be constant supervision of the defendant because the court can never be responsible for this. Whereas the court can order and supervise specific performance for the sale of land or a unique item, it would find it more difficult to supervise a contract which required continual supervision.

EXAMPLE

Luxury London Flats UK offer luxury flats with 24-hour porterage. Mr Wealthy arrives back at the flats one Saturday evening and finds his keys do not open the front door and he cannot enter the block. He rings the number he was given for the 24-hour porter only to be put through to an answer phone message which says that the message will be answered on Monday morning because there is no one on duty this evening. He claims that damages will not adequately compensate him because he purchased his flat on the basis that there was a 24-hour porterage service.

It is unlikely that the court will grant Mr Wealthy an order for specific performance because it would require constant supervision. These facts are similar to those in *Ryan* v. *Mutual Tontine Westminster Chambers Association* [1893] 1 Ch 116 where the defendants owned a block of flats and agreed to provide a resident porter for the tenants who would be on the premises throughout the day and night.

If the agreement for porterage services was limited to specific duties which could be monitored such as the removal of rubbish, the maintenance of services such as central heating and cleaning then there could be supervision by the court and the order would be granted.

So in *Posner* v. *Scott-Lewis* [1987] Ch 25 the court ordered specific performance of a contract to provide porterage services limited to such things as removal of rubbish which did not extend to 24-hour supervision of the premises.

The distinction between these cases has been explained in the later case of *Co-operative Insurance* v. *Argyll Stores (Holdings) Ltd* [1997] 3 All ER 297 on the basis that in *Posner* it was possible to show whether a result had been achieved whereas in *Ryan* this was not possible.

(e) Contracts to carry on a business

A contract to carry on a business may involve similar problems to those of contracts requiring constant supervision. *Co-operative Insurance* v. *Argyll Stores* (*Holdings*) *Ltd* (above) concerned the lease of premises by defendants who opened one of a number of supermarkets and covenanted to keep the store open during business hours. The premises were part of a shopping centre. The defendants decided to close the supermarket because it was not financially successful. This was part of a wider plan. The claimants sought an order for specific performance of the contract to force them to keep the store open as agreed under the contract because closure would have a significant effect on the viability of the shopping centre.

The Court of Appeal granted the order but it was later refused on appeal by the House of Lords which held that such an order would require constant supervision. The court also agreed with the view of the court at first instance that where a business was being run at a loss, specific relief would be too far-reaching and beyond the scope of control which the court should seek to impose.

(f) Illegal contracts

An illegal contract is a void contract and so there is no contract to enforce. Where a contract is valid but enforcement might produce a result which itself was contrary to public policy, then a court may not make the order.

An example can be seen in *Wroth* v. *Tyler* [1974] Ch 30 which concerned a contract for the sale of land. Specific performance would normally be granted because the contract concerned land. However, this was a sale from a husband to a purchaser where his wife had a statutory right of occupation. Vacant possession of the property was implied into the contract, so if an order for specific performance was granted the husband would have to bring action against his wife in order to force her to vacate the entry from the register and so give up her rights of occupation.

The court should be reluctant to make an order which requires a husband to take legal proceedings against his wife especially when they are living together. (Megarry, J)

The court refused to order specific performance but it had serious consequences for the defendant who had to pay damages which he could not afford and was subsequently made bankrupt. The result was that the trustee in bankruptcy took over the sale of the property and the wife's statutory right to occupy was subsequently lost.

(g) Mistake, misrepresentation and misdescription

Mistake and misrepresentation may affect the validity of the contract in which case specific performance will not be available but where it does not affect the contract's validity it may still be used as a defence to a claim for specific performance. This will depend on the circumstances of the case and the reasons for the mistake.

Compare the following two cases

In *Tamplin* v. *Jones* (1880) 15 Ch D 215 a purchaser had mistakenly believed that he was entering into a contract for the sale of a certain piece of land. The seller had described the land accurately but the purchaser who was already familiar with the land had not checked the plans. He could not avoid the contract under the doctrine of mistake and the court was prepared to order specific performance.

In *Webster* v. *Cecil* (1861) 30 Beav 62 the claimant tried to enforce a contract where the price had been wrongly stated on the contract by the defendant. The defendant had orally agreed to sell for £2,250 but wrote on the contract £1,250. The claimant was clearly aware of the mistake but claimed an order for specific performance. The court refused to make the order.

Where the property has been incorrectly described in the contract the availability of rescission will depend on the facts. The defendant will be entitled to rescind if the property or item was substantially different in substance but if the misdescription was not substantial then the court will enforce the contract but may order an abatement (reduction in price).

3 INJUNCTIONS

An injunction is an order of the court forbidding (*prohibitive*) or requiring (*mandatory*) an act to be done.

EXAMPLE

Danial lives in No. 23 the Blakelands, a house in Sandbach. His next-door neighbour Edie lives at No. 25. She has just started a new business as a beauty therapist. Cars constantly come to the house and disturb Danial and often block his drive. He seeks legal advice and his solicitor finds that he has a restrictive covenant entered against No. 25 Blakelands preventing any owner from running a business from the property. He is advised that he can take action against Edie and seek a prohibitive injunction which would be the most appropriate remedy. If the injunction is granted, Edie will have to stop working as a beauty therapist from her home.

(a) Principles on which an injunction will be granted:

1 An injunction will only be granted where there has been an infringement of the claimant's rights. The grant of an injunction is dependent on proof of legal rights. The court will not merely intervene because the claimant can prove an injustice has occurred.

Examples where the court has refused to grant an injunction because no legal right has been infringed are considered below.

Paton v. *Trustees of British Pregnancy Advisory* [1979] QB 276: an application by a husband trying to prevent his wife from seeking an abortion was refused because the court held he could not show that he had a legal right which had been infringed.

the first and basic principle is that there must be a legal right enforceable in law or in equity before the applicant can obtain an injunction from the court to restrain an infringement of that right.

(Sir George Baker P.)

Day v. *Brownrigg* (1978) 10 Ch D 294: the claimant lived in a house called 'Ashford Lodge' for a period of over sixty years. His next-door neighbour changed the name of his own house from 'Ashford Villa' to 'Ashford Lodge' causing the claimant loss through the confusion and as a result he sought an injunction from the court to restrain the defendants from using the same name. The application was refused by the Court of Appeal because there was no infringement of any legal or equitable right.

2 Damages must be inadequate as a remedy. An injunction will only be awarded if damages would prove to be an inadequate remedy. According to Lindley LJ 'the very first principle of injunction law is that prima facie you do not obtain injunctions to restrain actionable wrongs, for which damages are the proper remedy' (*London and Blackwell Rly Co.* v. *Cross* (1886) 31 Ch D 354).

The key issues for the court will be likely repetition of the behaviour, the rights and interests of both parties and the likely consequences of the interference of the court. The court should not be influenced by the means of the defendant to pay damages.

In a recent case *Secretary of State for the Environment, Food and Rural Affairs* (*respondent*) v. *Meier* [2009] UKSC 11, which concerned the application for an injunction against a group of travellers, it was observed by Lord Rodgers: 'admittedly, if the present defendants did fail to comply with the injunction, sequestration would not be a real option since they are unlikely to have any substantial assets'.

3 Delay and acquiescence. The court will consider the extent to which the claimant has delayed in bringing an action and also the extent to which the claimant has acquiesced in the behaviour. These are relevant matters that the court can consider and draw its own conclusions. As the award of the remedy is discretionary, different courts may come to different conclusions. The court has allowed an application for an injunction where there has been considerable delay but the delay is justified.

In *Shaw* v. *Applegate* [1977] 1 WLR 970 a claimant had delayed bringing action against the breach of a covenant because of uncertainty as to whether or not the covenant had in fact been breached. The claim succeeded but the court refused to order an injunction because there had been acquiescence by the claimant.

EXAMPLE

Ben purchased a house in 2007 which had a covenant prohibiting business use. He immediately set up business as a holiday letting agency for properties in Greece and other Mediterranean countries using part of the ground floor of the house. His neighbour Ivor is unaware of the business until he hears about it from some friends who used Ben's agency in 2010. Ivor is unsure whether this is a breach of the covenant. He makes inquiries at a local firm of solicitors who are also unsure whether this is a breach and tell him they will advise once they have instructed counsel. Ivor is concerned that the cost of this will be too great and he withdraws his instructions. Ben becomes aware of the inquiries that Ivor is making and is concerned that he will have to stop his business immediately but as he hears nothing from Ivor he continues to take bookings. Three months later Ivor instructs another firm who advise that this is in breach of the covenant.

Ivor brings an action for an injunction to prevent Ben from using the property for business purposes.

The court is likely to allow Ivor to pursue the application in spite of the four-year delay. The delay and subsequent apparent acquiescence may influence the court's decision on the award of the injunction.

4 The conduct of the claimant. This in an equitable remedy and the award is at the discretion of the court. The court can examine issues such as conduct of the claimant. This is based on the maxim of equity that 'he who comes to equity must come to court 'with clean hands'. This means that any breach of his own obligations under the contract or unfair conduct that is connected with the breach can be taken into account. Conduct not associated with the breach is not relevant.

(b) Injunctions and specific performance compared

There are similarities between a mandatory injunction and specific performance but there are certain advantages in bringing an action for an injunction rather than specific performance.

The main advantage is that there are fewer limitations on the type of situation where an injunction might be granted by a court and secondly there is also flexibility in the timing of the grant of the order.

(c) Interim injunctions

Injunctions can be ordered at different stages in court proceedings. An injunction can be ordered before final judgment. Such an injunction is called an interim injunction (formerly called interlocutory injunctions). Special rules apply to injunctions granted before the final outcome of the case. The grant of such injunctions can cause problems because they could prejudice the final outcome of the case.

Principles to be applied to the grant of an *interim injunction* were laid down by Lord Diplock in the case of *American Cyanamid* v. *Ethicon* [1975] 1 All ER 504:

1 there must be *a serious issue to be tried*, the court must be satisfied that the claim is not frivolous or vexatious;
2 the court must decide that on *a balance of convenience* an injunction should be granted; and
3 the claimant must give *an undertaking in damages* to be paid to the defendant for any loss he suffers from the grant of the interim injunction if at the full trial the court does not grant an injunction against the defendant.

This case heralded a change in the approach of the court in deciding whether to grant an interim injunction. The decision in *American Cyanamid* suggests that the court has to carry out a balancing act between the two parties in considering whether it should prevent a certain action from taking place or to wait and to allow the action to take place and so consider the issue at the final trial. Rather than attempting to consider the relative merits of both cases the court is looking at how best it can minimise the risk of loss to both of the parties.

An important issue will always be whether the claimant could be adequately compensated by damages if the court finds against the defendant or alternatively whether the defendant would be adequately compensated in damages if the claimant loses in the final hearing.

EXAMPLE

Medico UK is about to launch a new surgical product which it claims will revolutionise the treatment of second- and third-degree burns. Sanito Ltd is concerned that this new product will be in breach of its patent for a similar product which it registered two years ago. Medico UK has not started production yet but Sanito Ltd launched its product six months ago. It is concerned that if the new product from Medico UK is launched, then the doctors and patients will become used to the product and the award of a permanent injunction at the final trial will be unlikely. Sanito Ltd argues that an interim injunction is essential to preserve its position.

These facts are very similar to those of the case of *American Cyanamid* and the House of Lords were prepared to grant the interim injunction. It is therefore likely that Sanito Ltd will be successful in this case.

Lord Diplock recognised that there were other factors to be taken into consideration which included the public interest or the circumstances of the case before the court. There are some types of cases where the *American Cyanamid* principles are inappropriate in considering an award of an interim injunction for example in a trade dispute

The decision in *American Cyanamid* under scrutiny

The approach adopted in *American Cyanamid* has been subject to criticism because it appears to concentrate on balancing the interests of both parties rather than putting the onus on the claimant to make a strong prima facie case.

A number of judges in subsequent cases have been critical of this approach and have suggested that the principles of *American Cyanamid* were not principles but guidelines allowing the court discretion in whether or not to follow them:

The *American Cyanamid* case is no more than a set of useful guidelines which apply in many cases. It must never be used as a rule of thumb, let alone a straitjacket.

(*Cambridge Nutrition Ltd* v. *BBC* [1990] 3 All ER 523 Kerr LJ)

Cambridge Nutrition Ltd v. *BBC* [1990] 3 All ER 523

This case concerned the broadcast of a television programme. The claimants were the manufacturers of a special low-calorie diet and they agreed to the making of the programme by the defendants. They denied it was a contractual term of the agreement that it would not be broadcast until after the publication of a government report on the medical aspects of the diet and others similar to it. The claimants were concerned about the nature of the programme and applied to the court for an injunction preventing transmission until after the report had been published. The defendants argued that the broadcast of the programme was only appropriate before the report was published. The injunction was granted at first instance but lifted by the Court of Appeal. The court highlighted the fact that in this case neither side was interested in monetary compensation and the whole case turned on the grant of the interim injunction.

In *Series 5 Software Ltd* v. *Clarke* [1996] 1 All ER 853 Mr Justice Laddie reverted to the pre-*Cyanamid* approach. He suggested that Lord Diplock did not say that the court should not take into account the relative strengths of each of the parties' case in applications for an interim injunction. Although he applied the principles of *Cyanamid* he also added a further point that the decision will depend 'on any clear view that the court may come to based on evidence on the strength of each parties' case'.

He suggested that the court should consider the following matters:

1 The grant of an interlocutory injunction is a matter of discretion and depends on all the facts of the case.
2 There are no fixed rules as to when an injunction should or should not be granted. The relief must be kept flexible.
3 Because of the practice adopted on the hearing of applications for interlocutory relief, the court should rarely attempt to resolve complex issues of disputed fact or law.
4 Major factors the court can bear in mind are:
   (a) the extent to which damages are likely to be an adequate remedy for each party and the ability of the other party to pay;
   (b) the balance of convenience;
   (c) the maintenance of the status quo; and
   (d) any clear view the court may reach as to the relative strength of the parties' cases.

(d) Search orders and freezing injunctions

There are two special types of interim injunctions which have both evolved from case law.

(i) The *Anton Piller* order (the search order)

The *Anton Piller* order can be used where the claimant believes that the defendants are in possession of certain information and is unable to access this without an order from the court. The order is often made *ex parte* (without notice) being given to the other side.

The order is made under s.7 Civil Procedure Act 1997 which provides that the High Court may make an order for the purposes of securing:

(a) the preservation of evidence which is or may be relevant;
(b) the preservation of property which is or may be the subject matter of the proceedings or as to which any question may arise in the proceedings.

Under the provisions of the Act certain people are allowed to enter premises to search for, inspect, photograph, sample or record anything described in the order.

In *Anton Piller* v. *Manufacturing Processes Ltd* [1976] Ch 55 the claimants believed that the defendants were in possession of certain confidential information and were providing this information to the claimants' competitors. The order was granted to enable them to access the defendant's files in order to establish this.

(ii) What conditions must be satisfied in order for the order to be granted?

1 the claimant must have an *extremely strong prima facie case*;
2 the potential damage to the claimant in the event of no order being made must be *very serious*;
3 there must be clear evidence that the defendant has in his possession incriminating documents and *there must be a real possibility that he may destroy them* before any application with notice could be made so an *ex parte* application is essential; and
4 the order must do *no real harm* to the defendant or his case.

The grant of a search order can be seen as unfair from the point of view of the defendant. Unless it is carefully monitored it could allow the claimant considerable scope to search the premises of the defendant and perhaps take away material that he did not expect to see or suspect was there.

An example of excessive use can be seen in *Lock International* v. *Beswick* [1989] 1 WLR 1268 where the claimant used a search order as an opportunity to remove a large quantity of documents that belonged to three individual defendants as well as material that he was entitled to remove. On appeal the order was discharged and the judge accepted that it should not have been made.

(iii) Limitations and restrictions placed on the execution of the order under the Civil Procedure Rules

1 a supervising solicitor should be present (ideally not from the firm acting for the claimant); if the property is occupied by an unaccompanied woman a woman solicitor should be present;

2 the order should only be executed during office hours;

3 the search should be made in the presence of the defendant or a responsible employee;

4 a list should be drawn up of items that are to be removed and the list should be served on the defendant;

5 the claimant must give an undertaking in damages to compensate the defendant.

EXAMPLE

Stefan has run a very successful leather accessory business for a number of years. Recently, his profits have begun to fall and he suspects that his business is being affected by aggressive competition from a competitor, Shady Goods UK. He knows that it also makes cheaper leather goods but he believes it either makes or imports imitation goods which have some of Stefan's special design features and these goods sell at half the price of Stefan's goods. Stefan knows where Shady Goods UK's main factory is located and he would like to apply to court for a search order allowing him to gain access to files located at the factory and also the goods stored there.

Stefan should be advised that he will only be successful if he has an extremely strong prima facie case and he will suffer serious potential damage unless the order is made. He must also show that there is a real possibility that Shady Goods UK has the goods in its possession at the factory and is likely to destroy them. He must also show that if the order is granted, it will do no real harm to the defendant Shady Goods or its case. If the order is granted, then it can only be carried out in the presence of a solicitor (preferably not Stefan's solicitor) and only during office hours. Stefan must give a list of items he wishes to remove to Shady Goods' managing director and the search must be made in his presence or that of a responsible employee. Stefan must give an undertaking in damages that he will compensate Shady Goods if it suffers loss as a result of carrying out the order.

The *Mareva* injunction (the freezing order)

The freezing order prevents the defendant from taking assets from the jurisdiction. This is an important remedy because without assets in the jurisdiction the claimant may be unable to enforce a judgment against the defendant.

The order is usually granted as an *interim order* in anticipation of final judgment. It is also usual to apply for the order *ex parte*, i.e. without notice being given to the defendant.

The grant of a freezing order is governed by s.37 Supreme Court Act 1981:

s.37(1) the High Court may by order (whether interlocutory or final) grant an injunction or appoint a receiver in all cases in which it appears to the court to be just and convenient to do so;

s.37(3) the power of the High Court under subsection (1) to grant an interlocutory injunction restraining a party to any proceedings from removing from the jurisdiction of the High Court ... assets located within that jurisdiction shall be exercisable in cases where that party is, as well as in cases where he is not, domiciled, resident or present within that jurisdiction.

Principles on which the freezing order will be granted:

1 the claimant must show a *good arguable case*;
2 the defendant has *assets within the jurisdiction*;
3 there is a real risk that *any judgment will go unsatisfied* by reason of the disposal by the defendant of his assets, unless he is restrained by a court order from disposing of them; and
4 it would be just and convenient in all the circumstances of the case to grant the relief sought.

Where the order is granted the claimant must also give an undertaking in damages. If the claimant is unsuccessful at trial, then the defendant may be entitled to damages.

(i) Can the court grant a worldwide freezing order?

At first it was assumed that the order could only apply to assets within the court's jurisdiction. Subsequent cases have held that in exceptional cases the order can be made with worldwide effect.

(ii) When can the court grant a worldwide freezing order?

According to May LJ this can only be granted in exceptional cases where it can be made effectively, without oppression, and where there is no conflict with the ordinary principles of international law.

If the worldwide order is granted, it is usual to ask the claimant to give an undertaking not to seek to enforce the freezing injunction in any other country than England and Wales without first getting leave from the court. This is important to prevent the claimant from bringing successive actions across a number of different jurisdictions.

The most recent guidelines on the grant of a worldwide freezing order were made in *Dadourian Group International Inc. and Others* v. *Simms and Others* (*No. 2*) [2006] 1 WLR 2499 at 2502.

These principles known as '*the Dadourian principles*' cover a number of different issues to be used as guidance by any court in the grant of a worldwide freezing order (WFO) which include the following:

- The grant of permission to enforce a WFO should be 'just and convenient' for the purpose of ensuring that the WFO is effective and it must not be oppressive to the parties to the English proceedings or to third parties who may be joined to the foreign proceedings.
- All relevant circumstances and options should be considered. For example the proportionality of the steps proposed to be taken abroad.
- The interests of the parties should be balanced against the interests of the other parties to the proceedings and any new party likely to be joined to the foreign proceedings.
- Permission should not normally be given in terms that would enable the applicant to obtain relief in foreign proceedings superior to the WFO.
- There must be a real prospect that assets are located abroad and there must be a real risk they will be dissipated.
- In cases of urgency, proceedings can be brought without notice to the defendant but normally notice should be given.

4 RECTIFICATION

Rectification is a remedy allowing the parties to rectify a document which does not reflect the true intentions of the parties. Oral evidence can be introduced to prove that the contents of the written document are incorrect. Even wills have occasionally been rectified under this remedy.

The claimant must show that there has been a mistake in the written document which fails to reflect what the parties had intended to agree. This remedy will not normally extend to situations where there has been a misunderstanding between the parties. The parties must have both agreed on one conclusion and that must be omitted from the document or wrongly recorded.

EXAMPLE

Corrine is Max's daughter. Max allows Corrine to live in the flat in his property and Corrine agrees to pay for all the household expenses. They agree this and it is put into the form of a written contract but the term about payment of household expenses is left out by mistake. Corrine is now refusing to pay anything to Max.

These facts are similar to those in the case *Jocelyne* v. *Nissen* [1970] 2 QB 86 where the Court of Appeal granted an order of rectification to reflect the fact that the father and daughter had agreed a similar term orally and the written document failed to reflect their agreement.

5 RESCISSION

Rescission is a remedy which allows a contract to be set aside and the parties are restored to their pre-contract positions. The grounds on which equity will allow rescission are wider than those allowed under common law.

There are a number of circumstances when this remedy will be granted:

1 *Mistake*: contracts can be rescinded for mistake both at common law and also in equity. The range of circumstances under which common law will allow rescission is much more narrow than under equity. A contract will be void at common law if the subject matter of the contract no longer existed at the time of contracting. If the parties are mistaken as to a quality of the subject matter, this would not be a mistake at common law. In *Leaf* v. *International Galleries* [1950] 2 KB 86 rescission of a contract was not granted where it had been drawn up for the sale of a painting believed to be a Constable but which had been painted by a different artist.

 In equity a contract can be rescinded in a wider range of circumstances. The circumstances when a contract can be set aside in equity were described in *Solle* v. *Butcher* [1950] 1 KB 671 by Denning LJ as where the parties 'were under a common misapprehension either as to facts or as to their relative and respective rights, provided that the misapprehension was fundamental and that party seeking to set it aside was not himself at fault'.

2 *Misrepresentation*: a contract may be set aside where there has been a misrepresentation, either fraudulent or innocent. The misrepresentation itself does not render the contract void but it is possible for the other party to seek rescission.

3 *Undue influence*: rescission is available where one party has exerted undue influence over the other while negotiating the terms of the contract and one party has had pressure exerted over him so he has not acted under his own free will. In some cases undue influence is presumed because of the relationship of the parties. Examples include parties in a close relationship such as parent and child, married couples, cohabitants, solicitor and client. In other cases the contract can be set aside if actual undue influence can be proved.

Rescission will not be available in all circumstances

A contract cannot be rescinded if the parties cannot be returned to their former positions because it is now impossible to do so.

Rescission will not be granted to a party who has now affirmed the contract, which means he has accepted the goods.

There cannot be rescission where third parties would lose rights which they have acquired in property in good faith.

SUMMARY

This chapter examines the range of remedies which first arose under equity. Equity introduced a number of remedies to address the shortcomings of the common law. Common law was limited to the award of monetary damages which was often not the most suitable remedy as shown at the beginning of the chapter. The main remedies in equity are: specific performance, injunctions, rectification and rescission. Specific performance compels a party to carry out terms in a contract. It is not available in all types of contracts and even where it is available in a contract for unique property, land or other types of property, it may be refused if the defendant can raise one of a number of defences such as delay or hardship. Injunctions are granted in order to prevent or compel certain behaviour. The claimant must prove an infringement of rights and an injunction will not be granted where damages would be an adequate remedy. Injunctions are particularly appropriate in land law to prevent a defendant from breaching a covenant which limits his use of the land. It may be more valuable to prevent business use or building by a neighbour than to receive a sum of money in damages. Occasionally an injunction is given before the final hearing of the case. This is called an interim injunction and is awarded on strict principles. Injunctions can also be awarded to allow the claimant access to the defendants' premises to gather evidence and also to freeze assets either within the jurisdiction or in exceptional cases worldwide. In limited circumstances the court will grant an order to rectify a document where there has been a mistake in recording an agreement between the parties. Another remedy allowed under equity was rescission. Today a contract can be rescinded where the claimant can prove a mistake, a misrepresentation or undue influence.

3 The classification of trusts and powers

KEY POINTS

- a trust is an imperative obligation;
- trusts can arise either expressly or impliedly;
- an express trust can take effect as a bare trust or a fixed trust or a discretionary trust;
- a fixed trust arises where the beneficiaries have clearly identifiable interests in the trust property;
- a discretionary trust allows the trustees to choose from a group of beneficiaries who should benefit under the trust;
- a power is discretionary and the donee can choose whether or not to make an appointment;
- powers of appointment include bare powers and fiduciary powers;
- if a power of appointment is not exercised, the property will revert to the settlor's estate unless there is a gift over in default of appointment or a gift is implied in favour of all the objects;
- the court can intervene where the donee of the power exercises it fraudulently;
- a trust can be clearly distinguished from other legal concepts such as a debt, agency, bailment and a gift although there are also similarities; and
- trusts are used today for a wide variety of reasons including pension schemes, investment schemes, charities, ownership of land and protective trusts.

1 DIFFERENCES BETWEEN A TRUST AND A POWER

A trust imposes an imperative obligation on the trustee. This means that the trustee must carry out the wishes of the settlor. The trustee has no choice whether or not to act. If the trustee cannot act or refuses to act, the court can replace the trustee or step in and carry out the wishes of the trustee itself. A power of appointment is fundamentally different because the donee of a power has a discretion whether to act or not. No action can be brought if the power of appointment is not exercised, whereas the beneficiaries of a trust can bring an action whenever a trustee fails to act. There are similarities between the two and there may be a power imposed over a trust fund so the trustees act in both capacities. A power may be created where the donor wishes to allow the donee the right to choose among a group who is to benefit but does not wish the donee to carry all the responsibilities associated with trusteeship.

2 DIFFERENT TYPES OF TRUSTS

(a) Public and private trusts

Trusts can be divided into public and private trusts. A charitable trust is a public trust because it is deemed to benefit the public at large whereas a private trust benefits specified persons or groups of persons and importantly is not for the public benefit.

Private trusts can be subdivided into a number of further categories such as express and implied trusts; fixed and discretionary trusts and resulting and constructive trusts. Private trusts must have an obvious beneficiary to enforce but one group of private trusts, called private purpose trusts have been upheld by the courts although there are no named beneficiaries. This group of trusts is an exception and includes trusts for named animals and trusts for the erection of a tomb or monument in memory of the settlor.

(b) Express trusts and implied trusts

Trusts can be divided into express and implied trusts. An express trust is created when the owner of property (the settlor) either transfers the legal title to the property to a person (the trustee) to hold that property on trust for the benefit of another person (the beneficiary) or declares that he is now to hold property on behalf of another person. This is done deliberately. There must be clear evidence that the settlor intended to create a trust. An express trust will not be valid unless the *three certainties* are present. It may be created by deed or in writing or simply orally where the trust property does not require any special formalities. A trust may also be created under a will.

Clarence wishes his three children to have a share of the money held in his deposit account. He transfers the account to his friend Darius and asks him to hold the money on trust for his three children. He also wishes his nephew to have his flat in London. He writes this down on a piece of paper, which he signs. The children now have an interest in the money in the account and Clarence now owns the flat in London on behalf of his nephew. The nephew has an interest in equity in the property.

Express trusts can take several forms. They can be either fixed or discretionary or they can simply be bare trusts.

By contrast, implied trusts arise from circumstances and can be imposed by the courts. There are two types of implied trust: the resulting or constructive trust. They arise under different circumstances, either because they give effect to the presumed intention of the parties (a resulting trust) or they are imposed in the interests of justice and conscience (a constructive trust).

In some circumstances a trust is imposed under statute. An example would be where land is co-owned by two or more people, the law imposes a statutory trust of land under the Trusts of Land and Appointment of Trustees Act 1996. The statute lays down rules concerning the way the trust is managed and the resolution of disputes between the co-owners of the land.

(c) Bare trusts, fixed trusts and discretionary trusts

The simplest form of express trust is a *bare trust* where the trustee holds property for a sole beneficiary who is entitled to the whole of the estate. The important feature is that the trustee has no duties to perform in relation to the trust. The main duty of the trustee is to hold the property for the beneficiary usually as a nominee for him.

Mr Developer borrows a large sum of money from the Chartered Useful Bank to purchase a house from Mr Smith. Mr Developer uses a firm of solicitors, Careful and partners for the conveyancing of the property. Chartered Useful Bank could include a provision that the money can only be transferred to Mr Developer on completion and no earlier. When the bank transfers the money to Careful and partners to hold until completion they are nominees on behalf of the bank and are holding the money on bare trust for Mr Developer. They are trustees but they do not have any active duties in connection with the fund.

Under a *fixed trust* all the beneficiaries are clearly named or clearly identifiable as a group and also have identifiable interests in the property. The beneficiaries do not have to be individually named in order to be beneficiaries under a fixed trust, so long as they are a clearly identifiable group, each with an identifiable share.

EXAMPLE

Carl and Alan are named as trustees on behalf of their brother Winston who has named his grandchildren as beneficiaries under the trust. He directs Carl and Alan to hold his estate in equal shares for the grandchildren. This is a fixed trust. Each of the grandchildren will be identifiable and each can claim an equal share with the others. They can all enforce their interests against the trustees, Carl and Alan. Equity regards the grandchildren as owning an equitable interest as soon as the trust comes into operation.

A *discretionary trust* arises where the trustees are given the duty of choosing a beneficiary or beneficiaries from among a group named by the settlor. Unlike a fixed trust the beneficiaries in a discretionary trust do not hold interests in the property which they can enforce against the trustee until they have been chosen by the trustees. They merely hold a hope or a '*spes*' of being chosen and thereby acquiring an interest in property.

EXAMPLE

Carl and Alan are named as trustees on behalf of their brother Winston. He asks them to hold his entire estate on trust for such of his grandchildren as they shall select. There are nine grandchildren. None has an interest in the estate until he/she has been selected by Carl and Alan. They may choose any one of the nine or they may decide to choose them all. The choice however must be made and if Carl or Alan refuses to do so then another trustee must be selected or failing that the choice can be made by the court.

Discretionary trusts can be further subdivided between exhaustive and non-exhaustive discretionary trusts.

In an *exhaustive discretionary trust* the trustees are under a duty to distribute the income and or the capital to the beneficiaries. They must choose who is to benefit from among the group of beneficiaries. If the trustees fail to distribute the fund, they will be in breach of trust.

In a *non-exhaustive discretionary trust* the trustees are not under a duty to distribute the income and therefore have the power to accumulate the income.

McPhail v. Doulton [1971] AC 424

This case provides an example of a discretionary trust. The settlor Mr Baden set up a trust in favour of the staff at a company. Under the terms of the trust the trustees were to apply the income in their absolute discretion for the benefit of any of the 'officers and employees or ex-officers and ex-employees of the company or to any relative or dependants of any such person in such amounts ... as they think fit'. None within the group had a right to the property until the trustees had made their choice. They had nothing more than an expectation. This case is important in setting the tests to be used when making the choice and is discussed later in Chapter 4.

Discretionary trusts have been very useful in a number of areas. For a settlor who is uncertain who to choose among a group of beneficiaries the decision-making is left to named individuals who can make that decision and can vary it according to any change in circumstances. Discretionary trusts have been particularly useful as a tax-saving device although this is often thwarted by the government.

3 TYPES OF POWERS

A power of appointment gives someone who does not own property at law or in equity the authority to choose from among a group who shall own the property. The power of appointment is made by a donor and is granted to a donee to choose among a group of objects. It is purely discretionary and the donee cannot be forced to act and to make a choice. There is no breach of the power if the donee fails to make a choice during his lifetime. A breach would only occur if the power is used improperly by choosing someone from outside the group. The power of appointment may be restricted to a narrow class of objects (a special power) or it may extend to anyone except those within a specified class (a hybrid power) or unusually it may be made in favour of anyone whom the donee wishes (a general power). The reason why a donor may prefer to use a power is because it has flexibility of choice without imposing the duties of a trustee on the donee.

(a) Bare powers

A bare power is the simplest form of power of appointment. The donee is under no duty to exercise the power and unlike a discretionary trust the donee does not even have to decide whether or not to exercise the power. The objects would have no remedy against him if he decided not to do so.

EXAMPLE

Asif died last year. He left a sum of money to his wife Nandi to enjoy during her lifetime and on her death with power to appoint the fund among his three children Shilta, Tamsin and Panib. The power allows the wife to choose among them or alternatively she may decide not to choose among them at all. The children have no right to force their mother to make a decision.

In some cases the donor may state what should be done with the fund if the donee fails to make a choice during his or her lifetime. This is called *a gift over in default of appointment*. Asif may have made provision in the gift above that the fund will pass to, e.g. Hari on the death of Nandi if she has not exercised the power of appointment among the three children in which case if she dies without having made an appointment the fund will pass to Hari.

If no gift over in default of appointment has been made, then the court may hold that the fund should be divided among the objects. In order to do this the court must find 'a general intention' by the donee of the power to benefit the class.

In *Burrough* v. *Philcox* (1840) 5 My & Cr 72 a father granted to his daughter Ann a power of appointment over his property in favour of his nephews and nieces. She died without having made an appointment. The original power did not contain a gift over in default of appointment. The court implied a general intention that a trust would arise in favour of the group. This meant that the fund passed to the nephews and nieces as a group. Under the equitable maxim 'equity is equality' the fund would be shared equally between them.

The court will not always find a general intention to benefit the class. In *Re Weekes Settlement* [1897] 1 Ch 289 Mrs Slade granted a power of appointment to her husband over property contained in a marriage settlement, all their children being the potential objects. The husband died without having made an appointment. In this case the court found no general intention to benefit the class and the property passed to the eldest son.

EXAMPLE

Evie died in 2008 leaving a large fund of money for her husband Harold to enjoy during his lifetime. She also granted him a power of appointment over the fund in favour of their eight grandchildren. On his death he has not appointed any of the grandchildren. The fund could be divided equally between the grandchildren if they could show a general intention that they were to benefit if Harold did not appoint among them. Failing this the fund would revert back to Evie's estate and pass either to her residuary beneficiary (the person entitled to anything remaining in the estate after all bequests have been made) or it will pass under the intestacy rules and her surviving children will most likely benefit.

As a general rule there can be no general intention for the class to benefit where there is a gift over in default of appointment.

If appointments are made so that there is nothing left in the fund, then the person entitled to the gift over will receive nothing.

(b) Fiduciary powers

A fiduciary power arises where a power is held in a fiduciary capacity. It is also discretionary and the donee is not under a duty to exercise it. Unlike a bare power, the donee owes certain duties to the objects of the power.

Duties of a donee under a fiduciary power:

1 They should consider from time to time whether or not to exercise the power. The objects could enforce this duty against the donee who has not made an appointment if he/she has not first considered whether or not to act. They cannot force the donee to act but they can force the donee to consider whether or not to exercise the power.
2 They must 'survey the range' of objects within the group. This means that the donee must undertake an overview of all the objects by the donee but there is no obligation to consider everyone within the group.
3 They must consider whether an appointment is appropriate. This is to avoid 'excessive' use of the power where an appointment is made to someone outside the group and further to decide whether an appointment to one object is more appropriate than to others.

The fiduciary power usually arises where trustees hold a fund and they also have an additional power to appoint a surplus in the fund among a named group. It traditionally applied in a pension fund which had a surplus and the pension fund managers were given the power to choose how to appoint the fund among a group. It can also arise in a private trust.

In *Re Hay's Settlement Trusts* [1982] 1 WLR 202 a trust was created by the settlor under which she granted her trustees a general power of appointment over the property held subject to the trust. The trustees were under a fiduciary power in this case because they held as trustees. If they were not already trustees, they would not owe fiduciary duties in relation to the property.

(i) Can the court step in to exercise a fiduciary power?

This was an important issue in the following case.

Mettoy Pension Trustees Ltd v. *Evans* [1991] 2 All ER 513

Mettoy plc manufactured toys. The company went into liquidation and the question arose as to how the pension fund surplus should be distributed. This amounted to approximately £9 million. The company, rather than the trustees, held a power of appointment over any surplus held in the fund. Under the terms of the fund the power could be exercised in favour of the pensioners. Unless the power was exercised the surplus would pass into the assets of the company and would be used to pay the debts of the company. As the company was now in liquidation the pensioners wanted the court to exercise the power because the company was now incapable of exercising the power. Warner J. held that the power was a fiduciary power because although the company was not a trustee of the fund the relationship between the pensioners and the company could be fiduciary. He found that as the pensioners were not volunteers having contributed with their own pension contributions their relationship with the trustees was a fiduciary relationship. In this case the court could exercise the power on behalf of the company.

(ii) Can a donee release the power of appointment?

It is possible to release both bare powers and fiduciary powers but the fiduciary power can only be released if it has been authorised at the time the power was created. The effect on the property subject to the power of appointment is the same. Those entitled on default of appointment will become entitled to the property immediately. Their interest is accelerated.

In *Re Mills* [1930] 1 Ch 654 a power was granted to a donee, the brother of the deceased to make appointments among a group of objects and in default of appointment for the brother absolutely. The donee made a number of appointments and then released the power. The entire estate passed to him which was later challenged. The court held that this was a valid release of the power.

There are certain formalities associated with the release of a power. A bare power can only be released by using a deed under s.155 Law of Property Act 1925. Where a fiduciary power can be released a deed must also be used.

(c) Fraudulent use of a power

A fraudulent use of a power arises where a donee of a power exercises the power in favour of 'non-objects', i.e. those outside the class. This will be fraudulent even if the donee acted in good faith.

It merely means that the power has been exercised for a purpose or with an intention, beyond the scope of or not justified by the instrument creating the fraud.

(Lord Parker in *Vatcher* v. *Paull* [1915] AC 372)

In some cases, the exercise of the power may be to put into effect an agreement between the donee and the object whereby non-objects will gain an advantage. This would be seen as a fraudulent use of the power even though the exercise itself is valid.

In *Hillsdown Holdings plc* v. *Pensions Ombudsman* [1997] 1 All ER 862, Hillsdown provided a pension fund for its employees which had a surplus of over £20 million. The rules of the Hillsdown Pension Fund did not allow the trustees to appoint any surplus to the company. However the trustees could exercise the power in favour of another scheme which could appoint in favour of Hillsdown but only because it had changed the rules allowing it to do so. The power was exercised. The court held that this was a fraud on the power. The main purpose of the exercise of the power was to enable the trustees of the second fund to appoint to the company who were non-objects rather than the pensioners who were objects of the fund.

EXAMPLE

Lord Winter, a widower was granted a power to appoint over a fund of £1 million in favour of his children Leonora aged 12, Isolde aged 10 and Brunhilde aged 7. Isolde was born with serious health difficulties and had always been unwell. Lord Winter had financial problems. He made an appointment in favour of Isolde of £100,000 in 2010. Isolde died shortly afterwards. Lord Winter was administrator of his daughter's estate and benefited personally from any property she owned.

The court may regard this as a fraud on a power since the appointment appeared to be made with the intention that a non-object namely Lord Winter himself should benefit.

4 THE DISTINCTION BETWEEN A TRUST AND OTHER LEGAL CONCEPTS

A trust is similar to a number of other legal concepts but there are also clear differences and certain advantages, which can make it a very attractive means of holding property.

(a) Gifts

Under a trust the legal and equitable title are split so that the beneficiary receives the equitable title and the trustee holds the legal title. In contrast the donee of a gift receives both the legal and equitable title and once the gift is perfected the property is held by the donee absolutely. The donee is a volunteer so if the donor refuses to transfer the property the donee cannot enforce, whereas the beneficiary under a trust enjoys an interest in equity and therefore is entitled to enforce if the trustee refuses to transfer the property.

(b) Debts

Where money or property is lent from one person to another it creates a personal relationship of debtor and creditor which is enforceable under the rules of contract. The debtor can sue for recovery of the money which is enforceable personally against the debtor. If the debtor is insolvent, such a right will not take priority over others and the creditor will rank only among the other creditors. The rights of a beneficiary under a trust will take priority over others where the trustee is insolvent.

This difference is illustrated very well in the following case.

Barclays Bank Ltd v. *Quistclose Investments Ltd* [1970] AC 567

Rolls Razor was a limited company who owed money to Barclays Bank. The company borrowed money from Quistclose with the express purpose attached that it would be used to pay a dividend to the investors. Barclays Bank was aware of this arrangement. Before the investors could be paid the company went into liquidation. Barclays Bank claimed that the money lent by Quistclose could be used for the payment of the creditors of the company. Quistclose claimed that it was held on trust for a purpose, namely the payment of dividends and therefore since that purpose had not been carried out the money should be returned to them. The House of Lords held that the money had been impressed by a trust and therefore Quistclose was entitled to full recovery of the money.

(c) Bailment

Bailment arises whenever goods are entrusted to another for safekeeping. It could arise where a car is left at a garage for repairs or a coat is left at the dry cleaners. Alternatively it could arise where a book is lent to a friend. The relationship between the parties can therefore lie in contract. On delivery of the property certain duties arise which are enforceable. It is different from a trust because legal title does not transfer to the bailee and so he/she is not entitled to transfer the property to another. A trustee holds legal title and can sell the property although the proceeds will be held for the beneficiary.

(d) Agency

The agreement between an agent and his principal lies in contract but unlike other relationships such as bailment and contract the agent has the authority to deal on behalf of the principal. The agent can enter into a contract with a third party which will be binding on the principal. The agent can also attract liability in tort. The trustee cannot attract liability in this way on behalf of the beneficiaries. The relationship between the agent and principal has an important similarity with a trust which is that the agent owes fiduciary duties to the principal. These include such duties as not to allow his personal interests to conflict with those of his principal and any personal profit made out of his position would have to be repaid.

(e) Interests under a will or intestacy

An interest under a will or intestacy is enforceable against the personal representatives (either an executor where a person dies with a valid will or an administrator where a person dies intestate) as soon as the testator has died. However this does not give the claimant (either a legatee or devisee) a proprietary interest in the estate. By way of contrast, a beneficiary under a trust has a proprietary right as soon as the trust is fully constituted and can enforce his interest against the trustee. There are similarities. The personal representative owes fiduciary duties and both the trustee and personal representative hold property for others and not for themselves.

5 THE MODERN USE OF THE TRUST

Historically, a trust was used as a way of transferring property within a family for the benefit of others, usually to protect weaker members of the family from the duties associated with ownership of property.

Trusts are often used today in a family context but they are also used in a wide range of situations where the split between legal and equitable ownership is valuable. They are used in many different contexts.

Some examples are given in the following sections.

(a) Pension schemes

A pension scheme is usually set up with contributions from the employer and the employee. If the scheme were enforceable under contract, it would not be possible for the employer to pay into the fund because the contract would be between the employer and the employee. The use of a trust allows for both parties to pay into the fund which is held by the trustees on behalf of them both. The trustees can appoint managers of the fund who have the expertise to manage the fund efficiently.

There are many advantages of using a trust, not least that it ensures that the pension fund is separated from the assets of the company in case it becomes insolvent.

(b) Investment schemes

The trust is used for collective investments on behalf of groups of individuals. The unit trust allows the trustee of the unit trust to take decisions about sales and investments independently of the investor. The sale of assets of the trust will not attract tax because the sale is made by the trustee. Tax is only attracted when the units are sold by the investor. This differs from investing directly in companies where the shares are owned by each investor. Unit trusts benefit from experts being able to make decisions about investments.

(c) Purpose trusts providing security for the lender

Trusts can provide security where money is lent for a purpose and that purpose is not carried out. An example is the claim by Quistclose for the return of money lent to Rolls Razor expressly to pay dividends to investors. Quistclose could claim that the money should be returned to Quistclose and that it did not form part of the general assets of the company.

(d) Unincorporated associations

Unincorporated associations cannot hold money because they are not incorporated and have no legal personality. Many clubs and organisations have money transferred to them which they wish to keep on behalf of the members. The trust can be used and the money can be held by trustees who hold it according to the rules of the association.

(e) Ownership of land

Wherever land is owned by more than two people a statutory trust of land is imposed under the Trusts of Land and Appointment of Trustees Act 1996. The legal title will automatically be split from the equitable title. Statutory provisions govern the rights and duties of the trustees and anyone with an interest in the land.

Implied trusts are also important in the context of land ownership particularly where cohabitants live in a property together. No property rights arise on the basis of status for a cohabitant as they would for a married person or civil partner in spite of contributions made towards the family and the improvement of the property. However claims for a share in property may arise under a resulting or constructive trust. There are strict rules as to when such rights arise.

(f) Charitable trusts

Charitable trusts were one of the earliest uses of the trust. It continues to be one of the most important uses made of the trust. Charitable trusts are also called public trusts and although they may not have an obvious beneficiary to enforce they are upheld because if the trustees do not carry out their duties they can be enforced by the Attorney-General. The strict rules that are applied to private trusts about certainty and perpetuity are relaxed for charitable trusts.

(g) Protective trusts

A protective trust is a type of trust that protects certain beneficiaries who are regarded as incapable of looking after their own money sensibly. Income from a trust will normally be transferred to the trustee in bankruptcy if a beneficiary under a trust becomes bankrupt. In a protective trust the interest of the beneficiary will cease as soon as the beneficiary becomes bankrupt. Instead the income from the trust will be held by the trustees under a discretionary trust on behalf of a class of beneficiaries which will include the bankrupt.

The trustee in bankruptcy will only receive trust property if an appointment is made to the bankrupt. In the meantime the capital and remaining income will be safe.

A protective trust can be made expressly but not in favour of one's self in order to protect against one's own possible bankruptcy in the future. A statutory trust can also be imposed which brings about the same effect.

Under s.33 Trustee Act 1925 a primary trust is created under which the beneficiary has a life interest which will come to an end if the beneficiary becomes bankrupt and loses the right to retain any income under the trust. An important example would be bankruptcy but it could include other reasons.

In *Re Gourju* [1943] Ch 24 the principal beneficiary under a trust was in occupied France during the Second World War and therefore unable to receive income because income received would be diverted to the Custodian of Enemy Property under legislation. It was held that this was an event which triggered a forfeiture of the beneficiary's interest.

Once the primary trust has determined then the income is to be held on the terms of a secondary trust which takes the form of a discretionary trust. The trustees can then exercise their discretion to distribute income in favour of the bankrupt or members of the bankrupt's family as in any other discretionary trust.

EXAMPLE

Sean is aged 29 and for all of his adult life has gambled excessively. He has a wife Tara, and three small children under the age of 10. His father Mr O'Brady is aware of Sean's gambling habit and wants to ensure that if he leaves any money to Sean it will not ultimately be lost if at any time he became bankrupt. Mr O'Brady creates a trust whereby Sean has a life interest in a trust fund but his interest will determine if for any reason Sean loses his right to keep the income. Sean has gambled heavily all this year and he is made bankrupt in August. Sean's right under the trust immediately determines and a discretionary trust will replace the first trust. Under the discretionary trust Sean, his wife and three children are all beneficiaries and the trustees can choose to appoint income to any of them at any time. The trustee in bankruptcy will not have the right to claim the fund set up by Mr O'Brady for Sean.

SUMMARY

This chapter considers the main definitions of different types of trusts. It shows that there are many different categories of trusts. It looks at the difference between express and implied trusts and the different types of express trusts that can arise. It also considers in detail the difference between fixed and discretionary trusts. It shows that trusts are always imperative and the duty to act cannot be avoided whereas a power is discretionary and there is no duty to exercise a power. The difference between bare powers and fiduciary powers is also explored and the key features of fiduciary powers are considered in the context of case law. Fiduciary powers impose greater duties on donees including the duty to consider from time to time whether to exercise the power and the duty to 'survey the range' of objects within the group. Donees must also consider whether an appointment is appropriate. These duties were all set out in *Re Hay's Settlement Trusts*. The trust is compared to other concepts in law such as gifts, debts, agency and interests under a will or intestacy. The versatility of the trust is shown by comparing it to these other legal concepts. Finally, the modern use of the trust is explored which shows that it has become very significant in the commercial context as well as remaining very useful for solving disputes over property particularly between cohabitants. The trust also has an important use within pension funds and as a way of transferring property to charities.

4 The three certainties

KEY POINTS

- a private express trust must satisfy three certainties: certainty of intention, subject matter and object;
- it must be clear from the words used that the person holding the property is under a duty to hold it for others;
- precatory words will not create a trust;
- there must be certainty as to what property forms the subject matter of the trust;
- it must be possible to identify the objects of the trust with certainty;
- there are two aspects of certainty of objects: evidential and conceptual certainty;
- conceptual certainty is necessary for all types of trust;
- evidential certainty is not necessary for discretionary trusts;
- different tests for certainty of objects apply to fixed trusts, discretionary trusts and gifts subject to a condition precedent;
- the test for certainty for fixed trusts is the complete list;
- the test for certainty of objects for discretionary trusts is the 'given postulant test' which is the same test as applied for powers; and
- the test for certainty in a gift subject to a condition precedent is whether it could be said with certainty whether any one person falls within the class.

1 THE REQUIREMENT OF CERTAINTY: WHY IS IT NECESSARY?

A trust can be created in *two* ways:

1 it can be created by the settlor declaring that either he now holds all or part of his property on trust for others; or
2 the settlor transfers property to trustees to hold for the benefit of a beneficiary.

In both cases the law will only uphold the trust if it complies with the three certainties as laid down by Lord Langdale in the case of *Knight* v. *Knight* (1840) 3 Beav 171.

The three certainties are:

1 certainty of intention;
2 certainty of subject-matter; and
3 certainty of objects.

A trust will fail if it does not comply with each of the three certainties. If the property has been transferred to another but without showing sufficient certainty of intention that the property is to be held on trust, then the third party can keep the property for himself. If the property is still with the settlor, then the property is not held on trust but can be dealt with by the settlor as his own.

By contrast once *the three certainties* have been complied with as well as any other requirements such as *specific formalities* the trust is said to be constituted and the property will be held in trust. The settlor will no longer have rights in the property and cannot deal in it as his own.

The *three certainties* are strictly enforced. The main reason for this is that unless the trust is certain it would be impossible for the courts to enforce it.

It is also important that there is always someone who can step in and enforce the trust so a private express trust will usually fail if there is no human beneficiary. If the objects of the trust are not clearly identified, it would not be clear who can enforce the trust.

2 CERTAINTY OF INTENTION

(a) The word 'trust' does not have to be used

It must be clear that the person holding the property is obliged to hold it for the benefit of others. The actual words used do not matter. The words trust or trustee do not have to be used. What is important is that the property is held in one person's name for another person.

Paul v. Constance [1977] 1 All ER 195

Mr Constance held money in a bank deposit account. He had separated from his wife. He then formed a relationship with Mrs Paul and they lived together for seven years before his death in 1974. A year before he died Mr Constance received some money in damages. When the money was paid into the account he said to Mrs Paul 'the money is as much yours as it is mine'. Although Mr Constance had not used the words 'trust' at any time the court held that he held the money in the account on trust for them both. When Mr Constance died, Mrs Paul was entitled to claim half of the money in the account.

If the words used do not impose a duty on the person holding the property, then that person will not hold as trustee. The court will consider the effect of any words used rather than the actual words. So in *Paul* v. *Constance* the actual words used did not include the word trust but they did suggest that the money in the bank account was not held absolutely for Mr Constance but was to be held in part for Mrs Paul.

(b) Is the property held as a gift or a trust?

There may be evidence that the person intends to transfer the property as a gift. If a gift was intended, then the formalities of a gift must be shown to have been complied with.

Jones v. Lock (1865–66) LR 1 Ch App 25

Robert Jones returned from a business trip in Birmingham and he was criticised by his wife for not bringing back anything for his son. He went to his baby son and gave him a cheque for £900 saying in front of his wife and the nurse 'Look you here I give this to baby'. The boy held the cheque in his hands. There had been intention to make a gift but there was no evidence that he intended to hold the cheque on trust for the boy. However, the gift was not perfected as there was no delivery. Delivery of a cheque would have required endorsement on the back (Mr Jones would have had to have signed it himself on the back). He died shortly after this and it was held that the boy had no right to the cheque.

(c) Circumstances of the receipt of the property

Contrast the position where a trust can be found because of the circumstances of the receipt of property.

Re Kayford [1975] 1 All ER 604 HC

A mail-order company used a deposit account for deposits of money received from customers as advance payments for goods. The company was advised to call it the

'Customer Trust Deposit Account' but the company simply used the existing account for this purpose. The company went into liquidation within a few weeks and the liquidator sought to claim the money in the deposit account as part of the company's assets.

It was held that the intention of the company had been to create a trust of the money received by the customers.

It is well known that a trust can be created without using the words 'trust' or 'confidence' or the like: the question is whether a sufficient intention to create a trust has been manifested.

(Megarry VC)

(d) Precatory words

Certain words will not create a trust because they are precatory in nature. Precatory words are words that do not impose an obligation on the third party but instead impose a moral obligation which means they have a choice how to act.

EXAMPLE

Alice leaves some money to her brother Ben with the following words 'I leave £5,000 to my brother Ben hoping that he will use it for his children Chloe and Di'.

The key question here is: can Chloe and Di claim the money if their father Ben decides to spend it on himself? If there was a trust, then they have a right to the money as soon as Alice dies because at that moment the trust will be fully constituted and enforceable. However, if there is no trust but merely a moral obligation Ben can use the money for himself and he need not give anything to Chloe and Di. The words used by Alice suggest that no trust was intended.

Historically, in the early nineteenth century, precatory words could create a trust but later the courts took a different approach and in a number of decisions the courts found there was no trust because of the nature of the words used.

Consider the two cases below

In *Lambe* v. *Eames* (1870–71) LR 6 Ch App 597 a testator left his estate to his wife with the words that the estate 'be at her disposal in any way she may think best, for the benefit of herself and her family'. The court held that the wife could dispose of the property as she wished.

In *Adams* v. *Kensington Vestry* (1884) LR 27 Ch D 394 a testator left his property to his wife under his will on the following terms 'in full confidence that she will do what is right as to the disposal thereof between my children'.

The court had to decide whether a trust had been created over the property or whether the wife could deal with it as her own, giving part or all of the property to the children if she chose to do so. It was held that the wife was entitled to the property absolutely.

In both cases the testator had not shown an intention that the property should be held on trust.

(e) Can precatory words ever create a trust?

In some circumstances, precatory words *can* create a trust. The claimant must show that a trust was intended when the trust instrument or the will as a whole was considered. So, in these cases, it is the *context* of the words that would be important.

In *Comiskey* v. *Bowring-Hanbury* [1905] AC 84 a testator left property to his wife with a direction 'in full confidence that ... at her death she will devise it to such one or more of my nieces as she may think fit and in default ... I hereby direct that all my estate and property acquired by her under my will shall at her death be equally divided among my said surviving nieces.'

This gift used precatory words 'in full confidence' and normally the court would hold that no trust had been created. However, in this case, the wording of the gift over made it clear that a trust was intended by the testator after the death of his wife. The gift was in favour of the nieces either one or more chosen by his wife or to be divided equally between them and the wife had no right to enjoy the property absolutely.

Compare this case

Re Steele's Will Trusts [1948] Ch 603 also shows that precatory words can give rise to a trust. A testatrix left a diamond necklace to her son using precatory words which would not usually give rise to a trust: 'I request my said son to do all in his power by his will or otherwise to give effect to this wish.' The mother wanted to create a trust and she thought the words would impose a trust on her son because she had used the words from a gift some years earlier where the court had upheld a trust.

In this case the court considered what her true intention was at the time when she made the gift.

A development in the law of evidence now assists in the construction of gifts under a will to allow the court to decide their true meaning. Under s.21 Administration of Justice Act 1982, extrinsic evidence including evidence of the testator's intention, may be admitted to assist in the interpretation of a will and to resolve ambiguity.

(f) When will the court refuse to uphold a trust whatever words are used? Sham intentions

The court may not uphold a trust even where the word trust is included if it can be proved that no trust was intended. A trust can be a useful way of diverting funds particularly when bankruptcy is imminent. If the transfer of title to the property was not really intended and the beneficiaries were never intended to take an interest in the property, there can be no trust.

The following case provides a good illustration of this.

Midland Bank v. *Wyatt* [1995] 1 FLR 697

A husband executed a trust deed over the family home in favour of his wife and children. The house was in fact owned jointly by the husband and the wife. The wife was not told about the document and she did not see it. The husband's business failed and the bank obtained an order on the house. The husband relied on the trust deed and argued that he had given up his rights to it under the deed. The court found against the husband. They held the deed to be a sham or a pretence and the husband had never intended to give up his interest in favour of his wife and children. The bank had not been informed of the trust deed's existence.

EXAMPLE

Consider the following situations and decide whether a trust has arisen:

1 Freddie leaves his house to his sister hoping that she will leave it to the NSPCA.
2 Gia wins £50,000 in the National Lottery. She puts it into a bank account and says to her partner Luis 'this money is for us both'.
3 Hari writes his will copying an old precedent book he finds in the local library. 'I leave my collection of sports cars to my son Joe feeling confident that he will use them to take care of his sisters.'
4 Ike executes a trust deed over the house he shares with his partner Kia. The deed says that the house is held in trust for Kia and their twin sons. He does not tell Kia what he has done. He wants to divert his capital because he is worried that his company is in serious financial difficulties. Ike is made bankrupt the following year.

Note that in 1 precatory words are used so no trust is created and Freddie's sister can enjoy the house absolutely and has no obligation in law to leave it to the NSPCA.

In 2 the words used are similar to that of *Paul* v. *Constance* and the court is likely to find a trust in spite of the fact that the word trust is not used.

In 3 a trust may arise although precatory words are used if the evidence from the rest of the will suggests that Hari intended a trust.

The trust in 4 is unlikely to be upheld since it appears to be a 'sham'. The facts are similar to *Midland Bank* v. *Wyatt*.

3 CERTAINTY OF SUBJECT MATTER

(a) General issues

A beneficiary cannot enforce a trust unless the subject matter is clear. A settlor may have made it clear that he *intends* a trust but the property over which the trust is imposed must be clear to the trustees.

(b) How can subject matter be uncertain?

There are two ways that the subject matter may be uncertain:

1 *The trust property itself may be uncertain.* In *Palmer* v. *Simmonds* (1854) 2 Drew 221 where the testatrix attempted to create a trust of 'the bulk of my residuary estate' it was held to be uncertain because no one can describe with certainty what is the 'bulk' of anyone's property. Consider also *Sprange* v. *Barnard* (1789) 2 Bro CC 585 where a gift was made to a named beneficiary of property for his sole use and in addition 'the remaining part of what was left that he did not want for his own wants and use, to be divided equally' between two named persons. The two named persons were the brother and sister of the testatrix. In these cases the trust itself failed and the property could be kept by the recipient absolutely. So in *Sprange* v. *Barnard* the property could not be claimed by the brother and the sister because it was impossible to clearly identify what part of the property the beneficiary did not want for his own use. Likewise in *Palmer* v. *Simmonds* what constituted the bulk of the property would not be clear to someone administering the trust. Where a general term can itself be certain e.g. to provide a 'reasonable' income the courts will uphold the trust. Contrast the decision of *Re Golay's Wills Trusts* [1965] 1 WLR 969 where a testator directed that 'Tossy was to get a reasonable income from my ... properties'. This gift was upheld because according to Ungoed-Thomas J. 'the court was constantly involved in making such objective assessments of what is reasonable and is not to be deterred from doing so because subjective influences can never be wholly excluded'. In *Anthony* v. *Donges* [1998] 2 FLR 775 a gift made by a husband using the words 'such minimal part of my estate of whatsoever kind and wheresoever

situate save as aforesaid she may be entitled to under English law for maintenance purposes' failed. He was attempting to limit his wife's potential claims
under the law against his estate but the words used were too vague.

2 *The trust property may be certain but the extent of the beneficial interest may be
uncertain.* This means that although the whole of the subject matter is clear the
individual gifts may be uncertain. e.g. my two houses to my daughters Maria,
whichever she might choose and the other to Charlotte. This was the gift in
Boyce v. *Boyce* (1849) 16 Sim 476. Maria died before she had made a selection
and the court held that the gift failed and the houses resulted back on trust for
the testator's estate. It was not possible for Charlotte simply to make a selection
herself. She had been left a house after Maria had made a selection. In these
cases the property will result back to the testator's estate because it has already
been impressed with a trust. It cannot be an absolute gift.

(c) Issues arising on certainty of subject matter

(i) Unascertained property: tangible property

Where property forms part of a whole, a trust can only arise if it has been separated
from the whole. In a commercial setting a claimant may have superior rights if he
can argue that part of the whole has been set aside and he now has an equitable
interest in the property and it now forms the subject matter of a trust. The principles in these cases vary according to whether property is tangible, e.g. bottles of
wine or gold bullion or intangible, e.g. shares in a company or money in a bank
account.

EXAMPLE

Dan is a wine merchant. Fred orders 200 bottles of a special wine the '1990 burgundy' from Dan paying in advance for the order. There are 1,000 bottles of the
'1990 burgundy' in the warehouse. If Dan becomes bankrupt, it will be crucial to
find out whether or not the wine forms part of the assets of the business or whether
Fred can claim that the equitable interest passed to him once he placed his order
and paid for the wine and so he can claim the 200 bottles for himself. Unless Fred
can prove he has an equitable interest before Dan became bankrupt he will simply
rank as a creditor and it is unlikely that he will recover all his money back.

Re London Wine Co. (Shippers) Ltd (1986) PCC 121

Customers had paid for wine to be supplied by a wine merchant. The wine merchant
had not yet segregated the wine from the rest of the bottles in the warehouse. The

wine merchant went bankrupt and the court had to decide whether the customers could claim that their wine was held on trust for them once the order had been placed.

The court held that there was no trust until the wine had been physically separated from the rest of the bottles because until that had taken place the customers who had placed their orders could not physically identify which bottles belonged to them.

The trust failed for uncertainty of subject matter because the property was not ascertained.

Re Goldcorp Exchange Ltd [1995] 1 AC 74

A similar result occurred in this case. A gold bullion company supplying members of the public with gold bullion went into receivership. Members of the public purchasing gold bullion from the company were given certificates on receipt of their money. Gold bullion had been set aside for some of the customers but not for all. It was held by the Privy Council that a trust arose in favour of all customers where the gold bullion had been set aside, but not for the other customers.

(ii) Unascertained property: intangible goods

Where property is intangible such as shares in a company it is possible to claim that a trust has arisen even where the property has not been set aside and separated from the rest of the property. The logic governing this different approach stems from the fact that there is no discernible difference between the various items in the bulk, e.g. all ordinary shares are identical and all money in a bank account will be the same.

Hunter v. *Moss* [1994] 3 All ER 215

The holder of 950 shares in a company, Mr Moss orally declared that he now held 5 per cent of the shares on trust for Hunter. This represented 50 shares. Moss later refused to transfer the shares to Hunter. The Court of Appeal held that there was a trust over the shares and Hunter had a beneficial interest in the shares. The decision was based on the fact that as all the shares were of the same class it would have been impossible to distinguish between them and they could not be separated from the whole.

This decision can be criticised because the reasoning that all unascertained intangible property is the same has flaws particularly in relation to shares.

Consider this situation:

What if Moss had dealt in the shares so that some had been sold and some retained? Would Hunter now have a claim against the purchaser or against Moss?

Another problem surrounding this case is how the courts would approach the position if the company declared a rights issue. Could Hunter claim the shares or would the new shares belong to Moss? This is not clear from the reasoning in the judgment.

The case of *Hunter* v. *Moss* has been applied in later cases in particular *Re Harvard Securities Ltd* (*in Liquidation*) [1998] BCC 567 where a dealer in securities became insolvent and a number of purchasers claimed that shares held in Harvard's name were held on trust for them.

Relying on the reasoning in *Hunter* v. *Moss* it was held that the shares were held for the purchasers even though the shares had not yet been allocated to individuals.

4 CERTAINTY OF OBJECTS

(a) The need for certainty of objects in a trust

Beneficiaries in a fully constituted trust have an equitable interest in the trust property and can enforce their rights against the trustees. In order for a trust to be enforceable the objects of the trust must be certain. There are different tests for certainty of objects according to the type of trust involved.

(b) The key elements in certainty of objects

In considering certainty of objects there are two key elements to consider:

1 conceptual certainty; and
2 evidential certainty.

There must be conceptual certainty for all trusts but evidential certainty is not necessary for discretionary trusts.

(i) Conceptual certainty

Conceptual certainty concerns the question of whether or not the class of beneficiaries can be clearly defined. An example would be to leave property to 'my children'. Children are conceptually certain. Compare a gift to 'my friends in London'. The concept of who is 'a friend' of any named individual is not clear. There are no clear defining characteristics of 'friends' whereas 'children' have a clear meaning in law. A gift of property to friends will always be conceptually uncertain within a trust although property left subject to a condition precedent allowing 'friends' to purchase property belonging to the testatrix was upheld in *Re Barlow's Will Trusts*. This is discussed below.

All gifts under any type of trust must be conceptually certain.

(ii) Evidential certainty

Although the concept of who is within a class may be certain it may be difficult to prove who is within the group.

The gift may be to a group, such as employees at the BBC between the years 2000 and 2010. The group may be conceptually certain but there may be a problem in proving who is in the group of beneficiaries.

Evidential certainty is the means of proving who may be within the group of beneficiaries.

EXAMPLE

£100,000 to all employees of the BBC between 1990 and 2000. This would require evidential proof of the employer's records. The records would be in several different forms. Such as paper and computer records in the human resources department.

(iii) Administrative unworkability

Where a fund is relatively small and the number of potential beneficiaries to benefit within a discretionary trust is very large the court may not uphold the trust even where the objects are certain because the trust is administratively unworkable. The circumstances where a court will find a trust to be administratively unworkable will be, according to Lord Wilberforce in *McPhail* v. *Doulton* (*Re Baden's Deed Trusts No.1*) [1971] AC 424 'where the definition of the beneficiaries is so hopelessly wide as not to form anything like a class'.

The example given in this case by Lord Wilberforce was 'all the residents of Greater London'.

In *R* v. *District Auditor, ex parte West Yorkshire Metropolitan County Council* [1986] RVR 24 a trust set up 'for the benefit of any or all or some of the inhabitants of the county of West Yorkshire' was held to be administratively unworkable because the number of potential beneficiaries was so wide.

(iv) Tests for certainty of objects in different types of trusts

(a) A fixed trust

In a fixed trust the trustees have no discretion as to who to choose among the objects of the trust and they have no discretion as to the size of each beneficiary's interest. Each person within the class is entitled to call for their share so it is important to be able to say with certainty who is within this list. In a fixed trust there must be conceptual certainty and also evidential certainty.

EXAMPLE

Trevor leaves a gift of a fund of money to be divided between current members of the Penguin Club. The members will be conceptually certain as a 'current member of the Penguin Club' is conceptually certain. Evidential certainty will be provided by proof of who is a current member. This will either come from the club's database on their computer or a hard copy of a list of current members. If the database suffered some catastrophic problem rendering it impossible to be absolutely certain who is within the list of current members of the club, then the gift would fail.

The test for certainty of objects for a fixed trust is 'class ascertainability' or the 'complete list' test. It means that a trust will fail unless it is possible for the trustees to draw up a complete list of all the beneficiaries.

This principle was decided in the case of *IRC* v. *Broadway Cottages Trust* [1955] Ch 20 although the case itself concerned a discretionary trust. All those eligible under the trust have an equitable interest in the fund and if they do not receive their share, they can sue the trustees who will be personally liable to make good their loss.

A Benjamin Order
Where the beneficiaries are ascertainable and known but some cannot be found after enquiries have been made a trustee does not have to delay distributing the estate waiting for the return of the missing beneficiary. The trustees can apply to the court for a Benjamin Order allowing them to distribute the estate to the known beneficiaries, under the order any recovery of a share by the missing beneficiary can only be made against the other beneficiaries and not against the trustees. The procedure was first adopted in *Re Benjamin* [1902] Ch 723.

(b) A discretionary trust

A discretionary trust is a trust where the trustees make a selection among a class of beneficiaries. In such a trust it is not necessary to draw up a complete list of all beneficiaries because the trustees only choose one or more from the class of beneficiaries and many may not receive anything at all.

EXAMPLE

Jade leaves £100,000 on trust to be distributed at her trustees' discretion among her teaching colleagues at Barnet School.

This is a discretionary trust and only a selection of Jade's teaching colleagues will receive a gift under the trust. If the gift were worded to be divided equally between her colleagues at Barnet School, this would be a fixed trust. Every one of her colleagues would have a share in the fund and the trustees would have to be able to draw up a list of all their names. The trustees would apply the complete list test.

In a modern discretionary trust the test for certainty of objects is the 'any given postulant test'. It is also known as the 'is or is not' test or the individual ascertainability test or sometimes the 'class test'.

This test is based on the test for certainty of objects for a power. The test works in such a way that the trust will fail if it is not possible to identify anyone with sufficient certainty whether or not anyone comes within or outside the class.

The test for certainty of objects in a discretionary trust was laid down in *McPhail* v. *Doulton* [1970].

McPhail v. *Doulton* [1970] 2 All ER 228

This case concerned a trust set up by deed in 1941 by Mr Baden for his officers and employees or ex-officers and ex-employees of the company and their relatives and dependants. The trustees were directed to apply the income 'at their discretion in such amounts as they should think fit'.

Prior to this decision the test for certainty of objects was the 'complete list' test. The Baden trust in *McPhail* v. *Doulton* would have failed under this test as it would not have been possible to draw up a list of everyone in all the categories of potential beneficiaries.

The House of Lords considered two important questions in deciding whether the complete list test should apply:

1 Is the duty of a trustee of a discretionary trust only discharged where he has considered every possible claimant?
2 If the court has to administer a discretionary trust, must it split the fund equally between all the beneficiaries?

The House of Lords decided that the duty of a discretionary trustee is not to consider every possible claimant and the court was not bound by the maxim 'equality is equity' and it would be possible for the court to exercise its discretion and choose among the class of beneficiaries or ensure that the trust was carried out by appointing new trustees where none were able or willing to act.

The case of *McPhail* v. *Doulton* was referred back to the High Court and then to the Court of Appeal. The second case *Re Baden's Deed Trusts* (*No. 2*) [1972] 2 All ER 1304 revisited whether the trust in favour of the employees, ex-employees, their relatives and dependents should be upheld. Different members of the court took different approaches to the 'is or is not' test but the Court held the trust to be valid and it did not fail for uncertainty.

Sachs LJ: if the test for conceptual certainty is satisfied, then it is a question of fact whether any person is within the group. The gift will not fail merely because there may be uncertainty about certain people outside the class.

Megaw LJ: the test for conceptual certainty is satisfied if it can be said with certainty that a substantial number of objects fall within the group. It will not fail because there are persons who it is impossible to say with any certainty that they fall 'in or out' of the class.

Stamp LJ: the test for certainty of objects should be strictly applied and a gift will fail if it is not possible to say with any certainty whether any given person is within or without a class. He took a strict view and his interpretation is closer to the 'complete list' approach of a fixed trust.

Note that Stamp LJ took a much stricter approach to the test for certainty of objects than the other two judges.

EXAMPLE

Applying the 'is or is not' test:

Jade's gift of £100,000 on trust to be distributed at her trustee's discretion among her working colleagues at Barnet School will fail according to Stamp LJ if it is not possible to decide whether any person comes within or outside a class. The more lenient approach of Megaw LJ would allow the trustees to consider whether a substantial number of objects fell within the group and it would not fail if there were one or two people over whom there was some uncertainty such as someone who had taught at the school for one term and it was not certain whether she was a colleague.

There must be conceptual certainty as to who is within the class of 'teaching colleagues'. This will be considered objectively. Someone who worked as a teacher for many years may not be within the class because that teacher had little or nothing to do with Jade while she worked at the school but someone who worked for two months may qualify as a colleague because he was someone with whom Jade worked closely. If the objects of the trust are conceptually certain, then the gift will be upheld.

Can a third party decide who is within the class?

In some cases conceptual uncertainty could be cured by naming a third party to decide who is within the class but this can only be used where the person nominated has expertise or the uncertainty can be resolved by the person concerned.

Compare the following cases

In *Re Coxen* [1948] Ch 747 it was held that the testator could nominate the trustee as the person to resolve any issues with conceptual certainty but only because the testator had indicated how the uncertainty was to be resolved.

There was a different result in *Re Wright's WT* [1981] L S Gaz 841 where the testator had left property with instructions to the trustees 'to use the same at their absolute discretion for such people and institutions as they think have helped me or my late husband'. This failed for uncertainty.

Although the trustees were given the responsibility of choosing who was in the class, there was no obvious way that they could carry out this duty as they would have no idea who had helped the testatrix and her husband during their lives.

Where the trustees can make a decision because they have the expertise or knowledge or are told to refer the issue to a third party, then such a gift will be upheld because any uncertainty can be resolved.

In *Re Tuck's Settlement Trusts* [1978] Ch 49 any decisions in relation to who came within the class were to be resolved by a named person. In this case the Chief Rabbi was to decide whether a person was of the Jewish faith or not. The gift was a conditional gift discussed below but the principle can be applied to discretionary trusts as well.

However, unlike fixed trusts, evidential certainty is not necessary for a discretionary trust. This is because there is no requirement for a complete list of all the beneficiaries. The duty of the trustees in a discretionary trust is to 'survey the range' of beneficiaries.

This was discussed in *Re Hay's Settlement Trusts* [1981] 3 All ER 786 where Megarry VC outlined the duties of a trustee of a discretionary trust 'there is no need to compile a complete list of the objects or even to make an accurate assessment of the number of them: what is needed is an appreciation of the width of the field'.

There is no requirement that the trustees should consider every potential beneficiary.

(c) Gifts subject to a condition precedent

Sometimes a testator will not create a trust but instead will leave individual gifts of property to a group of people who must satisfy a condition before being able to claim the gift.

Therefore these are individual gifts and not trusts but they are not outright gifts because they each have a condition attached. Such gifts will fail if the condition attached fails for uncertainty.

The test for certainty of objects of a gift subject to a condition precedent is the test in *Re Allen* [1953] Ch 810 which is that 'the gift will be valid if it is possible to say of one or more persons that he or they undoubtedly qualify even though it may be difficult to say of others whether or not they qualify'.

The test was applied by Lord Browne-Wilkinson in *Re Barlow's Will Trusts* [1979] 1 All ER 296. In this case the testatrix left a number of paintings in her will and directed her executor to sell them but to first allow any of her family and friends to have the chance to purchase any of the paintings at below current market value. The court held that the gift would be upheld. It was for each claimant to show that he/she satisfied the condition to the executors.

By contrast a gift subject to a condition subsequent is a gift where the claimant will lose the gift once he fails to satisfy the condition attached.

An example would be where the testator left property to Alex while he is a student. The gift will end when Alex ceases to be a student. If a condition subsequent is uncertain, the gift will fail, e.g. £1,000 on trust for Alex so long as he remains happy.

In *Re Tepper's Wills Trusts* [1987] 1 All ER 970 a gift was made on the condition that the donee 'shall remain within the Jewish faith and shall not marry outside the Jewish faith'. The gift was upheld as valid because the term Jewish faith was certain from the outset.

It is sometimes difficult to distinguish between the various trusts and gifts which can be made by a testator.

EXAMPLE

Consider the examples below and decide if they are *fixed trusts*, *discretionary trusts* or *gifts subject to conditions precedent*.

1 Selina leaves her estate to all her friends at the tennis club;
2 Tanya leaves her car to her favourite friend;
3 Ursula leaves her collection of contemporary oil paintings to be purchased by any of her friends at half price;
4 Viv leaves his shares in Microsoft and Shell for the employees of his company and their relatives and dependents as his trustees in their absolute discretion may choose;
5 William leaves one of his two cars to his son Kumar who may choose which one he would like and the one he does not choose to my Godson Felix;
6 Xavier leaves the balance in his current account to be shared between any of his relatives who are practising Christians. Any doubt to be resolved by the Archbishop of Canterbury.

The gift in 1 is a fixed trust and the test for certainty is the complete list. The gift in 2 is a fixed trust. The gift of the contemporary oil paintings in 3 is a gift subject to a condition precedent. The gift in 4 is a discretionary trust and the test for certainty of objects is the 'is or is not' test. The gift in 5 is a fixed trust but the subject matter of the trust is uncertain. The gift in 6 is a fixed trust which appears to be conceptually uncertain but the nomination of a third party to resolve differences will allow the gift to be upheld. This is similar to *Re Tuck's Settlement*.

SUMMARY

This chapter considers the three certainties which are required by all trusts in order to be valid. The three certainties are: intention, subject matter and object. The trustee must be under an obligation to carry out the settlor's wishes (certainty of intention). If the gift allows the trustee some discretion as to whether or not to carry out the settlor's wishes, it cannot be a trust. Precatory words cannot create a trust as shown in *Adams* v. *Kensington Vestry*. The court will never uphold a trust where the intention is a 'sham' as shown in *Midland Bank* v. *Wyatt*. The subject matter of the trust must be clearly identifiable (certainty of subject matter). There are two ways that subject matter can be uncertain, either because the trust property is uncertain or the trust property is certain but the extent of the beneficial interest may be uncertain. Different rules apply to unascertained intangible and tangible goods. A trust of tangible goods can only arise where the property is separated from the whole such as the wine in *Re London Wine Co.* (*Shippers*) *Ltd*. A trust of intangible goods does not require the goods to be separated from the whole. This is because all the goods are the same as shown in *Hunter* v. *Moss*. The settlor must identify who is to be the beneficiary or beneficiaries of the trust (certainty of objects). It must be possible for any court to carry out the terms of the trust if the trustee is unable or unwilling to act. The court can only do so if the terms are sufficiently certain. Certainty of objects involves two aspects: conceptual and evidential certainty. The test for certainty of objects for fixed trusts is the 'complete list' test which requires the trustees to be able to draw up a list of all the beneficiaries in the class as laid down in *IRC* v. *Broadway Cottages Trust*. The test for discretionary trusts is more problematic. The test is the same test as that for certainty of objects of a power, the 'is or is not' test as laid down in *McPhail* v. *Doulton*. Different judges took a different approach to how strictly this test should be applied. The strictest application of the test is that a discretionary trust will fail if you cannot say with certainty whether any person is in the class. The less strict approach will allow a trust to be upheld where it can be said with certainty whether a substantial number fall within the group. The trustees are not required to consider all the beneficiaries when exercising their discretion but merely to survey the range. In some cases the property may be left as a series of separate gifts subject to a condition precedent rather than as property under a trust and the test for certainty of objects is different and is set at a lower standard which is whether one person is sufficiently certain.

5 Constitution of trusts

KEY POINTS

- equity will not assist a volunteer;
- a trust is fully constituted when the settlor either conveys the property to a trustee or declares that he holds the property on trust for named beneficiaries;
- a trust will be enforceable where a settlor has done everything in his power according to the nature of the property;
- according to *Pennington* v. *Waine* a trust will be enforceable even where the settlor has not done everything in his power if it would be unconscionable not to enforce it;
- an incompletely constituted trust may be enforceable by the beneficiaries under the rules of contract;
- an incompletely constituted trust may be enforceable as a trust of a promise;
- there are three exceptions to the rule that equity will not assist a volunteer:
  - the rule in *Strong* v. *Bird*;
  - a *donatio mortis causa*; and
  - proprietary estoppel.

key points

1 INTRODUCTION TO THE RULE EQUITY WILL NOT ASSIST A VOLUNTEER

It is very important for all parties to a trust to know when a trust is fully consti-tuted. Once the trust is constituted there is no right for the settlor to change his mind and claim the property for himself. The trustees are now under a duty to act and the beneficiaries have a right to enforce the trust. If the settlor has not trans-ferred the property to the trustees or properly declared that he holds the property as a trustee, then it is said to be incompletely constituted and the beneficiaries have no right to enforce it or to compel the settlor to constitute the trust. There may be good reasons why the trust is not fully constituted such as a change of mind by the settlor.

(a) The rule in *Milroy* v. *Lord*

According to Turner LJ a settlor can create a trust in one of two ways:

1 a declaration of self as trustee;
2 a transfer of the trust property to the trustees with instruction that they are to hold it upon trust for the beneficiaries.

In both cases the person making the transfer must do everything in his power to transfer the legal title to the property. In the case of a chattel this may be simple delivery with intention to transfer the property but in the case of shares or land the transfer may be more complicated and will involve specific formalities.

EXAMPLE

Eliza promises her granddaughter Didi that she will transfer £5,000 to Tom and Tim to hold on trust so Didi has some money for herself while she is at university. If Eliza fails to transfer the money to Tim and Tom, Didi cannot force Eliza to do so. This is because Didi is a volunteer. However, if Eliza transfers the money as agreed and then she falls out with Didi and does not want her to have access to the money, then Eliza cannot prevent her from claiming the money and Didi can enforce the trust.

(b) Outright transfer of the legal title to another

Alternatively, the property can be transferred directly to another in which case, subject to the satisfaction of any formalities, there will be a perfect gift. In this case there is no trust but the rules for enforcement are similar. Where property is transferred by way of a gift both legal and equitable title are transferred together to the donee.

EXAMPLE

Uncle Felix promises Greta, his niece, that he will transfer a diamond necklace to her that belonged to his grandmother.

Greta is a volunteer. According to *Milroy* v. *Lord* (discussed in detail below) equity will not assist Greta if Uncle Felix fails to transfer the necklace to her. She has not paid consideration for this and the necklace is not held for her benefit under a trust.

2 THE TRANSFER OF PROPERTY TO THE TRUSTEE UNDER A FULLY CONSTITUTED TRUST

If the settlor intends to create a trust by appointing trustees, then the property must be transferred to them in order to constitute the trust.

Milroy v. *Lord* (1862) 4 De GF & J 264

The settlor executed a deed in which he purported to transfer shares in a bank to Samuel Lord to be held on trust for the claimant, Mr Milroy. The transfer of the shares was not registered in the books of the company as was necessary according to the formalities of transfer of shares. Lord held power of attorney on behalf of the settlor and so he had the power to register the shares but he failed to do so. On the death of the settlor Milroy claimed the shares were held for him. The court held that the trust was not fully constituted because although there was sufficient intention shown there was no transfer of the shares and so the settlor had not done everything in his power to transfer the shares to the trustee.

The transfer of property must adhere to the correct formalities. Certain types of property require adherence to particular formalities:

1 Land. The legal title to land can only be transferred to another by the use of a deed of transfer from the settlor to the trustees (s.52 Law of Property Act 1925). This must be followed by registration of the title at the Land Registry in the name of the trustees.
2 Shares. The legal title to shares is recorded on the register of the company issuing the shares. It is the responsibility of the new owner of the shares to register

the shares. In order to transfer shares the owner must execute a transfer form and once this is in the hands of the transferee then the transferor cannot recover the shares on the principle that he has done everything in his power to transfer the shares.

3 Equitable interests in property. An equitable interest in property can only be disposed of in writing under s.53(1)(c) Law of Property Act 1925. Where an equitable interest is owned by a beneficiary it could form the subject matter of a trust if he/she wishes to transfer it to another for their enjoyment.

4 Chattels. Chattels must be physically transferred to the trustee and there must be an intention that the property should be held on trust.

3 SELF-DECLARATION OF A TRUST BY THE OWNER OF THE PROPERTY

A settlor may create a trust by declaring that property he owns is from now on to be held on trust for named beneficiaries. If this approach is adopted, there is no need to transfer the property as the settlor already has legal title. In these cases it is important that the settlor shows sufficient intention to create a trust otherwise the beneficiary could not claim an interest. Where the trust involves land or an equitable interest the declaration of trust must be put into writing.

(a) Has sufficient intention to create a trust been shown?

The settlor must show that he intended to create a trust over the property. Although the court does not expect the words 'trust' or 'trustee' to be used, the words must clearly show that the legal and equitable title to the property has now been divided and the settlor has transferred rights in equity to the beneficiary while retaining the legal title.

In *Jones* v. *Lock* (1865–6) 1 Ch App 25, as discussed in Chapter 4, a father (Jones) returned from a business trip and was criticised by his wife for not returning with a gift for his child. He then put a cheque for £900, which was made out to himself, in the hands of the child and declared 'this is for the baby'. He died shortly afterwards and the issue arose whether the cheque had passed to the child. The court held that there was no trust in favour of the baby because Jones had not declared an intention that the cheque should be held on trust. The transfer also failed as an outright gift because there was no delivery to the child. A cheque could be transferred to another person at that time but there had to be an endorsement on the back of the cheque in order for it to be enforceable and Jones had failed to endorse the cheque.

A similar result occurred in *Richards* v. *Delbridge* (1874) LR 18 Eq 11 where Mr Delbridge attempted to assign a lease into the name of his grandson. He signed a memorandum which read: 'This deed and all thereto I give to Edward Burnetto Richards from this time henceforth with all stock in trade.' This was held to be an imperfect gift. The assignment was not under seal so it could not transfer the lease and there was no trust because the grandfather did not declare himself to be trustee of the lease. It was clear that he had intended an outright gift but it had failed.

Compare the case of *Paul* v. *Constance* [1977] 1 WLR 527 where the court held sufficient intention was shown in order to create a trust of a bank account. Ms Paul and Mr Constance lived together. Mr C's marriage had broken down some years earlier and he was separated from his wife. Mr C received a sum of money by way of compensation for an injury. The money was put into a bank account and Mr C said on several occasions to Ms P that the money was as much hers as it was his. After his death, Mr C's first wife claimed all his assets but Ms P successfully claimed that she had a half share in the bank account because it was held on trust for them both.

A similar result to that in *Paul* v. *Constance* was reached in *Rowe* v. *Prance* [1999] 2 FLR 787. Ms Rowe and Mr Prance had a relationship together. Mr P owned a yacht in his sole name and he said on a number of occasions that the yacht would become their home and they would sail around the world together in it. When their relationship broke down Ms R successfully claimed that the yacht was held on trust in equal shares for them both. If these statements had been made in relation to a house, the result may have been different as formalities would be necessary for a declaration of trust over land whereas a declaration of trust over personal property (including the boat) would not require evidence in writing.

Compare the facts of the Examples (1) and (2).

EXAMPLE (1)

Shelley and Brad live together. Shelley owns an expensive car. Shelley often says to Brad 'this car is for us both'. If the relationship breaks down, the court is likely to follow *Paul* v. *Constance* and *Rowe* v. *Prance* and to hold that the car is owned by Shelley on trust for herself and Brad in equal shares.

EXAMPLE (2)

Tanya and Colin live together. Tanya owns an expensive car. She says to Colin 'I am going to give you my car'. However she continues to drive it herself and she does not transfer it to Colin. If the relationship breaks down, Colin cannot claim the car for himself as there has been no proper transfer as in the case of *Jones* v. *Lock* and there is insufficient intention shown to create a trust of the car.

There is no enforceable trust in Example (2) but in Example (1) the statement from Shelley to Brad suggests that there is an intention on Shelley's behalf to create a trust of the car for Brad.

What if the settlor is one of several trustees and there is a declaration of trust but no transfer to the remaining trustees? The court may uphold a self-declaration as sufficient to constitute the trust.

Choithram (T) International SA v. *Pagarani* [2001] 1 WLR 1

A wealthy donor wished to transfer some of his property consisting of shares and money in bank accounts into a charitable foundation. He became very ill and just before he died he signed a trust deed establishing the foundation, of which there were a number of trustees, including himself. He then orally declared that he was giving 'all my wealth' to the foundation. He did not transfer the title of the property to the other trustees and it remained in his name. After his death the foundation claimed the property arguing that the trust was fully constituted. The wife and children of the settlor challenged this, claiming the property passed to them under the intestacy rules. They argued that the transfer was ineffectual because the settlor had not transferred the property to the other trustees and further he had not declared that he held the property on trust for the foundation.

The Privy Council held that there was a gift of the property to himself in his capacity as trustee which effectively constituted the trust. There was a duty to transfer the property to the remaining trustees. Although the settlor had used words that were more appropriate for an outright gift the words were intended to create a gift to the trustees of the foundation.

There can in principle be no distinction between the case where the donor declares himself to be the sole trustee for a donee or a purpose and the case where he declares himself to be the one of the trustees for that donee or purpose.

(Lord Browne-Wilkinson)

Many might argue that this is a very generous interpretation of the transfer but the court was possibly influenced by the fact that the foundation had been set up for charitable purposes.

(b) Formalities for self-declaration

In most cases a trust will be enforceable where the settlor makes clear that he intends to hold property he owns for the enjoyment of others. If the declaration is clear, the trust is now fully enforceable by the beneficiaries.

Where the trust property comprises land then the beneficiaries can only enforce where the declaration by the trustee is evidenced in writing and signed by the settlor to comply with s.53(1)(b) Law of Property Act 1925.

EXAMPLE

Dinesh holds a party for his seventieth birthday. He tells his granddaughter Parveen that he wishes her to have his flat in Bournemouth. Parveen cannot enforce this promise against Dinesh unless he later puts the promise into writing and signs it himself.

4 THE RULE IN *RE ROSE*: 'THE SETTLOR HAS DONE EVERYTHING IN HIS POWER'

Under *Milroy* v. *Lord* it is accepted that a trust will be fully constituted where the settlor has done everything in his power to transfer the property to the trustee. The important point to consider is whether the settlor can recover the property if he changes his mind. It is very important to be clear as to what the settlor must do in connection with certain types of property in order for him to be regarded as having done everything in his power and for it to be regarded as an enforceable trust.

Where the trust property involves shares the settlor must have executed a stock transfer form which he must hand to the transferee. The transferee is then responsible for registering himself as the new owner of the shares and the company must consent to the new registration.

Re Rose [1952] Ch 499

Mr Rose executed two transfers of shares in favour of his wife on 30 March 1943. The transfer was registered at the company on 30 June 1943. He died five years later and in order to avoid estate duty his executors had to show that the shares had been transferred in March as opposed to June. The court held that the shares had passed in March since at that moment Mr Rose could not have recovered the shares if he had changed his mind about transferring them to his wife.

Mascall v. *Mascall* (1985) 50 P & CR 119

A similar result was held in this case with regard to land. Mr Mascall had executed a voluntary transfer of land to his son. It was for the son to register the property in his name at the Land Registry. Before this could be done the son had a row with his father and the father tried to argue that the transfer was not enforceable. Although the property was still registered under the father's name at the Land Registry it could not be recovered by him under the rule in *Re Rose* since title had already passed and it was for the son to take the final step of registration at the Land Registry.

What if there is a further step which must be taken by a third party before the settlor transfers the property?

Re Fry [1946] Ch 312

The transferor of shares lived in America. He wanted to transfer shares in a British company. However he needed the consent of the Treasury before this could be done. He executed share transfer forms and also applied for consent from the Treasury. At his death the necessary approval had not been granted and it was held that the shares had not passed to the transferee. He had not done everything in his power to transfer the shares, the transfer required the consent of a third party which he had not obtained.

5 THE RULE IN *PENNINGTON* V. *WAINE*

The rule in *Re Rose* has recently been revisited and a further possibility of enforcing an incompletely constituted trust or gift has been introduced.

Pennington v. *Waine* [2002] All ER (D) 24

Ada Crampton wished to transfer 400 shares to her nephew Harold. She executed a share transfer form in his favour and instead of forwarding this to Harold she sent it to the company's auditors. Ada wrote to Harold to tell him that she was going to transfer the shares to him and also that she wished him to become a director of the firm. In order to be a director he had to hold shares in the company. She added that he need not take any further steps himself. The form remained with the auditor and was never sent to Harold. At Ada's death the executors sought advice as to whether the shares passed with her estate or had been effectively transferred to Harold. According to the rule in *Re Rose* Ada had not done everything in her power to transfer the shares to Harold. Theoretically it would have been possible for her to recover the shares while she was still alive had she argued with Harold before her death unlike the father in *Mascall* v. *Mascall*. However the Court of Appeal upheld Harold's claim to the shares.

They held that it would have been *unconscionable* for Ada to have recovered the property from Harold. The grounds for this included such matters as: Harold's position as director was dependent on his owning shares, Ada told Harold about the transfer and also signed the share transfer form, Ada told Harold that he need take no further action.

The problem with allowing this transfer to be upheld on the basis of unconscionability is the danger that there will be an element of uncertainty as to whether the title to property has passed because different judges may take a different view of what constitutes unconscionability.

6 ENFORCING AN INCOMPLETELY CONSTITUTED TRUST IN CONTRACT

A beneficiary of an incompletely constituted trust may be able to enforce the trust if he can show that he has given *valuable consideration*.

Valuable consideration is defined as money or money's worth and will include 'marriage consideration'. Such consideration is rare today but was popular in the nineteenth century. Marriage consideration arises where a gift is made in contemplation or at the time of marriage. The potential beneficiaries include the husband and wife and the children of the marriage and are deemed to be within the settlement. More remote relatives are not included.

The case of *Pullan* v. *Koe* [1913] 1 Ch 9 illustrates how children may enforce a promise to settle under this rule. Under a marriage settlement a wife covenanted to settle after-acquired property which was valued in excess of £100. She failed to transfer a sum of £285 which she had received from her mother and instead it was held by her husband who purchased bonds with the money. On his death the children claimed that the money and now the bonds were held for them under the settlement. The court upheld their claim as they were not mere volunteers but were parties to the settlement and so had given consideration.

Compare the case of *Re Plumptre's Marriage Settlement* [1910] 1 Ch 609 where a wife had also agreed to transfer property she acquired after marriage under the terms of a marriage settlement. She failed to transfer property given to her by her husband. After her death her next of kin tried to enforce the promise. In this case they could not do so because they were not parties to the settlement and therefore they remained volunteers. The court held they had not given valuable consideration.

In *Re Cooks' Settlement Trusts* [1965] Ch 905 the settlor covenanted that he would settle the proceeds of sale for members of his family of any picture that he had received from his father and he later sold during his lifetime. He transferred a valuable picture to his wife and the trustees sought directions from the court whether the proceeds of sale of the picture could be claimed by the beneficiaries. The court held it would not enforce the trust in favour of the beneficiaries because they were volunteers.

7 ENFORCING AN INCOMPLETELY CONSTITUTED TRUST AS A TRUST OF A PROMISE UNDER *FLETCHER* V. *FLETCHER*

As a trust can be created in any type of existing property it can include a chose in action. If the beneficiary can show that there is a *trust of the promise to transfer property*, then this can constitute a chose in action. The beneficiary can show that this is a fully constituted trust and he then has the right to compel the trustees to compel performance by the settlor and enforce an incompletely constituted trust.

Fletcher v. *Fletcher* (1844) 4 Hare 67

This exception was used to enforce an incompletely constituted trust in this case. The settlor made a voluntary deed under which he covenanted to settle £60,000 in favour of his two illegitimate sons, Jacob and John on them attaining the age of 21. It included a provision that if one of the sons predeceased his father, then the trustees would hold the sum for the surviving son. The sons did not know of the covenant nor were the trustees aware of it either. At Fletcher's death only Jacob survived and he was already 21.

The executors of Fletcher's will argued that he was a mere volunteer and as the money had not been transferred to the trustees he could not enforce the trust.

It was argued on behalf of Jacob that there was a fully constituted trust.

It was held that Jacob was entitled to the sum not under the incompletely constituted trust but under a completely constituted covenant of a promise to settle a sum of money. The trust had not been constituted because the property had not been transferred to the trustees but by way of contrast Jacob could enforce because he already had an interest in the completely constituted trust of the promise and could enforce his rights under this. The court held that the executors held the benefit of the covenant on trust for him.

> **EXAMPLE**
>
> Alex covenants with Baz to transfer £60,000 to Baz as trustee so that he shall hold the benefit of the trust for Chaz and Dan if they attain the age of 21 years. In this example Alex has created a completely constituted trust of the benefit of the promise he made to Baz and in these circumstances Chaz and Dan can enforce. The trust would be deemed to be fully constituted and so the beneficiaries can enforce in these circumstances.

Fletcher v. *Fletcher* has been criticised because of the circumstances of the covenant. No one knew about the covenant except Fletcher himself. He kept the deed among his papers. It would be difficult to see how this covenant could be enforced by Jacob when he was unaware that he was the beneficiary of a promise to settle during his father's lifetime.

8 THE RULE IN *RE RALLI'S WILL TRUST*

If property reaches the hands of the trustee through another route however fortuitous, the trust is enforceable.

Re Ralli's Will Trust [1964] Ch 288

A testator left his residuary estate on trust for his wife and then to his two daughters absolutely. One daughter Helen had herself entered into a marriage settlement under which she covenanted to settle all property including after-acquired property on trust for her sister's children. She died before her mother and so could not transfer her share in the estate into her marriage settlement. In this case her brother in law was both her trustee and also trustee of her father and mother's trust and because of his dual role the court held that he could enforce her covenant to settle as he already held the title to her share under the residuary estate of her father.

These are unusual facts which have not occurred in any subsequent case and there is some doubt whether the decision would be followed.

There are similarities with the rule in *Strong* v. *Bird* (discussed below) but there are also some clear differences. The rule in *Strong* v. *Bird* has clearer guidelines and will only allow property to be claimed where the property passes to an executor rather than fortuitously where a trustee happens to be trustee of a similar trust.

9 EXCEPTIONS TO THE RULE 'EQUITY WILL NOT ASSIST A VOLUNTEER'

(a) The rule in *Strong* v. *Bird*

Where a donor makes an incomplete gift during his lifetime a donee may be able to enforce the gift if on the death of the donor he has been appointed as executor or he becomes the donor's administrator where the donor dies intestate.

Strong v. *Bird* (1874) LR 18 Eq 315

Mr Strong had borrowed money from his stepmother who lived in his house and who paid him rent. They agreed that his repayments could be deducted from the money she paid to him in rent each quarter. She did this for two quarterly payments and then she told him she did not expect him to repay the debt. In order to be enforceable a release from a debt should be put in the form of a deed but their agreement had been purely oral. The stepmother died and Strong was appointed her executor. In effect an executor steps into the shoes of the deceased. He was responsible for recovering all debts due to the estate which included the debt he owed to his stepmother.

The court held that his appointment as executor had the effect of perfecting the imperfect gift, in this case the release from the debt.

This principle has been extended further to include administrators as in *Re James* [1935] Ch 449 where a housekeeper had been promised by her employer before his death that the house and furniture would be hers after he died. After his death the son of the deceased gave her the title deeds but there was no transfer in her name so she did not own the legal estate. The son died intestate and the housekeeper was appointed his administrator. It was held that her appointment as administrator perfected the imperfect gift of the house to her.

(b) When will the rule in *Strong* v. *Bird* apply?

1 the donor must have manifested an immediate intention to make an *inter vivos* gift to the donee;
2 this intention must have continued until the death of the donor;
3 the donee of the gift must have been appointed executor for the donor or have been granted letters of administration if the donor died intestate; and
4 the subject matter of the gift must be capable of enduring the death of the donor.

EXAMPLE

Freddie promises Lilly that she need not repay the £2,000 she borrowed from him last year and that he will transfer his valuable collection of modern sculpture to her on his death. He does not put either promise in writing. On his death Lilly has been appointed his executor and she discovers that under his will all his estate has been left to charity.

Lilly cannot enforce his promise to transfer the paintings as the promise is not an *inter vivos* promise of the paintings but a promise of rights under the will.

However, Lilly can enforce the promise that she can be released from the debt she owed Freddie under the rule in *Strong* v. *Bird* because there is nothing to indicate that he had changed his mind about releasing her from the debt during his lifetime.

Note the following cases which show the limitations of the rule in *Strong* v. *Bird*.

In *Re Freeland* [1952] Ch 110 the owner of a car promised to transfer his car to one of his friends Hilda when it had been repaired. The car remained with the donor who then lent it to another friend May who still had the car on the donor's death. Both Hilda and May became executors to the deceased and both claimed the car. The court held that May had a better claim because the donor's original intention that Hilda should have the car had not continued until his death because he had lent it to May which was inconsistent with the need to show a continuing intention to transfer the property until the death of the donor.

A similar result occurred in *Re Gonin* [1979] Ch 16. A mother wished to transfer her house to her daughter but in error she had assumed that she could not do so because her daughter was illegitimate. Instead she wrote a cheque in her daughter's favour for £33,000. The cheque was found with the mother's property on her death. A cheque is no longer valid after the death of the transferor and although the daughter became executrix of her mother's estate she could not claim the house because the writing of the cheque by the mother undermined her continuing intention that the daughter should receive the house on her death.

(c) A *donatio mortis causa*

A *donatio mortis causa* (DMC) is an imperfect gift made in contemplation of death on the condition that it will be perfected on the death of the donor. The property is transferred to the donee but usually fails to satisfy the required formalities such as delivery or the requirement for written evidence. The gift is regarded as a conditional gift which then becomes unconditional on the death of the donor.

The conditions were laid down in the case of *Cain* v. *Moon* [1896] 2 QB 283:

1 the gift must be made in contemplation of death. It will still be effective if the donor dies from a different cause than that originally contemplated;

2 the gift must be made conditional on the death of the donor;

3 there must be delivery of the property or something symbolic of the property to the donee; and

4 the property must be capable of forming the subject matter of a *donatio mortis causa.*

EXAMPLE

Arlan is about to sail across the Atlantic with his friend Carlos in a small boat. He is not a confident sailor and he does not expect to return. He does not have time to make a will and instead he asks his close friend Sangit to visit. Arlan tells him that he wants Sangit to have some of his property. He gives him a key to a strongbox in which he says he has several share certificates, a quantity of money and the insurance documents for his car. Arlan is successful but soon after he arrives in America he becomes seriously ill with kidney failure and dies two months later. Sangit wishes to claim the property in the strongbox. He must prove that the gift of the property in the strongbox was made in contemplation of Arlan's death and that it was also conditional upon his death and had Arlan returned to England Sangit would not have a claim. He must also prove that there had been some transfer to him which could be seen as the transfer of the key and finally the property must be capable of being transferred in this way.

(i) The gift must be made in contemplation of death

There must be an impending risk of death occurring, not merely a premonition. Admission to hospital even for a routine rather than a dangerous operation will be sufficient, likewise fear of death as a result of a journey by plane. It would not be upheld where the deceased makes a gift when he is merely elderly with no reason to expect death immediately.

Death from a different cause than that expected would not prevent a DMC arising.

In *Wilkes* v. *Arlington* [1931] 2 Ch 104 the deceased was diagnosed with terminal cancer and he made a number of gifts in contemplation of his impending death although at the time he was still able to continue with his working life. He became ill with pneumonia and eventually died. The gifts made earlier in contemplation of death were upheld.

(ii) The gift must be made conditional on death

The donor must intend the gift to be absolute only on death. If the donor recovers, then it must be possible for the gift to be revoked by the donor. It will not be a valid DMC if the gift is intended to be an immediate gift. The law only upholds such gifts on the basis that the donor was unable to carry out the necessary formalities because circumstances made it impossible.

(iii) There must be delivery of the property or something symbolic of the property to the donee

The donor must deliver the property to the donee before his death. The important fact is that the donor no longer has control over the property which is now in the hands of the donee. The law accepts that the handing of a key to a locked box containing property intended to form the subject matter of the DMC may be sufficient for delivery to have taken place.

In *Re Lillingston* [1952] 2 All ER 184 the donor gave a key to the donee. It was the key to a trunk which contained a further key and eventually led to a safe deposit box containing property. The transfer of the key was sufficient delivery.

Compare the facts of the following case.

Reddel v. *Dobree* (1839) 10 Sim 244 where a donor delivered a locked cash box to the donee but he insisted that the box be returned every three months so he could check the contents. There could be no valid DMC as there had not been proper delivery.

What if the donor retains a spare set of keys?

It is difficult to accept that there can be a valid DMC where the donor retains a spare set of keys to the property transferred. This suggests there has not been transfer of control of the property by the donor to the donee.

In *Re Craven's Estate* [1937] 1 Ch 423 it was held that the retention of spare keys was not consistent with delivery of the property but the statement was obiter and the more recent decision of *Woodard* (see below) suggests that a second set of keys retained by the donor will not prevent a DMC arising.

In *Woodard* v. *Woodard* [1995] 3 All ER 980 the transfer of keys to a car from a father to his son was sufficient delivery although the donor retained a set of keys himself. The father told his son that the son could keep the keys as the father would not be driving the car anymore. The important point to consider would be why the spare keys were retained. If the donor intended to keep the keys so that the car should still be available for his own use, the position would be different but if they were retained inadvertently then there would be proper delivery.

(iv) The property must be capable of forming the subject matter of a *donatio mortis causa*

There are some forms of property which can never pass as a valid DMC. An example would be *a cheque* signed by the donor in favour of the donee. This is because a cheque is regarded as a mandate to the donor's bank and it will automatically terminate on the death of the donor.

There has also been doubt about whether *land* is capable of forming the subject matter of a DMC.

In *Sen* v. *Headley* [1991] 2 All ER 636 a seriously ill man was in hospital. He was visited in hospital by Mrs Sen who had lived with him for many years. He told her that the house was hers and he gave her a key to a strong box, which contained the title deeds and as the house had unregistered title the delivery of the deeds was significant.

The court held there had been a valid DMC and Mrs Sen could claim the house. This decision contradicted the earlier case of *Duffield* v. *Elwes* (1823) 1 Sim & St 239 which held that land could not form the subject matter of a valid DMC.

It is less likely that there could be a valid DMC today in registered land as there could not be delivery of anything symbolic of the title. It is unlikely that the delivery of keys would be held to be sufficient since they have less significance than the keys to a car.

It is also open to doubt as to whether *shares* could pass as a DMC. In *Staniland* v. *Willott* (1852) 3 Mac & G 664 it was decided that shares in a public company passed by a donor to a donee could have been a valid DMC although in this case the donor recovered and the transfer was revoked.

(d) Proprietary estoppel

The final exception to the rule that equity will not assist a volunteer is proprietary estoppel. It arises where a promise or assurance is made to a volunteer that he will acquire rights in land and as a consequence the volunteer relies on the promise and acts to his detriment. The law holds that the titleholder to the land is estopped from denying that rights have arisen.

The modern doctrine was laid down in *Taylor Fashions Ltd* v. *Liverpool Victoria Trustees Society Co. Ltd* [1981] 1 All ER 897 and showed that today it is based on the prevention of unconscionable conduct by the party where he relies on his strict legal rights to prevent the volunteer from making a claim.

An example of how proprietary estoppel can assist a volunteer is shown in *Greasley* v. *Cooke* [1980] 3 All ER 710 where a maid lived with a family for much of her life. She cared for a mentally disabled member of the family. She was promised the right to stay in the property as long as she wanted and in exchange she did not receive wages. When a member of the family later tried to evict her the court held that she had a right to occupy the property for the rest of her life.

The remedy is discretionary and according to *Jennings* v. *Rice* [2002] EWCA Civ 159 will be proportionate to the expectations of the claimant.

SUMMARY

This chapter considers the different ways in which property can be transferred to another. This could be by creating a trust in favour of the transferee or it could be by making an outright gift to him. Where a trust is created, legal title is retained by the trustee whereas in an outright gift, both legal and equitable title are passed to the transferee. A trust can be created in two ways: either by self-declaration or the transfer of the property to a third party to hold as trustee. For a trust to be valid there must be an intention to create a trust and the property must be transferred to the trustee according to any required formalities, e.g. under s.53(1)(b) Law of Property Act 1925 the declaration of a trust of land must be in writing. For a gift to be enforceable there must be proof of intention to create a gift as well as delivery of the property. A beneficiary or donee cannot enforce where the transfer is not perfect on the principle from *Milroy* v. *Lord* that equity will not perfect an imperfect gift. The rights of volunteers to enforce a promise of property are very limited. A court will enforce a transfer where the transferor has done everything in his power to transfer the property either to the trustee or the transferee under *Re Rose*. Under *Pennington* v. *Waine* the court decided that an incompletely constituted trust or gift would be enforceable if it would be unconscionable for the transferor not to transfer the property that had been promised. Over the years a small number of exceptions have arisen to the principle in *Milroy* v. *Lord*. There are however very few genuine exceptions and these are confined to the circumstances of the rule in *Strong* v. *Bird, donatio mortis causa* and proprietary estoppel. By contrast, where a beneficiary has given consideration he/she may enforce a trust and recover damages. This is not an exception because in this case the beneficiary is not a volunteer. The rule in *Strong* v. *Bird* will apply where the donor has manifested an immediate intention to make a gift which continues until the death of the donor and the donee has been appointed as executor or administrator of the estate of the donor and the subject matter of the gift must he capable of enduring the death of the donor. A *donatio mortis causa* is an imperfect gift made in contemplation of death on the condition that it will be perfected on the death of the donor. Under this exception, failure to satisfy the required formalities will not defeat the gift although there must be some symbolic delivery to the donee. Some property can never pass as a *donatio mortis causa* because it cannot survive the death of the donor, a good example is a cheque. Proprietary estoppel will allow a volunteer to claim rights in property where the formalities of transfer have not been upheld but only if the claimant can satisfy the requirements of *Taylor Fashions Ltd* v. *Liverpool Victoria Trustees Society Co. Ltd*. The remedy under proprietary estoppel is discretionary and is awarded on the basis that it is proportionate to the expectations of the claimant.

6 Formalities for the creation of a trust

KEY POINTS

- a trust can be created by either declaration of self as trustee or appointment of a third party as trustee;
- the settlor must have the capacity to create a trust;
- a trust must comply with the proper formalities on creation;
- property must be validly transferred to the trustee;
- the creation of a trust of land requires specific formalities;
- the transfer of an interest under a trust must comply with the proper formalities; and
- the formalities for the transfer of an interest under a trust can be avoided if the transfer is not a disposition of an interest under a trust.

key points

1 INTRODUCTION

A key feature of the trust is that it separates the legal and beneficial interest in the property so the trustee holds the legal title and the beneficiaries hold the equitable interest. This contrasts with sole ownership of property. Once a trust has been validly created and is fully constituted it can be enforced by the beneficiaries in court. The court will step in and enforce on behalf of the beneficiaries but it will only do so once all doubt has been removed that the trust is valid. The court must first consider whether any formalities were necessary in the creation for the trust and whether they have been adhered to. Unless such formalities are complied with the court will be unable to enforce the trust.

2 THE CREATION OF AN EXPRESS TRUST

The relationship of trustee and beneficiary under an express trust can arise in one of two situations:

1 *A declaration of self as trustee*: a person declares that property he/she owns will now be held on trust for another person. No transfer of property is required because the property is already in the hands of the trustee but there must be clear evidence that a trust was intended with all the consequences that this entails. In some cases, e.g. land, certain formalities must be followed even where the property is retained by the trustee.
2 *Transfer of property on trust to trustees*: in these cases the settlor will cease to have an interest in the property. The property must be transferred by the settlor to the trustees according to the required formalities and there may be a further requirement that the declaration of trust also complies with formalities. Once the trust is fully constituted the settlor cannot recover the property and the legal title now lies with the trustee.

An express trust will not be enforceable unless the settlor has capacity to create it and it satisfies any required formalities although it is a general rule of equity that it does not insist on formal requirements in order to create an express trust. The maxims of equity embrace the idea that equity looks more to the intention of the settlor than to the formalities necessary for the creation of a trust. An example is the maxim 'Equity looks at the intent rather than the form'.

Where the subject matter of the trust is either land or alternatively an equitable interest under a trust, specific statutory requirements must be complied with under the Law of Property Act 1925.

Constructive, implied and resulting trusts

Under s.53(2) Law of Property Act 1925 constructive, implied and resulting trusts operate informally and do not require compliance with formalities. Indeed they often arise in circumstances where the settlor is not aware that a trust has arisen so compliance with formalities would be impossible.

3 THE ROLE OF FORMALITIES IN THE CREATION OF A TRUST

Formalities have an important role in law because they promote certainty and reduce the possibility for fraud. First, formalities are important to make it clear when the interest in property has passed to the trustee and may clarify any dispute over the exact timing of when the trust has become fully constituted which are far more likely where transfers take place orally. Second, formalities may clarify the question of when an interest under a trust has been transferred from one beneficiary to another.

EXAMPLE

Bernard owns two farms. His nephew Alfred helps in one of the farms, Grove Farm and one day Bernard tells Alfred he wants him to have Grove Farm after his death but to reduce the tax payable on his death he is going to hold the farm as trustee for him.

    If Bernard and Alfred argue the following year, then it would be very difficult to prove that this conversation took place but if this is evidenced in writing and signed by Bernard he cannot later deny that Alfred has rights in Grove Farm.

4 WHO HAS THE CAPACITY TO CREATE A TRUST?

(a) Generally

In general, any person has the capacity to create a trust and the property can either be transferred to a third party or could be held on trust by the owner after making a declaration of trust. There are some exceptions to this general rule.

(b) Minors

A child under 18 may create a trust of personalty but it is voidable and he/she may repudiate it when he/she reaches the age of eighteen. A child under the age of 18 may hold personalty on resulting trust as shown in *Re Vinogradoff* [1935] WN 68 where a granddaughter was found to hold war loan stock on resulting trust for her grandmother's estate. Although the grandmother had transferred it into her granddaughter's name the grandmother continued to receive the dividends until her death and so the court held that the daughter held it on presumed resulting trust. This is discussed in more detail in Chapter 9.

Under s.1(6) Law of Property Act 1925 a child may not hold a legal estate in land so he/she cannot create a trust of realty under eighteen. The legal estate must be held in the name of the trustee.

(c) The mentally ill

There is no strict rule preventing a person who is mentally ill from creating a trust of any kind of property that he/she owns. If there is evidence, which suggests that a person does not have the mental capacity to create a trust, then a disposition made by him/her will not be effective to transfer the property.

Re Beaney [1978] (below) suggests that the law on mental capacity varies according to the size of the gift and the overall effect of such a gift.

Re Beaney [1978] 2 All ER 595

In this case the settlor was a woman who was suffering from senile dementia. She left her house to the daughter who had cared for her while she was ill. If the trust was upheld for the daughter who acted as carer, her other children would receive little from her estate as the house was her main asset.

It was held the settlor must be able to understand the nature of the gift and also its overall effect on the gift on the claims of the other children. The settlor could not understand the full nature of her gift as she could not understand its effect on the other children.

5 WHAT FORMALITIES ARE NECESSARY IN THE CREATION OF A TRUST?

(a) The general rule

As a general rule trusts do not require a specific form but merely proof that there is an intention that a trust is to be created.

For example the creation of a trust of personalty during the lifetime of the settlor merely requires proof that the settlor intends to create the trust.

EXAMPLE

Sheila wishes to create a trust in favour of her three daughters Ada, Belinda and Carrie. The trust property is her very extensive collection of valuable jewellery. She transfers the jewellery collection to her friend Teresa and tells her to hold the pieces on trust for the daughters. She tells Teresa which pieces of jewellery are to be given to each daughter. The following week she becomes seriously ill and eventually dies. Her executor, who is her second husband Tony, claims the jewellery forms part of the estate because there is nothing in writing about the creation of the trust. The trust is enforceable by the three daughters. This is a trust of personalty and does not require formalities to be complied with, other than proof of intention to create a trust. In this case the trustee Teresa will be able to give evidence that Sheila wished the property to be held on trust.

(b) This is a general rule and there are several situations where other rules apply

These depend on the type of property concerned and whether the trust is created during the settlor's lifetime or on death.

1 a lifetime trust of realty and other property;
2 a declaration of a trust under a will;
3 a disposition of an equitable interest.

(i) A lifetime of trust and other property

Under s.53(1)(b) Law of Property Act 1925 'a declaration of a trust of land or any interest therein must be manifested and proved by some writing signed by the person who is able to declare such a trust or by his will'.

The effect of this section is that the declaration of a trust of land does not need to be wholly in writing but it does require a piece of written evidence which could be executed at a later date and then signed by the settlor. It will not be a valid express trust of land without evidence in writing.

The written evidence must include certain key information such as the terms of the trust, the beneficiaries of the trust and also the trust property. The section does not explain the effect of failure to comply with the requirement of writing and it is presumed that the declaration will be *unenforceable* rather than *void*. So if the parties chose to uphold it then the law would recognise the rights of the beneficiary behind the trust.

EXAMPLE

Maria wishes to create a trust for her two children of her jewellery, which consists of two diamond necklaces and a pair of pearl earrings, and her house. She says to them both I want you to have my jewellery and my house. I am now holding them on trust for you both.

Under her will all her property has been left to a charity. Can the children claim all the property promised to them?

Maria has not complied with the formalities necessary to create a trust of land. Although she has manifested the intention to create a trust she has not satisfied the formalities laid down under s.53(1)(b) Law of Property Act 1925.

Under her will the house will pass to the charity. By contrast there are no formalities necessary for the transfer of a gift of personalty although the settlor must manifest an intention to create a trust. The jewellery will pass as she has shown an intention to hold the jewellery on trust. If she had merely said 'I want you to have my jewellery' and nothing more, the trust would not be enforceable but here she has expressly declared herself to be trustee.

(ii) Equity will not allow a statute to be used as an instrument of fraud

This maxim of equity was intended to prevent the formal requirements from acting as a barrier and preventing a claimant from asserting their rights where the legal owner tries to use the formalities in order to perpetrate a fraud.

The principle was expressed by Lindley LJ in *Rochefoucauld* v. *Boustead* [1897] 1 Ch 196: 'it is a fraud on the part of a person to whom land has been conveyed as a trustee, and who knows it was so conveyed, to deny the trust and claim the land for himself'.

In this case, an oral declaration of trust in land was later denied by the trustee who declared that no trust existed. The court found in favour of the claimant on the basis that the property had been transferred expressly subject to her rights and it would be inequitable for those rights to be denied in spite of the lack of written evidence necessary under the statute.

This case has been subject to criticism because it undermines the status of formalities.

As discussed earlier, formalities are necessary to ensure that there is certainty in transactions involving land and there should be no exceptions. In this case it would have been a better solution if the court found that the land was held on constructive trust because it would have been unconscionable for the trustee to deny the claimant rights in the property knowing that the land had not been transferred to him absolutely.

Other cases have been decided in similar circumstances on the basis of a *constructive trust*. An example is *Bannister* v. *Bannister* [1948] 2 All ER 133 where property was transferred to X on the oral understanding that Y, an elderly lady, could remain living there. Later X tried to evict her and the court held this action gave rise to a constructive trust in favour of Y because the denial of Y's rights was based on fraud.

EXAMPLE

Clarence wishes to create a trust of his small country cottage which he uses for weekend visits. He tells his friend Denzil that he is going to transfer his cottage to him but wishes him to hold it for his goddaughter, Viola. Clarence tells Viola that he is going to do this for her. The cottage is transferred to Denzil and a few months later Clarence becomes seriously ill and dies. Clarence has not made a will and all his estate will pass to his family. Viola has contacted Denzil to ask about the cottage.

Unless there is evidence in writing to comply with s.53(1)(b) Law of Property Act 1925 Viola is unable to enforce her rights as a beneficiary under a trust. Her only possibility is that she can claim that the rule in *Rochefoucauld* v. *Boustead* (discussed above) applies to her. Alternatively she could argue that there is a constructive trust in her favour. However it will be more difficult to argue that she has rights because the transfer to Denzil has not been made *expressly subject to her rights* as a term of the transfer as in *Bannister* v. *Bannister*.

(c) Formalities of transfer of trust property to the trustees (types of property)

(i) Transfer of land to trustees under s.52 Law of Property Act 1925

In cases where the real property is not to be held in trust by the settlor himself as trustee for the beneficiaries but is to be held on trust by another person as trustee then the real property must be transferred to the trustee. This must comply with s.52 Law of Property Act 1925 which requires a deed to be used for a disposition of an interest in land. A deed is defined in s.1 Law of Property (Miscellaneous Provisions) Act 1989. It is a document in writing that declares itself to be a deed, is signed by the transferor and is witnessed. The trustee will not own the land at law until he/she has been registered as owner at the Land Registry.

(ii) Transfer of shares to the trustees to be held on trust

If shares constitute trust property, their transfer to the trustees must follow specific formalities. The transfer of the legal ownership of shares requires registration of the trustee in place of the name of the settlor. It is important to note that if the settlor delivers the share certificates to the trustee with an oral declaration of trust this in itself will not be enough to create a valid trust.

(d) A declaration of a trust under a will

A settlor can declare a trust of any property including both land and personalty under a will. The requirements of a valid will are set out in s.9 Wills Act 1837.

A will is only valid if it is made in writing and it must be both signed by the testator or by some other person acting at his direction in his presence and also in the presence of two witnesses who must also attest and sign the will or alternatively acknowledge their signatures in the presence of the testator. There is no enforceable trust while the testator is alive because at any time he/she may revoke his will. The trust will be fully constituted on the death of the settlor and will only then become enforceable.

(e) A disposition of a subsisting equitable interest

Where a beneficiary receives an interest under a trust, it is property that the beneficiary can transfer to another either by sale or by gift or generally deal in. In some cases a beneficiary may wish to create a trust over his/her interest under a trust. Specific formalities are required in order to dispose of a subsisting equitable interest under a trust.

The Law of Property Act 1925 s.53(1)(c) provides that:

a disposition of an equitable interest or trust subsisting at the time of the disposition must be in writing signed by the person disposing of the same, or his agent thereunto lawfully authorised in writing or by will.

The section applies when a beneficiary under a trust tries to dispose of his or her interest under a trust. It is important to note that if the beneficiary does not comply with the formalities laid down in the statute no disposition takes place. The law regards it as a void disposition.

EXAMPLE

Sarah has an interest under a fixed trust. She is entitled to income under the trust every year. She receives approximately £2,500 each year. She wants her friend's daughter Karen to receive the money. She tells the trustees Len and Max to hold her interest on trust for Karen from now on. Unless this instruction is in writing it is a void transfer and Karen will have no right to the money. If it is in writing, the disposition will be enforceable and Karen can bring an action against the trustees if they fail to transfer the money to her.

(f) Why are formalities necessary for the disposition of an equitable interest under a trust?

The reasons why formalities were necessary in these circumstances were explained by Lord Upjohn in *Vandervell* v. *IRC* [1967] 2 AC 291: 'the object of this section, as was the object of the old Statute of Frauds is to prevent hidden oral transactions in equitable interests in fraud of those truly entitled, and making it difficult, if not impossible, for the trustees to ascertain who are in truth his beneficiaries'.

(g) What is a disposition of an equitable interest under s.53(1)(c)?

A declaration of a new trust is excluded from this section. It only applies to the *disposition* of a subsisting interest. Historically, if the transfer of an interest was seen as a disposition, then it could have fallen within the section and it would then be subject to various taxes. Parties to a transaction tried to prevent it from being seen as a disposition of an equitable interest and so attracting tax.

It was assumed at one time that the section could be avoided if it were possible to argue that the interest was transferred orally and then evidenced in writing as under s.53(1)(b) but this was found to be contrary to the requirements of the section.

The case below indicates what transactions may be seen as dispositions under s.53(1)(c).

(h) *Grey* v. *IRC*

Grey v. *IRC* [1960] AC 1

The appellants were bare trustees acting on behalf of Mr Hunter. In 1949 he created six settlements in favour of his five grandchildren and one for his future grandchildren. In February 1955 he transferred 18,000 shares to the trustees to be held on bare trust for himself. Two weeks later he indicated orally that the shares were to be held for his grandchildren. In March 1955, the trustees executed trust deeds which declared that the shares were held for the beneficiaries (the grandchildren).

The appellants argued that the disposition had taken place in February and not in March when the written document had been executed. Why did the appellants want to argue that the disposition took place in February and not March? The reason why the appellants wished to argue that the disposition had taken place in February was because they wished to argue that the oral instruction constituted the disposition of Mr Hunter's interest. If the disposition was deemed to take place in March, which was the time when the deed was executed, then the disposition would attract tax because stamp duty was payable on a written transfer of an interest.

The House of Lords held that there was no disposition in February when Mr Hunter gave an oral instruction to his trustees. The leading speech was delivered by Viscount Simonds who declared that if a disposition was 'given its natural meaning, it cannot, I think, be denied that a direction given by Mr Hunter, whereby the beneficial interest in the shares theretofore vested in him became vested in another or others, is a disposition'.

In the House of Lords' view the disposition by Mr Hunter took place in March on the execution of the deed. This was a disposition within the natural and ordinary meaning of the word. When Mr Hunter orally directed his trustees to transfer the interest in the shares, he was attempting to make a disposition of the interest and the only way he could do this would be by use of a written document to satisfy s.53(1)(c). However he could not then avoid attracting liability to stamp duty which was payable on certain written documents because the disposition took place when Mr Hunter executed the written document.

(i) What transfers of property do not constitute dispositions of an equitable interest under s.53(1)(c)?

There is no disposition if both the legal and the equitable interest are transferred together

This will occur where the settlor is still the owner of both the legal and the equitable title to the property. This will fall outside s.53(1)(c) because there is no separate transfer of the equitable interest. In this case the law regards the transferor as the sole legal owner and so the transfer will fall outside the section. This exception will include the situation where bare trustees hold the legal title. Here the trustees known as nominee trustees do not have control of the legal title and the settlor has the right to recall the legal title at any time. Since the law regards the transferor as retaining some interest in the legal title there is no separate disposition of the equitable title and the section will not apply. This is illustrated by *Vandervell* v. *IRC*, which is one of a series of cases concerning transactions carried out by Mr Vandervell.

(j) *Vandervell* v. *IRC*

Vandervell v. *IRC* [1967] 2 AC 291

Mr Vandervell wanted to transfer £150,000 to the Royal College of Surgeons (RCS) in order to establish a chair in pharmacology so he transferred shares to a bank to hold these shares as nominees. However he also wanted to set an upper limit on the amount transferred to them and he also wished to minimise his tax liability. He instructed the bank to transfer the shares to the RCS. The RCS was now able to register itself as owner of the shares but he also instructed the RCS to grant his own trust company (the Vandervell Trustees Ltd) an option to repurchase the shares for the sum of £5,000. Dividends were declared on the shares of over £145,000 and the Inland Revenue claimed income tax from Vandervell. He argued that he did not own the shares. The Inland Revenue argued that the transfer to the RCS required compliance with s.53(1)(c) and since it had not been declared in writing it was a void disposition.

The House of Lords however regarded the transfer to the RCS as part of one transaction, transferring both the legal and the equitable title to the transferee and it therefore fell outside s.53(1)(c).

According to Lord Upjohn: 'when the beneficial owner owns the whole beneficial interest and is in the position to give directions to his bare trustee with regard to the legal as well as the equitable estate there can be no possible ground for invoking the section where the beneficial owner wants to deal with the legal estate as well as the equitable estate'.

An important point in this case was that the legal title to the shares was held by the trustees and the equitable interest lay with Mr Vandervell but the House of Lords held that Mr Vandervell was the only person who could direct the transfer of both the legal and equitable interests. As a result the transaction did not constitute *a disposition of an equitable interest* and therefore it did not require writing and without a written disposition of the interest it did not attract stamp duty on the transaction.

EXAMPLE

Henry has a large number of shares in various companies which were held on bare trust by the London Bank as nominees. He decided to transfer these shares into a trust in order to raise a certain amount of money for his old school to build a new sports pavilion. He directed the bank to transfer the shares to the school. However, he does not want the school to have absolute ownership of the shares after the pavilion has been built. He therefore reserved an option to repurchase the shares. He transferred the option to a subsidiary company that he owns with the intention of exercising this option when the work is complete.

He wants to know whether the transfer of the shares constituted a disposition and whether it mattered that he had not put his instructions into writing. In this case the courts would not view this transaction as a disposition of an equitable interest because initially he transfers both the legal and the equitable interest. It would be similar to the facts of *Vandervell* v. *IRC*.

There was a second more complex point and that was whether the option to repurchase the shares constituted an interest in the shares for Mr Vandervell and if so, was he liable to tax on any income that he received from the shares?

The courts then considered the possibility that in granting the option to purchase to Vandervell Trustees Ltd, Mr Vandervell had not fully divested himself of the interest.

When the case eventually reached the House of Lords, Lord Upjohn considered whether Mr Vandervell had retained an option. He used the following example: 'where A transfers, or directs a trustee for him to transfer, the legal estate in property to B otherwise than for valuable consideration it is a question of the intention of A in making the transfer whether B was to take beneficially or on trust and if, the latter, on what trusts'.

He concluded that where the beneficial interest lies with one person and he fails to effectively transfer it to another then the interest must stay with that person. In this case it resulted in Mr Vandervell being liable to tax on the interest which he was said to retain.

(i) There is no disposition where a subsisting equitable interest is extinguished under a resulting trust

Re Vandervell's Trust (*No. 2*) [1974] Ch 269

There was however a further issue which was revisited some years later after the death of Mr Vandervell which also concerned the option to repurchase the shares.

Re Vandervell's Trust (No. 2) [1974] Ch 269

The trust company had exercised the option after the RCS had benefited sufficiently from the shares to establish the Chair in Pharmacology. Having purchased the shares, the trustees then informed the Revenue, that the shares were now held on trust for Mr Vandervell's children by Vandervell Trustees Ltd and all dividends were to be paid to these settlements. The Inland Revenue claimed that Mr Vandervell remained liable to tax because he still retained an interest in the shares. Again the court had to address the issue of whether or not the transfer constituted a disposition. If it was a disposition, then the transfer would need to comply with s.53(1)(c).

Megarry J. upheld the claim by the Revenue that Mr Vandervell retained an interest in the shares after he had directed the trustees to transfer the shares into the settlements for the children but the Court of Appeal reversed his finding.

It held that the transfer to the children was simply the extinguishment of an interest under a resulting trust and therefore it fell outside s.53(1)(c) since as Lord Denning declared 'a resulting trust for the settlor is born and dies without any writing at all'.

The declaration of trust in favour of the children simply extinguished Vandervell's interest under the resulting trust of the option and so never constituted a disposition within the statute.

On a practical note, if the Court of Appeal had not found that Mr Vandervell had divested himself of any interest in the shares when he directed the trust company to hold for the children, his estate would have been liable for an enormous tax bill which would have been taken from his children's interests and they were the very people Mr Vandervell had tried to benefit.

It could be supposed that the decision was driven by a perceived desire to protect the children from paying the tax liability of their father.

(ii) There is no disposition where the transfer of the subsisting equitable interest is a specifically enforceable contract

If a purchaser has entered into a specifically enforceable contract of sale, then the contract may be enforced by a decree of specific performance. In these circumstances the vendor or transferor will hold the property on constructive trust for the purchaser. If the property to be sold is an equitable interest behind a trust, then this may be a way of avoiding the need for writing under s.53(1)(c).

Oughtred v. IRC [1959]

This case illustrates the circumstances where a specifically enforceable contract for sale may arise.

Oughtred v. IRC [1959] 3 All ER 623

Shares in a private company were held for Mrs Oughtred for her life and then on her death for her son. There was an opportunity to save tax if the son transferred all his shareholding (an equitable interest under a trust) to his mother and in return she transferred another shareholding to nominees for him. This was agreed orally and then a deed of release was drawn up. The issue before the House of Lords was whether such a deed itself attracted stamp duty. It was argued on their behalf that the transfer took place when they orally agreed on the transfer and from then on the son held his interest on constructive trust for his mother.

The House of Lords did not accept this although there was a dissenting judgment from Lord Radcliffe who argued that there was a constructive trust of the shares and that would not require further evidence in writing in order to take effect.

The approach of Lord Radcliffe in this case was adopted in subsequent cases, e.g. *Neville v. Wilson* [1997] Ch 144 where an oral agreement between shareholders to share the assets of the company between themselves rateably was upheld on the basis that it arose under a constructive trust which did not require written evidence under s.53(1)(c).

(iii) Nomination by a member of an employees' pension fund

The potential pensioner had the chance to nominate a person who would benefit on his/her death. The nomination could be seen potentially as a disposition.

Re Danish Bacon Co. Ltd Staff Pension Fund [1971] 1 All ER 486

It was held by Megarry J. that a nomination of benefits to another is not a disposition of a subsisting interest since the interest is a future interest. On the facts of this case s.53(1)(c) would have been satisfied since there was written evidence of the nomination but it established the exception.

(a) Disclaimers of beneficial interests

If a beneficiary disclaims a beneficial interest, this will not be regarded as a disposition requiring written evidence

Re Paradise Motors Co. [1968] 2 All ER 625

A stepson disclaimed a gift of an interest in shares from his stepfather. The court held that since the gift had not been transferred to him, it had not passed into his hands. This could not constitute a disposition of an equitable interest but was avoidance of an interest and was therefore outside s.53(1)(c).

(b) Sub-trusts

A disposition is strictly interpreted so if the holder declares that he/she is holding his/her beneficial interest on trust for another this is not seen as a disposition. The law regards this as the declaration of a sub-trust. There are no formalities required unless it is land, which must be made in writing to comply with s.53(1)(b). A sub-trust will only come into existence where the beneficiary still has some role in the trust and has not dropped out of the picture altogether.

EXAMPLE

A large shareholding is left to Julian under a trust. Julian would like his three children to benefit from his interest during his lifetime and he may direct his trustees to transfer the income to any or all of his children during his lifetime. Julian wishes to decide which of the children is to benefit. The children can enforce against Julian if he fails to make a choice each year although their rights are only rights of discretionary beneficiaries. The property will revert back to Julian's estate on his death and will pass with his estate.

SUMMARY

This chapter explores the role of formalities in trusts. It shows that equity leans against the need for formalities and looks instead at intent rather than form. However there are a number of specific formalities that have been laid down in the Law of Property Act 1925 which must be complied with. A trust will not generally be valid unless on creation it upholds the statutory formalities. The creation of a trust of pure personalty does not require any formalities other than proof of intention to create a trust and where the trustee is a third party, rather than the settlor himself, the transfer of the trust property to the trustee. A trust of land requires evidence in writing according to s.53(1)(b) Law of Property Act. This is strictly enforced although where there is no evidence in writing the trust will be unenforceable rather than void. Where there is no evidence in writing but the trustee knows that the land is not for him absolutely, equity will intervene and allow the beneficiary to enforce his rights under the rule in *Rochefoucauld* v. *Boustead*.

Where a beneficiary wishes to dispose of his equitable interest behind a trust he must satisfy certain formalities under s.53(1)(c) in particular the need for the disposition to be in writing and signed. The disposition will be void if the formalities under this section have not been complied with. Many cases have been argued in the courts on the meaning of a disposition including *Vandervell* v. *IRC*, *Grey* v. *IRC* and *Oughtred* v. *IRC* and the possible ways to avoid the effects of the section. It is clear that a disposition of an interest must be made in writing and if it is made orally and later evidenced in writing it is the later written document that constitutes the disposition. There are a number of exceptions to s.53(1)(c) which include the disposition of both the legal and the equitable title at the same time as shown in *Vandervell* v. *IRC*. If a sub-trust is created where the beneficiary retains active duties, the need to satisfy s.53(1)(c) can also be avoided. Where the disposition of the interest is a specifically enforceable contract s.53(1)(c) will not apply because the court will hold that the property is held under a constructive trust and in this case s.53(2) applies which does not require formalities to be satisfied.

7 Private purpose trusts

KEY POINTS

- a trust cannot be enforced unless there is an ascertainable beneficiary;
- a trust for a purpose may fail because either the objects are uncertain or it infringes the perpetuity rule;
- a purpose trust may be saved if it comes within one of the anomalous exceptions which includes trusts for specific animals and trusts for the building of monuments;
- a purpose trust may be saved if there are hidden beneficiaries under the principle in *Re Denley's Trust Deed*;
- a purpose trust may be saved as a gift to an unincorporated association for the members of the association; and
- a purpose trust may be saved if the purpose of the trust is charitable.

key points

1 THE BENEFICIARY PRINCIPLE

One of the key rules in the creation of a valid trust is that a trust will only be valid if it has ascertainable beneficiaries. The reason for this is straightforward. The beneficial interest lies with the beneficiaries and it is only they who have the capacity to enforce the trust. Without beneficiaries the trust would have no one to enforce the trust and ensure that the trustees carry out their duties. Some examples of a private purpose trust are set out in the following sections.

EXAMPLE

Jason leaves £1,000 for the purpose of fishing and Sharon leaves a gift of £14,500 to build a beach hut on the beach at Aldeburgh for visitors to enjoy.

In both cases there is no obvious beneficiary to enforce. In the first case would it be to people who liked fishing or for those who wanted to teach others to fish or perhaps for people who wanted to conserve fish in the North Sea?

In the second case could the people of Aldeburgh enforce or would anyone who visited Aldeburgh regularly be able to enforce?

The rule against purpose trusts can be traced back to the early nineteenth century. In *Morice* v. *Bishop of Durham* (1804) 9 Ves Jr 399 a trust created for 'such objects of benevolence and liberality as the Bishop of Durham would approve of' failed as a charitable trust because the words used were not exclusively for charitable purposes.

However, it also failed as a private purpose trust because there were no obvious beneficiaries who could enforce the trust. 'Objects of benevolence and liberality' were not an ascertainable group who could be clearly defined.

The principle was later restated in *Re Astor's Settlement Trusts* [1952] Ch 534. A trust was created which included a provision that the trustees were to apply the income from a fund for a number of non-charitable purposes which included: 'the maintenance ... of good understanding ... between nations'; 'the preservation of the independence and integrity of newspapers'. The trusts were not charitable but they also each failed as a private purpose trust both for the lack of a beneficiary to enforce and also because the objects were void for uncertainty.

Roxburgh J. stated that: 'the only beneficiaries are purposes and at present unascertainable persons, it is difficult to see who could initiate proceedings. If the purposes are valid trusts, the settlors have retained no beneficial interest and could not initiate them.'

EXAMPLE

Fiola leaves £100,000 to Gary and Gordon in their absolute discretion to uphold peace initiatives within Europe.

There are *no obvious beneficiaries* to enforce the trust if Gary and Gordon refuse to carry out the wishes of Fiola or if they are uncertain how to carry out her wishes and even if they make an application to the court it would also be uncertain how to act.

The trust is also unenforceable because the *objects are not certain*. The certainty of objects test for this trust would be the 'given postulant test' or the 'is or is not test' under *McPhail v. Doulton* because it is a discretionary trust and the trustees could not say with certainty of any beneficiary that he/she comes within the group.

The other problem with such a trust is that it could potentially run forever. This would offend the *perpetuity rule*. This rule limits the maximum period in which property can vest in the beneficiary which means that the beneficiary becomes entitled to the property. It was assumed that to delay vesting could create uncertainty and property would be tied up for too long and without an effective 'owner' the property would lie dormant. Where a gift vested outside the perpetuity period it was void and the gift would fail and the property would revert back to the settlor. This issue has been partially addressed in the Perpetuities and Accumulations Act 2009. The reforms introduced under the act include the introduction of a single perpetuity period. This now applies to all lifetime trusts set up after the provisions of the 2009 Act came into force in April 2010. Non-charitable purpose trusts are expressly outside the new rules under s.18 of the Act.

The new perpetuity period is *125 years* although it will be possible for the settlor to specify a shorter trust period. There are special provisions for any trust already in existence.

The perpetuity period does not apply to charitable trusts although the rule against accumulations of income does apply. Income can only be accumulated for twenty-one years unless the Charity Commission orders otherwise. So if a purpose trust comes within the definition of charity these provisions will not apply.

2 THE ANOMALOUS EXCEPTIONS TO THE BENEFICIARY PRINCIPLE

For many years the courts have upheld *anomalous exceptions* to the beneficiary principle. Under these exceptions certain private purpose trusts can be upheld as valid. The exceptions do not have any obvious link with each other which explains why they are regarded as anomalous.

In the words of Roxburgh J. in *Re Astor's Settlement Trusts* the exceptions were 'anomalous and exceptional ... concessions to human weakness or sentiment'.

The exceptions fall into one of three groups:

1 care of single named animals;
2 tombs and monuments;
3 others, e.g. saying masses for the dead.

If a trust falls within one of the anomalous groups, it must still comply with the perpetuity period requirements, as mentioned above, previously a period of twenty-one years for private purpose trusts but is now 125 years.

(a) Care of single named animals

A trust for the care of animals in general has traditionally been upheld as a charitable trust but a trust for a single animal or small groups of animals would not be charitable because it would not fulfil the public benefit requirement for a charitable trust.

In *Pettingall* v. *Pettingall* (1842) 11 LJ Ch 176 a gift of £50 per annum to be used for the benefit of the care of the testator's black mare. There was a further provision that any surplus remaining after her death was to pass to the executor. This was upheld as a valid gift and the court held that the residuary legatees were able to supervise the performance of the trust.

Compare *Re Dean* (1889) LR 41 Ch D 552 where the gift was to be applied for the maintenance of the testator's horses and hounds 'should they live so long' to a maximum period of fifty years. The trust was valid although it clearly exceeded the perpetuity period in force at the time and secondly there was no obvious person who could enforce the trust as in the case of *Pettingall.*

(b) Tombs and monuments

A trust to erect and maintain a grave or a monument has usually been upheld as one of the anomalous exceptions where it complies with the perpetuity period.

The following trusts were upheld because they were left solely for the erection of a monument.

A gift of £1,000 in *Trimmer* v. *Danby* (1856) 25 LJ Ch 424 to be used for a monument in memory of the testator at St Paul's Cathedral was valid as it was a single instance of expenditure and the perpetuity period would not be affected.

The same view was taken in *Mitford* v. *Reynolds* (1848) 16 Sim 105 where a sum of money was left to erect a monument.

The following trusts were upheld because they were for the erection and maintenance of a monument and they complied with the perpetuity period.

The gift in *Pirbright* v. *Salway* [1896] WN 86 of £800 for the maintenance and upkeep of a burial enclosure dedicated to children 'for so long as the law permitted' was upheld.

Likewise in *Re Hooper* [1932] 1 Ch 38 income from a gift of £1000 was to be used by the executors for the upkeep of various graves and monuments for 'so long as they can legally do so' was also upheld.

Gifts under the anomalous exception which failed: *Re Endacott* [1960] Ch 232 a gift of money left by the settlor 'for the purposes of providing some useful memorial to myself' failed for lack of clarity of what would constitute a 'useful memorial'. Although a gift of £300 to be used for the purpose of erecting a monument in *Mussett* v. *Bingle* [1876] WN 170 was upheld a further sum of £200 for maintenance of the monument failed because it was void for perpetuity.

If the gift is found to be *capricious*, the courts will refuse to enforce it even where it is within one of the anomalous exceptions. Occasionally the courts have taken a view about whether the provision of funds to build a monument would be excessive. In *M'Caig* v. *University of Glasgow* [1907] SC 231 and *M'Caig's Trustees* v. *Kirk-Session of United Free Church of Lismore* [1915] 1 SLT 152 a gift for the building of multiple memorials in memory of some of the M'Caig family members was declared invalid by the Scottish courts.

In *Brown* v. *Burdett* (1882) 21 Ch D 667 a trust directing the executors to keep rooms in a house sealed up for twenty years was also declared capricious.

(c) Saying masses for the dead

A settlor may leave a sum of money solely for the purpose of paying for a mass to be said or a religious service to be held in his or her memory. This is a purpose trust and again it is not clear who would enforce this if the mass were not held. The courts have leaned in favour of upholding these gifts.

Where a gift is left for the saying of a mass in public it will be regarded as a charitable gift because it would fulfil the public benefit test. Where the mass is to be held in private it will be held as a valid private purpose trust as long as it does not exceed the perpetuity period. This was first accepted in *Bourne* v. *Keane* [1919] AC 815 and later extended to other non-Christian ceremonies in *Re Khoo Cheng Teow* [1932] Straits Settlements LR 226.

EXAMPLE

Ferdinand makes a will and includes the following terms:

1 £700 to erect a tasteful monument in favour of myself and my dear wife Clara;
2 £800 to be used to look after my dog Fido;

3 £600 to my church in order to say a mass in my memory after my death.

The gifts in 2 and 3 are likely to be upheld so long as they conform with the perpetuity period. Fido is a single named animal and the mass will also be enforceable. There is no possibility that Fido will live beyond the end of the perpetuity period. The gift to the church for the saying of a mass will be enforceable as it is a single mass and comes within the anomalous exceptions. The gift in 1 is unlikely to be upheld on the basis of *Re Endacott* because 'a tasteful monument' is unclear. The trustees could not carry this out and if they asked for directions from the court it will also be unable to direct what would be a tasteful monument.

3 THE *RE DENLEY* EXCEPTION AND TRUSTS FOR INDIVIDUALS WITH A PURPOSE ATTACHED

(a) The *Re Denley* exception

Many private trusts may appear to be for a purpose and should therefore fail but may in fact have hidden beneficiaries who could enforce them. It is rare to have a trust that is purely for a purpose.

EXAMPLE

Consider the following examples:

1 A gift of £4,000 to educate my two sons Sol and Tom;
2 Sum of £1,200 to be used to provide a tennis court for the employees of Barts and Co.

Both these examples are trusts for purposes and not for people but in both cases there are obvious beneficiaries who could enforce. In 1 the trust is set up for a purpose but it is possible to argue that Sol and Tom are hidden beneficiaries and in 2 the employees could be regarded as hidden beneficiaries. The tennis court is for the employees to enjoy. The law now accepts that a purpose trust with an obvious beneficiary or group of beneficiaries who could enforce will be upheld so long as it is within the perpetuity period.

Re Denley's Trust Deed [1969] 1 Ch 373

Land was given in trust for the purpose of a recreation or sports ground primarily for the benefit of the employees of a specified company. Goff J. held that although this appeared to be a private purpose trust it could be upheld because it was primarily for the benefit of an individual or individuals namely the employees. The employees could enforce the trust if the trustees failed to carry out the terms of the trust. The gift was expressly stated to be within the perpetuity period.

There are problems with the *Re Denley* approach and the decision has been criticised.

Issues arising from *Re Denley*

The employees in the case did not have the same interest as the beneficiaries in an ordinary private trust. Consider the following differences:

1 If the trust is upheld, then *who* owns the beneficial interest? The employees did not have an equitable interest enforceable against the trustees. They could not realise a share in the property. They merely had a right to use the sports ground. The employees were seen as the beneficiaries who were able to enforce against the trustees but could they demand a transfer of a share of the trust property?

2 As the trust concerned land owned by more than one person it would be a trust of land under which certain rights arise such as the right to occupy and under which the trustees have all the management powers such as the right to grant leases or to mortgage the property but the employees in this case could not have the right to occupy. This is less of a problem than the issue in 1 (i.e. who owns the beneficial interest) because under the *Trusts of Land and Appointment of Trustees Act 1996* the beneficiaries do not have the right to occupy property where the land is unsuitable for occupation.

3 If the employees had an interest in the trust property, then logically they could demand a transfer of the property under the rule in *Saunders* v. *Vautier* (1841) 4 Beav 115 but termination of the trust was never the intention of the settlor who had specified that it was to be used for a recreation ground so this could never have taken place in *Re Denley*.

The best interpretation is to allow such trusts to be upheld where there are beneficiaries who can benefit either directly or indirectly from the trust.

In *Re Denley* the benefit was indirect to the employees but it was sufficient for them to have the right to enforce the trust but not to claim a share of the beneficial interest.

(b) *Re Bowes*: is the purpose of the trust mandatory?

Alternatively, the law may hold that the purpose of the gift was not mandatory but merely indicative of the settlor's wishes. In the first example it could be held that this is a gift to Sol and Tom and the application of the money for their education was not imperative but merely a power to apply it for the purpose of education. In this case, Sol and Tom could keep the money for themselves.

In *Re Bowes* [1896] 1 Ch 507 it was held that a gift of money to two named individuals be used for the planting of trees on an estate could be claimed absolutely by the individuals. The court held that the planting of trees was merely intended to be the testator's motive behind the gift.

This principle has been extended to cases where the settlor has left property for the purpose of education as in the example of Sol and Tom. It may be possible that the trust is an absolute trust for the named individuals with a secondary purpose added to it.

In *Re Osoba* [1979] 1 WLR 247 a fund was left by a father for the education of his daughter up to university. The daughter completed her university education and there was a surplus of money left over. The court held that she was entitled to keep the money since education was no more than a motive for the gift. The money could be kept by the daughter rather than resulting back to the settlor's estate.

A similar result was held in *Re Andrew's* [1905] 2 Ch 48 where a trust was set up for the education of the children of a clergyman. There was a surplus left after they had all been educated and it was held that although the trust had been set up for their education the children could take the surplus for themselves for their own use.

Compare the following case

In *Re Trusts of the Abbott Fund* [1900] 2 Ch 326 a fund was collected for the care of two deaf and dumb old ladies by people who lived in the same village. After the death of the two old ladies there remained a sum of money in the fund. Who could claim the money:

1 the relatives of the old ladies; or
2 all the people who had subscribed to the fund?

If the case followed *Re Andrew's Trusts* and the later case of *re Osoba*, the money could be kept by the relatives but the judge found against them and the money was returned to the subscribers. The judge held that the money had never been given to the old ladies absolutely but expressly for their maintenance alone.

The decisions in these three cases are difficult to rationalise although the fact that the old ladies had died may have been a reason why the courts refused to give the money to relatives who would never have been in the contemplation of the settlor in this case the subscribers to the fund. In *Osoba* and *Andrew's* the children who were to benefit from the surplus were both still alive.

EXAMPLE

Salvador wants to ensure that his two children Bob and Eli are all educated to a high standard. He leaves a sum of £40,000 to be applied towards a university education for them all in a trust fund. Bob leaves school and decides not to go to university. Eli decides to go to university to study maths. After four terms he decides that studying is too dull for him and he leaves university to find a job.

There is £32,000 left in the fund. Can Bob and Eli both claim it absolutely? Would it make any difference if Bob had died in a motorbike accident earlier this year?

In this question the real issue is whether the settlor ever intended the claimants Bob and Eli to have the fund absolutely. If he did, then it can be concluded that the purpose of using it for university education was only a statement of the settlor's motive when he made the gift and the real motive was to benefit the two beneficiaries absolutely.

It may make a difference if Bob and Eli had both died leaving a surplus in the fund. This clearly influenced the court in *Re Trusts of the Abbott Fund* because it was the fact that the relatives of the old ladies would benefit rather than the old ladies themselves that seems to have persuaded the judge to find in favour of a resulting trust.

4 CAN UNINCORPORATED ASSOCIATIONS FORM AN EXCEPTION TO THE BENEFICIARY PRINCIPLE?

A further exception can be to find that the gift has been made to *an unincorporated association for its purposes*. This will be discussed in Chapter 8. The basis of this is that although the law does not recognise an unincorporated association as having a legal status it is prepared to accept that any funds can be held by a single member for all the members of the association for the purposes of the group according to the rules of the association.

5 WHY CHARITABLE TRUSTS CAN CREATE AN EXCEPTION

Charitable trusts are an exception to the beneficiary principle because unlike private purpose trusts there is always a person to enforce. *All charitable trusts can be enforced by the Attorney-General* so there is issue about enforcement. Where any problems concerning uncertainty arise the Charity Commissioners can resolve these. This contrasts with private purpose trusts because no one can enforce a private purpose trust that is uncertain because there is no one to resolve the uncertainty.

> ### EXAMPLE
>
> I leave £30,000 for the care of my Alsatian 'Rex'.
> I leave £30,000 for the care of all homeless dogs.
> I leave £30,000 for useful projects concerning animals.
>
> The first gift will be saved under the anomalous exceptions where a gift for a named animal will be upheld; the second gift by contrast is likely to be saved as a charitable gift because the care of homeless dogs will satisfy the public benefit test. The last gift is clearly a purpose trust and is unlikely to be saved unless the useful projects could come within one of the charitable purposes under the *Charities Act 2006*, possibly for the advancement of education.

6 ANOTHER POSSIBLE SOLUTION TO THE PROBLEMS CREATED BY PURPOSE TRUSTS

Where the settlor has created a detailed trust for express purposes the courts should strive to uphold it. Where it is not within one of the recognised exceptions to the beneficiary principle it will fail and the funds will *result* back to the settlor's estate. This is a failure because the court will not be carrying out the intentions of the settlor who clearly had not wished that part of his property to pass with his estate. Some other jurisdictions have tried to find other solutions to allow non-charitable purpose trusts to be enforceable.

Enforcer or protector trusts

A number of jurisdictions have found that a solution to this problem could be to create a mechanism for enforcement. In this way, the main criticism against purpose trusts would be removed. There would always be someone to enforce. The 'enforcer' or 'protector' could be someone appointed by the settlor in the trust instrument or alternatively it could be someone who the court considers to be competent to enforce the trust. If the trustees do not carry out their duties under the terms of the trust, the enforcer would step in and enforce on behalf of those with a sufficient interest.

The enforcer would not have a beneficial interest but merely a duty to ensure the purpose is carried out properly by the trustees.

Although the rules vary between different jurisdictions every trust has to comply with certain criteria: it must be sufficiently certain and it must not be contrary to public policy.

This approach has been adopted in a number of jurisdictions such as Bermuda, the Bahamas and Jersey but has not been adopted in the United Kingdom.

Criticism of 'enforcer' trusts

The main problem with this mechanism is that the enforcer of a purpose trust does not have a beneficial interest in the property or even an indirect interest as in *Re Denley* and so there is less incentive to enforce the trust. However there is a successful analogy in charitable trusts where the Attorney-General is responsible for enforcing charitable trusts. Critics may add that there is a difference between a single named individual empowered to supervise a purpose trust and a person appointed by the government to oversee all charitable trusts.

SUMMARY

This chapter considers the principle that all private trusts must have an ascertainable beneficiary who can enforce the trust in order to be valid. This principle was first identified in *Morice* v. *Bishop of Durham* and later reinforced in *Re Astor's Settlement Trusts*. Unless a trust has an identifiable beneficiary there is no one to enforce the trust. In a private trust, the beneficiaries have the sole right to enforce the trust against the trustees. A purpose trust can also fail because it is uncertain. A private trust will always fail where the objects are uncertain. There are a number of recognised exceptions to this including charitable trusts, gifts to unincorporated associations and gifts within the anomalous exceptions such as a gift to a single named animal, a gift to erect a monument or a gift for saying masses for the dead. These exceptions were described by Roxburgh J. as concessions to human weakness or sentiment in *Re Astor*. It is also recognised that some trusts may have hidden beneficiaries who can enforce the trust under the principle of *Re Denley* and so are not really purpose trusts at all and can be upheld if they satisfy the requirements of an express trust. Where this rule is applied the group of beneficiaries must be clearly identifiable. In recent years the failure of private purpose trusts has been addressed by the creation of enforcer or protector trusts where someone is appointed with the responsibility of enforcing the trust. The weakness of this solution is the fact that the enforcer does not have an interest in the trust and so would not have the incentive to enforce the trust.

8 Unincorporated associations

KEY POINTS

- an unincorporated association does not have legal personality;
- gifts to an unincorporated association will normally be regarded as invalid purpose trusts;
- a gift to an unincorporated association can be upheld in a number of different ways;
- the most popular theory is to uphold a gift to an unincorporated association in the contract-holding theory;
- an unincorporated association must have two or more persons bound together for one or more common purposes;
- persons within the association will have mutual rights and duties arising from the contract between them and rules concerning its control; and
- in order to be recognised the members must be able to join or leave the association at will.

1 INTRODUCTION

The law recognises private individuals and companies. They can both hold property and bring legal actions against others. The law does not recognise groups of people who do not have corporate status. Many groups of people join together for a common pursuit such as sport but do not want the difficulties and complications of registering as a company. This presents a problem where the group holds funds or is left a sum of money under a will, as it is difficult to see on what basis this property is held. There is a further difficulty in deciding what should be done with any surplus funds where the association is wound up. There are hundreds and hundreds of such associations so the law has had to find a way to recognise them.

EXAMPLE

Scott and his friends play football after work every Thursday. They hire a pitch at the local sports centre. At first there are only six of them but soon others join their group and eventually there are over twenty people. One day one of them suggests that it should be a proper club and each person who plays should pay a subscription every week. After a year they have £1,000 in subscriptions. Scott's employer thinks the football group is such a good idea he gives them an additional £3,000. They decide to call themselves Scott's Football Stars. One of the group thinks the money should be used for a party but someone else wants to use the money for a trip to watch a football match abroad. Some people only play once or twice a year, others play every week.

Who should make the decision about the use of the money?

If the group decided not to play football anymore, who should be able to claim the remaining money?

Could someone who only plays football once a year have a claim to a share of the money?

These are all difficult decisions because such a group of people, merely combined for a common purpose, is not normally recognised in law. The law has tried to create a solution to address the questions posed here but none of the solutions are totally satisfactory.

There is an overlap here with purpose trusts. If a sum of money is given to Scott's group for the football club, is this a trust for a purpose (and in which case likely to fail for lack of human beneficiaries)?

Alternatively, it could be a gift to the members of the association for the purposes of the association which may be upheld as an exception to the rule against purpose trusts but this interpretation has additional problems. Who can claim when this is a group where the membership is constantly changing and fluctuating?

2 DEFINITION OF AN UNINCORPORATED ASSOCIATION AND THE PROBLEMS THEY PRESENT

An unincorporated association was defined in the following case.

Conservative Association v. *Burrell* [1982] 1 WLR 522

This case concerned the status of the Conservative party. A sum of money had been left to the Conservative party and the issue before the courts was whether this sum attracted corporation tax. If the party were an unincorporated association, then it would attract tax. The Conservative party and the Labour party have a different status. The Conservative party traditionally attracts members to local branches rather than its central organisation. It is the local party that has a recognised status. The Court of Appeal regarded members of the Conservative party as being members of their local Conservative parties rather than members of one central party. For this reason the Conservative party was not held to be an unincorporated association.

The case importantly lays down the *key features* necessary in order for a group of people to be recognised as an unincorporated association:

1 *two or more persons* bound together for a *common purpose* not being a business organisation;
2 the group is bound by *mutual undertakings* each having mutual duties and obligations;
3 the organisation has *rules* identifying who has control over any funds and the terms of such control;
4 members can *leave and join at will.*

Unless a group has these key characteristics it will not be considered to be an unincorporated association. Even if it is a recognised group the issue of how funds can be kept must be addressed.

The definition looks at the need for rules for the group. If there are no formal rules, then rules can be implied. There is no requirement that the rules need to be in writing or formally agreed although where the rules are formally written down it is much easier to apply them and to interpret what was understood as the rules of the group by the members.

The problem of the status of unincorporated associations has been raised and discussed in a number of cases.

How can an unincorporated association hold funds?

The theoretical possibilities were raised in the following case.

Leahy v. Attorney-General of New South Wales [1959] AC 457

A gift of property had been made to whatever order of Roman Catholic nuns or Christian Brothers the settlor's executors and trustees may select. The gift was challenged by the widow and children of the testator. This could not be a charitable gift because the executors could select a purely contemplative order, which would not satisfy the public benefit test necessary for charitable gifts. It could only take effect as a private trust. However, the court found that the trust was not intended to benefit individual nuns or Christian brothers but instead it was a gift to create an endowment for the orders themselves.

This interpretation had two significant problems:

1 the members of the various orders were very numerous and located worldwide; and
2 the members could include future members. The effect of this would be that the trustees would hold the property indefinitely for future members.

The court found there were *three* different ways of construing the gift. These are recognised today as the three alternative ways of validating a gift to an unincorporated association:

1 a gift to the individual members who are members of the association at the date of the gift either as joint tenants or as tenants in common;
2 a gift to the members subject to their respective contractual rights and liabilities towards each other;
3 a gift for the purposes of the association which must necessarily be held on trust for present and future members.

The gift in *Leahy* was saved by legislation which validated the gift as a charitable trust but if this legislation had not been passed it could not have been held as a valid private purpose.

In *Neville Estates* v. *Madden* [1962] Ch 832 Cross J. accepted the three constructions laid down by the Privy Council but he also developed the second construction.

It may be a gift to the existing members not as joint tenants, but subject to their respective contractual rights and liabilities towards one another as members of the association. In such a case a member cannot sever his share. It will accrue to the other members on his death or resignation, even though such members include persons who became members after the gift took effect.

3 DIFFERENT CONSTRUCTIONS ON GIFTS TO UNINCORPORATED ASSOCIATIONS

(a) A gift to the present members

The simplest way of construing a gift to an unincorporated association is that it is an outright gift to them all and which then can be owned beneficially by all the existing members of the association. They will own absolutely as joint tenants or tenants in common. The members under this construction are regarded as separate and private individuals each with an outright share of the property.

EXAMPLE

If this construction is applied to the earlier example of Scott's Football Stars, the members of the group could all claim the property absolutely for themselves. If casual members are regarded as members, then they can also claim a share in the £4,000. They could simply ask for their percentage share to spend individually. If only annual members are regarded as members, then the casual members will be excluded.

What is the position if the property owned is not money and is not easily divisible?

The principle that all the members own the property equally is fairly simple where the property claimed is a sum of money and is easily divisible. It is far more complicated where the property that is given is a house or an object which cannot easily be split into individual shares. If the group were donated a football with the signatures of the current England football team, this theory would not easily solve claims of ownership between the members. Perhaps Scott wants to sell the football but others want it to be retained. Scott would have to sever his share and he would become a tenant in common. If he owned as a tenant in common, he would own a divisible share of the whole. He could leave his share in his will and he could also transfer it to another. However he could not realise his share unless he could sell it to another. Decisions would have to be taken jointly and where numbers are large as in the example of Scott's Football Stars then division is very difficult unless the whole group wish to sell.

If more money is given to the group and the membership has changed, then the rules would apply to the new group. So the changed membership would all have a share in the new property.

The problem with this construction is that it fails to take into account any increase in the membership. Everything would depend on the membership at the time of the gift.

It is also problematic where the membership is large. It is also very difficult to quantify each individual share where the property is not easily divisible.

(b) The contract-holding theory

This construction is the most popular approach to the ownership of assets in an unincorporated association. It replaces ideas of outright ownership of assets with the principle that a member only owns what the rules of the association lay down as his rights of ownership. This theory is based on the conclusion that when a person joins a group he or she will sign up to the rules of that group and it is those rules that govern ownership of property as well as more mundane issues about time and dates of meetings.

If the rules allow distribution to the members, then the members can claim but if the rules lay down that any money received by the club must be held for the purposes of the club no member can claim a share. It means that the rules of the association are paramount.

Under this construction any gift to the association is regarded as an accretion to the funds of the association to be held by an official appointed by the members.

EXAMPLE

The sum of £10,000 is left to Scott's Football Stars. The rules of the group say that half of any money received by way of bequests or in subscriptions must be transferred into the club's savings account and the other half can be used for any purpose if more than two-thirds of the current membership agree.

If there is agreement between more than two-thirds of the members that they can all share the fund, they can immediately claim the sum.

The contract-holding theory was discussed in the following case.

Re Recher's Will Trusts [1972] Ch 526

A testatrix left her residuary estate to the Anti-Vivisection Society but the theory was not applied on the facts of the case. The London and Provincial Anti-Vivisection Society had once operated from the address that she gave but the Society had ceased to exist having amalgamated with another group which no longer operated from the original offices. The court held that the gift could not be claimed by the new association because it had been specifically left to the Society operating from the address specified by the testatrix. Consequently the gift resulted back to the estate of the testatrix. Although the court did not uphold the gift, importantly, the court held that the gift would have been valid if the society had been in existence at the testatrix's death.

In his judgment Brightman J. suggested that the members could claim a sum left to an association if it was left without any direction which suggested that it was held on trust.

In the case of a donation which is not accompanied by any words which purport to impose a trust, it seems that the gift takes effect in favour of the existing members of the association not as joint tenants or tenants in common so as to entitle each member to an immediate share, but as an accretion to the funds of the organisation.

The contract-holding theory has been recently applied by the court.

Re Horley Town Football Club; Hunt v. Maclaren [2006] EWHC 2386

The testator Major Jennings left some land to the Horley Town Football Club in 1948 to ensure that the club had a permanent ground for playing football. In May 2002, the club sold the land for £4 million and the trustees used the proceeds to acquire another ground. The actual value of the land purchased was worth less than the acquisition value because of certain restrictive covenants which restricted its use to sports and leisure. In spite of this there was a surplus left from the sale of the original ground. The trustees asked the court for directions about the nature of the club, its rules and in whom the assets were vested.

It held:

1 the original gift from Major Jennings should be construed as a gift to the club for the members to be held on the basis of the rules of the club;
2 the members and subsequent members were entitled to that property according to the application of the rules. Members did not include temporary or associate members and therefore they were not entitled to a share of the assets;
3 the assets were vested in the trustees on behalf of the members who had a right to call for distribution of surplus assets among all the full members.

The contract-holding theory was further examined in the following case.

Hanchett–Stamford v. Attorney–General [2009] Ch 173

A society called the Performing and Captive Animals Defence League had once been a successful group who prevented cruelty to animals in productions and shows such as travelling circuses. The group had a formal constitution when it was formed but that had been lost. Membership had fallen over the years and eventually it was reduced to one member, Mrs Hanchett-Stamford. She became ill and moved into a nursing home. She wished to transfer the assets to a charity. At this time the League had assets worth £1.77 million. The court had to consider whether a sole surviving member of an unincorporated association can claim property absolutely for him/herself. It was accepted that she had absolute rights over the property as if she were the survivor of a joint tenancy and was therefore free to transfer the fund to a charity.

When does the contract-holding theory not apply?

The courts cannot apply the contract-holding theory where an association does not have total autonomy and for instance does not have the power to wind itself up.

Re Grant's Wills Trusts [1980] 1 WLR 360

A testator had left his estate to the Labour Party Property Committee for the benefit of the Chertsey Headquarters of the Chertsey and Walton Constituency Labour party providing that if the headquarters ceased to be in the Chertsey area his estate should pass to the Labour party absolutely. The gift failed because unlike the Conservative party, local branches of the Labour party do not have unincorporated status. The estate had been left to the Chertsey Branch of the Labour party but it did not exist as an independent organisation. It could not later amend its own constitution and wind itself up if it wished, such decisions had to be made by the Labour party itself. The gift had to be construed under an alternative construction, as a gift for the purposes of the Labour party as a whole but the testator had made no provision for the perpetuity rule. The gift could have been left with a provision that certain members of the association should be able to enforce it. Under these circumstances the gift could have been upheld under the principles in *Re Denley* and if it had complied with the perpetuity rules it could have been upheld.

Compare the decision in *Re Horley Town Football Club* above where changes to the football club's constitution had not affected its right to wind itself up should it wish at any time.

EXAMPLE

Scott and his friends in Scott's Football Stars have found arranging the hire of a pitch and the other arrangements are taking too much time. Scott's Football Stars decide to join a group called Local Football Heroes. Scott's Football Stars pay a fee to 'LFH' who then agree to organise the arrangements for them on Tuesday evenings and to arrange fixtures with other football clubs. Any member who joins Scott's team signs a form which says that no change can be made to the rules of Scott's Football Stars without prior agreement of the management of 'LFH' and should the group wish to wind itself up it could not do so without permission from 'LFH' who were at liberty to refuse.

Any money or assets transferred to Scott's Football Stars could not be construed under the contract-holding theory because they lack the key feature of being able to amend the rules of their club as they wish.

If Major Pemberton leaves a sum of money for Scott's Football Stars, then it could only be saved if it can be construed as a gift for the purposes of the Club and then it must conform with the rules of perpetuity and cannot last indefinitely.

Gifts under the contract-holding theory with purposes attached

If a testator leaves a gift to an unincorporated association with specific instructions attached, is it possible to apply the contract-holding theory?

Re Lipinski's Will Trusts [1976] Ch 235

The testator Harry Lipinski left his entire residuary estate to an unincorporated association called the Hull Judean (Maccabi) Association. He left the gift with specific instructions that it was 'to be used solely for the construction of new buildings for the association and/or improvements to the said buildings in memory of my late wife'.

The court applied the contract-holding theory. Although the terms of the gift were quite specific, Oliver J. held that the gift was to be held for the members according to the rules of the association and there was nothing to prevent the members from changing the constitution at any time to allow the whole of the sum to be spent immediately on the members or for any purpose they chose.

This construction by Oliver J. makes it very difficult for a testator to be sure that terms attached to any gift to an unincorporated association will be upheld by the trustees after his death.

EXAMPLE

Major Pemberton leaves £500,000 to Catford Football Club under his will to be used to build a clubhouse and bar for the members. Last year the club finished a two-year project refurbishing the bar and extending the already existing clubhouse and so they do not want to apply the money in the way Major Pemberton has laid down. However the pitch is in poor repair and the members of the club would like to use some of the money to resurface the pitch which the club owns and also to buy new strips for all the players. They would also like to pay the costs of sending some of the members to the next European Cup final.

The contract-holding theory could be applied and under the construction given by Oliver J. in *Re Lipinski's Will Trusts* the trustees do not have to apply the money according to the terms of Major Pemberton's will but they could instead use the money in any way permitted by the rules of the club. So if the rules of the club include it, the members are able to apply the funds for resurfacing the pitch or any other reason including a trip abroad to the final of the European Cup.

(c) A trust for present members

This construction is different because a trust is created for the present members rather than an outright gift. This would be a valid trust under the principles of *Re*

Denley. Any issues concerning perpetuities would be removed because the trust would be for present members rather than future members. The trust would not fail under the beneficiary principle because the trust will have beneficiaries to enforce, so it would not fail as a purpose trust. Some of the members would hold on trust for the other members.

EXAMPLE

Scott's Football Stars would not get the legal title to the property. They would have a share in equity under a trust. Trustees will have to be appointed to hold the property. It would address the problems of ownership of property that is not easily quantifiable such as the signed football given to Scott's Football Stars.

Although this has advantages because the trustees have the responsibility of decision-making it also has disadvantages. The main disadvantage is that there is nothing to stop the members ending the trust and demanding the transfer of the property to them in equal shares under the rule in *Saunders* v. *Vautier*.

According to Oliver J. in *Re Lipinski's Will Trusts* if the members under the rules of the association are able to wind up the association and then distribute the assets among themselves there is nothing to stop the members from disposing of the property in any way they wish even where the testator has stipulated a purpose for which the funds must be used.

(d) A trust for present and future members

The law will view a gift for present members and a gift for present and future members differently. Issues of perpetuity arise when the gift allows any future member to enjoy the property. The law will not uphold a gift which can last indefinitely. Where the gift is for present members they have an immediate right to enjoy the property. If the rights of future members have to be considered, the fund could not be distributed as they would have the right to challenge distributions for failing to take their rights into account.

Such a gift would be bound to fail whereas a gift to the association itself could be upheld under the contract-holding theory.

---

4 PROBLEMS ON DISTRIBUTION OF FUNDS ON THE DISSOLUTION OF AN UNINCORPORATED ASSOCIATION

Where an unincorporated association is wound up any remaining assets must be distributed. The question is raised as to who has the best claim to the funds.

The three constructions from *Neville Estates* v. *Madden* would produce different results. If property had been transferred specifically for a purpose connected with the association, then if that purpose has not been carried out there is an argument that the property should result back to the donor.

Re West Sussex Constabulary's Widows, Children and Benevolent (1930) Fund Trusts [1971] Ch 1

In this case Goff J. considered whether the contributors towards the funds of the association could claim the fund based on a resulting trust. He rejected this on the basis that in this case anyone who had contributed towards the fund through subscriptions, donations, payment for entertainments and through collecting-boxes, could not claim that the funds were held on resulting trust because the contributors had in fact received what they had bargained for, e.g. an entertainment which they had already attended. Anyone who had contributed by way of legacy could have a claim under a resulting trust since the purpose had failed and the property would result back to the estate. He did not apply the contractual analysis which would allow the contributors to claim based on their rights as members of the club. If the contributors could not claim the property and the members could not claim it, there was no one else who could claim; in this case most of the property held in the Friendly Societies accounts went to the Crown under the *bona vacantia* rules. These rules allow the Crown to claim property that is not legally owned by anyone.

However, if the property has been transferred to the association and rather than holding it for the purposes of the trust it is construed as being held for the members under the rules of the association the funds could then be distributed according to the rules.

Re Bucks Constabulary Funds Widows 'and Orphans' Fund Friendly Society (No. 2) [1979] 1 All ER 623

A surplus remained after a friendly society providing funds for the widows of police officers in a particular region was wound up. The court had to decide who could claim this fund. The funds could have been claimed by the Crown or by the members of the association before it was dissolved.

Walton J. held that the funds should be held for the members according to the rules and the members should have the right to claim that the fund could be divided equally between them.

This view was endorsed recently in *Hanchett-Stamford* (discussed above) where a sole surviving member was entitled to claim property of that unincorporated association and use it as she wished.

Size of shares

Where there is more than one remaining member the distribution of the assets will either be according to the rules of the association or according to the equitable maxim of 'equity is equality'.

The court can intervene and find another construction. In *Re Sick and Funeral Society of St John's Sunday School* v. *Golcar* [1973] Ch 51 a society which provided members with benefits, such as sickness benefits and benefits on death, was dissolved. The society had full members and half-members and although it did not provide for payments on dissolution the judge applied the differing membership to the distribution of the funds.

SUMMARY

This chapter examines the ownership of property by unincorporated associations. Property can be owned by individuals or companies but not by unincorporated associations, as they do not have legal personality. This presents a problem in law. The law does not recognise the right of any other group to own property. This causes difficulties for groups of people who do not wish to register as a company and yet they may be a group that wishes to own property and need recognition in law as a group. An unincorporated association has been defined in *Conservative Association* v. *Burrell* as a group of two or more people joined together for a purpose with mutually agreed rules and people can join or leave the group at will. There are three theories which can allow an unincorporated association to own property: that the group own the property jointly in law as co-owners; that the group can claim the property is held as an accretion to the funds of the group and that the group can claim that the property has been transferred on trust for the purposes of the group and there are ascertainable persons to enforce the trust. These theories were considered in *Leahy* v. *Attorney-General of New South Wales* and later developed in *Neville Estates* v. *Madden*. Each theory has its limitations but the most popular and successful theory is the contract-holding theory under which property is held for all the members according to the rules of the association. This theory was recently applied in *Re Horley Town Football Club* where there was a surplus of funds left after land owned by a football club was sold and this was distributed according to the rules of the club. The contract-holding theory does not apply where the club does not have total autonomy and cannot wind itself up as in *Re Grant's Wills Trusts*. Once the members decide to dissolve the association or there is only one surviving member then the property can be divided according to the rules. This was considered and applied in *Re Bucks Constabulary Fund (No. 2)*. In most cases any surplus will be divided between the surviving members in equal shares unless the rules determine otherwise.

9 Resulting trusts

KEY POINTS

- a resulting trust is an implied trust;
- resulting trusts are said to give effect to the implied intentions of the owner;
- there are two types of resulting trusts: presumed and automatic;
- a presumed resulting trust is based on the presumed intention of the transferor;
- a presumed resulting trust arises where the purchase money is provided by A or A and B together for the purchase of property in B's name;
- a presumed resulting trust can be rebutted by evidence that either a gift was intended or because of other circumstances;
- a presumed resulting trust could also be rebutted in some circumstances by the relationship of the parties but this principle has been abolished;
- a presumed resulting trust can be rebutted by evidence of a loan; and
- an automatic resulting trust arises where a trust fails or there is a surplus of funds after the purpose of the trust has been carried out.

1 DEFINITION OF A RESULTING TRUST

A resulting trust arises by operation of law and contrasts with an express trust which arises because the settlor has taken the proactive step of creating a trust. The trust arises informally without the need to satisfy formalities such as s.53(1) Law of Property Act 1925.

Resulting trusts were categorised in *Re Vandervell's Trusts* (*No. 2*) [1974] Ch 269 by Megarry J. into those that arose on the basis of the presumed intention of the parties which are known as presumed resulting trusts and those that arise because some or all of the beneficial interest remains undisposed of after the failure of a trust or because there is a surplus after the purpose of the trust has been carried out and does not depend on the presumed or actual intention of the parties.

A different view was taken by Lord Browne-Wilkinson in *Westdeutsche Landesbank* v. *Islington Borough Council* [1996] AC 669. He agreed with Megarry J. that such trusts arise on the operation of law but he disagreed with him on the true basis of resulting trusts declaring that both types of resulting trust are based on the intention of the parties.

He said:

Megarry J ... suggests that a resulting trust does not depend on intention but operates automatically. I am not convinced that this is right. If the settlor has expressly or by necessary implication, abandoned any beneficial interest in the trust property, there is in my view no resulting trust: the undisposed of equitable interest vests in the Crown as *bona vacantia*.

The case of *Westdeutsche* concerned loans made by a bank to Islington Borough Council. The contracts under which the loans were made were later found to be void and as a result the money had to be returned to the bank. The bank also claimed interest. If the relationship between the bank and the Borough Council was that of settlor and trustee, compound interest could be claimed, but if it lay in contract, only simple interest could be claimed. There was no evidence that either an express or implied trust had arisen and therefore only simple interest could be claimed.

2 PRESUMED RESULTING TRUSTS

It is important to see a resulting trust as based on conclusions to be drawn from facts rather than an express intention declared by the settlor. The court can draw the conclusion once the key features of a presumed resulting trust have been proved. It is often referred to as a default mechanism. If the settlor clearly expresses an intention concerning the transfer of property or there is evidence that a gift was intended, then the default mechanism can be ignored.

Compare the following two situations.

EXAMPLE (1)

Henri buys 1,000 shares in Shell. He decides to transfer them on trust for his niece Clemence. He transfers them to Eric and asks him to hold the shares for Clemence. This is an express trust. Henri does not need to put his request in writing because it concerns personalty rather than land but as soon as he transfers the shares to Eric the trust is said to be fully constituted.

EXAMPLE (2)

Suppose Henri pays for the purchase of 1,000 shares in Shell to be registered in Clemence's name. If nothing is said between them, the law will infer that the shares are held by Clemence for Henri. This is giving effect to the presumed intention of the parties. Henri has neither stated that he wishes Clemence to have the shares outright nor has he transferred the shares to another with the express wish that they are to be held on trust for Clemence so on the basis that he provided the money for the purchase the law infers that he retains an interest.

There are two types of situations which can give rise to a *presumed resulting trust*:

1 a voluntary conveyance of property in the name of another;
2 a purchase of property in the name of someone else (as above).

(a) Voluntary transfer into another's name

Where the legal title is voluntarily transferred to another the law will presume that the property is to be held on trust by the transferee for the transferor. This presumption can easily be rebutted by other evidence. The law distinguishes between personalty and land.

(i) Personalty

In cases involving personalty equitable principles apply. Whenever A provides the money for the purchase of personalty in the name of B it is assumed that A will retain an equitable interest *although* at law B will own the legal title.

Re Vinogradoff [1935] WN 68

A grandmother Mrs Vinogradoff voluntarily transferred war loan stock valued at £800 into the joint names of herself and her grandchild who at the time was 4 years old. The grandmother continued to receive the interest. After her death the court concluded that the stock was held by the granddaughter on resulting trust for the estate of Mrs Vinogradoff. It did not matter that the granddaughter was underage because it is possible to be a resulting trustee of personalty under the age of majority.

(ii) Land

The rules are slightly different in connection with a voluntary transfer of land. Before the Law of Property Act was passed in 1925, a voluntary transfer of land into the name of another had the effect of always creating a presumed resulting trust in favour of the transferor or grantor.

Where an outright gift was intended the law required the grantor to insert a trust expressly in favour of the transferee or grantee in order to prevent a resulting trust from arising. Certain prescribed words had to be used.

(iii) s.60(3) Law of Property Act 1925

Under s.60(3) Law of Property Act 1925 the possibility of a resulting trust arising as a result of a voluntary conveyance was addressed.

In a voluntary conveyance a resulting trust for the grantor shall not be implied merely by reason that the property is not expressed to be conveyed for the use or benefit of the grantee.

The section reflects the pre-1925 situation and concludes that failing to use the words that were compulsory before 1925 if an outright gift of land was to be made would not automatically imply a resulting trust.

This provision has been construed in different ways in subsequent cases. It could be construed strictly to suggest that it is no longer possible to imply a resulting trust simply because there has been a voluntary conveyance in the name of another.

A more practical construction is that the section is a word-saving device which means that it is possible to create an express trust of land in favour of another without using the words 'for the use or benefit of the grantee'. Prior to 1925 failure to use these words would mean that the land would result back to the grantor whatever the intention of the parties.

The question has rarely been raised in case law. It was addressed in *Lohia* v. *Lohia* [2001] WTLR 101 where Nicholas Strauss, QC, sitting as a high court judge, concluded that s.60(3) had abolished the presumption of a resulting trust in the case of a voluntary conveyance of land. He accepted that there could be a resulting trust but it would have to be proved by looking at other evidence such as any evidence that the grantor never intended that the grantee should have an absolute interest in the land.

The change to the law as a result of s.60(3) is that the court will still uphold a resulting trust in favour of the grantor after a voluntary transfer where there is other evidence that no outright transfer was intended.

This approach had already been taken in the earlier case of *Hodgson* v. *Marks* [1971] 2 All ER 682 but s.60(3) was not referred to in the case so no comment was made by the court as to its true meaning. This case involved an elderly lady Mrs Hodgson who transferred her property into the name of her lodger. It was orally agreed between them that the house would remain Mrs Hodgson's property. Four years later the lodger sold the property to Mr Marks who was unaware of the agreement. The Court of Appeal held that Mrs Hodgson was entitled to the property under a resulting trust.

(b) Presumption of advancement

Until recently the presumption of a resulting trust could be rebutted by evidence of the relationship of the parties which could mean the presumption of a resulting trust was automatically rebutted. This was called the *presumption of advancement.*

In a very limited number of cases the transferee was able to claim that title to property had been transferred absolutely to him or her simply by relying on the relationship between the transferor and him or herself.

The reasoning behind this is summed up by Lord Eldon who stated in *Murless* v. *Franklin* (1818) 1 Swan 13: 'The general rule that on a purchase by one man in the name of another, the nominee is a trustee for the purchaser is subject to an exception where the purchaser is under a species of natural obligation to provide for the nominee.'

He suggests that in certain cases the purchaser of property is under an obligation to provide for the other party in which case the presumption of a resulting trust is rebutted.

(i) When did the presumption of advancement arise?

The relationships in which the presumption would apply were very limited, e.g. father to either his own child or any child to whom he stood *in loco parentis*; and husband to wife. To stand *in loco parentis* to a child means anyone who the father is treating as his own child.

It did not extend to mother to child or wife to husband.

> Carlos transferred his London flat into the name of his son Pedro. Nothing was said between them. Later they fell out and Carlos tried to argue that he did not intend the flat to be Pedro's property absolutely. This would have been difficult for Carlos to challenge because he was Pedro's father.

The law held that in these cases a gift is presumed to have taken place based on the transferor's obligations to provide for the transferee.

(ii) Husband to wife

This presumption was based firmly in history and related to the common law obligation that a husband must provide for his wife. According to Malins VC: 'the law is perfectly settled that where a husband transfers money or other property into the name of his wife only, then the presumption is, that it is intended as a gift or advancement to the wife absolutely at once' (*Re Eykyn's Trusts* (1877) 6 Ch D 115).

However in modern times the obligation of a husband towards his wife lost its significance and the presumption in favour of a wife seemed outmoded. It was subject to considerable criticism over the years. In *Pettitt* v. *Pettitt* [1970] AC 777 Lord Diplock criticised the use of the presumption suggesting that 'these were inferences of intention which an earlier generation of judges drew as reflecting the propertied classes of a different social era'.

(iii) Father to child

The basis of the presumption of advancement between father and child lay with the father's obligation to provide for his child. It included anyone in whom the father was standing *in loco parentis* meaning anyone whom the father was treating as his own child. It only applied where the man provided more for the child than merely financial support which meant that the man took over responsibility for the child. The *loco parentis* rule was only applied to a man and not a woman.

An example arose in *Re Paradise Motor Co.* [1968] 1 WLR 1125 where a transfer of shares by a stepfather to his stepson treated by him as his own son was declared to be an outright transfer of property to him. Note the discussion in Chapter 6 about whether the disclaiming of this gift had to be in writing to satisfy s.53(1)(c) and the conclusion that it did not need to be in writing.

(iv) Abolition of the presumption of advancement

Attempts to reform these rules met with little success until very recently. The Family Law (Property and Maintenance) Bill, introduced in 2005, which would have abolished the presumption between husband and wife was dropped before it became law because of lack of time for debate.

Section 199 Equality Act 2010 has abolished the presumption of advancement although under s.199(2)(a)(b) anything done before the commencement of the section is not affected by the Act, and the presumption will continue for earlier transfers from a husband to wife or father to child.

(c) Purchase money resulting trusts

In cases where the property is purchased by one person in the name of the other or where the purchase money is provided jointly the presumption of advancement will apply.

The presumption arises from the basic assumption that outright gifts of money towards the purchase of property are not usually intended and should be expressly declared.

This was recognised in *Dyer* v. *Dyer* (1788) 2 Eq Cas 92 by Eyre CB:

> The clear result of all the cases, without a single exception is that the trust of a legal estate, whether taken in the names of the purchasers and others jointly, or in the name of others without that of the purchaser, whether in one name or several; whether jointly or successive – results to the man who advances the purchase money.

Centuries later in *Westdeutsche Girondesbank Girozentrale* v. *Islington Borough Council* (discussed above) Lord Browne-Wilkinson described a purchase money resulting trust in similar terms as arising whenever purchase money was provided by B for the purchase of property in A's sole name or provided by A and B for property purchased in A's name.

EXAMPLE

Terry and June purchase a house together. They both provide part of the purchase money but the house is registered in June's name. It is presumed that the house is held by June on trust for them both. This is the case irrespective of whether they ever discussed ownership of the property together.

The presumption can easily be rebutted by evidence that a gift was intended.

Fowkes v. *Pascoe* [1875] 10 Ch App 343

Three separate purchases of stock in the form of annuities had been made by Sarah Baker in the name of herself and John Pascoe. He was the son of her daughter-in-law. She had also purchased similar stock in her sole name and a further purchase in the name of herself and another. On her death, it was held that she had intended an outright gift of the stock she held with John Pascoe because there could be no other explanation of why she chose to buy three different holdings of stock.

Many people join together to purchase lottery tickets in a syndicate, if it wins then the provision of the purchase money may be relevant.

Abrahams v. *Trustee in Bankruptcy of Abrahams* [1999] BPIR 637

Mr and Mrs Abrahams regularly paid into a lottery syndicate. They each paid for their tickets but when the couple separated Mrs Abrahams started to pay towards her husband's share. He subsequently became bankrupt. The syndicate won the lottery and the trustee in bankruptcy claimed Mr Abraham's share. As the purchase money had been provided by Mrs Abrahams, the ticket in Mr Abraham's name was held on resulting trust for her. There was no presumption of advancement in favour of him because it did not operate from wife to husband.

Consider the following examples.

EXAMPLE (1)

Cherry and Richard live together. They are both part of a lottery syndicate and each pays separately each month towards the purchase of tickets. One day Richard has no money with him to pay and Cherry says she will pay this month for him. The syndicate won the lottery and Cherry is claiming Richard's share.

Cherry can claim the share on the basis of a presumed resulting trust and by applying the case of *Abrahams*.

EXAMPLE (2)

Donna and Kevin are married and they are both part of a lottery syndicate in the village where they live. Kevin always buys the lottery tickets. The syndicate won the lottery recently, before the Equality Act 2010 was in force. Kevin says he can claim Donna's share as he paid for the ticket.

> In this case the presumption of advancement will apply here. Kevin will be presumed to have made an outright gift to Donna, if there is evidence that he never intended to make an outright gift to Donna. Perhaps the syndicate has won a small amount of money previously and this has been kept by Kevin and not shared with Donna. This would rebut the presumption of advancement.

(d) Rebuttal of presumptions

Evidence that the transferor *did not* intend to retain an interest in the property or that the transferor *did* intend to retain an interest in the property can be brought to rebut the presumption of a resulting trust and could previously be brought to rebut the presumption of advancement.

(i) Personalty

In *Re Gooch* (1890) 62 LT 384 a father transferred shares into the name of his son but he had continued to receive dividends on the shares. Although the shares were registered in the name of the son, it was held that there was sufficient evidence to rebut the presumption of advancement.

(ii) Land

Warren v. Gurney [1944] 2 All ER 472

A father purchased a house for his daughter before she had got married. He retained the title deeds until he died. This had particular significance because the title was unregistered. The relationship of father and daughter would raise the presumption of advancement but this was rebutted on the basis of the father retaining the title deeds since it suggested that the father had not intended an outright gift to the daughter.

In the more recent case of *McGrath* v. *Wallis* [1995] 2 FLR 114 a similar result was reached where a father had purchased property in the sole name of his son intending them both to live there. The father provided the purchase money by way of capital from the sale of a previous house and also through a mortgage.

The son claimed the house absolutely but it was held that the presumption of advancement was rebutted first, by evidence that the father had intended to live there and second, by a written declaration of trust, which would have shared the beneficial ownership of the property although the declaration had not been signed thereby failing to satisfy the formalities necessary for an express declaration of a trust of land.

In *Lavelle* v. *Lavelle* [2004] 2 FCR 418 a father also purchased property for his daughter in her name. The daughter relied on the presumption of advancement to support her claim that she could claim it absolutely. The father successfully relied on the fact that he had only purchased it in order to reduce his liability to inheritance tax and the transfer was never intended to be a gift.

EXAMPLE

Frank has a large shareholding, considerable sums of money in the bank and several houses in which he has a number of tenants. Last year, in order to reduce his tax liability, he decided to transfer one of his houses to his son Eddie and to transfer part of his shareholding to his daughter Dana. When the dividends were declared on the shares this year Dana gave them to Frank. Recently, Frank suddenly died. He had not made a will because he had been discussing how to minimise his tax liability with his lawyer and nothing had been agreed.

At law Eddie owns the house transferred to him by Frank and Dana owns the shares and the transfer would have rebutted the presumed resulting trust by the presumption of advancement. However the presumption of advancement could also be rebutted by the fact that Frank had only transferred the shares and the house because he wanted to minimise his tax liability and the further evidence that Dana had continued to transfer the dividends she received on the shares to Frank rather than keep them for herself.

(iii) Loans

Where there is evidence that the relationship between the parties was never intended to be one of a trust but rather one of creditor and debtor any advance of money for the purchase of property will not raise the presumption of a resulting trust but instead it will be treated as a relationship in contract.

In *Re Sharpe (A Bankrupt)* [1980] 1 WLR 219 money advanced to Mr and Mrs Sharpe from Mr Sharpe's aunt was held to give rise to a loan because it was intended that the sum should be repaid. This prevented the aunt from claiming that she had a share in the property under a resulting trust.

(e) Illegality

In a number of cases, evidence to rebut either the resulting trust of the presumption of advancement constituted evidence of an illegal act or an illegal motive.

This area of law has its basis in equity and the equitable maxim 'he who comes to equity must come with clean hands' will be relevant. This means that the claimant cannot bring a claim where he has not acted in a lawful manner himself.

So traditionally the court would not allow a claimant to rely on an illegal act to rebut a presumption.

In more recent cases the court has taken a more pragmatic approach to the admissibility of illegal evidence.

(i) Illegal motives inadmissible to use to rebut a presumption

Gascoigne v. *Gascoigne* [1918] 1 KB 223 concerned a husband who had a lease registered in his wife's name in order to prevent his creditors from being able to claim it. He tried to rebut the presumption of advancement using evidence that he had only transferred it to her to defeat his creditors and he did not intend to make an outright gift to her. The court would not admit this evidence.

A similar view was taken in *Tinker* v. *Tinker* (*No. 1*) [1970] P 136 where the court would not allow a man to use evidence that he had conveyed property into the sole name of his wife because he wanted to protect his house in case anything happened to his business. The marriage broke down and he tried to argue that the presumption of advancement would not apply because he had never intended to transfer the property to his wife absolutely. However the court would not allow him to adduce this evidence in support of his claim.

Lord Denning summed up his difficulties as follows:

[T]he husband cannot have it both ways ... he is on the horns of a dilemma. He cannot say that the house is his own and, at one and the same time, say that it is his wife's. As against his wife he wants to say that it belongs to him and as against his creditors, that it belongs to her.

In a more extreme example *Chettiar* v. *Chettiar* [1962] AC 294 the court refused to allow a father to rebut the presumption of advancement where he had transferred a rubber estate into his son's name in order to circumvent rules concerning how many acres a plantation owner could own.

(ii) Illegal motives present but not relied on as evidence

Tinsley v. *Milligan* [1994] 1 AC 340

The court's more pragmatic approach to illegal motives is illustrated in this case. Ms Tinsley and Ms Milligan purchased property together but it was registered in the name of Tinsley because Milligan wanted to claim housing benefit by suggesting that she paid rent to Tinsley. The relationship broke down. Milligan had to repay the illegally claimed housing benefit but she claimed she had a share in the ownership of the house based on her contributions.

The House of Lords upheld Milligan's claim because although she had had an illegal motive for not having the house registered in her name this fact could be ignored and the bare evidence of her contributions towards the purchase price could be relied on to support her claim. This gave rise to a *presumed resulting trust* in her favour.

Lord Browne-Wilkinson summed this up as follows: 'the rule is the same whether a plaintiff founds himself on a legal or equitable title: he is entitled to recover if he is not forced to plead or rely on the illegality'.

The court went further in *Tribe* v. *Tribe* [1995] (see below) where it was prepared to uphold a rebuttal of a presumption of advancement based on an attempt to defraud creditors because the creditors had not been defrauded in this case.

Tribe v. *Tribe* [1995] All ER 236

The facts are complicated but illustrate the point well. A father transferred shares in a family company into his son's name because he had had notice that he had to carry out expensive repairs on the properties which he believed he could not afford to do. He later discovered that he did not have to carry out the repairs and tried to recover the shares from his son who refused basing his claim on the presumption of advancement. The court allowed evidence of the father's motive in support of his claim to the property and the shares were successfully recovered by the father.

Nourse LJ establishes an important rule in *Tribe*, i.e. that an illegal motive or purpose can be admitted in evidence to rebut a presumption only where it has not been carried into effect.

Tinsley and *Tribe* have both been followed in later cases including *Silverwood* v. *Silverwood* (1997) 74 P & CR 453 where a grandmother had transferred money into the names of her grandchildren in order to allow her to claim income support. When she died the court held that her grandchildren held the shares on resulting trust for her estate. Similarly in *Lowson* v. *Coombes* [1999] Ch 373 a man who had transferred property into the name of his partner could reclaim it although the primary purpose had been to defeat the claims of his former wife based on a presumed resulting trust.

(iii) Reform

In 1999 the Law Commission reviewed the whole area of admissibility of evidence of illegality and made a number of recommendations including:

1 the court should have discretion to decide whether illegality should act as a defence to normal rights and remedies;

2 the court should take into account a number of factors including the seriousness of the illegality involved; the knowledge and intention of the party relying on the illegality; the effect of denying the claim on the illegality.

The Law Commission has published a further consultative report called *The Illegality Defence: A Consultative Report* (2009) which in particular highlights the difficulties of allowing non-reliance as a reason for admitting evidence. It recommends legislative reform.

3 AUTOMATIC RESULTING TRUSTS

Lord Browne-Wilkinson also referred to another type of resulting trust in *Westdeutsche*: the automatic resulting trust. He differed from Megarry J. in *Vandervell's Trusts* (*No. 2*) who had suggested that this type of resulting trust did not give effect to the presumed intention of the parties but took effect on the operation of law. He thought that even automatic resulting trusts were based on the presumed intention of the parties.

(a) Failure of a purpose

Where an express trust has been validly created but later the purpose fails the law holds that the property in the hands of the trustees should 'result back' to the settlor's estate.

(i) *Quistclose*-type trusts

Barclays Bank v. *Quistclose Investments Ltd* [1970] AC 567

This case provides a good example of a failure of a purpose. Quistclose had transferred money to Rolls Razor, a firm close to bankruptcy, for the purpose of declaring dividends on shares. The company went into liquidation before the dividend was ever declared and Quistclose claimed that the money should be returned. Barclays Bank claimed that the money should simply pass into the general account of the company and should be used towards paying the general debts of the company. The trust failed and the property resulted back to Quistclose. The judgment of Lord Wilberforce suggested that there were two trusts in this case. First, a primary trust in favour of the objects of the trust, namely Rolls Razor to use the money for the purpose of the trust to pay dividends to the shareholders, then a secondary trust arose in favour of the lender Quistclose.

This has obvious problems of enforcement under the beneficiary principle as it is a purpose trust and the second problem lies in locating the beneficial interest. It is not clear whether this lay with the shareholders, the lender Quistclose or the borrowers Rolls Razor. In any event it was held to be a resulting trust.

(ii) *Quistclose* **reviewed in** *Twinsectra Ltd* v. *Yardley*

Twinsectra Ltd v. *Yardley* [1999] Lloyd's Rep Bank 438

Quistclose was considered and applied in this case. Twinsectra Ltd lent a large sum of money to a prospective purchaser of land. The money was paid over to the purchaser's solicitor to be paid into their account on the strict terms that it was only to be used for the purpose of acquiring land. The money was paid to a second solicitor and released and used for other purposes by the purchaser who subsequently went bankrupt. Unable to recover the money from the purchaser the lenders sought to recover the money from the second solicitor arguing that the money was held on trust for a specific purpose and he was therefore dishonestly assisting in a breach of trust. Although the House of Lords did not find the solicitor involved to be liable for dishonest assistance, it took the opportunity to review the facts of *Quistclose*.

Lord Millett explained that where a loan is made for a specific purpose the lender retains the beneficial interest. The borrower has very limited use of the money as he must apply it for the stated purpose and so the borrower has no beneficial interest in the money. If the purpose fails, then the money is returnable to the lender not under some new trust but under a resulting trust because the borrower is now unable to make use of the money.

EXAMPLE

Carrie wishes to build her own house and tells the rest of her family of her wish. Her very generous Uncle Dominic transfers £150,000 to her and writes her a note: 'Enjoy spending this money on building your new house. Love Uncle Dominic.' Carrie decides that she would like to refurbish an existing flat in London instead of building a new property and wants to know if she can keep the money from Uncle Dominic.

The money forwarded by Uncle Dominic has been earmarked for building a new house. It is not for general purposes and unless 'building' can be given a very wide interpretation this money must be returned. The law holds that Uncle Dominic retains an interest in the money until Carrie uses it for building a new house.

(b) Unexhausted beneficial interest

In some cases the purpose of the trust may be carried out and then a surplus remains. In these cases there could either be a resulting trust or the fund could be transferred absolutely to the original objects of the trust. The courts have adopted both these routes.

As discussed earlier in Chapter 7 in *Re Trusts of the Abbott Fund* [1900] 2 Ch 326 a fund collected for two deaf and dumb old ladies was held on their death to result back to the contributors and not to be taken absolutely for their estates. This case should be contrasted with the case of *Re Osoba* [1979] 1 WLR 247 where property in a trust set up for the testator's widow, his mother and also for the training of his daughter Abiola up to university grade was held absolutely for Abiola after she had left university because it was regarded as an absolute gift with merely a purpose attached. The difference between these two cases could be the fact that in *Re Osoba* the beneficiary was alive whereas in *Re Trusts of Abbott Fund* the old ladies had died and it would be their relatives who would benefit.

Disaster appeals

Many disaster appeals will qualify as charitable trusts and any surplus will pass under the *cy près* rules. Where the trust does not qualify in this way, usually because the fund could be applied for non-charitable objects, any surplus left after the purposes have been carried out may either result back to the contributors or will pass to the state under the *bona vacantia* rules.

Re Gillingham Bus Disaster Fund [1958] Ch 300

A large sum of money was collected for the survivors of an accident involving a number of sea cadets. Some had died and some had suffered very severe injuries. An appeal was held for the purpose of helping with funeral expenses, caring for boys who were disabled and then to such worthy causes in memory of the boys who lost their lives as the mayor may determine. There was a surplus left after these purposes had been carried out and the court held that this sum should be held on resulting trust for the contributors. This result may have been correct legally but it caused difficulties in practical terms because the contributions had come mainly from collecting tins and it was difficult to track down those who had given in this way. Harman J. felt that the contributors had given with one purpose in mind and so in this way it could be argued that they were similar to Quistclose who had earmarked the money lent to Rolls Razor for a particular use.

(c) Failure of a trust

Where a trust fails to conform to the key criteria such as certainty of objects or subject matter the property intended to be held on trust will result back to the settlor's estate. If there is no certainty of intention to create a trust, then the property is taken as an absolute gift.

Compare the following two situations in the Example below.

> ### EXAMPLE
>
> (1) Samson died last year. He left £50,000 to his wife Delilah in absolute confidence that she would use it for their two children Pearl and Rose.
>
> (2) Samson died last year. He left his two London flats to his wife Delilah to be held on trust for his daughters Pearl and Rose, Pearl to choose one of the flats first and Rose to have the other flat. Pearl recently died in a motorcycle accident before choosing a flat and Rose wishes to claim one of the London flats for herself.
>
> In (1) Samson has not created a trust because he uses precatory words only. Delilah can take the money absolutely and she can decide whether or not to give any money to the children. In the second example a trust has been created but the terms are now impossible to carry out so the trust has failed and both the flats will pass on resulting trust to Samson's estate.
>
> Example (2) is similar to the case of *Boyce* v. *Boyce* (1849) 6 Sim 476 where the testator left two houses on trust for his daughter Maria with instructions that she was to choose one house and the remaining house was to be held for her sister Charlotte. Maria died before choosing and both houses resulted back to the father's estate. Whereas (1) is similar to the case of *Adams* v. *Kensington Vestry* (1884) 27 Ch D 394 where property left to the testator's wife 'in full confidence' that she would do what is right did not create a trust and the wife took the property absolutely.

Re Ames' Settlement [1946] 1 All ER 689

This case is another example of the failure of a trust. Here a marriage settlement which had been created in 1908 failed because some years later the marriage was declared void. The court held that as the marriage had been declared void there was a total failure of consideration and any property that had passed into the purported marriage settlement simply resulted back to the settlor's estate. There was no question that the parties to the purported marriage could claim the property for themselves.

Another example however shows that rigid application of the rule can defeat what appears to be the original intention of the parties.

Re Cochrane [1955] 1 Ch 309

A marriage settlement had been made on terms that the income should be paid to the wife so long as she resided with her husband and in the event of the death of either of them the survivor was to take the capital absolutely. The wife left her husband and he later died. Under the terms of the settlement she should have been able to claim the property absolutely on his death but because she was no longer residing with her husband before his death the court held that the property should result back to the settlors.

Property left for a charitable trust that fails

Where property is left for a charitable purpose but that purpose fails because for example the purposes are not exclusively charitable the property will result back to the settlor as in the case of *Re Diplock* [1944] 2 All ER 60. A trust for benevolent or charitable purposes failed because benevolent purposes can include non-charitable objects. The trust failed absolutely and the property resulted back to the settlor's estate for his next of kin. This contrasts with other cases of charitable trusts which fail because the property can pass to a charity but it has ceased to exist or it has been taken over by another organisation. In these cases the law allows the property to pass to another charitable purpose under the *cy près* rules.

SUMMARY

This chapter considers the nature of a resulting trust. Resulting trusts are trusts implied in law. There are two types of resulting trust, the presumed and the automatic resulting trust. Although resulting trusts are not expressly created according to Lord Browne-Wilkinson in *Westdeutsche* they are said to give effect to the presumed intentions of the settlor. Megarry J. took a different view in *Re Vandervell's Trusts* because he considered only presumed resulting trusts give effect to the intentions of the parties. Presumed resulting trusts arise when property is purchased or conveyed voluntarily into the name of one person but another provides the purchase money. This was first recognised in 1788 in the case of *Dyer* v. *Dyer*. The presumption of a resulting trust can be rebutted with evidence of a gift as shown in *Fowkes* v. *Pascoe*. It can also be rebutted by evidence of a loan and until recently because of the relationship of the parties, e.g. where a father transferred property to a child or a husband transferred property to his wife. Where an illegal motive must be relied on in order to rebut the presumption either of a resulting trust or of advancement the courts will not admit the evidence in support of the claim. Where the illegal motive was never carried out then a claimant may bring such evidence to court in support of a rebuttal of a presumption as shown in *Tribe* v. *Tribe* and *Silverwood* v. *Silverwood*.

An automatic resulting trust arises in a number of circumstances. These include the failure of the purpose of a trust as shown in the case of *Barclays Bank* v. *Quistclose* where money had been lent for the purpose of paying dividends but before the dividends could be paid the company went bankrupt. The money lent resulted back to the lender. It also arises where there is a surplus after the purposes of a trust have been carried out such as in the case of *Re Abbott* where funds collected for the care of two deaf and dumb old ladies resulted back to the contributors after their death. Where there is a surplus after the purpose has been carried out it is possible to argue that the beneficiary can claim the surplus absolutely rather than allowing the money to result back to the settlor. This was successfully argued by the beneficiary in *Re Osoba*. This will usually apply where the purpose attached was a moral duty rather than an absolute term of the trust. Where a trust fails to conform to the key requirements such as certainty of subject matter and objects the property will result back to the settlor's estate. The rigid application of this rule may result in defeating the intention of the settlor as shown in *Boyce* v. *Boyce* where two houses had been left on trust for two sisters but one sister had to choose a house first. She died before making a selection and it was held that the surviving sister could not claim one of the houses for herself.

10 Constructive trusts

KEY POINTS

- a constructive trust is imposed by operation of law;
- it has a number of different definitions;
- it arises in a variety of different situations;
- the key feature of all types of constructive trust is to prevent unconscionability;
- in England and Wales the courts can only impose an institutional constructive trust; and
- other jurisdictions can impose a constructive trust as a remedy in the form of a remedial constructive trust.

1 INTRODUCTION. WHAT IS A CONSTRUCTIVE TRUST? PROBLEMS IN DEFINITION

A constructive trust is difficult to define. It is imposed by the court where it would be unconscionable for the legal owner of property to deny a beneficial interest to a claimant. It differs from a resulting trust because it does not usually give effect to the intentions of the parties but arises as a response to circumstances.

Constructive trusts have been imposed in a wide range of situations to remedy unconscionability showing that it is a very flexible response. However, it is the breadth of situations in which a constructive trust has been imposed that makes it difficult to define clearly.

This problem in definition is summed up by Edmund Davies LJ: 'English law provides no clear and all embracing definition of a constructive trust. Its boundaries have been left perhaps deliberately vague, so as not to restrict the court by technicalities in deciding what the justice of a particular case may demand' (*Carl Zeiss Stiftung* v. *Herbert Smith* (*No. 2*) [1969] 2 Ch 276).

There are other difficulties associated with a constructive trust. In many jurisdictions the constructive trust can be used as a remedy in response to unjust enrichment. In this form it is called a remedial constructive trust and it gives the courts flexibility. In England and Wales, the courts can only impose the institutional constructive trust in response to a number of well-defined situations. The courts have no flexibility to impose a constructive trust beyond the defined situations. The difference between the remedial and the institutional constructive trust is discussed later in the chapter.

Types of constructive trustee

In *Paragon Finance plc* v. *Thakerar* [1999] 1 All ER 400 Millett LJ distinguished between the two different types of constructive trustee as follows:

the constructive trustee really is a trustee. He does not receive trust property in his own right but by a transaction by which both parties intend to create a trust from the outset ... His possession of the property is coloured from the first by the trust and confidence by means of which he obtained it, and his subsequent appropriation of the property to his own use is a breach of trust.

The second class of case is different. It arises when the defendant is implicated in a fraud. Equity has always given relief against fraud by making any person sufficiently implicated in the fraud accountable in equity. In such a case he is traditionally ... described as constructive trustee and said to be liable to account as a constructive trustee. Such a person is in fact not a trustee at all, even though he may be liable to account as if he were.

Lord Justice Millett is distinguishing between the constructive trustee who receives trust property on behalf of another and if he deals with it for his own purposes then he will hold that property as a trustee because he is in breach of certain duties such as trust and confidence. The second category is different because he is implicated in a transaction by fraud but he has not received trust property in his own right and he was never supposed to take possession of property in his own right. An example of this second type of cases arises in Chapter 19 where someone who dishonestly *assists* in a breach of trust can be held liable as a constructive trustee although at no time did he/she hold the trust property in his own name.

The liability of constructive trustees is not the same as that of express trustees. They do not carry the same responsibilities as express trustees. Express trustees have a number of duties including the duty to invest the trust fund rather than merely safeguarding the trust property. Failure to invest will result in personal liability to compensate the beneficiaries. Express trustees must also act with care when delegating duties to others. Constructive trustees can be liable to the beneficiaries for loss caused to the trust property but they will rarely be expected to carry out duties such as investment.

2 DIFFERENT TYPES OF CONSTRUCTIVE TRUST

One of the features of the constructive trust is its *flexibility*. It has been used in a wide range of situations. These will be discussed below but some will be dealt with in more detail in later chapters.

The following list covers some of the situations in which a constructive trust will arise.

(a) Enforcing contracts for the sale of property

An agreement for the sale of land is not enforceable until the parties exchange contracts. The contracts must conform with s.2(1) Law of Property (Miscellaneous Provisions) Act 1989, i.e. must be in writing, comprise all the terms and be signed by both parties. Once the contracts have been exchanged then the sale of land is legally enforceable. The seller will hold the property on constructive trust for the purchaser who now has a beneficial interest in the property he is purchasing.

The position was summed up by Jessel MR in *Lysaght* v. *Edwards* (1876) 2 Ch D 449: 'the moment you have a valid contract for sale the vendor becomes in equity a trustee for the purchaser of the estate sold, and the beneficial ownership passes to the purchaser'.

A constructive trust also arises in the sale of other types of property particularly where it is unusual or rare, such as a valuable antique or painting.

Note that this type of constructive trust is slightly different from others because the constructive trustee still has a personal interest in the property whereas in other cases the entire beneficial interest will pass to the claimant. It means that the seller can retain the profit he makes on the sale of the land once sold to the purchaser but he is under a duty to care for the property.

If either the seller or the purchaser refuses to proceed with the sale after exchange of contracts, they can both claim a remedy in equity. An order for specific performance can be claimed because land is regarded as unique.

EXAMPLE

Fabian agrees to sell his house to Gerald. They agree terms and details of the sale. They do not want to use lawyers as they think that it will cost too much money and Gerald is a cash buyer and will not need to rely on a mortgage in order to raise money. They write the agreed terms on two separate pieces of paper and both sign each piece of paper.

Two weeks later Fabian changes his mind and refuses to sell to Gerald. Can Gerald force him to sell?

Fabian holds the property as constructive trustee on behalf of Gerald and Gerald can force Fabian to sell to him. If he refuses, the court may make an order for specific performance in favour of Gerald. Unlike damages, the remedy is at the discretion of the court.

(b) Family homes

The use of the constructive trust in the context of the family home is very important. It will be examined in detail later in Chapter 11 but it should be included in any list of the various uses of the constructive trust because it shows clearly how the courts view unconscionability in this context.

A constructive trust of land can only arise in the circumstances laid down by Lord Bridge in the key case of *Lloyds Bank* v. *Rosset* [1991] 1 AC 107.

According to Lord Bridge a constructive trust will only arise where there is evidence of 'common intention' to share the property between the parties. This can be proved either expressly or impliedly. He held that common intention can be implied by conduct but only contributions of money will be enough to imply such intention and contributions in kind would fall short. Express common intention can be implied by proof of an agreement between the parties. This does not need to be in writing but it must be an agreement that the property is to be shared between the parties beneficially.

An express common agreement was found in *Grant* v. *Edwards* [1986] Ch 638. In this case, a legal title owner told a woman with whom he was setting up home that he would have put her name on the legal title but as she was in the process of divorcing her husband ownership of property might prejudice her claim for financial provision so he thought it would be wrong to do so.

If the claimant can show that there was an express common agreement showing common intention between the parties that the property is to be shared between them, then it would be unconscionable for the legal title owner to deny the claimant a share. The agreement can be oral. Section 53(2) Law of Property Act 1925 expressly excludes constructive trusts from the need to comply with the formalities normally required for the declaration of a trust in land.

The constructive trust can be useful as an indication to the court of how the beneficial interest is to be shared between the parties, both where the property is in sole ownership and where it is jointly owned.

The case of *Midland Bank* v. *Cooke* [1995] 4 All ER 562 concerned property, which had been purchased in the name of the husband with contributions by both parties. The woman had contributed a small amount but the court found that there was a common intention to share the property and it also found that there was an intention to share the interests in the property equally. Waite LJ observed that the court was entitled to take into account all the circumstances of the parties' relationship and his duty was 'to undertake a survey of the whole course of dealing between the parties relevant to the ownership and occupation of the property and their sharing its burdens and advantages'.

(c) Unauthorised gains by a fiduciary

A court will impose a constructive trust whenever a person in a fiduciary relationship makes a personal profit from his position. This can arise in a range of situations and will be examined in detail in Chapter 18.

The rule was stated by Lord Herschell in the case of *Bray* v. *Ford* [1896] AC 44: 'it is an inflexible rule of a Court of Equity that a person in a fiduciary position ... is not, unless otherwise expressly provided, entitled to make a profit; he is not allowed to put himself in a position where his interest and duty conflict'.

Although a fiduciary relationship has always been regarded as very significant in equity and one to be afforded special protection the courts would not at first impose a constructive trust over bribes or secret profits.

The attitude of the courts to secret profits can be seen in the following two cases.

Lister & Co. v. *Stubbs* (1890) 45 Ch D 1

An employee of Lister & Co received bribes from another company from whom he received business on behalf of his employers. He invested the money he received and made a profit. When the bribe was discovered by his employers he was asked to return it, which he did. His employers also claimed the profit that he had made. The court held that he owed the money as a debtor in contract and did not hold it on constructive trust so he was entitled to retain the profit.

Attorney-General for Hong Kong v. Reid [1994] 1 AC 324

The *Lister* position was reversed in this case where an employee of the Hong Kong government, a Crown prosecutor, received bribes from defendants who asked him to use his position to drop proceedings against them. He kept the bribes for himself and invested them in property in New Zealand. The bribes were discovered by his employers who claimed that he should return both the bribes and the profit that he had made. He was held by the Privacy Council to be constructive trustee of the bribes and the Hong Kong government was entitled to claim the properties he owned because they had been purchased with bribes he had received.

This decision has recently been doubted in *Sinclair Investments UK Ltd* v. *Versailles Trade Finance Ltd (in Administration)* [2011] EWCA Civ 347. The Court of Appeal held in this case that a claimant could not claim proprietary ownership of an asset purchased by a fiduciary through his position but not beneficially owned by the claimant.

Why is a constructive trust imposed in these circumstances?

The fiduciary is treated differently from others because of the trust and faith that is placed in him by others. Fiduciary duties comprise duties of loyalty, good faith and trust and confidence which arise from the close nature of the relationship. The fiduciary may be party to special information because of his close working relationship and the law regards anyone who misuses this special position for his or her personal gain very harshly.

The approach is the same whether the fiduciary is acting in bad faith as in *Attorney-General* v. *Reid* or in good faith as in the case of *Boardman* v. *Phipps* [1967] 2 AC 44. In this case, a solicitor to a trust with a poor financial investment record made a profit for the beneficiaries using his knowledge from his personal position. He also made a personal gain and the court held that the personal gain was held on constructive trust and he must account for this to the beneficiaries notwithstanding the fact that he had acted in good faith and that large gains had been received by the beneficiaries of the trust. The court did order a discretionary payment to the solicitor in recognition of his contribution to the trust.

(d) Property rights acquired through unlawful killing

Where a person benefits from the unlawful killing of another and thereby acquires his or her property rights the courts apply the principle that 'no one should benefit from the commission of a criminal act'. As a result, the interest gained by the convicted person is held to be forfeited.

An early example of this principle arises in the case *Re Crippen* [1911] P 108 which involved the notorious murderer Crippen who, having murdered his wife, would have inherited her property under the intestacy rules. He was later hanged and on his death he left his estate to his mistress. The court declared that his mistress was not entitled to his wife's estate as Crippen was never beneficially entitled to it. He was not entitled to his wife's estate because the court had applied the forfeiture rule.

The Forfeiture Act 1982

The forfeiture rules can be modified to mitigate what can be a harsh effect in some circumstances. There may be special circumstances surrounding the unlawful killing which would make automatic forfeiture inappropriate.

Under s.2(1) Forfeiture Act 1982 the court can make an order modifying the effect of the rule where the forfeiture rule has precluded someone from acquiring an interest in property. The court must consider such issues as the conduct of the offender and of the deceased and other circumstances which appear to the court to be material. The Act applies to manslaughter but cannot apply to someone convicted of murder.

A good example of the application of the Forfeiture Act can be seen in *Re K* [1985] Ch 85 where the court was prepared to exercise its discretion in favour of a wife who had been subjected to years of violence from her husband. She was found guilty of his manslaughter and as a result she had forfeited his interest under a joint tenancy. This should have automatically vested in her allowing her to claim the family home absolutely after his death. A constructive trust would then have been imposed over the other half of the property in favour of her husband's next of kin. However, under the special circumstances of the case in particular because she had suffered such a high level of violence from her husband the court held that she was entitled to relief under the Act and as a result she was able to claim the entire estate for herself.

Dunbar v. *Plant* [1997] 4 All ER 289

The Forfeiture Act was applied again in this case. Miss Plant and Mr Dunbar had entered into a suicide pact together. The pair had decided on this step because she was awaiting trial for theft and faced the possibility of a prison sentence. Several attempts at joint suicide failed but then eventually in another attempt Dunbar died while Plant survived. Plant was later found guilty of aiding and abetting suicide under s.2(1) Suicide Act 1961. Dunbar had taken out an insurance policy in her favour before he died and his father argued that the forfeiture rules should apply preventing her from benefiting because of her role in his death.

The Court of Appeal held that she had forfeited her interest under the insurance policy because of her role in the circumstances of his death but it was prepared to apply its discretion under the Forfeiture Act and allow her claim under the policy to succeed.

EXAMPLE

Sally and Harry lived together in their jointly owned flat in Epping Forest which they purchased five years ago. Sally had a long-standing problem with addiction to drugs and alcohol which made their relationship very tense. She was often violent towards Harry and frequently attacked him. One night Harry came home to find that Sally had been drinking heavily. He accused her of drinking too much and wrecking both their lives and they began to fight. He pushed her against the kitchen table where she cut her head badly. Although he called an ambulance immediately she suffered severe swelling of the brain and died two days later. Harry was convicted of her manslaughter. Sally's family have now applied to the court for forfeiture of Sally's share in the flat which should have passed to Harry under the rules of survivorship under the joint tenancy. They wish the court to declare that he holds Sally's share on constructive trust for them.

Initially, the principle that no one should benefit from his or her wrong should be applied here so preventing the right of survivorship in Harry's favour. However *Re K* and *Dunbar* v. *Plant* may be applied to Harry's case in view of the violence he has received from Sally over the years and the court may exercise its discretion under the Forfeiture Act 1982 in his favour and thus allow him to claim the entire property for himself.

(e) Informal acquisition of property rights

The courts have sometimes been prepared to impose a constructive trust where the formalities of transfer have not been complied with in order to prevent fraud.

EXAMPLE

If Sachin sells and transfers property to Brian at undervalue but on the express understanding that Brian will hold the land on trust for Colin giving effect to rights granted to him by Sachin, Brian cannot deny Colin's rights. He will be holding the property on constructive trust which is imposed to protect Colin's rights. It would be unconscionable to deny Colin's rights because Brian purchased the property at undervalue and thereby gained a personal advantage at Colin's expense.

Binions v. *Evans* [1972] Ch 359

Mrs Evans lived in a cottage after her husband's death which was owned by his employers. They entered into an agreement with her allowing her to remain in the cottage rent free for the rest of her life and in return she agreed to keep the property in good repair. The employers sold the property to Mr and Mrs Binions expressly subject to Mrs Evans' rights and at undervalue. After the sale Mr and Mrs Binions tried to evict Mrs Evans. The Court of Appeal upheld Mrs Evans' rights. They held that because the purchasers bought expressly subject to her rights and at undervalue they were bound by her rights and they had become constructive trustees of her rights on purchase.

In later cases such as *Lyus* v. *Prowsa Developments* [1982] 1 WLR 1044 and *Ashburn Anstalt* v. *Arnold* [1989] Ch 1 it was emphasised that the constructive trust arising on the informal acquisition of property rights could only arise where the conscience of the estate holder has been affected such as where the property is sold at undervalue. In these circumstances it would be unconscionable to deny the claimant rights.

In *Ashburn Anstalt* v. *Arnold* it was said: 'the court will not impose a constructive trust unless it is satisfied that the conscience of the estate owner is affected'.

EXAMPLE

Polly has lived for many years in a flat provided by her employers. She works as a housekeeper for them. They have recently sold the property to Quentin. Quentin purchased the property knowing that Polly lived there and had rights to live there but it was not part of the agreement that she would be allowed to live there for the rest of her life. After the sale, he brings proceedings to evict her from the flat. Polly's right to live in the property is unlikely to be protected unless Quentin purchased at undervalue. She did not have a proprietary right in the property but merely a licence to live there which cannot bind third parties. If Quentin purchased at undervalue, then her rights would be enforceable against Quentin under a constructive trust and further if Quentin purchased expressly subject to her rights as a term of the purchase, her rights would also be enforceable.

(f) Mutual wills

The doctrine of mutual wills and secret trusts is discussed in detail in Chapter 12. Where two people enter into a contract to execute wills in a common form the survivor is bound by that contract. The courts distinguish between identical wills and mutual wills. Where the wills are considered mutual wills the survivor cannot change his/her will after the death of the other party. If he/she tries to do so, the court will impose a constructive trust on the property bound by the terms of the will in favour of the beneficiaries.

(g) Strangers as constructive trustees

Strangers to a trust are those persons who are not express trustees but have intermeddled in the trust in such a way that the law will regard them as trustees. Strangers to a trust are discussed in detail in Chapter 19. Where trust property is received by someone with the requisite knowledge or state of mind the court will view him as a constructive trustee and he will be liable to the beneficiaries. Similar liability is imposed on anyone who assists in a breach of trust although he does not actually receive the trust property into his hands. The rules for such liability are applied strictly to prevent an innocent volunteer who receives trust property from becoming liable.

3 INSTITUTIONAL AND REMEDIAL CONSTRUCTIVE TRUSTS

Constructive trusts take two forms, the institutional or the remedial constructive trust but unlike many other jurisdictions, English law only recognises the institutional constructive trust.

This difference between the two types of constructive trust was examined by Lord Browne-Wilkinson in *Westdeutsche Landesbank Girozentrale* v. *Islington BC* [1969] AC 669.

Under the institutional constructive trust, the trust arises by operation of law as from the date when the circumstances give rise to it. The function of the court is merely to declare that such a trust has arisen in the past ... A remedial constructive trust is different. It is a judicial remedy, giving rise to an enforceable equitable obligation; the extent to which it operates retrospectively to the prejudice of third parties lies in the discretion of the courts.

(a) The institutional constructive trust

The important feature of the institutional constructive trust is that rather than being imposed at the discretion of the court it is always imposed in response to a factual situation. So the court does not have the discretion to use the constructive trust as a remedy. The trust takes effect from the time that the relevant facts have occurred. In these circumstances the court confirms the existence of proprietary interests, i.e. the status quo. This type of constructive trust has the effect of binding third parties even though the trust is not declared by the court until judgment.

An example of when a constructive trust may be used is where a profit has been made by someone in a fiduciary position. This has already been briefly mentioned above and will be considered in greater detail in Chapter 18. Fiduciaries include trustees, executors, directors of companies and agents. The law regards a fiduciary as owing special duties to his principal and breach of those duties allows the law to impose a constructive trust over any profit made. This trust would be binding on third parties from the moment the facts gave rise to it. In bankruptcy, a claim under a trust will have priority over other creditors because the claimant is simply reclaiming his own property rather than making a claim in contract so the timing of the imposition of the constructive trust is very important.

EXAMPLE

Ahmed acts as agent for Darius selling biodegradable packaging for major supermarkets called JuiceBoxes. He has been given the task of asking for tenders for a new type of packaging for fresh fruit juices. One firm FreshJuzzes approaches him and offers him £30,000, if he agrees to put forward their tender to his principal. He accepts the money and persuades Darius to accept the tender. Ahmed uses the money to speculate on the stock market. He makes £100,000, which he uses to put down as a deposit on a house in 2010, which he buys as an investment. Later, he invests further sums of his own money but this time he loses a considerable amount of his savings and as a result he was made bankrupt this year. Darius has just heard about the bribe offered to Ahmed by FreshJuzzes and claims that it is owed to his company.

In this example, the law may regard Ahmed as a constructive trustee from the moment that he receives the bribe from FreshJuzzes. Ahmed must account for the increase in the money to Darius. This money could be regarded as belonging to Darius and JuiceBoxes as soon as the bribe is taken. When Ahmed becomes bankrupt his trustee in bankruptcy will want to maximise his assets to pay his creditors and claim that Darius only has a personal claim. If however the sum Ahmed received from FreshJuzzes can be claimed under a constructive trust, then Darius can claim that he had a beneficial interest in the money from the moment that Ahmed received it and thus claim he has an interest in the house that was purchased with it. Consider the facts of *Attorney-General for Hong Kong* v. *Reid* and *Sinclair Investments* v. *Versailles Trade Finance Ltd* in this context. The effect of the decision in *Versailles* is that Ahmed will be personally liable to Darius and Darius will have to claim as a creditor.

(b) The remedial constructive trust

The remedial constructive trust contrasts with the institutional constructive trust because it can be imposed by the court as a remedy and constitutes one of the remedies available to the court to reverse unjust enrichment. The remedy can be imposed where the court finds that the defendant has been unjustly enriched at the expense of the claimant. Alternatively, it may be used as a remedy where it would be unconscionable not to impose it.

(c) When does a remedial constructive trust arise?

A remedial constructive trust arises for the first time when the court orders it. In this way it differs quite specifically from the institutional constructive trust which is simply imposed in response to circumstances that are recognised as giving rise to a constructive trust.

EXAMPLE

Angie and Jez are in a relationship. They live together in Angie's house which she purchased last year. It needs considerable work in order to make it habitable. Jez carries out most of the work himself as he is a skilled painter and decorator and can also carry out some basic plumbing work. Jez works on the house for fifteen months. Their relationship breaks down and they agree to split up. Jez moves out but he claims that he should be entitled to a share in the property.

Under English law Jez cannot claim anything unless he can prove common agreement between himself and the legal title owner, Angie, that he is to have a share. There is no implied agreement because he did not contribute financially to the purchase and there is no evidence of an express agreement.

These are the facts necessary for an institutional constructive trust of land to arise. They cannot be altered because the court hearing Jez's claim thinks either that Angie has been unjustly enriched or that it would be unconscionable for Jez to be denied a share.

Under a remedial constructive trust the court could decide to impose a constructive trust on Angie's property as a remedy to prevent unconscionability. If Angie's property has risen in value, it would seem unfair on Jez that he should not receive anything from the property because much of the increase is attributable to his hard work on the house.

(d) The role of the remedial constructive trust in other jurisdictions

A number of jurisdictions across the world have been more ready to embrace the remedial constructive trust. One of the more enthusiastic countries has been Canada where the remedial constructive trust has been used in a variety of situations.

> The constructive trust has existed for over two hundred years as an equitable remedy for certain forms of unjust enrichment. In its earliest form, the constructive trust was used to provide a remedy to claimants alleging that others had made profits at their expense.
>
> (Dickson CJC, *Hunter Engineering Co. Inc* v. *Syncrude Canada Ltd*
> (1989) 57 DLR (4th) 321)

On the facts of this case a remedial constructive trust was not imposed because the court could not find evidence of unjust enrichment but the comments in the case showed that it was an option open to the court where unjust enrichment could be proved. Other cases show that once unjust enrichment has been proved, the Canadian courts are ready to impose a remedial constructive trust even in a commercial context.

This is illustrated by *LAC Minerals Ltd* v. *International Corona Resources Ltd* (1989) 61 DLR (4th) 14 where Corona had approached LAC Minerals in an attempt to negotiate an agreement to mine mineral resources. Corona owned the mining rights over the land. LAC Minerals received information about the possibility of mineral deposits also being found in neighbouring land. When the land was later sold Corona attempted to buy the land but it was defeated by a bid made by LAC Minerals. LAC Minerals carried out the mining operation on its own and made a profit.

The court held that LAC Minerals had been unjustly enriched at the expense of Corona and imposed a remedial constructive trust over the land in favour of Corona. This case shows the flexibility of the remedial constructive trust but illustrates that its effect can be fairly draconian.

Most of the examples of the Canadian courts imposing a remedial constructive trust have involved trusts of the family home. Its use by the Canadian courts in this area contrasts with the approach of the English courts. The Canadian courts consider the facts from the point of view of the legal title holder and they ask the question: has he or she been unjustly enriched at the expense of the claimant? This removes the difficulties encountered in the English courts of trying to establish common intention between the parties to accord with Lord Bridge's definition in *Lloyds Bank* v. *Rosset*. Common intention has always been notoriously difficult to prove unless there have been capital contributions towards the purchase price of property.

In one of the early cases in Canada, *Pettkus* v. *Becker* (1980) 117 DLR (3d) 257 the court granted a woman a half share of property comprising a honey farm where she had lived and worked with the owner for over fourteen years. The Supreme Court upheld her claim on the basis that she could prove an enrichment for the title holder and a corresponding deprivation and also the absence of any juristic reason for the enrichment.

Later cases have upheld claims based on enrichment based on contributions to the care of the family and home without the need to show contributions towards the family business as shown in *Peter* v. *Beblow* (1993) 101 DLR (4th) 621.

(e) The role of the remedial constructive trust in English law

(i) Cases which show support for the remedial constructive trust

English law does not recognise the remedial constructive trust but there have been a number of occasions when the judiciary have made comments on whether it should be part of English law.

In *Westdeutsche Landesbank Girozentrale* v. *Islington Borough Council* [1996] AC 669 Lord Browne-Wilkinson commented as follows: 'although the resulting trust is an unsuitable basis for developing proprietary restitutionary remedies, the remedial constructive trust, if introduced into English law, may provide a more satisfactory road forward. The court by way of remedy might impose a construct-ive trust on a defendant who knowingly retains property of which the plaintiff has been unjustly deprived.'

In *Westdeutsche* Lord Browne-Wilkinson showed he was sympathetic to the role of the remedial constructive trust and seemed to be ready to incorporate it into English law.

Other cases have also referred sympathetically to the remedial constructive trust although not actually adopting it.

One example arises in *Lipkin Gorman* v. *Karpnale* [1991] 2 AC 548 where the House of Lords considered the principle of unjust enrichment and applied it to the facts. A dishonest solicitor had taken money from his firm's accounts and used it to gamble at the Playboy Club. The House of Lords held the club strictly liable to return the money to the firm on the basis that the club had been unjustly enriched at the firm's expense. The club could raise a defence of change of position which reduced the amount payable to the firm. This is discussed later in Chapter 20.

A further example lies in *Re Goldcorp* [1995] 1 AC 74 where there the Privy Council made a reference to the remedial constructive trust as a way of recovering property from a company in receivership by claiming that an interest had been retained by the customers. The property in this case was gold bullion which had not been sepa-rated from the bulk and so would be viewed as unascertained goods. Although the remedial constructive trust was discussed it was not applied in the case.

A more recent judicial affirmation of the value of the remedial constructive trust can be seen in the judgment of Lord Scott in *Thorner* v. *Major* [2009] UKHL 18, a case decided on the principle of proprietary estoppel where he said: 'The possibility of a remedial constructive trust over property, created by common intention or understanding of the parties regarding the property on the basis of which the claimant has acted to his detriment, has been recognised at least since *Gissing* v. *Gissing* [1971] AC 886.' On the facts the courts did not impose a remedial constructive trust but upheld the claim under proprietary estoppel.

(ii) Cases which show a reluctance to support the remedial constructive trust

In other cases the court has been less ready to apply the remedial constructive trust.

Halifax Building Society v. *Thomas* [1996] Ch 217

The court refused to impose a remedial constructive trust where the defendant, a mortgagor, had obtained a profit at the expense of the mortgagee building society by purchasing a house with the aid of a mortgage which he had obtained fraudulently. The mortgagor defaulted on the mortgage repayments and the property was sold by the mortgagees. There was a surplus left after sale which the mortgagees claimed was held on constructive trust for them because they argued that the mortgagor would not have been able to purchase the property without the aid of the loan. The claim was rejected.

Peter Gibson LJ commented 'English law has not followed other jurisdictions where the constructive trust has become a remedy for unjust enrichment'.

Note that this case was decided after *Lipkin Gorman* v. *Karpnale*.

Re Polly Peck International plc (*in administration*) (*No. 2*) [1998] 3 All ER 812

The Court of Appeal revisited the use of the remedial constructive trust where the defendant was insolvent. The claimants owned land in Cyprus and they claimed that Polly Peck held profits under a remedial constructive trust which they had made by wrongfully exploiting the claimant's land. Polly Peck was insolvent and such a finding would allow the claimants to go to the front of the queue of creditors. The Court of Appeal refused to do so and Nourse LJ held that it was for Parliament to introduce the constructive trust into English law: 'you cannot grant a proprietary right to A without taking some proprietary right from B. No English court has ever had the power to do that, except with the authority of Parliament'.

The remedial constructive trust would therefore give the claimants under the trust priority over other creditors. Although there may be priority under the institutional constructive trust this would be because the claimant had come within the recognised situations giving rise to such a trust. An example would be the fiduciary who has misused his position and made a profit at the expense of his principal as in *Attorney-General for Hong Kong* v. *Reid*.

But the courts will not impose a constructive trust on the grounds that they feel it would be appropriate in the circumstances on the particular facts before them.

(f) Conclusions on the use of the remedial constructive trust

1 Although the remedial constructive trust has been used in a number of jurisdictions and clearly has had supporters in England both within the judiciary and without, it is still not part of English law. It is not possible to claim such a remedy in an application before the court.

2 The main reluctance lies with the uncertainty that the imposition of the remedial constructive trust creates. As it is based on judicial discretion it is difficult to monitor in what circumstances that discretion will be exercised.

3 If the remedial constructive trust is imposed to reverse unjust enrichment, then how will unjust enrichment be measured? It could introduce a significant element of uncertainty into English law. One judge may view unjust enrichment in one set of circumstances where another would not. It would bring in an unwelcome element of uncertainty to the law.

4 Practitioners would have difficulty in advising clients as to how a court will act because they would no longer be able to confidently predict the outcome of a case which can be done to some extent under the institutional constructive trust.

4 PERSONAL AND PROPRIETARY CLAIMS OVER PROPERTY

The difference between a personal and proprietary claim can be very significant. The important difference lies in the status of the rights.

Where a person has a proprietary right it is considered to be a right in a thing giving the claimant a right to sue for property rather than merely a right to the value in the form of damages.

A personal right merely gives a right against a person. The claimant can sue for a sum owed in the form of damages. The difference is not always important but in bankruptcy it is crucial.

EXAMPLE

Felicity has borrowed money from Alison to pay for a new carpet. She agrees to pay 6 per cent in interest over three years. This is a contractual agreement and gives Alison personal rights against Felicity. If Felicity goes bankrupt during the three years, then Alison will not be able to recover all the sums owing from Felicity. Alison will rank only as a creditor and is likely to only get a fraction of the amount back.

Compare the following example.

EXAMPLE

Felicity has promised to advance to Alison a sum of money towards a new computer. By mistake she forwards the money a second time to her before the agreement is signed and Alison notices this the following day. Alison has now gone bankrupt and Felicity wishes to know whether she can claim the money back in full or whether she will only rank as a creditor.

There are no facts in the first example to indicate that a constructive trust would be imposed whereas in the second example the recipient Alison knows that she has received this money twice and will therefore have to account for it back to the creditor Felicity in full. The advance of the money a second time raises a constructive trust because it would be unconscionable for Alison to retain the second payment and this will be binding on Alison. (Note here the facts of *Chase Manhattan Bank* v. *Israel-British Bank (London) Ltd* [1981] Ch 105.)

Where a creditor claims money from a debtor the claim usually lies in contract and will rank as a personal claim. In bankruptcy this means that the creditor will simply rank with other creditors and will not gain priority. If the claim is under a trust, the claimant will have priority because the claim lies under trust law giving the claimant a proprietary claim.

SUMMARY

This chapter examines the second type of implied trust, the constructive trust. The constructive trust is difficult to define although it can be defined as a trust imposed by law usually irrespective of the intentions of the parties. It has been imposed in a wide variety of situations. An example arises in the sale of land where the seller becomes a constructive trustee as soon as contracts are exchanged.

Another key example arises in the context of the family home where the intentions of the parties are important. Lord Bridge laid down the circumstances in which the sole legal owner of property becomes a constructive trustee of land in *Lloyds Bank* v. *Rosset*. A constructive trust of land will only arise where a common intention to share the property can be proved. Some of the other significant examples of constructive trusteeship include gains made by fiduciaries and the survivor where mutual wills have been drawn up. The trust arises in two different forms: the institutional and remedial constructive trust. Both types of constructive trust are imposed where there is unconscionability and it may be imposed against the wishes of the parties. England only recognises one type of constructive trust, the institutional constructive trust. Countries such as Canada will impose a remedial constructive trust as a remedy to reverse unjust enrichment. This was shown in *LAC Minerals Ltd* v. *International Corona Resources Ltd*. The institutional constructive trust is imposed by the court when certain facts have been proved. The contrast with the remedial constructive trust lies in the role of the court. The remedial constructive trust is discretionary and allows the court to intervene when there is a wish to reverse unjust enrichment at the claimant's expense. English courts are reluctant to impose the remedial constructive trust because it is concerned that it will introduce too great an element of uncertainty into the law. There has been sympathy towards the remedial constructive trust expressed by some members of the judiciary as shown by Lord Browne-Wilkinson in *Westdeutsche Landesbank Girozentrale* v. *Islington Borough Council* but such an attitude is not universal among the judiciary and the courts remain reluctant to impose such trusts.

11 Trusts of the family home

KEY POINTS

- there is no specific law concerning rights in the family home;
- married and civil partners can claim rights in the family home under statute;
- unmarried partners and family members must rely on property law in order to be awarded rights in the family home;
- rights in the family home may arise under an express trust if the declaration complies with formalities;
- rights may arise under an implied trust (either a constructive trust or a resulting trust);
- a constructive trust will only arise where there is proof of common intention that both parties are to share the property;
- a resulting trust is based on proof of contributions towards the purchase price;
- quantification of the shares under a resulting trust depend on the size of the contribution;
- quantification of the shares under a constructive trust depends on proof of the parties' intention; and
- rights in the family home may also arise under proprietary estoppel.

key points

1 INTRODUCTION TO TRUSTS OF THE FAMILY HOME

The family home is one of the most significant assets that people own. However, surprisingly unlike other jurisdictions there is no separate law in England and Wales concerning ownership of the family home. Rights in the family home do not arise automatically within a relationship where both parties are living or have lived together in the home in the past.

Married partners and civil partners have a statutory right to claim property on the breakdown of a relationship which depends on status where the court must award a share to the claimant.

For other relationships the picture is more complicated. Rights in the family home depend on proof that property rights have arisen either formally or informally. They depend on proof of such rights under property law and in particular proof of rights under a trust.

Rights can arise formally according to formalities laid down under statute or they can arise informally by showing that an implied trust has arisen or under the rules of proprietary estoppel.

Where rights are acquired formally, disputes between the owners are less likely since it will be relatively straightforward to prove what rights have arisen through written evidence of what was intended by the parties.

Where rights are acquired informally the situation is quite different. Disputes can easily arise over rights in property and proof may revolve around conversations and oral promises or agreements which are always difficult to prove.

Relationships giving rise to rights in the family home

Disputes concerning ownership of the family home can involve a variety of relationships including married couples, couples in a civil partnership, cohabitants or family members who purchase property together. Certain relationships allow property claims to be made upon breakdown. Married couples and civil partners can claim rights in property based on their status and specific legislation protects their property rights e.g. in the case of married couples the Matrimonial Causes Act 1973 gives a spouse the right to apply for the transfer of property and similar rights arise for civil partners under the Civil Partnership Act 2004.

By contrast, where parties are cohabiting or are family members there is no specific legislation that protects property rights in the family home and any dispute must be resolved by relying on proof that rights have arisen under a trust.

Rights can be acquired through the following means:

1 an express trust;
2 a common intention constructive trust;

3 a resulting trust; and

4 rights under proprietary estoppel.

2 AN EXPRESS TRUST

Occasionally a couple may expressly declare their interests in the family home under an express trust. It is unusual for the members of a family to use an express trust unless the parties have been given legal advice. This is because the rules are fairly complicated and require certain formalities to be followed.

Since the trust concerns land it must be declared or evidenced in writing in order to comply with s.53(1)(b) Law of Property Act 1925 (LPA 1925):

a declaration of a trust respecting any land or any interest therein must be manifested and proved by some writing signed by some person who is able to declare such a trust or by his will.

Where the parties are not married or in a civil partnership it is very important that the parties expressly declare their shares under a trust because there is no statutory framework by which a party can claim rights in property based on the status of a cohabitant.

If the relationship breaks down, then any claim must be based on the proof of rights under property law. If an express trust has been created over the family home, this will remove any doubt over whether each party has a right in the property. It may also address the issue of how the shares in the property should be divided if this has been expressly included in the terms of the trust.

EXAMPLE

Vernon and Wanda have lived together in rented accommodation for two years and now wish to buy somewhere to live together. Wanda does not have any money so Vernon purchases 29 Lark Rise, Banbury, a newly renovated flat in his name but he tells Wanda he wants her to have some security. Wanda's friend Leslie is a lawyer and he tells her that it would be better if Vernon put this in writing. Vernon writes the following on a piece of paper: 'I hold the flat 29 Lark Rise, Banbury in equal shares for Wanda and myself.' He signs it and puts it into a drawer. A year later Vernon and Wanda have a row and Wanda moves out claiming a share in the flat. As Vernon declared the trust of the flat in writing and signed it he has satisfied the requirements of s.53(1)(b) LPA 1925 and Wanda can enforce her claim for a share in the property. It would be more complicated for her to claim a share if he had merely declared the trust orally.

3 SOLE LEGAL OWNER: A COMMON INTENTION CONSTRUCTIVE TRUST OF LAND

If there is no express declaration of trust, informal rights may arise under an implied trust, either a *resulting* or a *constructive trust*. If the legal title to property is registered in the sole name of one person, another person can only claim rights in equity. If the rights are claimed under a trust, then the claimant is arguing that instead of enjoying rights for him/herself absolutely the titleholder owns as a trustee on behalf of both parties.

EXAMPLE

Harry and Joan have lived together for four years. Last year Harry purchased a house called Oak Cottage in his name. Joan had no money of her own but she has spent time decorating the property as it was in a poor state of repair. Last month Joan gave birth to a child Lulu. Joan wants to know if she has any rights in Oak Cottage.

Harry and Joan are cohabitants and any claim for rights in the family home must be based on property law because the law does not recognise their status as cohabitants. Harry is the legal owner of the property. He can sell the property any time he wishes and he can also take out a mortgage or create a lease. Joan may have rights in equity if she can prove that an express or implied trust has arisen. It is unlikely that they have any written evidence of their rights in the property but an oral agreement may be enough to prove she has rights under an implied trust. If Joan can show that she has rights in equity, Harry will be regarded as sole trustee of Oak Cottage holding the property on behalf of himself and Joan.

Constructive trusts were discussed in detail in Chapter 10 and it was shown that they arise in a wide variety of situations including rights in the family home.

A constructive trust of the family home is based on proof of common intention to share the property which means that this type of constructive trust has developed in a slightly different way from other types of constructive trust because they are usually imposed by the court against the wishes of the parties. The trust is used here to prevent the legal title owner from behaving in an unconscionable manner by denying rights of the claimant who has acted to his/her detriment.

The *constructive trust* is particularly important in the context of the family home because couples and families rarely draw up express trusts declaring their interests in property. If the courts held that only express trusts complying with the statutory requirements could give rise to property rights, it could be very unfair on parties who genuinely believed he or she had rights in the property and then acted to his/her detriment in reliance on this belief.

(a) Background to the common intention constructive trust

A series of cases in the 1970s laid down the grounds on which a court would be prepared to uphold a claim for rights under such a trust.

The two important cases of *Pettitt* v. *Pettitt* [1970] AC 777 and *Gissing* v. *Gissing* [1971] AC 886 both laid down the key features which must be proved in order to claim rights under a constructive trust but it was not until the decision in *Lloyds Bank* v. *Rosset* [1991] 1 AC 107 that the principles on which any claim must be based were clearly laid out.

In *Pettitt* the court declared that there must be proof of common intention that the claimant would be able to claim a share before a constructive trust could arise. On the facts of this case Mr Pettitt had carried out work on property owned by his wife. He was unsuccessful in his claim because there was no evidence of common intention between the parties that he was to acquire an interest in the property. The work on its own could not give rise to rights.

In *Gissing* Lord Diplock stated that a constructive trust would arise: 'whenever the trustee has so conducted himself that it would be inequitable to deny the *cestui que* trust a beneficial interest in the land acquired, and he will be held to have conducted himself if by words or conduct he has induced the *cestui que* trust to act to his own detriment in the reasonable belief that by so acting he was acquiring a beneficial interest in the land'.

In this case Mrs Gissing had not contributed financially to property purchased by her husband. He left her for a younger woman and she argued that she should have rights in the property based on her non-capital contributions. She was unsuccessful because she could not show that she had been induced by Mr Gissing to act to her detriment in the reasonable belief that she would acquire rights in the property. It was held that she had to link her contributions to a promise by or an agreement with Mr Gissing that she would acquire property rights.

(b) The key principles from *Lloyds Bank* v. *Rosset*

The principles from *Pettitt* and *Gissing* were developed much further in the important case of *Lloyds Bank* v. *Rosset* which laid down the key elements which a claimant must prove in order to establish rights under a constructive trust today.

More recently the case of *Stack* v. *Dowden* [2007] UKHL 17 has raised important issues in connection with these principles but as this case concerned joint ownership of the legal title it has not overruled the principles of *Lloyds Bank* v. *Rosset* which concerned sole ownership of property.

Lloyds Bank v. *Rosset* [1991] 1 AC 107

This case concerned a married couple. A semi-derelict property was purchased by Mr Rosset in his sole name. The reason for this was that the purchase monies came from a family trust in Switzerland which stipulated that any property purchased using money from the fund must be held in the sole ownership of Mr Rosset. The wife did not contribute financially to the purchase but she did contribute in kind by improving the property and she relied on these contributions to prove that she had acquired property rights. Mr Rosset had taken out a mortgage with Lloyds Bank over the property to pay for the works being carried out but he had not discussed this with his wife. The work was finished and the couple moved in but the husband failed to pay the mortgage instalments. The key issue was whether the wife had rights in the property which took priority over the mortgagee, Lloyds Bank. Unusually this was not a case about unmarried cohabitants but priority between the claims of a spouse and a mortgagee. Her rights could not take priority unless she could establish rights under a trust because the property had been purchased by the husband in his sole name. In order to claim rights Mrs Rosset had to prove that there was a common intention that she was to have a share in the property. Mrs Rosset relied on the fact that she had renovated the property and also supervised building work over a period of time.

Lord Bridge considered Mrs Rosset's case and he laid down how common intention can be proved, thus giving rise to a beneficial interest in her favour.

He held that such a claim arises in two circumstances:

1 *Express common intention.* This can only be proved by any express agreement, arrangement or understanding between the parties that the property is to be shared beneficially. In his words such an agreement will support the claim 'however imperfectly remembered or however imprecise the terms'. Lord Bridge continued 'once a finding to this effect is made, it will only be necessary for the partner asserting a claim to a beneficial interest against the partner entitled to the legal estate to show that he or she has acted to his or her detriment or significantly altered his or her position in reliance on the agreement'.

2 *Implied common intention.* This rule applies where there is no evidence of express common intention but there is evidence from which the court can infer common intention to share the property. Lord Bridge was quite clear that the only evidence that would support such a claim would be direct financial contributions. Even evidence of a small financial contribution would be enough. It would not have to be substantial. However evidence of contributions in kind would not be sufficient to support a claim.

Lord Bridge could not find any proof of any 'agreement, arrangement or understanding' between the parties giving rise to rights in Mrs Rosset's favour. There was also no evidence that she had made direct financial contributions towards the purchase of the property.

(c) How does proof of common intention work in practice?

(i) Express common intention

Lord Bridge gave *two examples of cases* which both show what the court might regard as evidence of express common intention.

Eves v. Eves [1975] 1 WLR 1338

Property was purchased by Mr Eves in his sole name. He told his partner Janet that he would not put her name on the title because she was too young to own property. She was 18 at the time but since 1970 the age at which property can be owned has been 21. However the fact that he had told her that she could have had a share if she were older was sufficient for the court to hold that there was evidence of express common intention. The court found that he had led her to believe that she would derive a share and on the basis of that she had carried out work on the property and thus found in her favour declaring that she had a share in the property.

Grant v. Edwards [1986] Ch 638

Property was purchased by Edwards to provide a home for himself and Grant. At the time both parties were married to different people. Edwards suggested to Grant that he would not put her name on the title deeds because she was going through a difficult divorce and claiming maintenance from her husband and it would prejudice her claim if she were seen by the court to own property of her own. It was held that this constituted a promise of rights by Edwards to Grant as he would have put her name on the title deeds in any other circumstances and Grant was able to claim a share in the property.

Hammond v. Mitchell [1991] 1 WLR 1127

This case concerned a couple who had been living together in a bungalow owned solely by Mr Hammond. He told his partner Ms Mitchell that he would not put the title of the bungalow in his partner's name because he wanted to avoid tax, and owning the property in his sole name would help. He told her: 'Don't worry about the future because when we are married it will be half yours anyway.' Ms Mitchell helped Mr Hammond in his business. After eleven years together the relationship broke down and Ms Mitchell claimed a share in the property based on a common intention constructive trust. The court upheld the partner's claim because of the evidence of express common intention that the property was to be shared between them.

EXAMPLE

Holly and Dave met in a bar in December three years ago. They became friends and Dave suggested to Holly that they move in together. He was in the process of buying a house. Holly did not have any savings and as she was a student and did not have a job she could not make any financial contribution to the purchase. Holly had told him that her godmother Carly had promised to buy her a house on her twenty-fifth birthday if she had not bought a house before then. As Holly was 24 she hoped that Carly was going to fulfil her promise to her. Dave said to Holly: 'I will not put your name on the title to the new property because otherwise Carly will not purchase you a property on your birthday.' After three years together Dave and Holly started to argue incessantly and eventually they split up. Holly is claiming a share in the property.

The court is likely to find in Holly's favour because of Dave's discussion with her about the reasons for not putting her name on the title at the Land Registry. The discussion is similar to discussions that took place in *Eves, Grant* v. *Edwards* and *Hammond* v. *Mitchell*.

James v. *Thomas* [2007] EWCA Civ 1212

This case concerned a claim by a cohabitant Ms James for rights in property solely owned by Mr Thomas. Ms James and Mr Thomas cohabited for over fifteen years together and during this time Ms James had worked without payment for Mr Thomas in his business which he ran from home. At one time they had worked under a partnership but that had been dissolved. On one occasion Mr Thomas had told Ms James that she would be well provided for after his death. When the relationship broke down Ms James claimed a share based on an express common intention. She relied on his promise that she would be provided for after his death and also the work that she had carried out to support her claim for a share in the property.

The Court of Appeal rejected her claim. It held that the discussion about provision for Ms James after Mr Thomas's death did not relate to rights in the property. Further, the improvements to the property could not alone give rise to property rights.

(ii) Implied common intention

Lord Bridge held that the grounds for inferring common intention are very limited. The court must look at the conduct of the parties and under these grounds only evidence of financial contributions would count as evidence in order to imply common intention to share.

The criticism that has been aimed at these grounds is that it fails to take into account any other evidence, in particular evidence of contributions in kind and any other non-capital contribution.

In cases where the couple have not had any discussions that can be classed as showing an express common intention and the claimant has not contributed financially then a claim is bound to fail.

What contributions count as direct financial contributions?

The House of Lords in *Lloyds Bank* v. *Rosset* held that only direct contributions towards the purchase price can imply a common intention to share. Lord Bridge accepted that these could be either initial payments or payments towards the mortgage instalments but it was extremely doubtful whether anything less would do.

Oxley v. *Hiscock* [2004] 3 WLR 715

This case concerned an unmarried couple who lived together in property owned by Mr Hiscock. Ms Oxley had made contributions towards the purchase which amounted to 20 per cent of the purchase price. This allowed the court to infer a common intention to share but the couple disagreed about what share she should derive from the property. She claimed she was entitled to a half-share but Mr Hiscock argued she should get a share equivalent to the amount she had contributed. The court awarded her just under 40 per cent.

Even a very small contribution will be enough to infer a common intention to share. In *Midland Bank* v. *Cooke* [1995] 4 All ER 562 the wife relied on a contribution of less than 7 per cent to infer common intention to share. The contribution made by the wife was a half-share in a wedding present made by her parents-in-law to her and her husband.

Burns v. *Burns* [1984] Ch 317

A couple had cohabited for over nineteen years in property owned in the sole name of Mr Burns. They had had two children and Ms Burns had not worked but devoted herself to their care and care of the family home. Ms Burns had not made any financial contribution towards the purchase of the property or mortgage instalments but she had made indirect contributions towards household expenses. There was no evidence of an express agreement to share and without proof of direct financial contributions she was unable to claim an interest in the family home despite her indirect contributions towards the home and care for the children.

The Court of Appeal found no right to a beneficial entitlement to the family home:

It seems to me that at the time of the acquisition of the house nothing occurred between the parties to raise an equity which would prevent the defendant from denying the plaintiff's claim. She provided no money for the purchase; she assumed no responsibility in respect of the mortgage; there was no understanding or arrangement that the plaintiff would go out to work to assist with the family finances; the defendant did nothing to lead her to change her position in the belief that she would have an interest in the house.

(Fox LJ)

EXAMPLE

Ursula met Victor at a volunteer centre run by the RSPCA eighteen years ago and after six months he asked Ursula if she would like to move into his house, Barrabrigg. Ursula was training to be a veterinary nurse and Victor was a driving instructor. They never discussed ownership of Barrabrigg. After a year Ursula gave birth to twins and she decided to give up her veterinary nurse training and to stay at home to care for the twins. She occasionally worked at a call centre and any money she earned she put towards clothes for the children and household purchases. Victor paid all instalments towards the mortgage. Recently, Victor met Cilla who was also a driving instructor and they have decided that they would like to live together in Barrabrigg. Ursula knew nothing of their relationship until last week. She is shocked and also very worried about her rights in the house.

Consider here the fact that Victor owns the house at law so Ursula must prove she has rights in equity under a trust. Ursula has very little chance of proving that she has rights under a constructive trust because she has not made any financial contributions towards the purchase nor will she be able to prove that there has been an express discussion about rights in the property. Without an express or implied common agreement that she is to acquire a right in the property any detriment she has suffered such as her contributions towards the household expenses will be irrelevant.

(d) Detriment

Once the claimant has shown either an express or implied common intention to share the property the next step is to prove detriment or change of position. The standard for this is lower than that necessary to prove common intention itself.

In *Grant* v. *Edwards* Nourse LJ explained that the conduct required should be 'conduct on which the woman could not reasonably have been expected to embark unless she was to have an interest in the house'.

In this case the care of children and indirect contributions towards the housekeeping expenses were sufficient to prove detriment.

Browne-Wilkinson VC commented further in the case that in his opinion 'any act done by [the claimant] to her detriment relating to the joint lives of the parties is, in my judgment, sufficient detriment to qualify. The acts do not have to be referable to the house.'

The approach of Browne-Wilkinson VC as to what constitutes detriment is more liberal than that of Nourse LJ.

(e) Has the law moved on since *Rosset*?

Although as stated above *Stack* v. *Dowden* concerned property owned jointly at law where there is no need to show common intention the comments made in the House of Lords suggest that this case will affect even cases of sole ownership.

Baroness Hale stated that the law has moved on since *Lloyds Bank* v. *Rosset* in response to changing social and economic conditions. She suggested in her judgment that it was for the court to take a 'holistic approach' to ownership of the family home and that the 'search is to ascertain the parties' shared intentions, actual inferred or imputed with respect to the property in the light of their whole course of conduct in relation to it'.

(f) Quantifying a share under a common intention constructive trust

Once a claimant can establish that a constructive trust has arisen the court has complete discretion as to how the shares should be quantified unless the parties have already reached express agreement about the size of their respective shares.

The court works on the principle that it is trying *to give effect to the intentions of the parties*. Unlike quantification under a resulting trust the court is not limited to giving effect to the size of the respective contributions of the parties.

A number of different approaches have emerged from case law:

1 The approach in *Midland Bank* v. *Cooke* which is to look at the 'whole course of dealing of the parties' taking in every aspect of their financial commitments.
2 The approach in *Oxley* v. *Hiscock* where the court could decide the shares according to what was 'fair'.
3 The approach in *Stack* v. *Dowden* where the court can take into account a range of matters such as how the parties arranged their finances, how they discharged their outgoings and how the purchase was financed.

In *Stack* v. *Dowden* the court expressly disapproved of the approach of abandoning the search for common intention in favour of a result which was deemed to be 'fair'. Therefore the approach in *Oxley* v. *Hiscock* would no longer be taken by the courts.

Baroness Hale summed up the duty of the court in considering shares in the family home in *Stack* v. *Dowden* as a 'search to ascertain the parties' shared intentions' (see above). It is assumed from the dicta in that case that the court is able to look at a much wider range of issues when quantifying an interest than they could previously both in cases of sole legal ownership and joint legal ownership.

4 SOLE LEGAL OWNER: RESULTING TRUSTS OF LAND

The resulting trust of land arises where one party makes a contribution towards the purchase price of property. Under a resulting trust the person making a contribution will have a share in the property. This is based on the presumption that a contribution to the purchase price of property would not be made unless the purchaser had presumed that he or she would retain an interest in the property. It is often called a 'purchase money resulting trust'.

Resulting trusts were discussed in detail in Chapter 9.

EXAMPLE

Keira and Kevin purchase a house together. It is registered in Keira's sole name but Kevin contributes 35 per cent of the purchase price. Keira will be deemed to hold the house as resulting trustee for Kevin even if they had not discussed ownership of the house together.

However where there is evidence of express common intention or a common intention to share can be inferred the law will consider the property to be held on constructive trust.

In *Midland Bank* v. *Cooke* (see above) the court took the view that a constructive trust rather than a resulting trust had arisen because there was clear evidence in the way the parties dealt with their finances that they intended to share the ownership of the property.

The presumption of a resulting trust is rebuttable by proof of:

1 *presumption of advancement* such as when it is presumed that the purchase money has been advanced as a gift either because of the relationship between the parties e.g. father to child or because of the circumstances of the advance; or
2 the money has been provided by *loan* giving rise to a contractual relationship between the parties (note that this has been recently abolished by the Equality Act 2010); or
3 the money have been transferred as an outright *gift*.

(a) What contributions give rise to a presumed resulting trust?

The presumption will arise when direct payments towards the purchase price have been made. These are interpreted fairly generously but certain contributions will never count.

(i) Contributions made after purchase

Financial contributions will only be relevant where they are made at the time of purchase. Any contribution made after purchase could give rise to a constructive trust.

(ii) Contributions in kind

A contribution towards the cost of improvements to the property will never count as a direct contribution to the purchase and will not give rise to an interest in property. In *Burns* v. *Burns* [1984] Ch 317 the contributions of the woman towards the home were held not to be referable to an interest in the property under a resulting trust.

This has been criticised. It constitutes a very narrow view of contributions towards the property. The decision whether to contribute towards the purchase price or towards improvements to the property may be a lifestyle decision but it will dramatically affect the rights of the claimant to an interest in property.

(iii) Right to buy under the Housing Act 1985

The Housing Act 1985 gives certain tenants the right to buy property which they have rented for a period of time at a discounted price. The discount is regarded as a direct financial contribution. In *Springette* v. *Defoe* [1992] 2 FLR 388 the claimant qualified for a discount of 41 per cent on the purchase price of a local authority owned house because of the length of time she had occupied it as a tenant. The court held this to be a direct contribution towards the purchase price.

(iv) Mortgage repayments

The role of mortgage repayments has been controversial. They can be deemed as contributions towards the purchase price because it can be seen as simply delayed payments of the purchase price. The courts have taken a different attitude according to whether there is a prior agreement as to who is to be responsible for the payment of the mortgage or whether the repayments are made subsequent to the purchase without a prior agreement between the parties.

Curley v. Parkes [2004] EWCA Civ 1515

The case concerned a couple who lived together in a house purchased in the sole name of Ms Parkes. The purchase monies consisted of the proceeds of sale of a previous house of Ms Parkes, some cash and the rest from a mortgage taken out in Ms Parkes' sole name. Mr Curley paid a sum amounting to over £9,000 into Ms Parkes' bank account from which some of the mortgage instalments were paid. When the relationship broke down he claimed that this constituted a contribution towards the purchase price and should give rise to a share under a resulting trust.

Contributions to mortgage repayments were held by Peter Gibson LJ not to give rise to an interest under a resulting trust, because 'subsequent payments of the mortgage instalments are not part of the purchase price already paid to the vendor, but are sums paid for discharging the mortgagor's obligations under the mortgage'.

(b) Quantification of a share under a resulting trust

The court will quantify a share under a resulting trust according to the amount contributed by the claimant. This is a simple calculation based on size of contribution.

> **EXAMPLE**
>
> Theo and Rose have decided to purchase a house together. Theo purchases Sunny Rise for £300,000 and it is registered in his sole name. At the time of purchase Rose makes a contribution of £30,000 towards the purchase price. Rose will have a 10 per cent interest in the property. If she had contributed £3,000, she would have a 1 per cent share in the property.
>
> The strict arithmetical approach to quantification is regarded as a drawback of the resulting trust approach. The court does not have discretion to calculate the share according to the intentions of the parties as it can under a common intention constructive trust. It cannot take into account other relevant factors. For this reason, the courts prefer to use the constructive trust in considering rights in the family home.

(c) A continuing role for resulting trusts?

In recent years, the courts have preferred not to use the resulting trust in assessing shares in the family home on the basis that it is an inflexible tool in this context. This was affirmed in *Stack* v. *Dowden* where the House of Lords, with the exception of Lord Neuberger, rejected its value in this area of law. In a dissenting judgment Lord Neuberger supported the use of the resulting trust in the context of the family home.

There has been other judicial support for its continued use. Where property is purchased by way of an investment, particularly if the purchasers are members of the same family, the resulting trust may be an appropriate solution.

Laskar v. Laskar [2008] EWCA Civ 347

A mother and daughter purchased a house as an investment. The mother had the benefit of a discounted price under the 'right to buy' scheme. She purchased the property in joint names with one of her daughters. The purchase price of just over £50,000 was raised by the large discount that the mother could claim and also a cash contribution from the daughter and a mortgage taken out in joint names. The property was let to tenants and the rent was used to discharge the mortgage repayments. Later the mother and daughter disagreed and the daughter claimed a half-share in the property based on the fact that they were joint owners of the property at law.

The Court of Appeal applied a resulting trust giving the daughter a 30 per cent share in the property. Lord Neuberger sitting in the Court of Appeal repeated comments that he had made earlier in *Stack* v. *Dowden* in the House of Lords about the continuing value of resulting trusts:

I can see no reason not to fall back on the resulting trust analysis, namely that in the absence of any relevant discussion between the parties their respective beneficial shares should reflect the size of their contributions to the purchase price.

5 JOINT LEGAL OWNERS OF THE FAMILY HOME. IMPLICATIONS OF *STACK* V. *DOWDEN*

The legal title to property may be conveyed into joint names. In such cases, any dispute will revolve around the size of share that each party may claim rather than whether rights in equity have arisen at all. As the land is jointly owned the property will be owned under a trust of land. The beneficial ownership may be as tenants in common or as joint tenants.

Where the parties own as *joint tenants* each owns everything and nothing and in the event of a dispute the maxim 'equity is equality' will be applied and the parties will be deemed to own in equal shares when the property is divided. The parties may declare that they own as joint tenants in law and equity and any other presumption giving rise to unequal shares will then be overridden.

(a) An express declaration at the time of purchase of joint tenancy or tenancy in common

In *Goodman* v. *Gallant* [1986] 2 WLR 236 a couple purchased property in joint names as joint tenants. The contributions were unequal, the claimant having made a contribution of three-quarters of the purchase price. When the relationship broke down the claimant argued that she was entitled to a share equivalent to her contribution. The court held that she was only entitled to half because of the declaration of the joint tenancy at the time of purchase.

Where the parties own the property as *tenants in common* each owns a 'share' in the sense that each can deal in a share in the property. The share can be sold or mortgaged in equity or left under a will.

If the parties do not declare whether they hold as joint tenants or tenants in common, the court must decide the issue using surrounding facts and also applying equitable presumptions.

(b) No express declaration at the time of purchase

Stack v. *Dowden* [2007] 2 AC 432

This case concerned a couple, Ms Dowden and Mr Stack who purchased a family home in joint names in 1993. The purchase price was £190,000. This was funded partly by a mortgage advance of £65,000 for which both parties were liable, partly by cash which was derived from the sale of a previous property which had been registered in the sole name of Ms Dowden and also by funds from a building society account in the name of Ms Dowden. The transfer did not include a declaration of trust, nor was ownership of the interests in equity expressly declared at the time of purchase so it was not clear whether they held as joint tenants or tenants in common. They did not discuss their shares at the time of purchase. The relationship broke down in 2003 the couple having been together for over twenty-five years and living in the same house since 1983. Mr Stack claimed a half share in the property.

The Court of Appeal held that the shares should be 65 per cent for Ms Dowden and 35 per cent for Mr Stack. The House of Lords upheld this decision. Their reasoning gives the courts an indication of how to approach quantification of shares where the parties jointly own the legal title.

The leading judgment was given by Baroness Hale. It can be broken down into separate parts:

(i) Step one

Where parties own property jointly at law the presumption is that the parties own the beneficial interests jointly. The presumption is that 'equity follows the law'.

(ii) Step two

The claimant must prove that the parties intended the beneficial interests to be different from their legal interests.

The burden lies with the claimant to show that the beneficial interests were intended to be different from the legal interests.

(iii) Step three

The context of the relationship must be considered. A number of factors suggesting that the parties intended the shares to be other than equal will be relevant. Relevant factors are listed by Baroness Hale. Those factors include such things as: any advice or discussions at the time of the transfer which casts light on their intentions; the reasons why the home was acquired in joint names; the purpose for which the home was acquired; the nature of the parties' relationship; whether they had children for whom they had a responsibility to provide a home; how the purchase was financed, both initially and subsequently; how the parties arranged their finances, whether separately or together or a bit of both; how the parties discharged outgoings on the property and their other household expenses.

(iv) Step four

Where there is evidence that a contrary inference should be drawn then the court can conclude that the property was to be held in unequal shares.

In applying this approach the House of Lords concluded that the couple did not intend the property to be held equally. They had always treated their finances separately and had always held separate bank accounts. This indicated that the couple did not intend to share the property equally.

(v) An alternative approach

Lord Neuberger preferred to adopt a resulting trust in *Stack* v. *Dowden* and using this approach he concluded that the shares should be in the same proportions as the contributions of the parties. So Mr Stack could claim a share equivalent to his contribution and Ms Dowden could also claim a share equivalent to her contribution. Lord Neuberger's approach produced a very similar result to that produced under the constructive trust approach.

(c) Comments on *Stack* v. *Dowden*

Baroness Hale makes it clear that where property is owned jointly at law it is presumed that the equitable interests in the property are to be held under a joint tenancy.

The burden rests with the claimant to show that the parties intended their beneficial interests to be different from their legal interests. Baroness Hale suggested that such cases would be very unusual. This means in practice the claimant must show, by reference to the list of factors cited in the case, that they intended to hold the beneficial interest as tenants in common.

Once the claimant has rebutted the presumption that the beneficial interests are to be held as a tenancy in common, then the court can consider how the shares are to be quantified.

This approach has been welcomed since it allows the court to ignore the purely arithmetical approach of the resulting trust and instead to look at a range of factors surrounding each case which should produce a result which more accurately reflects the intentions of the parties.

(d) Cases decided after *Stack* v. *Dowden*

Cases decided after *Stack* v. *Dowden* show that the approach adopted by the House of Lords can extend to cases where the family home is purchased for family members, such as a parent and child.

Adekunle v. *Ritchie* [2007] WTLR 1505

A mother and son purchased property together. The mother needed her son's contributions as she could not afford to purchase the property under the 'right to buy' scheme on her own. There was no evidence that they intended to live there together. Although the purchase was in joint names the finances of the couple were kept separate. The judge held that the beneficial interests can follow the law but where there are unusual circumstances as in this case then the court can rebut the presumption of equality and quantify the shares in a different way.

Lord Neuberger's dissenting judgment has received some support and it does suggest that the approach advocated by Baroness Hale is not necessarily the approach to be taken in all cases of joint legal ownership.

Laskar v. *Laskar* (above) shows us that there may be situations where the resulting trust approach is preferable and will bring a result which more accurately reflects the intentions of the parties.

Fowler v. *Barron* [2008] 2 FLR 1

This case was decided after *Stack* v. *Dowden* but before the judgment of *Stack* was available to the court. The facts are very similar.

An unmarried couple lived together for over twenty-three years. In 1998 they purchased a house in joint names to provide a home for themselves and their children. There was no express declaration of trust although the transfer suggested that either party could give a valid receipt for the capital proceeds. Mr Barron paid the deposit on the house and also arranged the mortgage. He paid all the utility bills and costs of the house including the instalments on the mortgage. Ms Fowler used her earnings to pay for items for household costs and costs of the two children. When the relationship broke down Ms Fowler claimed a half-share in the property based on her joint ownership at law.

At first instance the court found that Ms Fowler had no interest in the property because she had not contributed towards the purchase. On appeal the Court of Appeal found in favour of Ms Fowler and upheld her claim for a share of 50 per cent. The court inferred from the behaviour of the parties that there was nothing to indicate that Ms Fowler was not to derive a share in the property and that although they had spent their income in different ways the parties' intentions were such that it made no difference who incurred a particular expense.

EXAMPLE

Marie and Ned have lived together for twenty-five years and have three children. Recently they decided to split up. Marie claims that she should have a 50 per cent share in the family home which they purchased in joint names in 2000. Ned paid for the deposit and also contributed £50,000 from a legacy that he had received from a relative. Ned arranged a mortgage and paid all the instalments. Marie has a part-time job and paid for the household shopping and she bought all the children's clothes. Ned argues that her share should reflect the fact that she has not contributed towards the mortgage and did not contribute towards the purchase and so it should be reduced.

The court will follow Baroness Hale's judgment in *Stack* v. *Dowden*. Unless Ned can show any reason why equity should not follow the law the court will award Marie a 50 per cent share. He may argue that the payment of £50,000 towards the purchase price from the legacy left to him is evidence of the separate finances of the parties especially if the money had been kept in a separate bank account.

Jones v. *Kermott* [2011] UKSC 53

The Supreme Court held that the beneficial interest in jointly held property should be split 90 per cent to Ms Jones and 10 per cent to Mr Kermott. There was no express declaration of the shares and following *Stack* v. *Dowden* it was held that the presumption of equality could be rebutted by contrary evidence which was not shown in this case.

6 EFFECT OF TRUSTS OF LAND (APPOINTMENT OF TRUSTEES) ACT 1996

Where two or more people own an interest in property a trust of land automatically arises. This is a statutory trust arising under the Trusts of Land (Appointment of Trustees) Act 1996 (TOLATA 1996). Anyone with an interest in the property who does not own at law has certain important rights such as a right to be consulted about decisions relating to the property s.11 TOLATA 1996 and also a right to bring an action in court such as an application for sale of the property under s.14 TOLATA 1996.

7 THE ROLE OF PROPRIETARY ESTOPPEL

Rights in property can also be acquired informally under proprietary estoppel. According to *Taylor Fashions Ltd* v. *Liverpool Victoria Trustees Co. Ltd* the claimant must prove that he/she has received *an assurance* which he/she has acted on to his/her detriment. The assurance must concern rights in land and the claimant must act in such a way that he/she suffers detriment in reliance on the promise. This approach may be relevant in considering rights in the family home. There appears to be an overlap with constructive trusts. In a number of decisions the courts have suggested that the two routes are similar and at times indistinguishable. This was the view of Lord Justice Chadwick in *Oxley* v. *Hiscock*. The differences between the two are still clear:

1 proprietary estoppel is based on an assurance of rights whereas a constructive trust is based on common intention;
2 the remedies available to the court under a constructive trust are limited to awarding a share in the beneficial interest whereas the court can award a range of remedies under proprietary estoppel;
3 the timing of when the rights arise is different. Under a constructive trust the rights of the claimant arise as soon as the circumstances giving rise to those rights exist, e.g. as soon as there is common intention to share the property whereas under estoppel the rights of the claimant do not arise until they are declared by the court.

8 THE FUTURE FOR RIGHTS IN THE FAMILY HOME

The law relating to rights in the family home is often complex and for unmarried couples much depends on whether a trust can be established in cases of sole ownership. The Law Commission has considered the reform of this area and in particular, the rights of cohabitants, on two separate occasions since the start of the twenty-first century. It is a controversial area. The most recent Law Commission report *Cohabitation: The Financial Consequences of Relationship Breakdown* (Law Comm. No. 207, Parts I and II, 2007) makes a number of suggestions including that rights in the family home should accrue on the basis of proof of length of relationship and whether the couple had children. This would not go as far as the financial provisions for civil partners and married couples. The scheme would only extend to couples with children or who have lived together for at least two years. It would be possible for couples to contract out of the scheme should they wish. The court could then exercise its discretion as to what relief to grant but it would have no discretion to award periodic payments as in marriage. There is no indication at present that the government wishes to take up the Law Commission's suggestions.

SUMMARY

This chapter examines rights in the family home. Although the family home is often the most significant asset most people own, there are no separate rules of law governing rights in the family home. Where a party to a relationship wishes to establish rights in property because he/she does not own the legal title he/she must establish rights under a trust or alternatively under the rules of proprietary estoppel. Rights can arise under an express or implied trust. Rights can only arise under an express trust where the formalities laid down in s.53(1)(b) LPA 1925 are complied with. Rights under an implied trust can either arise under a resulting or a constructive trust. Rights under a resulting trust depend on direct financial contributions made at the time of purchase as laid down in *Dyer* v. *Dyer*. Rights under a constructive trust depend on establishing a common intention to share the property which can either be implied or express according to Lord Bridge in *Lloyds Bank* v. *Rosset*. An implied common intention constructive trust can only arise where there have been direct financial contributions but an express common intention constructive trust will arise where there is evidence of an express agreement to share the property as illustrated in *Eves* v. *Eves* and *Grant* v. *Edwards*. Contributions in kind are not considered to be direct financial contributions as shown in *Burns* v. *Burns*. The claimant must also prove that he or she has suffered detriment which according to Nourse LJ does not have to be referable to the property itself. Once rights have been established the court has to quantify the shares. In a resulting trust the shares will be quantified according to the size of contribution. In a constructive trust the court is bound by any express agreement of the parties but where there is no express agreement as to the size of each, the court must try to give effect to the intentions of the parties. Baroness Hale established in *Stack* v. *Dowden* that the duty of the court when quantifying the interests of the parties is to ascertain the parties' shared intentions, actual, inferred or imputed with respect to the property. Where property is jointly owned at law a trust automatically arises but according to Baroness Hale in *Stack* v. *Dowden* unless the claimant can prove exceptional circumstances equity follows the law and the parties will own their interests in equity as joint tenants. Exceptional circumstances include where the parties have kept their finances separate and how the purchase of the property was financed as shown in *Stack* v. *Dowden*.

12 Secret trusts and mutual wills

A SECRET TRUSTS

KEY POINTS

- secret trusts operate outside the will;
- secret trusts do not have to adhere strictly to formalities;
- secret trusts exist in two forms: the fully secret trust and the half-secret trust;
- both fully secret and half-secret trusts require compliance with *three* requirements:
  - intention by the settlor to create a trust;
  - communication of that intention to the secret trustee; and
  - acceptance of that obligation by the trustee either expressly or impliedly;
- the rules for the timing of the communication of the intention varies between a half-secret trust and a fully secret trust;
- the intention to create a fully secret trust must be communicated any time before the death of the testator;
- the intention to create a half-secret trust must be communicated any time before the will is executed; and
- historically secret trusts were upheld in order to prevent fraud.

1 WHAT ARE SECRET TRUSTS?

A secret trust is a trust imposed on a beneficiary who receives property under a will but is later told by the testator that the gift under the will is to be held on trust for another person. The secondary beneficiary is not named in the will. If this instruction is made orally, it will not comply with the formalities laid down in the Wills Act 1837. However it may be upheld as a secret trust.

Under s.9 Wills Act 1837 a will must comply with certain key formalities without which a will cannot be upheld.

(a) s.9 Wills Act

No will shall be valid unless –
(a) it is in writing, and signed by the testator, or by some other person in his presence and by his direction; and
(b) it appears that the testator intended by his signature to give effect to the will; and
(c) the signature is made or acknowledged by the testator in the presence of two or more witnesses present at the same time; and
(d) each witness either –
  (i) attests and signs the will; or
  (ii) acknowledges his signature, in the presence of the testator (but not necessarily in the presence of any other witness), but no form of attestation shall be necessary.

These formalities are fairly simple to comply with but they are strictly enforced and so exclude oral declarations concerning the destination of one's property after death. If the formalities of the Wills Act are not complied with, then a testator will die intestate. To die intestate means to die without making formal provision for one's estate that is enforceable in law.

In these cases the law will impose statutory rules under the Administration of Estates Act 1925 as to who should inherit the property of the deceased person.

EXAMPLE

Terry decides to make a will leaving his entire estate to his friend Shelley. He writes a will at home and invites his two neighbours to come in. Terry signs the will in front of them both and both the witnesses sign the will themselves. After his death the will is enforceable in Shelley's favour.

(b) Compare this Example

> **EXAMPLE**
>
> Terry decides to make his will in favour of his friend Shelley. He tells his two neighbours that he is writing his will and asks them to come to his house to sign the will. Neither can come to the house that evening but he tells them both that he is leaving everything to Shelley. After his death the will is unenforceable because it does not comply with the Wills Act.

If the testator says to the beneficiary of the property under the will that he is not to keep the property for himself but to hold it on behalf of someone else, then this instruction will not comply with the Wills Act since it is a purely oral communication. However the law may uphold the promise as a secret trust.

Trusts of personalty do not require any formal documentation and are based purely on intention to create a trust and transfer of property to the trustee. However the courts have also upheld secret trusts of land where there is no documentary evidence. The reason that such trusts are upheld is traditionally the prevention of fraud. This is because where the beneficiary knows that he is not to enjoy the property for himself absolutely under the law of trusts he must either hold it for another or the property must result back to the estate of the testator.

> **EXAMPLE**
>
> Terry leaves £100,000 to his friend Sam. Before his death he asks Sam to come and see him. He says to him that the money left to him under the will is not for him but for his mistress Rosie. He says he does not want anyone to know about this. Sam agrees. This is now enforceable as a secret trust but it is not on the face of the will so no one knows about the gift.

(c) Why create a secret trust?

A will is a public document and so can be seen by any member of the public. If the testator wishes to leave property to someone whom he wishes to keep off the face of the will, a secret trust can avoid any unwelcome publicity. This is particularly valuable where the testator is a well-known person.

There are *two* types of secret trust:

1 the fully secret trust; and
2 the half-secret trust.

2 FULLY SECRET TRUSTS

A fully secret trust is one where neither the trust nor the terms are shown on the face of the will. Anyone reading the will would be unaware that the testator has no intention of making an absolute gift to the beneficiary.

According to Brightman J. in *Ottaway* v. *Norman* [1971] 3 All ER 1325 there are *three* requirements for a fully secret trust:

1 there must be an intention to create a trust;
2 that intention must be communicated to the secret trustee; and
3 the secret trustee must accept the trust.

(i) Intention to create a trust

Intention to create a secret trust is the same as proving intention for any express trust. In *McCormick* v. *Grogan* (1869–70) LR 4 HL 82 the testator told Grogan who was his sole beneficiary that he would find a letter with his will on his death and the letter would contain instructions concerning his property. The letter named certain people and the amounts that each was to inherit but it also said that the trustee was to act solely according to his own discretion. The House of Lords held that there was no trust in this case because it left the decision whether to act or not to the trustee.

(ii) Intention must be communicated to secret trustee

In a fully secret trust the timing of the communication of the terms of the trust can be any time up until the death of the testator. If communication of the secret trust takes place after the death of the testator, for example, a letter is found with the testator's papers with instructions that a gift is to be held on a secret trust, the courts will not enforce. The reason for this is that since there had been no communication of the trust during the life of the testator there was no opportunity for the trustee to accept or refuse the trust. In *Wallgrave* v. *Tebbs* (1855) 2 K & J 313 it was held that documents found after the death of the testator could not be deemed to be the communication of a secret trust since the communication did not take place before the testator had died. If the testator makes an incomplete communication, e.g. he tells the secret trustee that he is to hold as trustee but he does not tell him of the terms the trustee will hold on resulting trust for the testator's estate.

Re Boyes (1884) 26 Ch D 531

The testator George Boyes told the trustee that he was to hold as a trustee but he did not tell him about the terms. After his death papers were found which directed the trustee to hold the property on behalf of the testator's mistress and an illegitimate child. The court held that no trust arose because the trustee was not told about the terms of the trust before the death of the testator.

This case is difficult to explain since the trustee was aware that he held as a trustee but without knowing the names of the beneficiaries the trustee had no opportunity to reject the trust if he did not wish to hold as trustee for the named beneficiaries.

A testator cannot reserve to himself a power of making future unwitnessed dispositions by merely naming a trustee and leaving the purposes of the trust to be supplied afterwards.

(Viscount Sumner in Blackwell v. Blackwell [1929] AC 318)

(iii) Instructions in sealed letters

Compare the later decision of *Re Keen* [1937] Ch 236 where the trustees were told that they held as trustees, but the terms were not communicated expressly, the testator instead handing the trustees a sealed letter. This was a half-secret trust because there was some reference to the trust on the face of the will. The trust failed because as it was a half-secret trust, the timing of the communication of the trust had to take place before or at the time of execution of the will.

However, had the timing been at the time of the execution of the will, the secret trust would have been enforceable as the means of communication were held to be sufficient.

To take a parallel, a ship that sails under sealed orders is sailing under orders though the exact terms are not ascertained by the Captain till later.

(Wright MR)

EXAMPLE

Mimi is unwell. She made her will a week ago. Under the terms of her will she has left £25,000 to Adolpho her brother. Adolpho comes to see her and Mimi tells him that any property he is to receive under her will is not for him absolutely but he must apply it according to the terms of a letter that she hands him. Mimi dies the following day. Adolpho opens the letter and finds instructions from Mimi that the property is to be given to her two nieces, Cara and Della, the children of Mimi and Adolpho's sister Flora. Adolpho does not wish to give the money to Cara and Della because he had a bitter quarrel with Flora five years ago and he has not spoken to her since.

In spite of his objections Adolpho will be bound by the terms of the secret trust. The terms have been communicated to him when the letter was handed to him.

(iv) Secret trustee must accept the terms of the trust

The secret trustee must accept the terms of the trust. Silence can constitute acceptance. In *Moss* v. *Cooper* (1861) 1 J & H 352 one of three trustees remained silent when the terms of the trust were communicated to the trustees. This was held to be acceptance. The trustee must be aware that any written communication is of terms of a trust and the trustee must also be aware of the effects of the communication fully. However, there is no requirement for the trustee to expressly state that he accepts the trust.

3 HALF-SECRET TRUSTS

A half-secret trust is a secret trust where the testator makes it clear on the face of the will that the beneficiary is not to benefit personally from the gift under the will but to hold the property as a secret trustee.

EXAMPLE

Under his will Tariq made the following gifts:

1 to Imran £5,000;
2 to Hanif my collection of First World War memorabilia;
3 to Hassan my shares in Unilever for the purposes I have communicated to him.

The gift to Imran and also to Hanif would be both fully secret trusts whereas the gift to Hassan would be a half-secret trust. On the face of the will Hassan is clearly not intended to benefit from the gift to him. However the testator may have told Imran that he is to hold the £5,000 on trust for Leila. It is not clear from the face of the will that Imran is not to have the money for his own enjoyment.

The requirements for a half-secret trust are very similar to those required for a fully secret trust. The difference lies in the timing of the communication to the secret trustee. In a half-secret trust the timing of the communication must be before or at the same time as the execution of the will.

EXAMPLE

Consider the example above again. Tariq wrote his will on 4 March. It was signed and executed on 10 March. Tariq did not tell Hassan the terms of the gift under the will until 14 March. He told Hassan that the shares were to be given to Leila, his lifelong friend. The communication is too late. Hassan cannot claim the gift for himself because it is clear from the will that he is not to benefit personally but the gift to Leila is not enforceable. The shares will result back to Tariq's estate and pass either to the residuary legatee or on intestacy to his next of kin.

4 ISSUES ARISING IN SECRET TRUSTS

(a) The secret beneficiary predeceases the testator

If the beneficiary dies before the testator, then the gift will lapse. This is because the secret trust is not fully constituted until the testator has died. Until the testator dies there is no trust under which the beneficiary can take a benefit. The property will only pass to the trustee on the death of the testator.

In *Re Gardner* (*No. 2*) (1923) 2 Ch 230 Romer J. came to the unusual decision that a secret beneficiary's gift would not lapse on death and would pass to the secret beneficiary's heirs. Property had been left to the testatrix's husband and then to two nieces and a nephew. One of the nieces predeceased the testatrix. The court held that the deceased niece's estate had acquired an interest in the property and would be entitled to one-third of the estate on the death of the husband.

There has been considerable criticism of the approach of the court in this case because it appears to allow an unconstituted trust to be enforceable. When the niece died the trust was not fully constituted. There was nothing to stop the testator revoking the trust.

(b) The secret trustee predeceases the testator

If the secret trustee dies before the testator, then in some cases the trust will still be enforceable. This question may depend on whether there is a secret or half-secret trust. In a fully secret trust, the trust will fail. The trust will not be fully constituted until the testator has died and the gift to the beneficiary will lapse.

If the legatee renounces and disclaims, or dies in the lifetime of the testator, the persons claiming under the memorandum can take nothing.

(Cozens-Hardy LJ in *Re Maddox* [1902] 2 Ch 220)

In this case the judge is suggesting that the secret beneficiaries have no right because the property has not passed to the secret trustee and the trust will not be fully constituted. However, if the trust has been fully constituted, the trust may be enforceable on the basis that no trust should fail for the want of a trustee.

(c) Can a secret trustee ever benefit from a secret trust?

The secret trustee may argue that he can retain any surplus from the testator's estate for himself once the terms of the trust have been carried out. Alternatively in some cases the secret trustee may argue that the testator had expressly provided a sum by way of gift to him under the terms of the will.

If the secret trustee can argue that the gift was an absolute gift but subject to the terms of the trust, then the courts will allow him to keep the surplus. If the secret trustee is left the entire gift, it is more difficult to argue that any surplus can be retained and instead it will be held on resulting trust for the estate.

In *Re Rees* [1950] Ch 204 the court held that half-secret trustees who had been left the testator's whole estate absolutely on the following terms: 'they well knowing my wishes concerning the same' were not permitted to keep the surplus for themselves. In this case the trustee was also the testator's solicitor and it is thought that that fact influenced the court when it came to its decision. A lay trustee may be able to retain the surplus where a professional trustee may not do so because he owes a higher standard of care to the beneficiaries than a lay trustee.

Evidence may be admissible to indicate to the court the wishes of the testator concerning the surplus. In *Re Rees*, the court would not admit evidence that contradicted the terms of the will.

It may be possible for a fully secret trustee to claim the surplus because in this case there would be no contradiction with the terms of the will.

(d) A secret beneficiary acts as witness to the will of the testator

A witness to a will cannot claim any benefit under that will according to s.15 Wills Act 1837 neither can a spouse of the witness claim a benefit.

Re Young (Dec'd) [1951] Ch 344

A testator left his entire estate to his wife. Before the will had been executed the wife had accepted an instruction from her husband that the chauffeur, Mr Cobb was to receive a legacy of £2,000 payable out of her gift. The chauffeur had witnessed the will. The question for the court was whether such a gift should be forfeited under s.15 Wills Act 1837. The court decided that the gift to the chauffeur should be upheld.

As Danckwerts J. commented in this case:

> The whole theory of the formulation of a secret trust is that the Wills Act has nothing to do with the matter because the forms required by the Wills Act are entirely disregarded, since the persons do not take by virtue of the gift in the will, but by virtue of the secret trusts imposed upon the beneficiary who does in fact take under the will.

It is quite an arbitrary decision however that a beneficiary under the will is allowed to derive a benefit under these circumstances. In *Re Young* it appears that the chauffeur was unaware of the gift under the will but it would not have affected his right had there been evidence that he was aware of the testator's instruction to his wife. Although the need for an impartial witness to the will as required under the Wills Act would be compromised in this situation.

EXAMPLE

Mr Wong has just written and signed his will and it has been witnessed by two friends Mr Greenaway and Mrs Pinkney. The day before he signs it, he tells his daughter Kate that she was to be the main beneficiary under the will and Mr Wong asks her to give £25,000 to his neighbour Mr Greenaway. If Mr Greenaway had been left £25,000 under the will, then he would have had to forfeit his gift because he was a witness to the will but in this case the gift is under a fully secret trust and can be enforced by him. The gift to Mr Wong will only take effect outside the will and the requirements of the Wills Act are not compromised.

(e) A gift of property to two people either as joint tenants or tenants in common

If property is transferred to two or more people to be held on secret trusts but the testator only discloses the terms to some but not all of the trustees, then the trustees will all be bound if they hold as joint tenants if the communication is made before or at the execution of the will but it will only bind those who have been told of the secret trust if they hold as tenants in common.

The reason for the distinction lies in the nature of a joint tenancy and a tenancy in common.

A joint tenant of property is not regarded as holding a separate interest in the property so disclosure of terms of the trust to one party will bind both.

EXAMPLE

I leave my house Blackstones to A and B as joint tenants. If B dies first, A will own the entire interest even if B has already made a will.

Property can also be held by two or more people as tenants in common. The law regards them as having shares in property, which can be dealt with on death.

EXAMPLE

I leave my house Greenacres to A and B as tenants in common. If B dies, having made a will before his death leaving his property to C, B's share of the property will pass to C on B's death.

Where jointly held property is the subject of the secret trust and only one of the two or more owners who hold as tenants in common is told about the trust the others will not be bound by the terms of the trust.

EXAMPLE

Under the terms of his will, Dan leaves Greenacres to Anif and Ben as tenants in common. This is a fully secret trust. If Dan tells Ben that the property is to be held by Anif and himself for the benefit of Claude, Anif's share will not be subject to the trust unless Dan also tells him that he is to hold the property for Claude. After Dan's death, Anif and Ben will own the property jointly as a tenants in common but Anif's share will be held on trust for Claude.

Consider *Re Stead* [1900] 1 Ch 237 in this context. Farwell J. held that it was appropriate that the tenant in common who knew nothing of the secret trust not to be bound by the trust because: 'to hold otherwise would be to enable one beneficiary to deprive the rest, of their benefits, by setting up a secret trust'.

There is a distinction here between half-secret and fully secret trusts. In a half-secret trust there must be communication before or at the same time of the execution of the will in order for the trust to be enforceable. However in a fully secret trust, communication can take place any time up until the death of the testator. In a fully secret trust if there has been communication to a tenant in common after the execution of the will, he will not be bound by the terms of the trust.

The point here is that the reason why these rules are upheld at all is the rule that a person cannot claim property beneficially if the gift has been induced by a promise to hold for another.

In the case of a gift to a joint tenant under a fully secret trust where the will has been executed there is no risk of this because the gift was made before the communication of the gift.

5 THE THEORETICAL BASIS FOR SECRET TRUSTS

(a) What kind of trust is a secret trust?

A secret trust takes effect under the law of trusts as a trust rather than as a testamentary disposition but what kind of trust is a secret trust?

Is a secret trust an express trust; or
Is a secret trust a constructive trust?

(i) Is a secret trust an express trust?

Express trusts require adherence to certain formalities in particular the need for compliance with s.53(1)(b) Law of Property Act 1925. Under this section evidence in writing is required in order to create a trust of land. This suggests that if secret trusts were express trusts, no trust of land could take effect unless the testator communicated with the secret trustee in writing at the time of the creation of the trust or at a later date.

A half-secret trust of land was unenforceable in *Re Baillie* (1886) 2 TLR 660 because the communication between the testator and the secret trustee was oral rather than in writing. This case suggests that secret trusts must adhere to certain formalities of transfer.

However there are other examples of cases where a secret trust of land has been upheld without the instruction being put into writing.

(ii) Is the secret trust a constructive trust?

Under s.53(2) Law of Property Act 1925 constructive trusts do not require evidence in writing even where the trust concerns land. If a secret trust of land were to be considered as a constructive trust, then this would allow a secret trust of land, created orally to be upheld in spite of the lack of written evidence.

The nature of a fully secret trust is that it must operate outside the will as there is no evidence that there is a trust on its face.

(b) Why are secret trusts enforced by the courts?

Why are secret trusts enforced when they so clearly contradict the formalities of the Wills Act 1837?

The lack of formality in this area is dangerous as it could lead to uncertainty and confusion.

There are two main theories about why secret trusts can be enforced:

1 The prevention of fraud;
2 Secret trusts arise outside the will.

(i) The prevention of fraud

The main reason why secret trusts have traditionally been upheld, is the prevention of fraud. If a gift is made under a will to a named legatee who knows that the gift is not really for him or her but for another person, then it would be a fraud to claim the property for him or herself on the basis that the gift was not put into writing as laid down in the Wills Act.

EXAMPLE

Fleur has written her will and she leaves £25,000 and her diamond necklace to her friend Greta. She secretly tells Greta that she is to give the money and the diamond necklace to Hana. Hana is Fleur's child but born while Fleur was still at school. Hana was adopted at birth by Mr and Mrs Leaf. Fleur has secretly followed Hana's progress and although she has never met her, she wants her to have the money and necklace after she has died.

Greta does not want to give the necklace to Hana as she rather likes it herself and she also wants to keep the money for herself.

Under the statute Greta is the beneficiary of the will and it appears on the face of the will that she can retain the property. However Greta knows the property is not for her and she would be misusing the statute for her own benefit if she denied Hana the property.

The courts will apply the maxim 'equity will not allow the statute to be used as an instrument of fraud'.

The statute is the Wills Act 1837 and although a testamentary gift must be made in writing it would be a fraud on the estate if the testator's wishes were not upheld.

(ii) Secret trusts operate outside the will

An alternative theory for fully secret trusts is that they operate outside the will and so they do not need to comply with the Wills Act.

The secret trust therefore is a trust which comes into existence only when the property is received by the legatee which will be on the death of the testator. The legatee then becomes a secret trustee on behalf of the testator because at that stage the trust is fully constituted.

EXAMPLE

Fleur leaves £50,000 and a diamond necklace to Greta under her will. She tells Greta a few days before she dies that the money and the necklace are not Greta's absolutely but are to be held for Hana.

In this example the secret trust does not come into existence until Fleur dies and then as the property under the will passes to Greta the trust becomes fully constituted and at that stage is enforceable by the beneficiary. The Wills Act is not compromised because the trust does not require writing in order to come into existence.

B MUTUAL WILLS

KEY POINTS

- mutual wills are wills entered into by two parties in identical form which are intended to be binding on the survivor after the death of the first party;
- identical wills are not always mutual wills;
- a mutual will can only be binding if it is proved that the parties intended to be bound by the terms; and
- the survivor holds the property on constructive trust on the death of the first party in favour of the beneficiary.

1 WHAT IS A MUTUAL WILL?

Mutual wills are testamentary documents based on an agreement between husband and wife to create an irrevocable interest in favour of agreed beneficiaries.

EXAMPLE

Hari and Wanda have been married for thirty years. They visit their solicitor and make wills that are identical leaving their property to each other on their death and then to their children Ros and Tom. Hari dies in 2009 and Wanda later decides to marry an old friend Ian. Wanda makes a new will in favour of Ian. However, when Wanda dies, the first will takes effect. In entering into the mutual wills they have agreed that neither will revoke their wills after the death of the first party.

Re Walters, dec'd; Olins v. Walters [2009] Ch 212

This case is a recent example of how mutual wills operate. Mr Walters and his wife had married in 1934. In 1988 they made identical wills in favour of each other which replaced earlier wills made in 1954. They later made codicils in similar terms. (A codicil is a written document which is intended to add a further provision to the will. It must comply with the Wills Act.) Under the codicils made by Mr and Mrs Walters the property was to be divided between their five grandchildren with life interests of two-thirds of the property in favour of their two daughters. After the death of his wife, the grandfather fell out with his grandson and he no longer wished him to benefit under his will. He argued that the wills were not mutual wills as they lacked contractual certainty and so he was not bound by their terms.

The Court of Appeal held that mutual wills do not require the level of certainty necessary in a commercial contract. Lord Justice Mummery quoted from *Snell's Equity*: 'Mutual wills provide an instance of a trust arising by operation of law to give effect to an express intention of the two testators.'

2 THE AGREEMENT BETWEEN THE PARTIES

Mutual wills can only take effect where two individuals have entered into a binding agreement not to revoke their wills after the death of the first party. The agreement must be a mutually binding agreement so both parties are bound by it.

The key feature is not whether or not the wills are identical but the fact that both parties intend to be bound by the terms after the death of the other party.

Re Goodchild [1997] 1 WLR 1216

A couple had made similar wills both leaving their property to their son. When the wife died, the husband made a new will leaving his property to his second wife. The son argued that the original wills had been mutual wills and therefore it was binding on his father. The court found that although the wills were similar in form the wills were not intended to be binding. There was no evidence that the parties intended to enter into an agreement to create mutual wills. In this case the father was able to leave the property to his new wife.

3 THE APPLICATION OF THE CONSTRUCTIVE TRUST IN A MUTUAL WILL

The operation of mutual wills will give rise to a constructive trust in favour of the beneficiary of the identical wills. The survivor of the parties to the mutual wills holds as constructive trustee.

It has long been established that a contract between persons to make corresponding wills gives rise to equitable obligations when one acts on faith of such an agreement and dies leaving his will unrevoked so that the other takes property under its dispositions.

(Dixon J. in *Birmingham* v. *Renfrew* (1936) 57 CLR 666)

This was an Australian case which laid down the principle that the rights of the beneficiary of the mutual wills take effect as rights in equity.

The other key issue is when the constructive trust arises. There are *three* possible occasions when the constructive trust can arise.

1 The date when the mutual wills are created. This cannot give rise to a constructive trust because the parties remain free at any time up until the death of the first party to revoke and amend their will.

2 The death of the first party. The constructive trust arises on this date because the trust is constituted as soon as the parties lose their right to amend the will. The agreement is enforceable on the death of the first party. In *Re Hagger* [1930] 2 Ch 190 a husband and wife made mutual wills leaving property to three named beneficiaries. The wife died but soon after all the three beneficiaries also died. The court held that the estates of the three beneficiaries could take the property on the death of the husband. Their interests had crystallised as soon as the first party had died.

3 The death of the second party. The trust has already taken effect and it would generally be too late to wait until this moment for the trust to take effect.

SUMMARY

This chapter considers the role of the secret trust and also mutual wills.

The law on secret trusts allows testamentary trusts to be enforced over property where the strict formalities of trusts have been ignored. Secret trusts can either take effect as fully secret where the existence of the trust is not disclosed on the face of the will or half-secret where the existence of the trust is shown on the will but the names of the beneficiaries are not disclosed. According to Brightman J. in *Ottaway* v. *Norman* three requirements must first be proved for both types of secret trusts: intention to create a trust; that the trust has been communicated to the trustee; and that the trustee accepts the trust. The rules for communication of the terms of a secret trust vary according to whether it is a half-secret or fully secret trust. In the case of a fully secret trust the terms must be communicated any time up until the death of the testator. Although communication to the trustee can take place anytime up until the death of the settlor a secret trust will fail if communication takes place after the death of the testator. For instance in *Wallgrave* v. *Tebbs* information regarding the intentions of the testator was found with the papers of the testator after his death and it was held that this was not sufficient communication. Communication of the terms of the trust can be made to the trustee by a sealed letter as held in *Re Keen*. If the secret beneficiary predeceases the testator, the gift will lapse (although *Re Gardner No. 2* upheld such a gift). It is generally believed that this decision was wrongly decided. Where a secret trustee acts as a witness to the will of the testator the gift under the secret trust will be upheld as it is deemed to take place outside the will. It does not contravene the provision of the Wills Act that prevents a witness to a will from benefiting under that will. Secret trusts are not express trusts but are generally upheld on the basis of constructive trusts where formalities are not adhered to strictly. They are upheld in order to prevent fraud on the part of the secret trustee.

Mutual wills are wills created during the lifetime of two or more persons who agree to be bound by an agreement made during their lifetime, on the death of the first party. Mutual wills are enforceable because the survivor holds the property as a constructive trustee which can be enforced by the survivor.

13 Charities; the Charities Act and the rules of *cy près*

KEY POINTS

- charitable trusts are different from private trusts;
- charitable trusts must be exclusively charitable;
- charitable trusts enjoy a number of advantages;
- a charitable trust must satisfy certain requirements;
- the definition of a charitable trust is laid down in the Charities Act 2006;
- the definition of charity now comprises thirteen different heads of charity;
- all charitable trusts must satisfy the public benefit requirement; and
- if a charitable trust fails the funds may be transferred to another charity under the rules of *cy près*.

key points

1 INTRODUCTION TO CHARITABLE TRUSTS

Charitable trusts are public trusts which carry a number of advantages. They are enforceable by the Attorney-General.

2 THE ADVANTAGES OF CHARITABLE STATUS

There are a number of advantages of having charitable status. Charities have always been regarded as beneficial to the public so the law has treated them in a more lenient way than private purpose trusts. The most significant of the advantages lie in the more lenient rules on taxation.

(a) Purpose trusts

All trusts must have an identifiable beneficiary who can enforce the trust. A non-charitable purpose trust is void unless there is a beneficiary to enforce or it comes within one of the anomalous exceptions. The beneficiary principle does not apply to charitable trusts. They do not require a beneficiary to enforce because the Attorney-General has the responsibility of enforcement of all charitable trusts.

(b) Certainty of objects

The objects of a private trust must be certain. Uncertainty of objects will cause a trust to fail. The objects of a charitable trust must be exclusively charitable but they do not need to be certain. Any uncertainty can be addressed by the Charity Commission. Where a trust has both charitable and non-charitable purposes and the objects are uncertain the gift will fail.

(c) The perpetuity rules

Charitable trusts are not subject to the rules against alienability that apply to private trusts. These rules make it impossible for a gift to last indefinitely. Charitable gifts can be perpetual and those with very large funds may last for many years indeed centuries. The Charity Commission can prepare a scheme to remedy any possibility that the perpetuity rules will affect the validity of the gift.

(d) The rules of *cy près*

If a private purpose trust fails, the funds will be held on resulting trust for the settlor's estate. There is no possibility that the court can take the decision to transfer the funds to another purpose.

Where a charitable trust fails it is possible to transfer the funds to another similar charity if the settlor has shown a general charitable intention. The court will consider whether there has been initial or subsequent failure of the trust. In cases of subsequent failure, i.e. where the charitable body ceases to exist after the death of the settlor but before the gift has been transferred. The *cy près* rules will always apply because a general charitable intention will be implied. Where there has been initial failure because a charitable body has ceased to exist at the time when the gift was vested the funds can only be applied *cy près* if a general charitable intention can be proved. This is discussed in greater detail at the end of the chapter.

(e) Taxation

A charity has a number of taxation advantages. These include the following:

1 relief from income tax on profits gained from trading activities such as charity shops;
2 charities are also entitled to Gift Aid which enables a charity to claim the basic rate on income tax on a gift made to them by a taxpayer;
3 relief from corporation tax;
4 exemption from capital gains tax;
5 they receive an 80 per cent exemption from non-domestic rates on properties they occupy which are used wholly or mainly for charitable purposes;
6 exemption from stamp duty.

The value of these tax advantages is huge running into billions of pounds of tax savings for individual charities each year. There is some debate as to whether all charities should receive all the taxation advantages.

3 THE DEFINITION OF CHARITY

Charity has been a difficult concept to define over the centuries and until the Charities Act 2006 there had never been a statutory definition of charity. A charitable trust involves a number of different requirements.

1 the trust must be for charitable purposes;
2 the trust must be exclusively charitable;
3 the trust must satisfy the public benefit test.

(a) The trust must be for charitable purposes

Over the centuries the definition of charity developed from the application of the Charitable Uses Act 1601. This Act contained a preamble which included a detailed list of charitable purposes. For many years this list was used as a starting point to consider whether a purpose was charitable or not. As the Preamble became less and less relevant to life hundreds of years after it was passed, the courts used the charitable purposes by analogy.

Under the Preamble, the repair of churches was held to be charitable and so by analogy a gift for the provision of a crematorium was held to be charitable in *Scottish Burial Reform and Cremation Society* v. *Glasgow City Corporation* [1968] AC 138. The link was tenuous but sufficient for the courts to regard it as charitable.

The case of *Commissioners for Special Purposes of Income Tax* v. *Pemsel* [1981] AC 531 introduced a different approach. Lord MacNaghten held that there were four categories of charitable purpose: the relief of poverty; the advancement of education; the advancement of religion; and trusts for other purposes beneficial to the community not falling under any of the preceding heads. Since the passage of the Charities Act 2006 a purpose will be charitable if it comes within one of the heads of charity included in the Act. The heads of charity in *Pemsel's Case* have all been included within the statutory definition as well as many new heads of charity.

(b) The trust must be exclusively charitable

The issue here is whether the funds can be applied to a non-charitable purpose. Many charitable trusts have failed because non-charitable objects have been entitled to benefit.

(i) Trusts that have failed because the objects are not exclusively charitable

These include the following cases:

> *IRC* v. *Oldham Training and Enterprise Council* [1996] STC 1218: A training and enterprise council was held not to be a charitable body because it could include some non-charitable objects or causes.
>
> *Chichester Diocesan Fund* v. *Simpson* [1944] AC 341: A trust which contained the words 'for such charitable ... institutions or other benevolent objects ... as my executors ... may ... select' failed because it was held that benevolent objects could include non-charitable objects whereas if the words had been charitable 'and' benevolent objects the benevolent objects would have been charitable because they were connected always with charitable objects.

Attorney-General of the Bahamas v. *Royal Trust Co.* [1986] 1 WLR 1001: In this case a gift for the education and welfare of Bahamian children failed. Although here the word 'and' was used, the problem lay with the word 'welfare', which may include a non-educational purpose and may not be a purpose that at the time was within the fourth head of charity.

A trust may fail because of the particular wording used in a trust.

EXAMPLE

Dermot leaves £400,000 to educate and enrich children under the age of 15 in a certain area of Bradford.

Although a trust to educate children would be charitable it is unlikely that a trust to enrich children could be charitable as it could include non-charitable objects. It would depend on how the word 'enrich' was interpreted.

(ii) Compare the following cases

Re Simson [1946] Ch 299: A gift was left to a vicar 'for his work in the parish'.
Farley v. *Westminster Bank* [1939] AC 430: A gift was left to a vicar 'for parish work'.

The wording of these two cases seems very similar but the gift in the first case was upheld whereas the gift in the second case failed. The wording of the first gift was held to limit the vicar to carrying out purposes associated with his work as a vicar and so was deemed to be charitable under advancement of religion. The second gift opened up the possibility of using the money for purposes which were not exclusively charitable. Parish work could include a non-charitable purpose whereas if the vicar was carrying out his work as a vicar it would necessarily be charitable as it would be for religious purposes.

(iii) Trusts that have been upheld because the non-charitable purpose is incidental to the charitable purpose

These include the following case:

London Hospital Medical College v. *IRC* [1976] 1 WLR 613: A students' union that provided social and recreational facilities for students at a London teaching hospital was upheld as charitable although it was observed by Brightman J. that students who were members of the student union could derive a personal benefit by using the facilities.

(iv) Trusts that have failed because the non-charitable purpose was not incidental to the charitable purpose

These include the following case:

> *IRC* v. *City of Glasgow Police Athletic Association* [1953] AC 380: An athletic association whose objects were to provide sporting and recreational and other facilities within a sports club was not held to be charitable. It was claimed that it should be charitable on the basis that it promoted the efficiency of the police force. It failed because it was held that efficiency of the police force was not merely ancillary to the charitable purpose.

(v) Trusts that have been upheld by applying severance to the words used by the settlor

These include the following cases:

> *Salusbury* v. *Denton* (1857) 3 K & J 529: A testator left property to his widow partly to be transferred to the foundation of a charity school and the rest to be used for the testator's relatives. On the death of the widow no appointments had been made. The fund was divided equally by the court with the part transferred to the school deemed to be a charitable gift and the second part to ascertainable beneficiaries as a private trust.
>
> *Re Coxen* [1948] Ch 747: A large sum of money was left by a past Lord Mayor of London for three purposes:
>
> 1 to provide a dinner for aldermen of the City of London meeting on trust business;
> 2 to pay the sum of one guinea to each alderman attending the meeting;
> 3 to pay the remaining sum to certain hospitals.

All three sums were upheld as charitable gifts but Jenkins J. suggested that he would have upheld the gift anyway because he would have been able to sever the non-charitable element namely the dinner and the payment to the aldermen from the charitable element which was the provision of funds to certain hospitals.

(c) The trust must satisfy the public benefit test

A charitable trust will fail unless it can satisfy the public benefit test.

There are two aspects to public benefit: (a) there must be an identifiable benefit or benefits; and (b) the benefit must be to the public or a sufficient section of the public. This is discussed in more detail later.

4 CHARITABLE PURPOSES

Charitable purposes are listed in s.2(2) Charities Act 2006. Unless the purpose of any potentially charitable trust falls within the list of charitable purposes within the Act it will fail to be charitable. Although the list is much wider and more detailed than the purposes laid down in *Pemsel's Case*, it includes the heads of charity described in *Pemsel* but the fourth head has been expanded to include a number of new heads of charity.

There has been very little case law since the Charities Act was passed and previous case law still has some relevance in deciding what the courts would regard as charitable.

(a) The prevention and relief of poverty

The relief of poverty was the first head of charity described in *Pemsel*. It has always been interpreted broadly so it is not necessary for the relief of poverty to be confined to the destitute.

The Charity Commission has commented on how poverty should be defined in their guidance issued in 2008 (*Public Benefit and the Prevention or Relief of Poverty: Draft Supplementary Guidance for Consultation*):

Poverty does not just include people who are destitute, but also those who cannot satisfy a basic need without assistance.

In *Re Coulthurst* [1951] Ch 661 poverty was defined as 'to go short' in the ordinary meaning of that term with due regard being had to their status in life.

The relief of poverty includes the provision of basic necessities of life such as clothes, food and somewhere to live.

Another example of how the courts approach the relief of poverty arose in *Joseph Rowntree Memorial Trust Housing Association Ltd* v. *Attorney-General* [1983] Ch 159 where a housing association wanted to build housing for elderly people for rent. The occupiers would pay 70 per cent of the rent with the housing association paying the remainder. This was held to be charitable because it was held to relieve a need, which was the need for specialist housing for the elderly.

Gifts for the relief of poverty that have failed

If it is possible for someone who is not deemed 'poor' to benefit, then the gift will fail.

Re Gwyon [1930] 1 Ch 225

Money was left for the provision of short trousers for boys in the Farnham area. As the terms of the will were not sufficiently specific, there was nothing to prevent children from more affluent homes from benefiting from the gift so the courts held that it failed.

Re Sanders' Will Trusts [1954] Ch 265

Part of the residuary estate of the testator was left to be used to provide or assist in the provision of dwellings for the working class of a certain part of Pembrokeshire in Wales. This failed because Harman J. held that the working classes were not necessarily to be classed as 'poor people'. He commented that it was no longer appropriate to regard working class people as a section of poor persons.

(b) The advancement of education

Trusts for the advancement of education have been held to be charitable for many centuries and they were expressly mentioned in the Preamble to the Charitable Uses Act 1601. The advancement of education has included learning and education in a very wide sense and has not been restricted to the provision of education in schools and universities.

Education includes research. Mr Justice Slade set out principles to be satisfied in order for research to be regarded as charitable in *Re Besterman's Wills Trusts* (1980) The Times 21 January:

1 the research must be a useful subject of study;
2 the knowledge acquired must be disseminated to others; and
3 the trust must be for the benefit of the public, or a sufficiently important section of the public.

The research in *Re Besterman's Wills Trusts* was held to be charitable although it was restricted to research in just the two philosophers Voltaire and Rousseau. Likewise research in *Re Hopkins Will Trusts* [1965] Ch 669 restricted to finding the Bacon–Shakespeare manuscripts was also held to be charitable.

Compare

Re Shaw [1957] 1 WLR 729 where a trust set up by George Bernard Shaw to be used to research the benefits of a 40-letter alphabet was held not to be charitable. Mr Justice Harman held that such research 'did not increase the sum of communicable knowledge in an area which education may cover'.

The provision of facilities for sport was regarded as charitable if linked with education as in *IRC* v. *McMullen* [1981] AC 1 which allowed a trust set up by the Football Association which had among its aims: 'to organise or provide or assist in the organisation or provision of facilities which will enable and encourage pupils at schools and universities ... to play association football or other games or sport'.

This head of charity also traditionally included the promotion of the arts such as the provision of a fund left by the wife of Frederick Delius, the composer, to be used for the advancement of his works (*Re Delius' Will Trust* [1957] Ch 299).

The Charities Act 2006 now expressly includes a separate category of trusts for the advancement of the arts.

EXAMPLE

Cedric Johnson was a keen member of a club for local historians. He left £300,000 for research into the life histories of people who had lived in a small village in Wiltshire. He never married. His close relatives argued that the gift was not a useful subject of study and therefore it was not charitable. Further it could not be charitable because there was no requirement that the work was to be published. The relatives have a very good argument based on *Re Besterman* that research that is not published cannot be charitable in spite of the fact that it probably does increase the sum of communicable knowledge as mentioned by Mr Justice Wilberforce in *Re Hopkins*.

(c) The advancement of religion

The law has always taken a very liberal approach to trusts for the advancement of religion. Even small groups with few followers have been given charitable status. In *Funnell* v. *Stewart* [1996] 1 WLR 288 a gift to faith healers was upheld.

Likewise, in *Thornton* v. *Howe* (1862) 31 Beav 14 a gift to enable the works of Joanna Southcote who alleged that she had been impregnated by the Holy Ghost and would give birth to the second Messiah was upheld despite criticism from Romilly MR who described the writings as foolish.

Traditionally a religion was only acceptable to the courts if it had a belief in a supreme being. In *Re South Place Ethical Society* [1980] 1 WLR 1565 a trust to 'study and disseminate ethical principles' failed because it was an agnostic society where the members neither believed in nor denied that a god existed. The requirement of belief in a god caused problems to a number of religions and many well-known religions struggled to satisfy this, e.g. Buddhism.

The Charities Act 2006 has removed this requirement. Under s.2(3)(a)(ii) the Act states 'religion [which] does not involve belief in a god'. The Act also states that a religion can involve belief in more than one god.

Gifts for purposes associated with religion have been held to be charitable. These could include a trust for the repair of the church, the organ or to provide a stained glass window.

Gifts under this heading include the advancement of religious purposes. In *United Grand Lodge of Ancient, Free and Accepted Masons of England* v. *Holborn BC* [1957] 1 WLR 1080 Donovan J. described advancement in this way 'to advance religion means to promote it, to spread the message ever wider among mankind; to take some positive steps to sustain and increase religious belief'.

(d) The advancement of health or the saving of lives

This is a new head of charity although it was mentioned in the Preamble which includes the relief of the aged, impotent and poor as well as trusts for the maintenance of the sick or maimed soldiers or mariners. The reference in the Preamble allowed the relief of the sick always to be regarded as a head of charity and this includes the provision of any item, service and facility for the sick.

It has always been acceptable that fees can be charged for a charitable purpose such as a school or a hospital. In *Re Resch's Will Trusts* [1969] 1 AC 514 a gift of a large sum of money to a private hospital was upheld as charitable on the basis that the private hospital supplements the service provided by the general hospital.

The key feature arising in this context and which also arises in the context of fee paying schools is that the hospital or school must not be run as a purely commercial venture.

EXAMPLE

Conran has left £500,000 to St Hilda's Nursing Home which provides nursing care to the elderly with certain conditions associated with arthritis and rheumatism. St Hilda's charges for the nursing care but 20 per cent of the charges are subsidised out of a trust fund. St Hilda's is open to anyone with the relevant health conditions.

This is likely to be upheld as charitable.

(e) The advancement of citizenship or community development

This is another new head of charity and involves issues that had come within the fourth head such as urban or rural regeneration. An example might be the provision of advice to the unemployed in an area, or the provision of assistance to homeless people. The Charity Commission has commented that the organisation must seek to maintain or improve 'the physical, social and economic infrastructure ... and assist people at a disadvantage because of their social and economic circumstances' (Charity Commission RR 2 Promotion of Urban and Rural Regeneration).

(f) The advancement of the arts, culture, heritage or science

The advancement of the arts, culture and heritage were incorporated under the advancement of education or under the fourth head of *Pemsel's Case* before the Charities Act 2006. Now the advancement of the arts including the support of museums, choirs and historic buildings have become a dedicated head of charity.

The support of arts and culture carries with it a value judgement about whether or not the purpose has merit.

The value of the works of Frederick Delius was not in doubt in *Re Delius (Dec'd)*, nor were the value of choral works in *Royal Choral Society* v. *IRC* [1943]. The main aim of the Choral Society was declared to be to form and maintain a choir in order to promote the practice and performance of choral works. The gift to the Choral Society was held to be charitable.

Re Pinion (Dec'd) [1965] Ch 85

A collector left a collection of objects that he had collected during his lifetime to trustees with the direction that they were to open his house as a museum after his death. The objects included furniture, paintings, glass and china as well as other objects. The court had to decide whether this was charitable under the advancement of education. The court decided that the objects had no artistic merit and no value and held that it was not charitable.

I can conceive of no useful object to be served in foisting upon the public this mass of junk.

(Harman LJ)

Monuments

Also, under this head a trust to erect a monument to an important person may have charitable status. The Charity Commissioner cited a monument to Earl Mountbatten of Burma as an example (Charity Commentary on the Descriptions of Charitable Purposes in the Charities Act 2006).

A monument to a private individual would not be charitable as shown in *Re Endacott* [1960] Ch 232 (see Chapter 7 on private purpose trusts).

(g) The advancement of amateur sport

Until the enactment of the Charities Act 2006, the advancement of amateur sport was not charitable per se. It could be held to be charitable if it could be linked with education, or under the fourth head as a purpose beneficial to the community.

Non-charitable trusts for sport

> *Re Nottage* [1885] 2 Ch 649: A trust to provide annually a prize to be awarded to the most successful yacht of the season was not charitable in spite of the motive for the gift which was to encourage the sport of yacht-racing.

Trusts for sport held to be charitable

These include the following cases:

> *IRC* v. *McMullen* (as discussed above) held that the provision of facilities in schools and colleges to play association football was charitable.
> *Re Gray* [1925] Ch 362: A gift to an army regiment 'for the promotion of sport (including in that term only shooting, fishing, cricket, football and polo)' was held to be charitable because it promoted efficiency of the armed forces.

The Charities Act allows a trust for the advancement of sport to be charitable but it must satisfy the public benefit requirement. The advice of the Charity Commissioners is that: (a) the sport must be capable of improving the physical health and fitness of a person; (b) the club must have open membership which means that the club's facilities must be genuinely available to anyone who wishes to take advantage of them (Charity Commission RR11: Charitable Status and Sport).

(h) The advancement of human rights, conflict resolution, or reconciliation, or the promotion of religious harmony or equality and diversity

This category is genuinely new in the context of charitable purposes. Traditionally, charitable trusts cannot have a political objective, i.e. one that involves bringing about a change in the law but it is accepted that in introducing this category some political campaigning by a charity can be allowed.

Charities are able to engage in political campaigning in order to further their charitable purposes. Charity law draws a distinction between political purposes and political activities.

(Charity Commission RR 12: The Promotion of
Human Rights, January 2005)

(i) The advancement of environmental protection or improvement

Environmental protection was recognised under the fourth head and the work done by organisations such as the National Trust in preserving the environment particularly on the coastline was recognised by the Charity Commission. In their guidance of 2001 the Charity Commission explained that a trust to promote preservation or conservation must have merit and also satisfy the public benefit. This is a similar issue as seen under trusts for the arts, culture, heritage and science as it requires a value judgement as to what is worth preserving.

(j) The relief of those in need by reason of youth, age, ill health, disability, financial hardship or other disadvantage

The relief of need was recognised in the preamble to the Statute of Charitable Uses Act 1601 and included relief of the aged, impotent and the infirm. These words can be read as separate heads as stated in *Joseph Rowntree Memorial Trust Housing Association Ltd* v. *Attorney-General* [1983] Ch 159. This case, discussed earlier under the relief of poverty, concerned the provision of housing for the elderly where they made payments towards the cost. It was held to be charitable because it relieved the need of a particular group, namely the elderly, who needed the facilities by reason of their age.

(k) The advancement of animal welfare

The protection of animals has always been recognised as charitable under the fourth head although all trusts must satisfy the public benefit test.

In *Re Wedgwood* [1915] 1 Ch 113 it was held that a public benefit was provided in a trust 'for the protection and benefit of animals'. It was upheld as charitable by the judge because he believed 'a gift for the benefit and protection of animals tends to promote and encourage kindness towards them, to discourage cruelty ... and thus to stimulate humane and generous sentiments in man towards the lower animals'.

Similarly in *Re Murawski's Will Trusts* [1971] 1 WLR 707 an animal sanctuary which provided care and shelter for stray, neglected and unwanted animals of all kinds which aimed to protect the animals from ill-usage, cruelty and suffering was deemed to be charitable. The public benefit came from the fact that the sanctuary relieved animal cruelty.

(i) Compare this case

Re Grove-Grady [1929] 1 Ch 557

A trust to provide 'a refuge ... for animals, birds or other creatures not human ... and so that all such animals, birds or other creatures not human shall there be safe from molestation or destruction by man' failed as a charitable trust because the Court of Appeal held that it was not for the public benefit. The fact that the public had no access to the refuge was an important factor as well as the fact that the animals and birds and other creatures would be left to defend themselves. If the animals are kept from human access it was suggested that the public benefit test could not be satisfied. This case was decided in 1929 and perhaps the court would now come to a different conclusion and uphold the value of such a refuge even if the public did not have access.

(ii) Anti-vivisection and political objectives

The courts have had difficulty with the status of societies whose aim is anti-vivisection.

Re Foveaux [1895] 2 Ch 501

The court held that gifts to two anti-vivisection societies were charitable. Chitty J. commented that 'if a society for the prevention of cruelty to animals is a charitable society, it would seem to follow that an institution for the prevention of a particular form of cruelty to animals is also charitable'.

The problem with a society whose aim is anti-vivisection is that the objects of such a society are political because their primary aim is to change the law and a trust whose primary aim is political cannot be charitable.

The decision in *Re Foveaux* was reversed in *National Anti-Vivisection Society* v. *IRC* [1948] AC 31. The House of Lords refused charitable status to the National Anti-Vivisection Society (NAVS) on two grounds:

1 the benefits to the public in carrying out research by experimenting on animals outweighed the harm that was caused to the animals used in such an experiment;
2 the objects of the NAVS were to bring about a change in the law and were therefore political.

Where an organisation has, as its main aim, to bring about a change in the law it is regarded as a political objective and charitable status will be denied.

A more recent example lies in *Hanchett-Stamford* v. *Attorney-General* [2009] Ch 173 where the Performing and Captive Animals Defence League whose main objective was to prevent cruelty to animals used in film productions, an objective that could only be achieved by a change in the law, was denied charitable status.

Since the League did not have charitable status it could only be recognised as an unincorporated association (see Chapter 8 on unincorporated associations).

Doris Weeks left £20,000 to the Unwanted and Mistreated Dogs League, a group whose objective was to prevent dogs from being mistreated or abandoned. Amongst their objectives the league wants to persuade the government to introduce a registration scheme which would require dog owners to register dogs with the local council. This will be regarded as a charitable group if the change in the law is ancillary to the main objectives of the group but if it is the primary objective it will fail.

(l) The promotion of the efficiency of the armed forces of the Crown, or of the efficiency of the police, fire and rescue services or ambulance services

The main emphasis in this aim is to promote efficiency of the forces and a trust set up where efficiency of the forces is only a secondary aim will fail.

In *IRC* v. *City of Glasgow Police Athletic Association* [1953] AC 380 an athletic association which had as its main object the provision of sporting and recreational and pastime facilities for police officers in a sports club was not charitable. The main aim of the association was to provide sporting facilities rather than to promote efficiency.

This compares with *Re Gray* (discussed earlier), where a gift for the promotion of various sports such as shooting, fishing and polo was held to be charitable because in this case it promoted efficiency in the army.

(m) Any other purposes

The list of charitable purposes under the Charities Act 2006 is comprehensive but it also includes a heading 'any other purpose' which is similar to the fourth head of charitable purposes included in *Pemsel's Case* and so recognises that the list of charitable purposes is not fully comprehensive and it also allows flexibility. Therefore new charitable purposes could be included at a later date.

5 HOW WILL THE COURTS CONSIDER A NEW CHARITABLE PURPOSE?

(a) The 'analogy approach'

Section 2(4) Charities Act gives guidance on how this category should be applied to future cases. Traditionally the analogy approach was applied to purposes that had not been considered to be charitable before 2006.

The preamble to the Charitable Uses Act 1601 was applied before 2006 and if by analogy the purpose could be considered to lie within the 'spirit and intendment of the Act' the charitable purpose would be upheld.

An example is found in *Scottish Burial Reform and Cremation Society Ltd* v. *Glasgow City Corporation* [1968] AC 138 (discussed earlier), where the court had to consider whether a society set up to provide crematorium facilities was charitable. The court used the 'analogy' approach and considered whether such an aim was included in the preamble. Although it contained no provision for cremation it did include burial within churchyards and this was sufficient to allow the court to find that it was charitable by analogy.

(b) New charitable purposes where no analogy exists

The analogy approach was criticised in *Incorporated Council of Law Reporting of England and Wales* v. *Attorney-General* [1972] Ch 73 where Russell LJ suggested this approach had serious shortcomings because it could only apply where there was a possible analogy and there were cases where none could possibly exist. In this case the production of law reports by a company had no obvious analogy within the preamble and yet the court found it to be charitable because they felt that a comprehensive set of law reports was in the interests of the public and in the interests of the government in ensuring the due administration of the law.

The approach of Russell LJ was as follows: 'if a purpose is then shown to be beneficial or of such utility it is prima facie charitable in law ... [and] the proper question to ask is whether there are any grounds for holding it to be outside the equity of the statute'.

This approach suggests that the courts are not confined purely to the analogy approach when considering a new charitable purpose.

6 TRUSTS WITH POLITICAL OBJECTS

A trust that has purely political objects or includes purely political purposes cannot be charitable.

(a) Why are trusts for political purposes deemed not to be charitable?

The reasoning behind this is clearly stated by Lord Parker in *Bowman* v. *Secular Society* [1917] AC 406:

a trust for the attainment of political objects has always been invalid, not because it is illegal, for everyone is at liberty to advocate or promote by any lawful means, a change in the law, but because the Court has no means of judging whether a proposed change in the law will or will not be for the public benefit, and therefore cannot say that a gift to secure the change is a charitable gift.

(b) When will a trust be deemed to have political objects?

According to Slade J. in *McGovern* v. *Attorney-General* [1982] Ch 321 a trust is deemed to have a political purpose if it has one of the following principal purposes:

1 to further the interests of a particular political party; or
2 to procure changes in the laws of this country; or
3 to procure changes in the laws of a foreign country; or
4 to procure a reversal of government policy or of particular decisions of governmental authorities in this country; or
5 to procure a reversal of government policy or of particular decisions of governmental authorities in a foreign country.

This case concerned Amnesty International (AI) which had as two of its objectives an attempt to secure the release of prisoners of conscience and the abolition of torture or inhumane or degrading treatment or punishment. The issue was whether AI could have charitable status when its main aims were to procure changes in the law both in the United Kingdom and also abroad. It was held that it could not be a charitable trust because its primary aims were to bring about a change in the law.

The introduction of s.2(2)(h) Charities Act 2006 and guidance from the Charity Commission suggests that there has been some relaxation of the strict rules against a charity having political purposes as part of its aims. Under guidance issued in March 2008 it was accepted that a charity can carry out campaigning and political activity and this can be part of its governing document. A charity can also carry out political activity for a change in the law and it can try to influence government or other bodies. However charities cannot support a political party and any attempt to change the law must not be their primary purpose, it must be a subsidiary purpose (Charity Commission CC9 – Speaking Out – guidance on campaigning and political activity by Charities).

(c) Political objectives and education

There is a possibility that a trust that has political objects will try to conceal them with an educational charity and so be able to gain charitable status. The courts have monitored this carefully.

(d) Compare the decisions in the following cases

Re Hopkinson [1949] 1 All ER 346 concerned a trust for the advancement of adult education with particular reference to the values laid out in a Labour party memorandum on education. It was held not to be charitable because in the words of the judge 'it was not education in the proper sense of the word but the furtherance of political views and the better equipping of those who make it their business to further them'.

Southwood v. *Attorney-General* [2000] WTLR 1199 concerned a trust designed to educate the public that peace is best secured by disarmament and pacifism was held not to be charitable. One judge in the Court of Appeal commented that 'the court is in no position to determine that promotion of one view rather than the other is for the public benefit'.

By way of contrast in *Re Koeppler's Will Trusts* [1986] Ch 423 a gift made to Wilton Park which was an organisation with no allegiance to a political party founded to carry out research into foreign affairs was held to be charitable. The court considered the nature of its activities and held that although its activities involved research into matters which could be considered to be political the work could not be described as furthering political objects and it was not actively engaged in seeking a change in the law.

EXAMPLE

Higher Education for All is a group which seeks to widen education opportunities for all school leavers as well as adults. Since the introduction of higher university fees it has started to campaign for their reduction and their eventual abolition. It now seeks charitable status. The fact that it carries out some political campaigning will not prevent it from being regarded as a charity but if at a later date it revises its objectives and makes university fee reduction its primary purpose it may lose its charitable status.

7 CHARITABLE PURPOSES OVERSEAS

A charity can carry out its charitable works abroad as well as at home. However there is an issue in trying to discover whether the works are for the public benefit. The question is whether the public benefit test is satisfied if the trust benefits a sufficient section of the public in the United Kingdom or abroad. The Charity Commission had originally specified that there must be some discernible benefit to the community of the United Kingdom as well as the foreign country (*Report of the Charity Commissioners for England and Wales 1963*).

The position is more pragmatic today. In its report in 1992 the Charity Commission held that a charity operating abroad would in future be presumed to be charitable in the same way as if its operation were confined to the United Kingdom provided that there is no offence to public policy.

8 THE REQUIREMENT OF PUBLIC BENEFIT

Under s.2(1)(b) Charities Act 2006 a charitable purpose is a purpose that is for the public benefit. The Act does not define what is meant by public benefit but under s3(3) it does state that: 'public benefit is a reference to the public benefit as that term is understood for the purposes of the law relating to England and Wales'.

An important change brought about by the Charities Act is that it can no longer be presumed that a purpose of any charitable trust is for the public benefit. Previously, trusts under the first three heads of charity (relief of poverty, advancement of education and advancement of religion) were presumed to be for the public benefit. Every charitable trust now has a duty to show that it satisfies the public benefit requirement.

(a) What is meant by public benefit?

There are two aspects to public benefit: (a) there must be an identifiable benefit or benefits; and (b) the benefit must be to the public or a sufficient section of the public. Instead of attempting to define what is meant by 'a benefit' the Charity Commission has given guidelines that comprise some principles to be applied across the range of different charitable purposes.

(b) Approach of the courts to public benefit pre-2006

The courts applied a different test to public benefit under the different heads of charity. The most relaxed test was applied to trusts for the relief of poverty. In *Re Segelman* (see below) a trust for the relief of poverty among the testator's relations, a group who numbered less than thirty, was held to be charitable. A less generous approach was taken towards charitable trusts for the purpose of education, where any personal connection or 'nexus' with the testator was not allowed. Trusts falling under the fourth head were also treated strictly.

(c) Charity Commission guidance post-2006

The Charity Commission sets out the principles for both aspects of public benefit in its guidance: Charity Commission Charities and Public Benefit (January 2008):

There must be an identifiable benefit or benefits
1a It must be clear what the benefits are
1b The benefits must be related to the aims [of the charity]
1c Benefits must be balanced against any detriment or harm.

The benefit must be to the public, or a section of the public
2a The beneficiaries must be appropriate to the aims
2b Where benefit is to a section of the public, the opportunity to benefit must not be unreasonably restricted:

- By geographical or other restrictions; or
- By ability to pay any fees charged

2c People in poverty must not be excluded from the opportunity to benefit
2d any private benefits must be incidental.

(i) How can benefit be assessed?

Assessment of whether there is a benefit from a charitable trust can be difficult. Different people will have different views as to what is a benefit.

(a) There must be an identifiable benefit

The Charity Commission has set out that under this head there must be a real connection between the charitable purpose and the other benefits derived under it. If the benefits are ancillary to the purpose it cannot be charitable and if there is also detriment to be suffered it must not outweigh any benefit derived from the charitable purpose.

(b) The benefit must be to the public, or to a section of the public

It has always been accepted that a trust can be for the public benefit even where it is only available for a section of the public such as in a small geographical area.

Where unreasonable restrictions are placed on groups then the purpose may no longer be regarded as charitable.

In *IRC* v. *Baddeley* [1955] AC 572 the courts refused charitable status to a gift to promote 'religious, social and physical training' of Methodists or those likely to become Methodists in West Ham and Leyton.

It failed both on the lack of exclusivity of charitable purpose because it could include non-charitable purposes and also because the group was not 'a section of the public'.

(ii) Personal nexus with the testator

Where the group of charitable objects has a personal nexus with the testator it can cause the charitable trusts to fail. It depended under which head the charitable trust fell.

In *Oppenheim* v. *Tobacco Securities Trust Co. Ltd* [1951] AC 297 a trust set up for the education of the children of a group of employees who numbered over 110,000 failed because the court held they had a personal nexus with their employer and therefore failed the public benefit test.

Compare *Re Segelman* [1996] 2 WLR 173 where the section of the public was the testator's relatives but it was upheld because it was a trust for the relief of poverty where a personal nexus was acceptable. The Charity Commission guidance does not prevent a trust with a personal nexus from gaining charitable status but only in certain circumstances in particular where there is a sufficient section of the public. This suggests that post-2006 *Re Segelman* would have failed whereas *Oppenheim* may have been upheld on the basis of the large numbers involved.

In *R (Independent Schools Council)* v. *Charity Commission for England and Wales* [2011] WLR (D) 301 it was held that in assessing the public benefit requirement for independent schools each case would depend on its facts. There was no reason why the provision of bursaries to students who could pay some but not all of the fees should not be seen as for the public benefit.

9 THE RULES OF *CY PRÈS*

If a charitable trust fails, it may be possible to save the gift and transfer the funds to another charitable purpose under the *cy près* rules. This contrasts with the failure of a private trust where the funds will always result back to the settlor's estate. If the funds can be applied in this way, it is for the Charity Commission to draw up a scheme for use of the funds.

10 THE MEANING OF *CY PRÈS*

Cy près means 'as near as possible' and to apply the funds of a failed charitable trust *cy près* means to apply the funds to another charitable trust close to the purpose intended by the settlor. The law will allow this to happen if it can be shown that the settlor had dedicated the funds to charity as a whole showing a general charitable intention.

EXAMPLE

Tyrone leaves £100,000 to Bridley Children's Home. The home ceased to exist shortly before Tyrone's death. Members of Tyrone's family are claiming that as

> the home has closed the funds should result back to his estate but the executors believe that the funds could be transferred to another children's home in the area. The funds may be applied *cy près* in these circumstances if a general charitable intention can be shown.

Before the Charities Act 1993 it was only possible to apply funds *cy près* if a charitable purpose had become impossible or impracticable. These are both very narrow grounds and the Charities Act 1993 widened the circumstances for the application of *cy près* to include a list of five circumstances in which property given for a charitable purpose that was not impossible or impracticable to carry out but nevertheless was difficult to carry out could still be applied *cy près*. These include where the original purposes cannot be carried out according to the directions of the settlor, where the property left could be used more effectively for another purpose or where the original purpose has been adequately provided for by other means.

The Charities Act 2006 has widened the circumstances further and under s.15 it is possible to take full account of current social and economic circumstances when applying funds *cy près*. This replaces the emphasis of the Charities Act 1993, which focuses on 'the basic intentions underlying the gift' and 'the spirit of the gift'. The practical effect of this is that when the Charity Commission decides on a scheme to replace the original purpose it must take into account prevailing social and economic conditions as well as the 'basic intentions' and 'spirit' underlying the gift.

The application of funds *cy près* will usually depend on whether the charitable gift failed initially or subsequently.

(a) Initial and subsequent failure of a charitable trust

Initial failure

Initial failure occurs where the charity ceases to exist before the death of the testator. In these circumstances any property left to it by the testator can only pass to another charity if it can be shown that he/she had a general charitable intent rather than an intention to benefit only the particular charity named. If no general charitable intention can be shown, then the property will result back to the testator's estate or alternatively to those who contributed to the fund.

(b) What is regarded as initial failure?

Where the charity ceases to exist before the death of the testator

In *Re Rymer* [1895] 1 Ch 19 a gift was left to the rector for the time being of St Thomas seminary 'for the education of priests in the diocese of Westminster and for the purposes of such seminary'. The seminary had ceased to exist before the testator died. The funds were not applied for another charitable purpose because the purpose of the gift was so specific, both for a named institution and also for a specific purpose.

There will be failure if the testator leaves property with very specific instructions as to how the funds are to be applied and the charity ceases to exist before the testator's death.

Similarly in *Re Spence* (1979) Ch 483 funds were left to the 'Old Folks Home at Hillworth Lodge Keighley' which had closed a year before the testatrix died. The gift failed because the gift was very specific and the funds could not be transferred *cy près*.

(c) Gifts to charitable corporations

A gift to a corporate charity is regarded differently from a gift to an unincorporated association because a company has a legal personality. If the company ceases to exist before the death of the testator, then the charitable gift is likely to fail as a gift cannot be construed as a gift for the purposes of the company as these will no longer continue once the company winds up.

In *Re Finger's Will Trusts* [1982] Ch 286 several gifts were made by the testatrix including gifts to an unincorporated charity and a corporate charity both of which had failed. The gift to the unincorporated association was considered to be a gift for the purposes of the association and was saved, whereas the gift to the corporate body was regarded as a gift to the company and the gift failed. However, in this case the court later found a general charitable intention from the wording of the gift and it was saved.

(d) No failure of the charity

(i) Amalgamation with another charity

Where a charity has amalgamated with another charity it will not be regarded as failure but merely continuation in a new form. A good example of amalgamation occurred in *Re Faraker* [1912] 2 Ch 488. The testatrix left funds to Hannah Bayly's charity which was set up to benefit the poor widows of Rotherhithe but the charity had amalgamated with other charities some years before. It was held that the charity had not failed and it was not necessary to show general charitable intent.

(ii) Gifts to unincorporated associations

The law distinguishes between gifts to incorporated and unincorporated associations. A gift to an unincorporated association, which ceases to exist before the death of the testator, will not fail because the gift is considered to be a gift for the purposes of an unincorporated association which can continue to exist even after the association has itself ceased to exist.

Where a charitable gift fails initially it may still be saved where a general charitable intention is found as in *Re Finger's Will Trusts* (discussed above).

(e) Finding a general charitable intention

Underlying general charitable intention

The gift may be worded in such a way that the court can find a general charitable intention underlying the gift although it has been left for a specific purpose which fails. In *Biscoe* v. *Jackson* (1887) 35 Ch D 460 a general charitable intention was found where funds had been left to establish a soup kitchen but underlying the gift was a gift to benefit the poor of the area.

(f) Gifts to charities that never existed

The courts have been prepared to find a general charitable intention where a gift is left to a specific charity which has never existed. In *Re Harwood* [1936] Ch 285 several gifts were left by the testatrix for charitable purposes. One gift was to the Peace Society of Belfast which had never existed and this was upheld whereas a gift to a society which had ceased to exist before her death failed. Leaving a gift to a society which had never existed demonstrated a general charitable intent.

Subsequent failure

Subsequent failure occurs where the charity ceases to exist between the death of the testator and the administration of the estate. There may also be subsequent failure where the purposes of the charity are impossible to carry out. In these cases a general charitable intent will be assumed because the gift will be fully dedicated to charity on the death of the testator because at the time the charity was still in existence or the charitable purpose could still be carried out.

In *Re Slevin* [1891] 2 Ch 236 funds were left to St Dominic's Orphanage which had closed after the testator had died but before the money could be distributed. It was held that the money could be applied *cy près* because it had already been dedicated to charity on the death of the testator.

EXAMPLE

Hatty King, an eccentric old lady who died last month, left the following gifts in her will:

(1)   Her house in London to the Needlewomen of Hackney;

(2)   £40,000 to the Peacemaking Society of Stratford;

(3)   £100,000 to the National Society of BeeKeepers;

The Needlewomen of Hackney no longer exists as it joined the Needlewomen of Tower Hamlets last week. The Peacemaking Society of Stratford never existed. The National Society of BeeKeepers was an unincorporated association but due to the drastic reduction of bees in the country wound themselves up last year.

The gift in (1) has not failed as there has been an amalgamation and the house can be claimed by the new combined group. The gift in (2) may be upheld as although there has been initial failure, a general charitable intention can normally be found where the charity never existed at all. In (3) the gift may be upheld because where an unincorporated association winds up the purposes of the association can continue.

SUMMARY

This chapter considers the special status given to charitable trusts. A charitable trust has a number of advantages compared to a private trust such as taxation advantages, the relaxation of the need for the trust to have certain objects or identifiable beneficiaries and also a relaxation of the perpetuity rules and the application of the *cy près* rules when a charitable trust fails. In order to be regarded as charitable such a trust must satisfy three key requirements: it must be for a charitable purpose; it must be exclusively charitable and it must be for the public benefit. Charitable purposes have traditionally been defined very narrowly and have been based on common law. Charitable purposes have now been given a statutory definition in s.2(2) Charities Act 2006. The statutory purposes include the four recognised heads of charity from *Pemsel's Case*: relief of poverty, advancement of education and religion and other purposes as well as a number of new heads of charity. The new heads of charity include the advancement of health or saving lives, citizenship, arts, culture, heritage or science, amateur sport and animal welfare. One of the most controversial new heads is the advancement of human rights, conflict resolution or reconciliation or the promotion of religious harmony or equality. This suggests that a trust which has some political objectives will be upheld. The change in the law under the 2006 Act can be illustrated by the case of *McGovern* v. *Attorney-General* [1982] Ch 321 where it was held that a trust which had political purposes as its main object could not be charitable. The Charity Commission makes it clear that it now draws a distinction between political purposes and political activities. Political activities will not be upheld as charitable. A charitable trust will fail if the funds can be applied for a non-charitable purpose. All charitable trusts must satisfy the public benefit test. The Charities Act 2006 does not specifically define what is meant by public benefit but the Act does refer to the previous law. Traditionally it was held that in order to satisfy the public benefit test, a trust must be shown to be 'of benefit' and also must benefit 'the public as a whole or a section of it'. The Charity Commission has laid down guidance as to what it regards as the public benefit which includes showing an identifiable benefit, which must be related to the charity and that benefit must be to the public or a section of it. An important benefit to charitable trusts is the ability to apply the funds *cy près*. This contrasts and makes it possible to apply funds to another charity if a charitable trust has failed. It is important first to distinguish between an initial failure and a subsequent failure. In the case of initial failure, e.g. where the charity ceased to exist before the death of the testator the gift will only be saved if a general charitable intention can be shown. This is assumed in subsequent failure where the charity fails after the death of the testator. There is no failure of the charity where it has amalgamated with another charity or the gift has been made to a charitable unincorporated association.

14 Trustees: appointment, retirement and capacity

KEY POINTS

- the settlor can expressly appoint trustees either to an *inter vivos* trust or under a will;
- a maximum of four trustees can be trustees of land;
- there is no limit to how many people can act as trustees of personalty;
- the Trustee Act 1925 s.36 provides for the retirement and removal of trustees and the appointment of a new trustee;
- the Trustee Act 1925 s.39 provides for the retirement of trustees without replacement;
- trustees are not generally paid but exceptionally a trustee can be paid; and
- the Trustee Act 2000 provides for some limited payment and payment can be made in other limited circumstances.

1 APPOINTMENT OF THE TRUSTEES

(a) Creation of the trust

A trust requires at least one trustee to hold the legal title to the property of the trust. When a settlor creates a trust during his lifetime the first trustees will be named in the trust instrument. He may even choose to appoint himself as a trustee in which case there is no necessity to transfer the assets of the trust as these are held already in his name.

Where the trust is created by will, the trustees will be appointed by the settlor under the will, which constitutes the trust instrument. In many cases the executors of the will act as trustees on the death of the settlor and where no trustees are named the executors will automatically act as trustees of the trust property.

(b) Appointment of further trustees

Often the original trustees of a trust will need to be replaced. This could be for a variety of reasons such as death of the trustee or perhaps a trustee no longer wishes to act. There are many rules about who has the power to appoint new trustees. Sometimes the settlor may have expressly chosen certain people to appoint replacement trustees or the court may make the appointment or alternatively there are a number of statutory provisions which provide for this.

In some cases a trustee may refuse to act or 'disclaim' the trust after appointment while the trustee is still alive in which case the property will be held by the remaining trustees and where all disclaim then the property will be held by the settlor until other trustees can be appointed. The trust will not automatically end because the law holds that no trust will fail for the want of a trustee.

Where however the trust has been created on the basis that a particular individual will act as trustee and that person refuses to act the trust will fail as held in *Re Lysaght* [1966] 1 Ch 191. A gift was made by the testator to the Royal College of Surgeons to create medical scholarships. The scholarships had a condition, which was that no scholarship should be made to someone who was Jewish, Roman Catholic or not British born. The Royal College of Surgeons refused the gift because it regarded the restrictions as offensive. It was held that the trust must fail as the Royal College of Surgeons had been expressly appointed and in the view of Buckley J. no one else could act as a trustee to replace it.

(c) Who has the power to appoint further trustees?

The initial appointment of trustees is usually reserved to the settlor himself but the law allows others to become involved after the initial appointment.

(i) Settlor

After the first appointment the settlor can only appoint further trustees himself if he reserves to himself the right in the trust instrument. This will be an express term of the trust and allows the settlor some continuing influence over the trustees.

(ii) Trust instrument

The appointment of further trustees will usually be provided for by the settlor in the trust instrument.

(iii) Named person with power to appoint trustees

Alternatively the power to appoint trustees could be given to a named person, usually someone close to the settlor who he knows he can trust.

(iv) Appointment by a person nominated by the settlor in the trust instrument

In most cases the person appointed will have the power to appoint trustees in any circumstance but if the trust instrument specifies that the power is limited to a certain set of circumstances such as only in the event of the death of a trustee then the power is limited to those circumstances.

In *Re Wheeler* [1896] 1 Ch 315 the power to appoint a new trustee was given to a named individual but only if a trustee became 'incapable'. A trustee became bankrupt which is viewed as merely rendering a trustee 'unfit to act' and not 'incapable' so the appointed person could not appoint another trustee.

The donee of the power to appoint should not appoint himself to the position of trustee although the court could sanction such an appointment.

(v) Compare these cases

In *Re Skeats' Settlement* (1889) 42 Ch D 522 individuals who had been granted the power to appoint trustees decided to appoint themselves. This was held to be an improper exercise of the power since the power was a fiduciary power.

In *Montefiore* v. *Guedalla* [1903] 2 Ch 723 Buckley J. held that it could be possible in exceptional circumstances for a person appointed to appoint a trustee to appoint himself and it would not be an improper use of the power.

(vi) Statutory power to appoint

If the settlor does not provide for the appointment of further trustees in the trust instrument or grants the power to a named person, the appointment of trustees is covered by various statutory provisions such as the Trustee Act 1925 s.36; Trustee Act 1925 s.41 and the Trusts of Land and Appointment of Trustees Act 1996 s.19.

Today these are the more usual means of appointing replacement trustees.

(vii) Appointment under s.36 Trustee Act 1925

Where the settlor has not nominated anyone to hold the power to appoint new trustees under the trust instrument the surviving or continuing trustees have the power to appoint further trustees under s.36 Trustee Act 1925. This provision applies to all trusts. An issue has occasionally been raised as to who is a 'surviving or continuing trustee'. Under s.36(8) Trustee Act 1925 this may include a trustee who has refused to act or wishes to retire from the trust. Section 36 is discussed in more detail later in the chapter.

(viii) Appointment by the court

Where there is no express provision for the appointment of trustees the court may appoint the trustees under s.41 Trustee Act 1925. The circumstances when the court can appoint are limited.

(ix) s.41(1) Trustee Act

The court may, whenever it is expedient to appoint a new trustee or new trustees, and it is found inexpedient, difficult or impracticable so to do without the assistance of the court, make an order appointing a new trustee or new trustees either in substitution for or in addition to any existing trustees, or where there is no existing trustee.

The court's power is generally regarded as a last resort and is not usually used where one of the other methods is still available.

The application to appoint is made either by the beneficiaries or a trustee.

The court has complete discretion as to who to choose as a trustee but in appointing a new trustee the court should consider certain criteria laid down by Turner LJ in the nineteenth century case of *Re Tempest* (1866) 1 Ch App 485.

The court will have regard to:

(a) the wishes of the person who created the trust if expressed in the trust instrument;

(b) the court will not appoint someone in opposition to the interests of beneficiaries under the trust;

(c) the court will be reluctant to appoint a beneficiary because there may be a possible conflict of interest;

(d) the court will have regard to the question whether his appointment will promote or impede the execution of the trust.

A more recent example of where the court has appointed a trustee can be seen in the case of *Re Weston's Settlement Trust* [1969] 1 Ch 223. In this case the court would not appoint a trustee who was non-resident because it perceived the appointment as impeding the administration and so the execution of the trust.

(x) Appointment of trustees by the beneficiaries

Under s.19 of the Appointment of Trustees Act 1996 the beneficiaries of a trust have some statutory powers to appoint or replace trustees for any trust although they are limited. These powers are not just restricted to a trust of land. It was intended that the power to appoint under this section was to be exercised only where there was no one specified by the settlor under the trust instrument to appoint trustees.

Under s.19 where all the beneficiaries are of full age and capacity and are together absolutely entitled to the trust property they may in writing direct the trustees to appoint such person or persons as may be specified to be a trustee.

This power may be exercised by the beneficiaries to direct certain trustees to retire and to replace a trustee and they also have the power to appoint an additional trustee.

EXAMPLE

Trudi, Umma and Val were appointed by Arthur in 2008 to act as trustees of a trust under which Arthur's children Lee, aged 20 and Mo, aged 25 are the sole beneficiaries. The trust assets comprise some shares, money in a bank account and a house. Arthur died last year and now Lee and Mo wish to replace Val, one of the trustees with Winnie. If the beneficiaries are of full age, both in agreement and can show that they are absolutely entitled to the property they can do so but in order to make the appointment they must write to Trudi, Umma and Val and direct them to act on their behalf.

They would not have the power to appoint trustees in the following situations:

(a) Mo was 19 but Lee was still 17 years old;

(b) Lee and Mo's mother had a life interest in the property and she was entitled to go on living there during her lifetime;

(c) Sam had been named by Arthur in the trust instrument as having the power to nominate additional or replacement trustees to the trust.

Under s.20 Trusts of Land and Appointment of Trustees Act 1996 the beneficiaries have an additional power to appoint trustees where a trustee is incapable of carrying out his duties as trustee because of a mental disorder. This power will only be exercisable where there is no person willing or capable to make an appointment of another trustee under s.36(1) Trustee Act 1925.

This power can only be exercised by the beneficiaries under the same circumstances as under s.19, i.e. they are of full age and capacity and together they are all entitled to the trust property. Any continuing trustee must consent.

The right to appoint under s.19 and also under s.20 may be expressly excluded under the trust instrument.

(xi) Refusal to act

A trustee can refuse to act on appointment or can agree to act as trustee on condition that the office is limited in a certain way. This would limit his/her liability as trustee. The most obvious way to limit liability is to insert an exclusion clause into the trust instrument. Once the office has been accepted the trustee must carry out his/her duties until he formally retires from the office.

2 WHO CAN BE APPOINTED AS A TRUSTEE?

Anyone can be appointed a trustee of a settlement although there are special rules in the cases of charities and pension trusts and for minors and those without legal capacity.

(a) Minors

Different rules apply to minors, i.e. anyone under the age of 18. Under s.1(6) Law of Property Act 1925 a minor cannot hold a legal estate in land, so a minor cannot be a trustee of land.

Further, a minor may not be expressly appointed as a trustee in relation to any trust or settlement under s.20 Law of Property Act 1925. So a minor cannot hold a legal estate in personalty as an express trustee. If a minor has been appointed as an express trustee, the minor can be removed and replaced under s.36 Law of Property Act 1925. It is possible for a minor to hold personal property as a trustee under a resulting trust.

In *Re Vinogradoff* [1935] WN 68 a grandmother transferred £800 of war loan stock into the joint names of herself and her granddaughter but continued to receive the interest for herself. After her death it was held that the granddaughter held the stock on resulting trust for her grandmother's estate. The granddaughter could not claim it for herself.

(b) Who should be appointed as trustee?

(i) Lay trustees

For many people the obvious choice of trustee is a close family member or friend who is able to carry out the wishes of the settlor. The advantage of appointing a lay trustee lies in the confidence that the settlor may have when the trustee exercises any discretion within the trust instrument. The disadvantage lies in the fact that a lay trustee may lack expertise and experience. Decisions may be delayed and expert advice may be required when duties such as the duty to invest are undertaken.

(ii) Professional trustees

In many trusts, professional trustees such as solicitors or trust corporations (discussed below) are appointed. Professional trustees have expertise in administering trusts which a lay trustee may not hold and therefore they are more likely to be able to cope with the demands of trusteeship. Professional trustees can charge for their services whereas a lay trustee does not have the right to charge unless either it is expressly provided for in the trust instrument or certain limited common law and statutory provisions apply. Professional trustees are therefore often inappropriate for a small family trust where the assets are limited.

(iii) Trust corporations

A trust corporation has a special status and has additional powers compared to other trustees. An example of a trust corporation is a bank. It will be appointed for its special expertise and management skills. An important additional power held by a trust corporation is the power to give receipt for trust money received under a trust of land where normally two trustees are required. A trust corporation is able to charge for its services as it is regarded as a professional trustee. Not all corporate bodies are entitled to act as a trust corporation. It must be given the power to undertake trust business and must have issued capital of at least £250,000

(iv) Judicial trustees

Under the Judicial Trustee Act 1896 a Judicial Trustee can be appointed by the court who will usually be an officer of the court but will act separately from the court so the trust is not actually administered by the court.

Section 1 Judicial Trustee Act:

> any fit and proper person nominated for the purpose in the application may be appointed a judicial trustee, and in the absence of such nomination, an official of the court may be appointed, and in any case a judicial trustee shall be subject to the control and supervision of the court as an officer thereof.

One of the advantages of having a judicial trustee is that he can obtain directions from the court informally without having to make a formal application.

The circumstances when a judicial trustee will be appointed are exceptional and will usually occur when proper administration of the trust has broken down. This may be caused by a major disagreement between the trustees that cannot be addressed by the appointment of new trustees or by obvious poor management of the trust that then leads to litigation.

A disadvantage of a judicial trustee lies in the possible high cost because a judicial trustee can request remuneration.

EXAMPLE

Oswald died four years ago leaving a trust fund of over a million pounds. This was to be held in trust, partly for his wife and the remainder for his four children when they reach the age of 25. At his death, none of the children had reached 25 and the youngest was 16. The trustees were Bazz, Mazz and Tazzer who were all relatives of Oswald. The three have made some disastrous investment decisions and the value of the estate has fallen heavily. The three trustees are all blaming each other and Tazzer is also suspected of taking some of the trust property himself and he is currently being investigated by the police. None of the rest of the family wishes to become a trustee.

In this case the judicial trustee could be approached and asked to act, as there is evidence of serious mismanagement.

(v) The Public Trustee

There has also been provision since the Public Trustee Act 1906 for a Public Trustee. The public trustee is a corporation sole which can act in several capacities including as an ordinary trustee or a judicial trustee but can act on behalf of certain individuals as a trustee in the last resort. This means the Public Trustee will step in when there is no one else suitable, able or willing to act and an injustice would result if the Public Trustee did not accept the post. As the Public Trustee is a corporation sole no one individual will be regarded as acting for the estate so there will never be any requirement to appoint a replacement trustee.

When will it be appropriate to appoint the public trustee?

The Public Trustee generally acts for estates, which are very small or have very low monetary value. The Public Trustee is also used when someone dies intestate (without making a valid will) and an administrator has not yet been appointed to take over the administration of the estate. An application for the appointment of the Public Trustee can be made by the settlor, the trustees or the beneficiaries. Once appointed, the public trustee has all the same powers as any ordinary trustee. It is possible for the Public Trustee to act with an existing trustee. Although the Public Trustee acts for small estates he is allowed to charge for its services. A further advantage of using the Public Trustee is that the Lord Chancellor's Department will be liable for any loss, which results from a breach of trust.

The Public Trustee cannot administer charitable trusts and he cannot act as an administrator of an insolvent estate or deal with a trust that involves an arrangement with creditors.

The Public Trustee can decline to act but never on the grounds that an estate is too small.

EXAMPLE

Edwin is an elderly widower who is finding it difficult to live alone and also to manage his financial affairs. He has no children but one niece Tara who comes to visit him from time to time. He does not own his own home but he has some savings. He tells Tara that he is thinking of going into residential accommodation and he wants to put all his savings into a trust fund. He asks her if she would agree to becoming trustee for him. She does not think she has sufficient expertise and so refuses.

Edwin could seek help from the Public Trustee who could step in and take over his financial affairs.

---

3 NUMBER OF TRUSTEES

(a) Personalty

There is no limit on the number of trustees that can be appointed to a trust of personal property. In practical terms it may be difficult administratively for too many trustees to attempt to work together, particularly as any decision among trustees must be unanimous.

A recommendation was made by the Law Reform Committee 23rd Report ('The Powers and Duties of Trustees') (Cmnd 8733) (1982) that where the settlor has not stated otherwise not more than four trustees should be appointed whatever the nature of the trust property. This recommendation was based on the practicalities of a large number of trustees being involved in decision-making. This recommendation has not been acted on.

(b) Land

Under s.34 Trustees Act 1925 no more than four people can act as trustees of land.

A sole trustee of land is allowed by law but there are limitations on his capacity to deal in the land.

1. Under s.14(2) Trustee Act 1925 a sole trustee cannot give a valid receipt for capital monies arising out of a sale of land unless the sole trustee is a trust corporation;
2. A sole trustee cannot benefit from the overreaching provisions on the sale of land. Overreaching can be described as the process whereby equitable rights in land are transferred from the land into the purchase monies. Under s.27 Law of Property Act 1925 it is held that a purchaser is not to be concerned with the trusts affecting land if the proceeds of sale are paid to no fewer than two trustees of land. If a sole trustee sells land, the purchaser will be bound by any equitable rights in the land under a trust of land. This will have a very serious effect on the purchaser who will be bound by those rights and could allow a claimant with an equitable interest the right to remain living in the property.

4 DUTIES OF A TRUSTEE ON APPOINTMENT

The first duty of any new trustee will be to acquaint himself with the trust instrument and the terms of the trust as well as any trust documentation. A trustee is liable for any breach of trust from the day of appointment and may be liable for breaches that occurred before his appointment. However, if the trustee has checked the documentation thoroughly and taken every step to acquaint himself with the trust, liability for any breaches of previous trustees will be minimised.

Transfer of trust property

The trust property must be transferred into the name of the new trustee. Under s.40 Trustee Act 1925 where an appointment to trustee is made by deed all property including land and chattels such as shares will be automatically vested in the new trustee. There are some exceptions to the automatic transfer of property under the vesting deed to the new trustee.

1 Land: where trust property includes registered land the name of the new trustee must be registered on the proprietorship register at the Land Registry;

2 Shares: where the trust property consists of shares title can only be transferred by effective registration of the name of the new trustee in the register;

3 Leases: where land is held under lease and consent is required of the legal owner before there can be an assignment. The legal owner must consent to the transfer of the lease into the new trustee's name.

5 APPOINTMENT OF NEW TRUSTEES UNDER S.36

Trustees have the right to retire from the trust at any time. Trusteeship is an onerous responsibility and the law makes provision for trustees to leave the trust. The law is concerned that the trust can continue to operate once a trustee has retired so under certain statutory provisions retirement can only be allowed where there is another trustee to step into the retiring trustee's shoes.

Section 36(1) Trustee Act lays down extensive statutory provision for the appointment of new trustees in certain situations. The Act covers situations where the trustee desires to be discharged or a new trustee must be appointed because the trustee cannot continue to discharge his duties. Under this section a new trustee must be appointed in the place of the retiring trustee.

Section 36 lists eight situations where a new trustee can be appointed:

1 the trustee is dead. As mentioned earlier this may also include a trustee who is named in the will but dies before the settlor;

2 the trustee remains out of the United Kingdom for a continuous period of more than 12 months (note that the United Kingdom includes England, Wales, Scotland and Northern Ireland but not the Channel Islands or the Isle of Man);

3 the trustee wishes to be discharged from the trust;

4 the trustee refuses to act. This also includes a trustee who disclaims the trusteeship initially;

5 the trustee is 'unfit to act'. This refers to a trustee who is bankrupt or alternatively has been dishonest including a criminal conviction;

6 the trustee is 'incapable of acting'. This includes anyone under a mental or physical disability or who is unable to act through old age;

7 the trustee is an infant;

8 the trustee has been removed under an express power.

As discussed earlier under s.36(1)(a) and s.36(1)(b) Trustee Act 1925 the appointment of a new trustee can be made by the following persons in the following order:

(a) the person named in the trust instrument by the settlor to make appointments;
(b) the surviving or continuing trustees;
(c) if there are no continuing or surviving trustees then the appointment is made by the personal representatives of the last surviving trustee.

EXAMPLE

Consider the following situations and the application of s.36 to the different situations:

1 Stan has appointed Leah and Tom to be trustees. He nominates Cilla under the trust instrument to have the power to appoint trustees. Leah is under age and cannot act as a trustee and Cilla will have the power to appoint a new trustee;

2 Connie has appointed Ellie, Fran and Gia to be trustees. Ellie and Fran are killed in a road accident. Gia will appoint the new trustees because she is the surviving trustee;

3 Dave has appointed Felix and Kwok to be his trustees. Felix is killed in a car crash and Kwok dies in a freak accident the following day. Kwok's personal representatives will appoint the new trustees. This is because Kwok was the last surviving trustee and it is his personal representatives who have the power to appoint further trustees;

4 Ed has appointed Jasper and Hari to be his trustees. Hari wants to go abroad and wishes to be discharged. Jasper becomes mentally ill and is incapable of acting as a trustee. If there is no provision in the trust instrument for someone to appoint a trustee and Jasper becomes mentally ill before Hari decides to go abroad, Hari would be regarded as a continuing trustee and would be able to appoint another trustee. In such a case Hari could go abroad and the new trustee could then make the appointment to appoint a new trustee to replace Jasper.

Under s.36(6) it is possible to use the statutory provision to appoint further trustees so long as the total number does not exceed four, where the assets include land.

There has been some dispute about who may take part in the decision to appoint a new trustee. Under s.36(1)(b) the appointment should be made by surviving or continuing trustees.

Who is a continuing or surviving trustee?

Re Stoneham Settlement Trust [1953] Ch 59

A trustee had been out of the United Kingdom for over twelve months so a new trustee was appointed. When the trustee who had been replaced returned to the United Kingdom he sought to have the appointment set aside on the grounds that he was not consulted over the appointment of the new trustee making the appointment invalid. The court held that he did not have the right to take part in the decision-making since he was a 'removed trustee' under the Act and not a 'refusing or retiring trustee'.

6 RETIREMENT OF TRUSTEES UNDER S.39

The law allows a trustee to retire from the trust under a number of circumstances. Under s.36 a trustee can retire where another trustee has been appointed to take his place. A trustee can also retire under s.19 Trusts of Land and Appointment of Trustees Act. In this case the new trustee will be appointed by the beneficiaries. Section 39 allows a trustee to retire without the appointment of another trustee.

However there are certain requirements to be satisfied.

1 the retirement must be by deed;
2 the trustee must first obtain the consent of the other trustees;
3 the consent of the other trustees must be by deed which expressly approves of the retirement; and
4 two trustees or a trust corporation must remain after the retirement.

This section would not be available where the trustee wishing to retire was only one of two trustees when first appointed.

After retirement a trustee continues to be liable for breaches of trust which occurred during his trusteeship. Retirement can never be a defence to an action for breach of trust in such actions.

EXAMPLE

Consider the situations below and decide under which statutory provision a new trustee could be appointed:

1 Last year Cyril appointed Kai and Lei to be trustees of his settlement in favour of his three children A (aged 21), B (aged 18) and C (aged 16). Kai wishes to retire from the trust because he finds he does not have enough time to devote to the trust. A and B would like their Uncle Finn to be appointed;

> 2 Cyril creates an *inter vivos* trust and appoints Xin, Yang, Zin and Wang to be trustees. Wang wishes to retire from the trust;
> 3 Cyril created a trust under his will appointing his two friends Simon and Tim to be trustees. Cyril died last year. Tim has recently become bankrupt and Simon has been diagnosed with depression. Who can appoint new trustees?

Note under (1) the beneficiaries cannot influence the choice of new trustee because C is under age and s.19 TOLATA only applies where all the beneficiaries are *sui juris*. Under (2) Wang can retire under s.39 as there are two or more trustees remaining after his retirement. Under (3) the issue here is who is a continuing trustee and who of the trustees remains able to appoint a new trustee. As Tim is bankrupt he will be regarded as unfit to act whereas Simon will be regarded as incapable of acting through his illness but this will depend on the severity of his condition.

A trustee may also retire if the trust instrument contains a power of retirement or by consent of the beneficiaries if they are of full age and capacity. A trustee can also retire with consent of the court.

7 REMOVAL OF TRUSTEES

A trustee can only be removed if one of circumstances set out in s.36 applies or the trust instrument contains an express power to remove a trustee or the court retains inherent power to remove a trustee. Of course recourse to the court will be expensive.

8 REMUNERATION OF TRUSTEES

Trusteeship is often an onerous responsibility but there is no presumption either under common law or under statute that a trustee will be paid. There are circumstances when a trustee can claim payment but it is rare for lay trustees to be paid unless the settlor has made express provision for payment in the trust instrument.

The rationale behind this is that payment for a trustee's work may compromise their decision-making and they may unnecessarily delay the work in order to increase their payment.

(a) Payment pre-Trustee Act 2000

(i) The court's inherent jurisdiction

The court has always had inherent jurisdiction to authorise payment for work carried out by a trustee. However it will only do so where there is evidence that the work carried out is exceptional.

Unusually payment was ordered in *Boardman* v. *Phipps* [1967].

Boardman v. *Phipps* [1967] 2 AC 46

In this case a solicitor had breached the fiduciary duty he owed to the beneficiaries of a trust. He purchased shares in a private company which was the main asset of the trust and took a controlling share eventually making the company profitable. The beneficiaries profited from his actions but the solicitor also made a personal profit and under the strict rules of breach of fiduciary duty the court ordered him to transfer his personal profit to the trust. However because the increase in value of the shares was due to the expertise of the solicitor without which the trust would not have profited, the court ordered remuneration for the solicitor.

(ii) Provision for payment in the trust instrument

The trust instrument may specifically allow a trustee to receive remuneration. These are referred to as 'charging clauses' and were construed very strictly against the trustee. The Trustee Act 2000 has relaxed the circumstances which allow charges to be made.

(iii) Solicitor-trustees

A solicitor-trustee is entitled to claim the costs of litigation under the rule in *Cradock* v. *Piper* (1850) 1 Mac & G 664 if he acts on behalf of himself and his co-trustees. This rule was sometimes criticised. In *Re Worthington* [1954] 1 All ER 677 Upjohn J. commented that it was 'exceptional and anomalous and not to be extended'. It has been overtaken by provision for such payments in the Trustee Act 2000.

(iv) Statutory authority under various statutes before 2000

Payment to such bodies as trust corporations, the judicial trustee and the Public Trustee is authorised under various statutes (s.42 Trustee Act 1925; s.1 Judicial Trustee Act 1896 and s.9 Public Trustee Act 1906).

Payment under the Trustee Act 2000

Under ss.28, 29 Trustee Act 2000 more extensive remuneration for trustees has been allowed although this does not include payment to lay trustees.

- s.28 allows remuneration for any trustee acting in a professional capacity on behalf of the trust even if the services could be provided by one of the lay trustees.
- s.29 provides that remuneration may be claimed by a trust corporation or a professional trustee for services provided to the trust where payment has not been expressly authorised in the trust instrument. However payment cannot be made until the other trustees have agreed in writing that he should be paid.

SUMMARY

This chapter examines the appointment, retirement and capacity of trustees. Trustees are initially appointed in the trust instrument by the settlor but provision must be made for changes in the body of trustees. There may be many reasons why someone can no longer act as a trustee including his or her own choice or because he or she is no longer capable of acting as a trustee and the law must accommodate all these reasons. Where someone ceases to act as a trustee, further trustees can be appointed by a person named in the trust instrument or by the continuing trustees themselves or where there is no surviving trustee, the personal representative of the last surviving trustee. The statutory power to appoint further trustees lies in s.36 Trustee Act 1925 and also s.19 Trusts of Land and Appointment of Trustees Act which allows the beneficiaries some control over who is to be appointed. Where the beneficiaries are of full age and are in agreement and are already entitled to the trust property they can appoint new trustees. In the last resort, the court can appoint a trustee under s.41 Trustee Act 1925. Guidelines for the appointment of trustees by the court were laid down by Turner LJ in *Re Tempest*. In some cases a professional trustee will be appointed as opposed to a lay trustee. The court may appoint the Public Trustee in cases where there is a very small estate and no one is willing to act as a trustee. In cases where the administration of the trust has broken down the judicial trustee may be appointed who can take directions from the court without having to make a formal application to court with all the high cost involved. There is no limit on the number of trustees who can be appointed in a trust of personalty but no more than four people can be trustees of land. Trustees can retire from the trust and can also be removed in limited circumstances such as where they are no longer capable of acting because of ill-health or are considered to be unfit to act because of bankruptcy. In some circumstances trustees can retire without being replaced. This is laid down in s.39 Trustee Act 1925. The general rule is that trustees cannot be paid for their services. There are a number of exceptions including where the trustee has made provision for payment in the trust instrument but since the Trustee Act 2000 this strict rule has been relaxed although it is mainly allowed where the trustee provides professional services.

15 Duties and powers of trustees

KEY POINTS

- trustees owe a duty of care to the beneficiaries both under common law and under statute;
- trustees have a duty to provide the beneficiaries certain information including accounts;
- the beneficiaries have no inherent right to disclosure of the trust documents;
- disclosure of trust documents lies with the court's discretion;
- trustees have a duty to preserve and maximise trust assets;
- the trustees' power to invest is governed by the Trustee Act 2000;
- trustees can delegate their powers to others but will remain liable unless the delegation complies with the general duty of care;
- certain duties of a trustee can never be delegated such as the exercise of a trustee's discretion;
- trustees have the power to advance income to infant beneficiaries for their maintenance and to all beneficiaries with a vested interest; and
- trustees have the power to advance capital to all beneficiaries if they can prove it is for their benefit.

1 INTRODUCTION: THE OFFICE OF TRUSTEE

The office of trustee carries with it a wide range of duties. Overriding all duties and powers of a trustee is the duty to carry out the terms of the trust and to act in the beneficiaries' best interests at all times. The duties of a trustee must be carried out with care because failure to carry out a duty may make the trustee personally liable in an action for breach of trust.

The role of a trustee involves two main aspects:

1 A managerial role which involves the administration and management of the trust property.
2 A distributive role which involves ensuring that the trust property is distributed to those entitled under the terms of the trust.

2 DUTY OF CARE

All trustees owe a duty of care to the beneficiaries. This duty involves taking care of the assets of the trust and acting in the best interests of the beneficiaries.

The duty of care comprises both a common law and a statutory duty as laid down in the Trustee Act 2000.

(a) Common law

Under common law, the duty of care owed by all trustees was 'to take such care as would an ordinary prudent man of business would exercise in the management of his own affairs' (*Speight* v. *Gaunt* (1883) 9 App Cas 1).

A higher standard of care was required where a trustee was involved in the investment of trust funds. Echoed in *Learoyd* v. *Whiteley* (1887) 12 AC 727 by Lord Watson: 'As a general rule the law requires of a trustee no higher degree of diligence in the execution of his office than a man of ordinary prudence would exercise in the management of his own private affairs.'

Under *Re Whiteley* (1886) 33 Ch D 347 the duty is one 'to take such care as an ordinary prudent man would take if he were minded to make an investment for the benefit of other people for whom he felt morally bound to provide' (Lindley LJ).

This prevents the trustee from taking risks with the trust assets, risks which a trustee may take with his/her own personal assets.

The common law duty of care has little relevance today although it still serves to fill any gaps left by the Trustee Act 2000.

(b) Trustee Act 2000

Under the Trustee Act 2000 the statutory duty of care owed by trustees differs according to whether a trustee is a professional or a lay trustee.

s.1 a trustee must exercise such care and skill as is reasonable in the circumstances, having regard in particular –

(a) to any special knowledge or experience that he has or holds himself out as having, and

(b) if he acts as trustee in the course of a business or profession, to any special knowledge or experience that it is reasonable to expect of a person acting in the course of that kind of business or profession.

Under this section there is a higher duty of care placed on professionals such as solicitors and accountants.

The statutory duty of care applies in all circumstances specifically listed in schedule 1 Trustee Act 2000. These include the exercise of statutory powers of investment by the trustees, the purchase of land and the delegation of certain powers to agents.

It is possible to exclude the statutory duty to invest and in these cases the common law duty of care will still apply.

EXAMPLE

Pradeep, Afnan and Priya have been appointed as trustees of the Robinson family trust. Pradeep is a solicitor who specialises in criminal litigation and Afnan is a trainee accountant. Priya has a degree in economics and works for a charity helping to raise funds for victims of natural disasters. Will each of the trustees owe the same duty of care to the beneficiaries?

Section 1(b) will not apply to any of the three trustees because none of them is acting as a trustee in the course of a business or profession such as a solicitor or anyone working within a trust corporation. It is also unlikely that s.1(a) will apply a higher standard of care to any of them because none have any special knowledge or experience. As Afnan is a trainee accountant the court cannot expect him to have the expertise of a fully trained accountant and the expertise he will have is therefore limited. Priya's degree in economics is not enough to suggest that she has any specialist knowledge and therefore she would not owe a higher standard of care to the beneficiaries. Pradeep is a solicitor but he is unlikely to be regarded as having the expertise necessary to act in a professional capacity.

3 GENERAL DUTIES OWED BY TRUSTEES: TO PROVIDE ACCOUNTS; TO PROVIDE INFORMATION; TO ACT UNANIMOUSLY; TO ACT IMPARTIALLY

The trustees have a number of administrative duties in connection with the trust.

(a) The duty to provide accounts

The trustees have a duty to provide the beneficiaries under both fixed and discretionary trusts with accounts in order to allow them a chance to check that all is in order and no breach of trust has occurred. However, if the beneficiaries wish to be supplied with copies of the accounts they must pay for these themselves.

The trustees are allowed to employ an agent, usually an accountant, to assist with the preparation of the trust accounts.

(b) The duty to provide information

The trustees have a duty to provide the beneficiaries with trust documents concerning the trust. There has been litigation over what information beneficiaries are entitled to demand and who among the beneficiaries has a right to see the documentation. The question will be particularly difficult where the trust is a discretionary rather than a fixed trust. It is also questionable whether an object of a power of appointment should have the right to access trust documents.

Can objects of a discretionary trust demand to see information concerning the trust?

(i) The traditional approach to beneficiaries' right to see trust documents

In *O'Rourke* v. *Darbishire* [1920] AC 581 Lord Parmoor stated categorically that beneficiaries have a right to see all trust documents which relate to affairs of the trust because they have proprietary rights in the trust property and therefore they have proprietary rights in such documents.

the beneficiary is entitled to see all trust documents because they are trust documents and because he is a beneficiary. They are in this sense his own. Action or no action, he is entitled to access them.

The courts did not differentiate between beneficiaries of a fixed trust and a discretionary trust.

(ii) What is a trust document?

Re Londonderry's Settlement [1964] 3 All ER 855 considered what was meant by a 'trust document'. Salmon LJ accepted that there was no statutory definition of a trust document but he highlighted certain key characteristics that included the following:

1 they are documents in the possession of trustees;
2 they contain certain information about the trust which the beneficiaries are entitled to know;
3 the beneficiaries have a proprietary interest in the documents; and are therefore entitled to see the documents.

Salmon LJ here is equating ownership of the trust property, giving proprietary rights in the trust property with rights in the documentation of the trust.

(iii) The new approach to the beneficiaries' right to see trust documents

Schmidt v. *Rosewood Trust Ltd* [2003] 3 All ER 76

This case concerns two settlements created by a settlor in the Isle of Man. Rosewood Trust Ltd was appointed as the sole trustee of both settlements. The trust consisted of a discretionary trust giving the trustees a power to appoint the property to a group of objects. One of the objects of the trust, a child of the settlor and the administrator of his father's estate claimed the right to see the trust documents. He particularly wished to see documentation concerning the trust assets. The trustees refused to allow him access arguing that the trust documents need only be disclosed to beneficiaries with a proprietary interest in the property. A court in the Isle of Man refused disclosure to the claimant, he then appealed to the Privy Council.

The court addressed a number of questions covered in the following sections.

Has an object of a discretionary trust and an object under a power of appointment a right to see trust documentation?

Under Lord Parmoor's approach in *O'Rourke* v. *Darbishire* (above) such objects of a power of appointment would not have such a right because such an object would not have a proprietary right in the trust documents. The Privy Council in *Schmidt* adopted a new approach.

In the court's view, the right to see documents did not depend on having a proprietary interest but instead in all cases, including fixed trusts, the right of beneficiaries to see trust documents depended on the exercise of the inherent discretion of the court.

The effect of *Schmidt* is that no beneficiary has the absolute right to see trust documents.

> no beneficiary (and least of all a discretionary object) has any entitlement as of right to disclosure of anything which can plausibly be described as a trust document.
>
> (Lord Walker)

Today, access to documents by the beneficiaries or objects of a power will depend on the exercise of the jurisdiction of the court.

The Privy Council laid down certain guidelines concerning the exercise of that jurisdiction including some that had previously been adopted:

1 The beneficiaries will not have any right to information where there are issues as to personal or commercial confidentiality. In these cases the court may have to balance the competing interests of different beneficiaries, the trustees themselves and third parties and as a result some limitations must be imposed.

2 The principle that no beneficiary should have the right to see documents relating to the exercise of the trustees' discretion was reinforced in *Schmidt*. This was described by Lord Walker as 'the need to protect confidentiality in communications between trustees as to the exercise of their dispositive discretions, and in communications made to the trustees by other beneficiaries'.

EXAMPLE

Sara created a discretionary trust in favour of her two children Glen and Hatty, her three nephews and her eight godchildren. The trustees, Cedric and Roderick, are both friends of Sara. The main assets of the trust are: shares in a private company run by Sara's brother Terry, a house in Wales and £500,000. The trustees exercise their discretion in favour of two of the godchildren awarding each the sum of £50,000. Glen wishes to see the documentation concerning the exercise of the discretion. He also wishes to see the trust accounts and to have copies for himself and Hatty.

Glen's right to see trust documentation is dependent on the exercise of the court's inherent jurisdiction and discretion. He can apply to see trust documentation in the same way as a beneficiary under a fixed trust and it is not dependent on proof of any proprietary right in the documents. Under the guidelines given in *Schmidt* there is no right for any beneficiary to see documents relating to the exercise of a discretion so Glen will be refused access to this.

He will be able to ask to see the trust accounts but if Glen wishes to have a copy of the accounts he must pay for the production of them himself.

(c) Duty to act jointly and to make decisions unanimously

Trustees are obliged to act unanimously when making decisions. Decisions must be made together and all trustees are jointly liable for any decision that is made. In *Tempest* v. *Lord Camoys* (1882) 22 Ch D 640 it was held that where one trustee had taken a decision to exercise his discretion to purchase land but without the agreement of his co-trustee, the purchase was improper and could be set aside.

A trustee cannot claim that he did not take part in a decision and therefore should escape a breach of trust because trustees are jointly and severally liable and can commit a breach of trust by omission as well as commission. A passive trustee commits a breach of trust in his passivity in the same way as an active trustee takes positive action to commit a breach of trust.

This is illustrated in the case of *Bahin* v. *Hughes* (1886) 31 Ch D 390 where Miss Hughes, one of three trustees actively committed a breach of trust by investing in unauthorised investments which resulted in a loss. The two passive trustees tried to argue that they should not be liable for the breach because they had not taken an active part in it. Fry LJ found that all three trustees were liable for the breach of trust.

This is discussed in more detail later in Chapter 18 on breach of trust. When can the trustees act by majority? There may be provision in the trust instrument for majority decision-making. Certain types of trustees can act by majority, these include trustees of charitable trusts and pension fund trusts.

However it is possible for one trustee to sanction action taken by another trustee. This would be regarded as a joint decision.

(d) Duty to act impartially

In performing their duties trustees have a duty to act impartially and not to show any favour towards a single beneficiary. They must act in the best interests of all the beneficiaries. Investment decisions must be taken with the interests of all the beneficiaries in mind so that both capital and income are maximised and neither the beneficiary with a life interest nor the remainderman has preferential treatment.

4 DUTY TO EXERCISE DISCRETION

(a) The duties of trustees in exercising their discretion

In a discretionary trust the trustees have a duty to exercise their discretion. They have to exercise their discretion in favour of one or more of the beneficiaries in an exhaustive discretionary trust. In the case of a non-exhaustive discretionary trust where income can be accumulated they have a duty to consider whether or not to exercise their discretion.

EXAMPLE

Emma and George are trustees of a non-exhaustive discretionary trust which means they can accumulate the income of the trust. The objects of the trust are members of the settlor's family. Every year Emma and George meet together to consider the exercise of the discretion. Even if they choose not to appoint to any beneficiary they will have discharged their duties as trustees.

In both an exhaustive and a non-exhaustive discretionary trust the trustees cannot ignore the discretion and refuse to act. However once a decision has been made the courts have jealously guarded the trustees' right to refuse to disclose the reasons why a decision has been made.

(b) Can the beneficiaries force the trustees to give reasons for their decisions?

Trustees cannot be forced to give reasons for the exercise of their discretion. This principle has been upheld by the courts over a long period of time.

Re Beloved Wilkes Charity (1851) 3 Mac & G 440

Trustees had the power to select any boy to be educated at Oxford in order to become a minister in the Church of England, preference to be given to several named parishes. A boy was selected but not from one of the named parishes and a challenge was made as to how the selection had been made. It was held that the trustees did not have to give reasons for their selection.

EXAMPLE

Dylan and Chris have been appointed trustees of a discretionary trust of £250,000 by their friend Bryon. The beneficiaries are Bryon's three children Lara, Keira and Josie. The trustees appoint £50,000 to Josie. Keira and Lara are concerned that the appointment has been made improperly because Chris once had a brief affair with Josie but they have no evidence to support their concerns.

Unless they have substantive evidence to support this claim the court cannot force the trustees to give reasons for their choice of beneficiary.

(c) When can the court intervene in the decision making of trustees?

The court can intervene:

1 where the trustees have failed to consider whether or not to exercise their discretion at all; or
2 whenever there is evidence that the selection has been made improperly; or
3 in cases where it is clear that the trustees have failed to take into account all relevant matters.

(i) Failure by the trustees to consider whether to exercise the discretion at all

Although the court will not intervene in the trustees' exercise of their discretion, a court will intervene if the trustees have failed even to consider whether or not to exercise their discretion.

> it is settled law that when a settlor has given a pure discretion to trustees as to the exercise of a power, the court does not enforce the exercise of the power against the wish of the trustees, but it does prevent them from exercising it improperly.
>
> (Jessel MR in *Tempest* v. *Lord Camoys*)

In *Tempest* v. *Lord Camoys* (discussed above) one trustee had exercised his discretion to purchase land and the other trustee had considered this course of action but did not support it. The court could not intervene in the exercise of the discretion as it had been exercised properly but it could set aside the purchase on the basis that it was improper because only one trustee had consented to the purchase and the trustees had not acted unanimously.

Turner v. *Turner* [1983] 2 All ER 745

Three trustees held a power of appointment over the settlor's property. The settlor had created a trust for tax-planning purposes although he still considered himself in control of his property. The trustees were the settlor's father who was elderly, his sister-in-law and her husband and they were all inexperienced in financial matters. The trustees signed deeds of appointment which were made by the settlor himself, failing even to read them or fully understand their significance. The court held that it had power to set the appointments aside.

(ii) Improper selection by the trustees

If the trustees do not have to give reasons for the exercise of a discretion, then it is difficult for a beneficiary to argue that the selection was made improperly.

However where a trustee voluntarily gives reasons why a decision has been taken and the reason can be criticised for being improper then it is possible for the court to intervene.

Klug v. *Klug* [1918] 2 Ch 67

A decision was taken by the trustee not to advance funds to a beneficiary under the power of advancement. The reason given was that the trustee did not approve of the choice of husband of the beneficiary, who was her daughter and she had married without gaining her mother's consent. The court regarded this as an improper exercise of a power. In this case the court intervened and ordered payment to the daughter.

EXAMPLE

Edgar and Felix have been appointed as trustees by their friend Gregory. They hold £250,000 on discretionary trust for Gregory's three daughters Hana, Isla and Jan. Edgar and Felix exercise their discretion in favour of Hana. They write to all three beneficiaries saying that they have made the appointment to Hana because she is much prettier than the others.

Although the trustees cannot be forced to give reasons for the exercise of their discretion, where they do give reasons, which are improper the court can intervene and set aside the discretion as in *Klug* v. *Klug* [1918] (discussed above).

(iii) Failure to take into account all relevant matters

In more recent cases attempts have been made to open trustees' decision-making to scrutiny. The power of the courts to intervene in trustees' decision-making was recognised by Lord Reid in *Dundee General Hospital Board of Management* v. *Walker* [1952] 1 All ER 896 who concluded that the court can intervene if 'it can be shown that the trustees considered the wrong question, or that, although they purported to consider the right question they did not really apply their minds to it or perversely shut their eyes to the facts or that they did not act honestly or in good faith, then there was no true decision and the court will intervene'.

This suggests that there will be circumstances when the courts can investigate the process of decision-making.

(d) The rule in *Hastings-Bass* [1975]

Under the rule in *Hastings-Bass* [1975] Ch 25 the court has also been prepared to overturn the exercise of their discretion by trustees in good faith where the result is one that they did not intend. The rule has traditionally been applied either where the trustees would not or might not have acted in a particular way had they not taken into account certain considerations which they should not have taken into account or they failed to take into account considerations which they ought to have taken into account.

When will the court intervene under the rule in *Hastings-Bass*?

The exact circumstances when a court would be prepared to intervene on the basis of the rule in *Hastings-Bass* has been subject to some uncertainty. The judgment in the case suggested that it would apply where:

1 what has been achieved is not authorised by the power conferred upon him; or
2 it is clear that he took into account irrelevant considerations; and
3 he failed to take into account considerations which he should have taken into account.

These principles were considered in the following case.

Sieff v. *Fox* [2005] 1 WLR 3811

This case concerned the exercise of a power of appointment by trustees to the Duke of Bedford. They exercised a discretionary power of appointment to transfer property from one settlement to another intending to reduce liability to inheritance tax. The trustees had taken legal advice but it later turned out to be incorrect and although inheritance tax was saved the transfer brought about liability to capital gains tax of £1 million which would not have been imposed before the transfer of the property. The trustees sought to have the appointment set aside.

In his judgment Lloyd LJ set out the circumstances when the principle can be applied as follows:

> where trustees act under a discretion given to them by the terms of the trust, in circumstances in which they are free to decide whether or not to exercise that discretion, but the effect of the exercise is different from that which they intended, the court will interfere with their action if it is clear that they would not have acted as they did had they not failed to take into account considerations which they ought not to have taken into account.

The Court of Appeal agreed to set aside the appointments.

In spite of Lloyd LJ's approval of the application of the rule in *Hastings-Bass* in *Fox* v. *Sieff* he has recently restricted its use in two cases heard contemporaneously in the Court of Appeal and narrowed the circumstances when trustees can rely on the court to reverse a decision which has unintended consequences.

Futter v. Futter; Pitt v. Holt [2011] EWCA Civ 197

In a joint action of two cases, which although had very different facts, in both cases the trustees had taken advice on the exercise of their power to make capital payments and the advice was incorrect and attracted liability to tax which had not been foreseen by the solicitors. The trustees successfully argued in the High Court in separate actions that the exercise of their discretion was void and of no effect which then resulted in no liability to tax. The Inland Revenue in turn successfully appealed to the Court of Appeal and the trustees' liability to tax was reinstated. The Court of Appeal limited the application of the rule in *Hastings-Bass*. It held that the rule had been misinterpreted in previous cases. It held that where a trustee acts outside his powers any action taken by the trustee will be void. Where a trustee acts within his powers but he either takes into account an irrelevant factor or fails to take into account a relevant factor his act may be voidable. It is only where the action taken by the trustee is a breach of his fiduciary duty that it will be voidable. The court concluded that unless the trustee's actions were void or voidable the court would not set aside the exercise of a trustee's discretion.

Where a trustee has taken advice from a professional adviser such as a solicitor or an accountant which turns out later to be incorrect it will not be a breach of the trustee's fiduciary duty. In these cases the trustee should sue the adviser for negligence.

(e) Consequences of *Pitt v. Holt; Futter v. Futter*

The use of the rule in *Hastings-Bass* by trustees who wish to undo an action which has resulted in loss to the trust has now been severely restricted. The beneficiaries will have to resort to suing the trustees if the trustees' actions result in a loss to the trust fund or the professional person who gave the advice. However the trustees may have an exemption clause inserted in the trust deed which may protect them from an action for negligence.

The parties in both cases have been given leave to appeal to the Supreme Court so the rule will be considered for the first time by a court at this level.

(f) Application of the rule to pension fund trustees

The rule was often applied more strictly to trustees in pension funds as illustrated by the approach of the court in the following case.

Smithson v. Hamilton [2007] EWHC 2900 Ch

In this case a change in the rules of a pension scheme allowing early withdrawal by members had inadvertently given rise to greater benefits to these members than if they had withdrawn at a later age. The trustees asked the court to sanction an alteration of the rules of the pension scheme under the rule in *Hastings-Bass*. The court was not prepared to do so holding that this was not within the remit of the rule. The mistake was with the employers who had drafted the scheme and the correct remedy would be rectification.

(g) Unreasonableness

The second way that the court may have the jurisdiction to interfere with a trustee's action is on the principle of reasonableness. This now also incorporates the wider public law *Wednesbury* test of reasonableness.

Dundee General Hospitals v. Walker [1952] 1 All ER 896

In this case the House of Lords considered an appeal from the Scottish appeal courts. The case concerned a discretion held by trustees to apply a legacy to a hospital but only if it was not in state control. The trustees did not apply the legacy because they believed the hospital was in state control and the hospital challenged this conclusion.

The House of Lords considered in what circumstances a court would be able to intervene with a trustee's decision on the grounds of unreasonableness:

1 where the trustees have made a decision in bad faith; or
2 where the trustees can be shown not to have fully considered all the relevant facts.

Lord Reid described the grounds for a court to intervene with the trustees' decisions as follows: 'if it can be shown that the trustees considered the wrong question, or that, although they purported to consider the right question, they did not really apply their minds to it or perversely shut their eyes to the facts, or that they did not act honestly or in good faith, then there was no true decision and the court will intervene'.

These principles were further considered by Scott VC in the later case of *Edge* v. *Pensions Ombudsman* [1998] Ch 512. He concluded that a court cannot intervene on the grounds of unreasonableness except in very limited circumstances.

the judge may disagree with the manner in which the trustees have exercised their discretion, but unless they can be seen to have taken into account irrelevant, improper or irrational factors, or unless their decision can be said to be one that no reasonable body of trustees properly directing themselves could have reached the judge cannot intervene.

(h) Trustees must give reasons where the beneficiaries have a legitimate expectation

The general rule is that trustees do not have to give reasons for the exercise of their discretion. However the general rule can be displaced where a discretion has been exercised in favour of a beneficiary over a period of time and the trustees change their policy. In these circumstances the beneficiaries are entitled to an explanation of this change of policy on the basis that they now have a legitimate expectation that the discretion will be exercised in their favour.

This principle was stated in *Scott* v. *National Trust* [1998] 2 All ER 705. The case concerned a change of policy by the National Trust in allowing hunting to take place over National Trust properties. A challenge was made to this change of policy and the court held that where it was made after a period of time it must be supported by reasons.

EXAMPLE

Tom and Tim are appointed trustees for a discretionary family trust in favour of the four children Len, Ken, Jan and Mo. For five years the trustees split the income of the trust equally between the four beneficiaries. The following year they split the income between Len and Ken. Jan and Mo received nothing and were not given a reason why the trustees had changed their policy. Under *Scott* v. *National Trust* Jan and Mo are entitled to an explanation of the change of policy.

(i) Can beneficiaries compel disclosure of 'letters of wishes' by the settlor?

A letter of wishes is a letter written by the settlor when he creates the trust which would not be binding on the trustees but would show the settlor's wishes about the exercise of a discretion or other powers under the trust instrument. A settlor who had decided not to transfer property to a beneficiary under a fixed trust because of a specific reason such as the immediate tax implications may instead make him/her a beneficiary under a discretionary trust and could indicate to the trustees how he wishes them to exercise their discretion.

Breakspear v. *Ackland* [2008] 3 WLR 698

Three beneficiaries applied to the court for disclosure of a letter of wishes written by the settlor, their father. They wanted disclosure hoping to reveal how the settlor had wished the discretion to be exercised. Briggs J. used the case as an opportunity to review the issues concerning 'letters of wishes' as there had been no English decision on this point. He decided that no beneficiary had a right to see trust documents. Further no beneficiary can demand to see any document that discloses the reasons for the exercise of a trustee's discretion; this follows the principles from *Re Londonderry's Settlement* [1965]. Following case law from other jurisdictions, in particular Jersey, he concluded that where a settlor had made it clear that a letter of wishes is to remain confidential then those wishes must be honoured. On the facts of this case Briggs J. authorised disclosure of the letter of wishes but he made it clear that such a letter would not normally be disclosed.

5 POWER TO INVEST

(a) Sources of trustees' power to invest

Trustees have a duty to preserve the trust property for the beneficiaries which involves a duty to invest the assets on their behalf. The nature of that duty may vary because the trust instrument may be specific about investment. There are three sources of the nature of investment powers:

1 the trust instrument;
2 common law powers;
3 statutory powers.

(i) The trust instrument

The trust instrument may extend the powers of a trustee to invest beyond those powers allowed under statute or common law. This power was far more important for trustees before the Trustee Act 2000 and the Trustee Investment Act 1961 were passed because trustees' powers to invest were more restrictive.

Re Harari's Settlement Trusts [1949] 1 All ER 430

This case shows that the court will try to construe an investment clause in a trust instrument widely. A clause had been inserted in a settlement allowing the trustees to invest 'in or upon such investments as to them may seem fit'. The existing investments in the settlement included Egyptian bonds and securities which were not authorised by law at the time. Before this case the law was construed narrowly and an invest-ment clause would only give power to invest in investments which were authorised by law which would not include investments beyond the range authorised under law.

Jenkins J. applied a less restrictive interpretation and authorised investment by the trustees in a wider range. He commented: 'I think the trustees have, under the plain meaning of those words to invest in any investments which ... they honestly think are desirable'.

(ii) Common law powers

The common law lays down the duties of trustees in relation to their power to invest which includes the duty of care. The common law duties are less important in the light of the very specific statutory duties laid down in the Trustee Act 2000. The common law duties include the duty to act as a prudent man of business acting on behalf of someone for whom one feels morally bound and the duty to act fairly between the beneficiaries.

(iii) Statutory powers

The powers of the trustees with regard to investment are now largely governed by ss1–10 Trustee Act 2000. The main provisions of the Act concern trustees' duty of care; the general power of investment and the standard investment criteria; the need to take advice when exercising the power of investment; the power to acquire freehold and leasehold land. Trustees have the power to invest widely. Section 3 Trustee Act 2000 allows the trustee to make investment in 'any kind of investment that he could make if he were absolutely entitled to the assets of the trust'.

(b) The statutory duty of care

Section 1 Trustee Act 2000 imposes on trustees a statutory duty of care. Under this duty trustees are required to exercise such care and skill in relation to investments as is reasonable in the circumstances, having regard in particular to:

(a) to any special knowledge or experience that he has or holds himself out as having, and
(b) if he acts as trustee in the course of a business or profession, to any special knowledge or experience that it is reasonable to expect of a person acting in the course of that kind of business or profession.

Under s.1(1)(b) where a professional trustee acts for a trust a higher standard of care will be imposed on him.

(c) The standard investment criteria

Whenever trustees exercise their statutory power of investment they are expected to have regard to what is regarded as the 'standard investment criteria'.
    This comprises two aspects:

1 the suitability of any investment either proposed or already held under the trust;
2 the need for diversification of investments of the trust, in so far as is appropriate to the circumstances of the trust.

There is also a requirement under the section to keep the investments under review and to consider whether they should be varied.

EXAMPLE

Trudy and Sindy are sisters and are trustees of a small trust set up by their father for their children. The trust assets consist of £50,000 which has been placed in a building society account and a portfolio of shares in several public companies. They are concerned that they have not met the requirements of the standard investment criteria.

In this case the trust assets are relatively small. The trustees must consider whether the investments are suitable and sufficiently diverse. The assets have been split between two different investments. There is also a combination of risk from the portfolio of shares which may carry a higher yield and the building society account which is lower risk but the return will also be lower.

(d) The obligation to take advice before making an investment decision

Under s.5 trustees have a statutory obligation to take advice before they make any investment decision.

The relevance of this section is that trustees who fail to take advice before making an investment decision which results in a loss leave themselves liable for an action for breach of trust.

EXAMPLE

Hilda, Isla and Joe are trustees of a trust fund, which comprises money in a bank deposit account, a small number of shares in Shell plc and a semi-detached house. Will they need advice on the nature of the investments?

They will discharge their responsibility if they consider whether to take advice and they do not require advice under the Act if it is unnecessary or inappropriate to do so. In this case the fund is relatively small and the investments are in low-risk investments. It is unlikely that they will need to take professional advice.

Under s.5(4) proper advice is advice from someone 'who is reasonably believed by the trustee to be qualified to give it by his ability in and practical experience of financial and other matters relating to the proposed investment'.

EXAMPLE

Frankie and Joey are trustees of a trust set up by Georgio Marvello, a very successful entrepreneur, for his employees and their families. The trust assets are worth over £2 million. They are mainly invested in shareholdings but also include some paintings purchased over a period of time by Georgio's father and a sum of money. Frankie and Joey are wondering whether it would be sensible to invest some of the assets in property. Will they require professional advice?

The trustees have a statutory duty under s.5(1) Trustee Act 2000 to obtain and consider proper advice about the way in which, having regard to the standard investment criteria, the power should be exercised. Trustees also have a duty under s.5(2) to have regard to advice when reviewing the investments. The only exception to this statutory duty is that it is unnecessary or inappropriate to take the advice. The size of the fund and the range of the assets suggest that advice is necessary here in order to transfer assets into property. The advice must be given by someone suitably qualified under s.5(4). There is no requirement that Frankie and Joey follow the advice given.

(e) The relevance of moral and ethical considerations in investment decisions

Trustees have a duty to make a maximum return on the trust assets. This means that they must invest in such a way that they achieve this. The question has arisen in several cases whether moral and ethical considerations should be relevant in decisions with regard to investments.

Cowan v. *Scargill* [1985] Ch 270

Arthur Scargill, the General Secretary of the National Union of Mineworkers challenged investments made by the National Coal Board because he believed that the investments were unethical. He objected to investments in South Africa because its government still allowed apartheid and he objected to investments in companies working in oil who were direct competitors of the coal industry.

Megarry VC refused his application on the basis that the trustees were under a duty to maximise the profits of the trust and ethical considerations were only secondary to this duty: 'Trustees must put on one side their own personal interests and views'.

Megarry VC outlined one set of circumstances where he thought it may be possible for trustees to follow ethical considerations which was when a group of adults who were all of age and the same moral values who 'might well consider that it was far better to receive less than to receive more money from what they consider to be evil and tainted sources'.

Harries v. *Church Commissioners* [1992] 1 WLR 1241

This case is an example of the exception described by Megarry VC (in *Cowan* v. *Scargill*). It concerned investments made by the Church Commissioners which holds funds on behalf of the Church of England. The Church Commissioners applied ethical considerations when making investment decisions. Under this policy they refused to invest in armaments, gambling, tobacco, newspapers and South Africa. This policy was upheld by the court as being appropriate in the circumstances.

There will be some cases, I suspect comparatively rare, when the objects of the charity are such that investments of a particular type would conflict with the aims of the charity. Much cited examples are those of cancer research companies and tobacco shares, trustees of temperance societies and brewery and distillery shares, and trustees of charities of the Society of Friends and shares in companies engaged in production of armaments.

(Nicholls VC)

However adopting ethical considerations could only be justified if trustees were left with a sufficiently wide range of investments.

(f) Financial considerations and risk management

Trustees owe both the statutory duty of care when making investment decisions, which means they must exercise such skill and care as is reasonable under the circumstances which largely replaces the common law duty that a trustee acts as a prudent man of business. The new test takes into account the specific knowledge and experience of any trustee. If the trustee is a professional person, then the court will take this into account when considering whether a trustee is in breach of his duty.

Any action by a beneficiary with regard to the trustee's handling of investments will be centred around one of the following statutory issues:

1 the trustee's failure to discharge the duty of care;
2 his failure to adhere to the standard investment criteria such as reviewing the investments and checking to see that they are sufficiently diverse and are suitable;
3 the trustee's failure to take advice.

Under common law the trustee also owes a duty to act impartially between the beneficiaries. In relation to investments this means that the investments should not overly favour the person with a life interest at the expense of the person entitled in remainder.

Nestle v. *National Westminster Bank plc* [1994] 1 All ER 118

The beneficiary claimed that the trustees, the National Westminster Bank, were in breach of their duty to invest by failing to review the fund from time to time, failing to diversify and also their duty to act impartially between the beneficiaries.

Miss Nestle the claimant had been left an interest in a trust fund which was worth £54,000 at the time the trust was created and worth £269,000 in 1986 when she became entitled to the fund. The claimant alleged that the fund should have been worth £1 million when she inherited the fund if the trustees had taken different investment decisions. The claimant failed to convince the court that the bank was in breach of trust.

The Court of Appeal criticised the bank's overall handling of the investments commenting that it was 'inexcusable that the bank took no steps at any time to obtain legal advice as to the scope of its power to invest in ordinary shares'.

However, it also held that although the trustees had failed to review the investments and had also been very conservative in their investment decisions they had a duty to balance the needs of all the beneficiaries. The trustees had tried to balance the needs of all the beneficiaries which meant that they had tried to ensure that the life tenant had sufficient income as well as the needs of the beneficiary entitled in remainder, Miss Nestle the granddaughter of the settlor.

The fact that the trust failed to increase over the intervening years also did not found a breach of trust.

Staughton LJ outlined what the beneficiary would have to do in order to be successful:

The plaintiff must show that, through one or other or both of these causes, the trustees made decisions which they should not have made or failed to make decisions which they should have made. If that were proved, and if at first sight loss resulted, it would be appropriate to order an inquiry as to the loss suffered by the trust fund.

6 DELEGATION OF DUTIES

(a) General principles

A trustee has a duty to act personally when carrying out the duties as a trustee. The trustee has been chosen personally by the settlor to carry out the functions as a trustee so generally delegation to another conflicts with the trustee's appointment. This general principle against delegation must occasionally be compromised either because there are certain duties that a trustee cannot carry out personally or because the trustee cannot carry out any of the duties of a trustee, e.g. because he or she has left the country.

An example of when delegation of a single function is appropriate is the preparation of accounts, few lay trustees would have the necessary expertise to prepare satisfactory accounts. It has been accepted that certain functions of trustees can be delegated to others.

Although a trustee can delegate certain functions associated with the administration of the trust generally there is an absolute prohibition on the delegation of certain powers and the exercise of any discretion to another including to another trustee. There are some statutory exceptions allowing delegation even of the trustee's discretion.

There are two types of delegation:

1 Individual delegation where a single trustee delegates his function to another for a limited period of time, perhaps while the trustee is abroad.
2 Collective delegation where trustees acting together and collectively delegate certain functions to an agent such as an accountant.

(i) Individual delegation

There is limited power for a trustee to delegate even his/her discretions. Section 25 Trustee Act 1925 and s.1 Trustee Delegation Act 1999 allow limited delegation of functions and discretions of an individual trustee to another by power of attorney.

Section 25 Trustee Act 1925 allows a trustee to delegate powers to another for a period of twelve months and may be used where a trustee leaves the country to live abroad either permanently or for a short period. The delegation must be by deed. When powers are delegated under this section the trustee remains liable for any losses as a result of the acts of the donee. The continued liability of the trustee means this section is rarely used.

Section 1 Trustee Delegation Act 1999 allows a trustee of land to delegate indefinitely his powers to an agent. The trustee remains liable for the acts of the donee throughout the whole period.

EXAMPLE

Mr and Mrs Stanley jointly own a large house and garden. They have two sons Albert and Bernard who both live a short distance away. Mr and Mrs Stanley are both over 70 years old and conscious that they are both failing in health but are reluctant to move. Under s.1 Trustee Delegation Act 1999 they can appoint their sons as donees and the sons will be entitled to act on their behalf should they wish to sell their house and move at a later date.

(ii) Collective delegation

Section 9 Trusts of Land and Appointment Act 1996 allows collective delegation by trustees of land to a beneficiary. If the delegation has been carried out properly, the trustee will not be liable for the actions of the agent but if the delegation is outside the statutory powers of delegation the trustee remains liable for any act as if he had carried it out personally.

(b) Trustee Act 2000

Under s.11(1) trustees 'may authorise any person to exercise any or all of their delegable functions as their agent'. This mainly covers management and administration and does not include delegation of the trustee's discretion.

The Act defines delegable functions in a very broad way to include any function of the trustee subject to several restrictions.

The following functions cannot be delegated:

1 any decision concerning the distribution of trust assets;
2 any decision as to whether costs or fees should be debited to capital or income;
3 the appointment of new trustees;
4 any power to delegate trustee functions or to appoint a nominee or custodian.

The Act allows the appointment of agents who may carry out trustees' management functions and also nominees and custodians who may take custody of the trust assets. Agents are entitled to be paid by trustees for any function carried out, e.g. preparation of accounts. Appointments of agents, nominees and custodians must be made in writing.

7 POWERS OF MAINTENANCE AND ADVANCEMENT

The Trustee Act 1925 gives trustees wide powers to apply income for the maintenance of minor beneficiaries and to advance capital for the benefit of all beneficiaries.

(a) The power of maintenance

Under s.31 Trustee Act 1925 trustees have a statutory power to advance income to a beneficiary who is an infant whether the interest of the minor is vested or contingent for their maintenance, education or benefit.

EXAMPLE

For Henry £25,000 on trust when he attains the age of 25. This is a contingent interest as the fund is not payable to him until he satisfies the age contingency and reaches the age of 25. He wishes to have income applied to him for the payment of school fees. The trustees have the power to apply income in this situation because it is for his education which is covered under s.31 Trustee Act 1925.

(i) Limitations on the payment of maintenance under s31

1 The power is subject to exclusion, modification or even extension by the settlor in the trust instrument.
2 The power is subject to the absolute discretion of the trustees.
3 The gift must carry the right to income. This means that the income from the fund must be available for the payment of maintenance. 'Carrying the right to income' depends on the type of gift. A vested gift is a gift where the beneficiary is left property without the need to satisfy a contingency the gift is said to be vested as soon as the beneficiary reaches the age of 18 and the beneficiary can claim the income under such a gift. For contingent gifts the law regards gifts of personalty differently from gifts of realty and also treats gifts made during the settlor's lifetime differently from gifts made on the settlor's death. Where a specific gift of personalty or realty is made on the settlor's death it automatically carries the income whether it is dependent on a contingency or not but pecuniary legacies are excluded. Where a gift of the settlor's residuary property is made, it will carry the income on the settlor's death. Finally, a pecuniary legacy will not carry the intermediate income unless the gift is made by the infant's father or any person standing *in loco parentis* and no other fund is set aside for the infant's maintenance.
4 The beneficiary is over 18.
5 There is a prior interest.

An adult who has attained the age of majority but has not satisfied a contingency is able to claim an advance of income automatically until he/she attains the contingency unless it has been excluded or there is a direction that the income is to be accumulated by the trustees.

An example can be seen in *Re Turner's Will Trust* [1937] Ch 15 where it was decided that the beneficiary was not entitled to the income because the settlor had directed that it should be accumulated.

Maintenance is usually payable under the statutory power under the Act but the court also has inherent power to authorise maintenance. Further there may be authorisation under the trust instrument.

(ii) The power to advance capital

The power of advancement allows trustees to apply capital to the beneficiaries even in cases where they are not yet entitled to the fund. This power is available to both infant and adult beneficiaries.

(b) Statutory power of advancement

Under s.32 Trustee Act 1925 a trustee has the power to advance capital to a beneficiary who has an absolute or contingent interest in the fund.

(i) Restrictions on the power to advance

1 Permission must first be given by any beneficiary in writing who has a prior interest and will be prejudiced by the payment. This would include a life tenant who will receive less income as a result of the advancement.
2 The trustees can only apply half of the beneficiaries' presumptive or vested share. This is strictly applied. In the *Marquess of Abergavenny's Estate Act Trust* [1981] 2 All ER 643 a beneficiary had received half her share but requested a further sum after the value of the estate had risen. The trustees applied to the court but it was held that the rise in the value of the estate was irrelevant.
3 There is also a requirement that a beneficiary who receives capital by way of advancement must account for this when the fund is finally distributed. This is called the hotchpot rule.

EXAMPLE

Phil has a contingent interest in a trust fund. He wishes to start a small business. Can he call for an advance of capital? He can claim up to one-half of his share if he gets written permission from anyone with a prior life interest. At a later date, he must account for this advance when the fund is eventually distributed. It will also depend on whether there is any contrary intention in the trust instrument.

(ii) Benefit

Capital can only be advanced if the sum is to be applied for the benefit of the beneficiary. Benefit was defined in *Pilkington* v. *IRC* [1964] AC 612 by Lord Radcliffe: 'means any use of the money which will improve the material situation of the beneficiary'.

Case law shows that the courts are prepared to consider a wide variety of instances as being of 'benefit' to a beneficiary including the saving of death duties (inheritance tax) in *Pilkington* and the payment of a sum to a charitable trust in *Re Clore's Settlement Trusts* [1966] 1 WLR 955.

X v. *A* [2005] EWHC 2706

The beneficiary had been given several sums from a trust all of which she had applied to charitable causes. The court held that no further sums would be authorised because the sum requested was too large a part of the entire fund. Hart J. commented: 'it cannot be said that the proposed advance is relieving the wife of an obligation she would otherwise have to discharge out of her own resources if only because the amount proposed exceeds the amount of her own free resources'.

It should be noted that the power to advance capital and also to make maintenance payments to beneficiaries is always subject to trustees' discretion.

SUMMARY

This chapter considers the wide range of powers and duties held by trustees. These duties can be grouped together as managerial and distributive powers. All trustees are under a duty of care which is governed both by common law and statute. The statutory duty of care laid down in the Trustee Act 2000 is to exercise such care and skill as is reasonable in all circumstances but it will be higher for professional trustees. Trustees are jointly and severally liable for their acts and must act personally which means they cannot normally delegate the exercise of their discretions but can delegate some administrative and managerial powers. Trustees have a range of discretions which include making an appointment under a discretionary trust and making an appointment of capital or income to beneficiaries. Trustees cannot be compelled to give reasons for the exercise of a discretion but in some circumstances the court can consider those reasons such as where the discretion has been exercised in bad faith and the trustee discloses the reasons as in *Klug* v. *Klug*. The courts have been prepared to reconsider a trustee's actions where it was made without fully considering relevant matters. No beneficiary has a proprietary right to trust documents, and cannot compel the trustees to disclose them. It was held in *Schmidt* v. *Rosewood* that disclosure of trust documents to any beneficiary is at the discretion of the court. Beneficiaries can ask the trustees for an advance of their share of the capital if they can show that it is needed for their benefit as laid down in s.32 Trustee Act 1925. Benefit is widely interpreted. Infant beneficiaries can ask for a share of the income under s.31 Trustee Act 1925 if they can show it is for their education, maintenance or benefit. Trustees have a range of managerial duties and powers including a duty to preserve trust assets. They have the power to invest trust property but must work within the statutory criteria in the Trustee Act 2000, which includes the duty to take advice and to apply the standard investment criteria ensuring that investments are sufficiently diverse and are suitable for the fund. Investment decisions should be made in order to maximise the trust fund and as shown in *Cowan* v. *Scargill* should not take into account moral or ethical views of the trustees.

16 Variation of trusts

KEY POINTS

- once a trust is fully constituted the trustees are under a duty to carry out its terms;
- the court has some jurisdiction to vary a trust under its inherent jurisdiction;
- the court's jurisdiction to vary is limited and only applies to a case of emergency or compromise;
- a number of statutory provisions give limited power to vary the terms of a trust to the trustees;
- the rule in *Saunders* v. *Vautier* gives the beneficiaries power to terminate the trust prematurely;
- the right of the beneficiaries to terminate the trust depends on whether they are all of age, in agreement and together are fully entitled to the property;
- the Variation of Trusts Act 1958 gives the court wide powers to vary a trust but only where a benefit is derived;
- the powers of the court to vary under the Variation of Trusts Act extends to unborn and minor beneficiaries; and
- a variation will not be approved if it is deemed to be a complete resettlement of the trust property.

1 INTRODUCTION

Once a trust is fully constituted the terms are binding on the trustees and the provisions of the trust must be carried out as set out by the settlor. If a trustee does not carry out the terms as set out in the trust instrument, he/she would be vulnerable to an action for breach of trust. However there has always been some limited scope to vary the terms of a trust usually in the event of an unforeseen event arising.

1 The court holds inherent jurisdiction to vary the terms of a trust in certain circumstances but this jurisdiction is limited.
2 There were several statutory provisions to vary a trust even before the Variation of Trusts Act 1958 was introduced.
3 Although strictly not usually a variation the beneficiaries could always combine together and bring the trust to an end under the rule in *Saunders* v. *Vautier* (1841) 4 Beav 115.

2 COURT'S INHERENT JURISDICTION

The court has always had inherent jurisdiction to allow variation to the terms of a trust in a number of situations.

(a) Cases of emergency

Here the court steps in to authorise action by the trustees which would otherwise be unlawful. This would extend to any exercise of the trustees' powers. An emergency is generally regarded as a situation for which the trust instrument has not made provision and the circumstances could not have been foreseen by the settlor. It was used to vary investment powers of trustees which until the Trustee Investment Act 1961 and the Trustee Act 2000 were strictly limited.

Re New [1901] 2 Ch 534

This jurisdiction is illustrated by this case which concerned a shareholding of a trust. The shares were invested in a mining company which restructured and issued new shares. The trustees found that they did not have the authority to invest in the new shares and so they needed a change in investment policy to allow the trust funds to be held in what were now non-authorised investments. The court was prepared to authorise this change of policy because it was in the interests of the beneficiaries.

The court has limited its power to act in this way so it will only arise in circumstances where there is a genuine emergency.

EXAMPLE

The settlor Francis leaves his large country house on trust for his three children with a provision that the property must be sold by January 2012. Francis died in 2009. Property prices fall during the autumn of 2011 and the trustees consider that it is an inappropriate time to sell the house and not in the best interests of the trust. The trustees can apply to the court to have the term concerning the time of sale to be varied so that they are entitled to sell at a later date when prices have risen.

In *Re Tollemache* [1903] 1 Ch 547 the court refused to authorise a variation where the application concerned authorisation for the life tenant to take out a mortgage in order to provide an increased income for the beneficiary. The court refused because although this would benefit the trust, it was held that this was not a genuine emergency.

(b) 'Compromise arrangements'

The right was reserved to the court to allow it to vary the terms of a trust governing the rights of beneficiaries. The jurisdiction extended to infants and unborn persons under trusts. The right could be exercised where there was a dispute about the rights of the beneficiaries and the courts can step in to approve a compromise.

What is a compromise arrangement?

Chapman v. *Chapman* [1954] AC 429

The trustees of a settlement applied to the court for leave to vary the terms of a trust allowing the trustees to release property in order to avoid estate duty. The beneficiaries included minors and also unborn beneficiaries and any variation in the terms of the trust would therefore need sanction of the court.

The House of Lords had to consider whether the arrangement proposed was a compromise and so within the court's jurisdiction.

It commented that the court had power to approve arrangements varying beneficial interests but only where there was a 'genuine dispute' about the rights of beneficiaries. It was reluctant to intervene in other circumstances.

In this case the settlors themselves wished to vary the terms but the court was not influenced by their views. The House of Lords held the view that a fully constituted trust could not be reopened even by the settlor himself except in cases of genuine dispute and in this case there was no genuine dispute.

the wishes of the grandparents, as settlers, are entirely irrelevant on the question of jurisdiction. By settling the property on certain trusts they have put it out of their power to alter these trusts, however much they may wish to do so.

(Lord Morton)

Chapman v. *Chapman* was criticised because it clearly laid down serious limitations on the circumstances when the court could intervene. According to Lord Simonds: 'It was not the function of the court to alter a trust because alteration is thought to be advantageous to an infant beneficiary.'

It seemed the only way that the court's jurisdiction could be invoked would be to create a dispute about the beneficiaries' rights under the trust.

(c) Maintenance

The court has inherent power to award maintenance from income to a beneficiary where there is a direction that income is to be accumulated by the trustees. This power is limited to advancing the income and does not strictly extend to the power to vary the interests. However it may result in a variation of interests because after the power has been applied a person may receive a share of the trust property who was not a beneficiary under the trust.

Re Collins (1886) 32 Ch D 229

A testator had directed his trustees to accumulate the income from a trust to be accumulated for a period of twenty-one years and then it was to be paid to the settlor's sister for her life and then on her death to her sons. The sister requested that she should receive the income early so she could use it to educate her children. The court held that the court had the power to authorise her to receive the income early.

Farwell J. commented 'it is assumed that [the settlor] did not intend that these children should not be left un-provided for or in a state of such moderate means that they should not be educated properly'.

The trustees have statutory power to advance income under s.31 Trustee Act so this provision has fairly limited effect today and many trusts include express powers of maintenance.

3 STATUTORY PROVISIONS

There are a number of statutory provisions other than the Variation of Trusts Act that give the court jurisdiction to authorise a variation of the terms of a trust. Some statutes are restricted to authorising administrative powers of the trust only, e.g. s.57 Trustee Act 1925 while others extend to giving the court the power to vary the beneficial interests, e.g. s.53 Trustee Act 1925.

(a) Section 53 Trustee Act 1925

This section gives the court power to make an order in favour of an infant beneficiary who is absolutely entitled to the property for his/her maintenance, education or benefit. This power includes both capital and income. Section s.31 Trustee Act 1925 also allows trustees to apply income and capital in this way but this section confers wider powers because benefit is not restricted to material benefit. The jurisdiction has been used mainly to reduce tax liability or to increase the share that a beneficiary will eventually receive.

Re Meux [1958] Ch 154 illustrates when the court may intervene. The court sanctioned the sale of the interest of a minor beneficiary entitled to a reversionary interest to the tenant for life. The proceeds were then settled on new trusts for the minor. The advantage was that the beneficiary would receive more after the sale than if the property had been left on the terms of the original trust.

EXAMPLE

Dominic is aged 14 and has a reversionary interest in property called Keepers Rest in which his Uncle Terry has a life interest and is currently living there. The property is in a poor state of repair but Uncle Terry is keen to buy it and improve it. He is willing to pay one-third more than its current value. Dominic lives with his parents. The trustees wish to gain approval of the court to allow the sale of the property and for the funds to be placed on trust in a high-interest long-term savings account. The court has the power to sanction this if the court believes that it will be for the benefit of Dominic.

It cannot be used to vary the beneficial interests under the trust as pointed out by Upjohn J. in *Re Heyworth* [1956] 2 WLR 1044 where he commented on a proposed scheme to accelerate the share of a beneficiary so it could be received absolutely 'if I sanctioned such a scheme on behalf of the infant I should be reading the section as though it empowered the court to convey the property of an infant whenever it was for her benefit'.

(b) Section 57(1) Trustee Act 1925

This section allows trustees to do any act relating to the management or administration of the trust which the court thinks is expedient to the trust. This section is limited to administration and does not allow variation of beneficial interests.

The limits of the purpose was described by Evershed MR in *Re Downshire Settled Estates* [1953] Ch 218: 'it was no part of the legislative aim to disturb the rule that a court will not rewrite a trust'.

However it has wider scope than the court's inherent jurisdiction which is generally limited to intervening in an emergency situation.

The courts have only been prepared to sanction a variation which benefits the trust as a whole and have refused to sanction a scheme which only benefits a single beneficiary.

Re Craven's Estate (No. 2) [1937] Ch 431

The powers available to the court are illustrated by this case where the court refused to sanction a scheme which appeared only to benefit a single beneficiary rather than the trust as a whole. A scheme was proposed to allow an advancement of funds to a beneficiary to allow him to become a Lloyd's underwriter. He needed a large sum of money as a deposit for this. The trust included a number of beneficiaries and the advancement to the single beneficiary would not benefit them as a group.

More recent cases have involved an application to vary investment powers which were important before the passing of the Trustee Act 2000.

An application was made by the trustees of a pension fund under this section for permission to invest in non-authorised investments in *Mason* v. *Farbrother* [1983] 2 All ER 1078.

(c) Section 64 Settled Land Act 1925

This section is far less important today than it was before the reforms introduced in relation to trusts involving land in the Trusts of Land and Appointment of Trustees Act 1996. The section is restricted to settled land, which was considerably limited by the 1996 Act. It allows the court jurisdiction to authorise any transaction which would benefit settled land.

Before the 1996 Act a settlor who created a trust had two choices. Property would either be put into a trust for sale or alternatively into a settlement. A settlement made provision for property to be left on successive trusts. Property in a settlement was owned by the tenant for life and would be transferred on his death to the beneficiaries entitled in remainder. After 1996 trusts could no longer be created as a settlement and could only be created as a trust of land. However all existing settlements could continue so the Settled Land Act continues to apply to these settlements. Section 64 Settled Land Act allows the court very extensive powers to vary the terms of the trust which extend beyond management.

I bequeath my house, Badgers Rest to my wife Harriet for life, with remainder to my children George and Elspeth. While Harriet is alive she has control of the property as tenant for life but on her death the property will pass automatically to George and Elspeth. Harriet cannot leave the property with the rest of her personal estate as she only owns an interest in it for the duration of her life.

Under s.64 Settled Land Act 1925 the court can authorise any transaction which affects the settled land if in the opinion of the court 'it is for the benefit of the settled land'.

Hambro v. Duke of Marlborough [1994] Ch 158

The court authorised a scheme to vary the beneficial interests of the Marquess of Blandford the eldest son of the Duke of Marlborough. The property was held on trust under the terms of the 1706 parliamentary settlement. Under the settlement the marquess was entitled to the estate on the death of the Duke of Marlborough who held the estate as tenant for life. The trustees decided that the Marquess of Blandford was not an appropriate person to inherit the Blenheim estate on the death of the duke because he had shown lack of judgement in financial matters and he had been profligate with money. A scheme was devised which prevented the Marquess from inheriting but instead the property would pass to the trustees on the death of the duke and the property would be held on protective trusts for the Marquess for life. Under the terms of a protective trust the trust property is held on discretionary trusts for the beneficiaries who in this case would include the Marquess and his family. On his death the property would revert back to the terms of the original settlement. The trustees argued that the scheme would protect the land under the settlement. The court upheld the new scheme in spite of opposition of the Marquess of Blandford. The court concluded that it was not necessary to have the support of the beneficiaries when exercising its powers under s.64. The decision of the court depended on whether the scheme was in the best interest of the trust.

A further example of the scope of s.64 can be seen in *Re Scarisbrick Settlements Estates* [1944] Ch 229 where the tenant for life of a stately home, Scarisbrick Hall was authorised to sell investments and to raise a sum of money to enable repairs to be carried out on the fabric of the hall. The tenant for life was limited to the income of the investments which was not sufficient to cover the cost of the repairs.

(d) Section 24 Matrimonial Causes Act 1973

This section confers powers on the court to make property adjustment orders on divorce, separation or nullity. The powers include variation of trusts which were contained in any settlement made for the benefit of the parties to a marriage or for children of the marriage. It also extends to varying the provisions of any ante-nuptial or post-nuptial settlement. The court has used its powers in relation to the family home and also to vary the rights of the parties under a pension scheme.

E v. E (Financial Provision) [1990] 2 FLR 333

The court used its powers under s.24 to make an order that a wife should receive money from a discretionary trust under which the husband, the wife and the children were the beneficiaries. The terms of the order were that the wife was to receive a sum of £1.25 million under the trust.

Brooks v. Brooks [1996] AC 375

This case which allowed the court to make provision for a wife out of a pension scheme provides a further example of the range of powers available to the court. The terms of the pension scheme were that part of the benefit under the scheme was to be paid to the wife and the children on his death if he were to die prematurely. The House of Lords decided that a pension scheme was a post-nuptial settlement and so it had jurisdiction to decide on the shares under the fund. It held that the wife should be entitled to a share of the pension. However there is legislation which specifically deals with entitlement of the parties to a pension on divorce which is the Pensions Act 1995 and it is only in exceptional cases that s.24 Matrimonial Causes Act 1973 would be used.

The exceptional circumstances of Brooks v. Brooks were outlined by Lord Nicholls:

This decision should not be seen as a solution to the overall pensions problem ... a feature of the instant case is that there is only one scheme member and, moreover, the wife has earnings of her own from the same employer which will sustain provision of an immediate pension for her.

More recently the courts considered the right to occupy the matrimonial home in Ben Hashem v. Ali Shaif [2009] 1 FLR 115 where a wife was granted a right to occupy property owned by a company.

This order was considered to be a settlement and so within s.24 Matrimonial Causes Act 1973.

(e) Section 16 Mental Capacity Act 2005

Section 16 Mental Capacity Act gives the Court of Protection the power to make a settlement of a patient's property where that person does not have capacity to do so. Mental incapacity is defined in the Act under s. 2(1) as 'lacking the required mental capacity to dispose of property ... if he is unable to make a decision himself in relation to the matter because of an impairment of, or disturbance in the functioning of, the mind or the brain'.

The Act also contains power to vary the settlement 'in such manner as it thinks fit in the best interests of the person' and with regard to the statutory principles listed in the Act. The circumstances where this power will be invoked would be where a material fact has not been disclosed or where the circumstances have materially changed.

4 THE RULE IN *SAUNDERS* V. *VAUTIER*

The rule in *Saunders* v. *Vautier* gives power to beneficiaries of full age and sound mind the power to call for the trustees to transfer the trust property to the beneficiaries provided as a group they are entitled to call for the entire equitable interests. This will bring the trust to an end.

Saunders v. *Vautier* (1841) 4 Beav 115

The case concerned a testator who left East India stock worth £2,000 on trust for Mr Vautier his great-nephew. The terms of the trust were that the income was to be accumulated until he reached the age of 25. When he reached his twenty-first birthday Mr Vautier claimed the entire trust fund. The court upheld his right to claim the property in spite of the provision by the settlor that the interest was to be postponed until he reached 25.

Where a legacy is directed to be accumulated for a certain period, or where the payment is postponed, the legatee, if he has an absolute indefeasible interest in the legacy, is not bound to wait until the expiration of that period, but may require payment the moment he is competent to give valid discharge.

(Lord Langdale)

This rule has been applied in both fixed trusts as well as discretionary trusts.

Re Smith [1928] Ch 915

A discretionary trust of income was created in favour of a mother, Mrs Aspinall. Any surplus income was to be accumulated and on her death a fixed trust of the capital combined with the accumulated income was to pass to her three children. Later after all the children had reached the age of majority, mortgages were taken out by the mother, two of her children and the executor of a child who had predeceased her. The mortgagees sought permission to have the interest paid out of the income payable to the mother and the children under the discretionary trust until the mortgage had been paid off. The court held that this could be authorised under the rule in *Saunders* v. *Vautier* because they were collectively entitled to the fund and could require the trustee (who in this case was the public trustee) to transfer the whole of the fund to them. This could be done because the beneficiaries were all in agreement, of age and together were beneficially entitled to the entire interest.

(a) What does this rule entitle the beneficiaries to do?

Where a beneficiary is of age and is entitled to call for the property at any time the interest held can be accelerated and the trust brought to an end. It is often used where there is an age contingency to be met.

EXAMPLE

Shona and Bridget are beneficiaries under a trust which consists of a number of shareholdings and a sum of money in a savings account. The trust was created by their father and one of the terms was that the fund should be held on trust until they both reached the age of 25. Shona is now aged 21 and Bridget is 23. They wish to bring the trust to an end so they may immediately have access to the funds as they are both keen to purchase property for themselves. They are both of age and they agree on this action so they can bring the trust to an end without the cost of taking the case to the court.

The rule in *Saunders* v. *Vautier* cannot be used in every trust and in all circumstances. The rule could not be used where the beneficiaries are not in agreement.

EXAMPLE

Connie, Brenda and Annie are sisters and they are all beneficiaries under a discretionary trust. They are all over 18 years of age. The trust property consists of a shareholding and some money in an investment savings account. Connie and Brenda would like to claim the property now, knowing that if the trust was ended now the fund would be divided equally between them but Annie is aware that there is still a chance that she could receive the entire fund if the trustees decide to appoint it to her under the discretionary trust. As they are not all in agreement the rule in *Saunders* v. *Vautier* will not apply to them.

The rule in *Saunders* v. *Vautier* will also not apply if one or more of the beneficiaries is under the age of 18.

> **EXAMPLE**
>
> Cassie, Debbie and Eliza are sisters and are beneficiaries under a discretionary trust. Cassie and Debbie are over 18 but Eliza is only aged 16. The beneficiaries cannot bring the trust to an end under the rule in *Saunders* v. *Vautier* because the rule can only apply where the beneficiaries are all of age. If the beneficiaries wish the trust to be varied, they must seek authorisation from the court.

(b) The rule in *Saunders* v. *Vautier* allows the beneficiaries to bring a trust to an end but it cannot be used as a way of resettling the trust or varying the terms

Stephenson v. *Barclays Bank Trust Co. Ltd* [1975] 882 concerned two adult beneficiaries who applied to the court to make changes to the way a trust was administered. The court held that the rule did not give the beneficiaries any control over the trustee's actions. It merely allowed them to call for what was lawfully theirs.

In *Re Brockbank* [1948] Ch 206 the courts had to consider an application by the beneficiaries who wished to appoint a new trustee. The trustees had a statutory discretion under s.36 Trustee Act 1925 to appoint a further trustee but the beneficiaries wished someone of their choice to be appointed. The court held that the rule did not allow the beneficiaries to compel a trustee to appoint a particular trustee.

(c) How can the rule in *Saunders* v. *Vautier* be justified?

The rule appears to allow the beneficiaries to step in and terminate the trust and so ignore the terms laid down by the settlor.

1 The justification lies in the fact that where the beneficiaries are absolutely entitled to the fund: 'the gift cannot be fettered by terms governing mode of enjoyment'. So if there is an age contingency to be met it is only a mode of enjoyment. The beneficiary has absolute rights in the property which cannot be removed.

2 The rationale behind allowing the beneficiaries to call for their shares has been supported by the principle that interests in property should be freely alienable.

This means that the shares should not be tied up and the freedom to enjoy shares should not be limited. So if the beneficiaries wish their rights in property to be accelerated this should not be prevented.

3 The rule can also be based on the absolute ownership of the equitable interests in the property by the beneficiaries which should allow them the right to enjoy the property. The trustees merely held the legal title on the beneficiaries' behalf, they should not have the right to delay the beneficiaries' enjoyment of the property.

5 THE VARIATION OF TRUSTS ACT 1958

The Act introduced a wide range of changes including the range of circumstances in which a court may intervene and approve a scheme to vary the terms of a trust.

The powers conferred on the court were described by Evershed MR as 'a wide and, indeed, revolutionary discretion' in *Re Steed's Will Trusts* [1960] Ch 407, one of the early cases decided under the new jurisdiction.

(a) Why was the Act passed?

The Variation of Trusts Act 1958 was introduced after the Law Reform Committee Report was published in 1957. The committee had criticised the case of *Chapman* v. *Chapman* [1954] AC 429 and the limitations placed on the circumstances when the court can intervene and vary the terms of a trust. These limitations arose mainly as a result of the limited definition given by the House of Lords as to what constitutes 'a compromise'. Such limitations had not applied to courts when authorising a variation before *Chapman* v. *Chapman*. The Law Reform Committee suggested that a variation should be allowed even where the principal reason was reduction in tax liability.

(b) Main changes introduced by the Act

Under s.1(1) the court has the power to vary or revoke all or any of the trusts or enlarge the powers of the trustees of managing or administering any of the property subject to the trusts. Property includes both real and personal property.

The Act can be applied retrospectively so it can apply to any trust including those created before the Act was passed.

The court can intervene and approve any scheme on behalf of beneficiaries who cannot consent on behalf of themselves but where a beneficiary can consent on his or her own behalf the court will not act.

Save for one category of applicant any variation must be for the 'benefit' of the beneficiaries. Benefit has been widely defined.

(c) Categories of people on whose behalf the court can act

Under the Act a court may make an order approving a scheme varying a trust on behalf of the following categories of people:

s.1(1)(a) any person having, directly or indirectly, an interest, whether vested or contingent, under the trusts who by reason of infancy or other incapacity is incapable of assenting.

This category includes both children and also anyone suffering from a mental disability. It is the section that will apply whenever the beneficiaries cannot assent to a variation because they are either too young or mentally incapable of assenting.

s.1(1)(b) any person (whether ascertained or not) who may become entitled, directly or indirectly, to an interest under the trusts as being at a future date or on the happening of a future event a person of any specified description or a member of any specified class of persons, so however that this paragraph shall not include any person who would be of that description, or member of that class, as the case may be, if the said date had fallen or the said event had happened at the date of the application to the court.

This category is the most complex of all the categories as it covers possible beneficiaries who may arise in the future if certain events occur or arise. This section is intended to cover situations where the entitlement of a beneficiary is dependent on the happening of some future event.

(d) Who is excluded from this section?

The Act does not allow the court to authorise a variation on behalf of an adult beneficiary who could give consent personally but it is difficult in practical terms to gain consent from them.

Knocker v. *Youle* [1986] 1 WLR 934

An example arose in this case where a complex trust had been created in favour of a number of beneficiaries including the settlor's daughter who held a power of appointment and then in default of appointment ultimately the property was to pass to the daughter's cousins. She had many cousins including a number in Australia. An application was brought by the daughter to vary the terms of the will under s.1(1)(b). However the court held that it would be possible to gain the consent of the cousins as they were already ascertained under the will and they were alive and so the court was unable to give its consent to the variation. In spite of the fact that in this case it would have been very difficult to find the various cousins and to gain their consent.

EXAMPLE

Stella leaves her house on trust for her sister Peta for life and on her death to anyone of the family who is a practising lawyer at the time of her death. At the time the trust was created it would not have been possible to know who were going to be practising lawyers at the time of Stella's death. The court would be able to give consent.

Compare the facts of the case below.

Re Suffert [1961] Ch 1

A settlement had been created in 1935 in favour of the settlor for life and on his death on protective trusts for the settlor's daughter and eventually for the daughter's statutory next of kin. The daughter applied to vary the trust. At the time of the application there were three people alive who would be her statutory next of kin. The court had to consider whether it could give consent on their behalf. The cousins were in existence at the time of the application and if the daughter had died just before the application was heard the cousins would have been able to claim the share. For this reason the court held that they could not give consent.

The court cannot give consent on behalf of a beneficiary who is in existence and who would be entitled had the event occurred at the time of the application.

(e) Section 1(1)(c) 'any person unborn'

The court will only consent under this section where there is a genuine possibility that children could be born after the variation and thereby be affected by it. However the court will not consent where the likelihood of children being born to the beneficiary is impossible.

This can be illustrated by the approach taken in *Re Pettifor's Will Trusts* [1966] Ch 257 where the court held that it was not necessary to seek approval on behalf of unborn children of a woman aged 78. Pennycuick J. described the way the trustees should proceed in such cases: 'Trustees can with complete safety and propriety deal with their funds on the basis that a woman of 70 will not have a further child.'

Of course in a world where science has enabled children to be born to older and older mothers such a view may have to be revised.

(f) Section (1)(d) 'any person in respect of any discretionary interest of his under protective trusts where the interest of the principal beneficiary has not failed or determined'

The approach of the court to applications under this section are slightly different from applications under the other three subsections because there is no necessity to prove that the variation is for the benefit of the trust:

the court may, if it likes, disregard the question whether any benefit is provided or not.
(Danckwerts J. in *Re Turner's Will Trusts*
[1960] Ch 122)

However the court will still consider the application as a whole before exercising its discretion.

EXAMPLE

Damien is 38 years old. He is married with two children Rocky and Sasha. He has had a gambling problem all his life and his father is concerned about the way he might deal with any money if he transfers it to him outright. He creates a protective trust on the following terms: 'To Damien for life until he becomes bankrupt and remainder to be held on discretionary trust for Rocky and Sasha.' Damien has a life interest and Rocky and Sasha both have a discretionary interest under a protective trust until Damien becomes bankrupt in which case he must forfeit his interest in their favour.

If Damien undergoes treatment for his gambling condition, he may apply to the court to authorise his determinable life interest to become an absolute interest.

Alternatively if Damien suddenly becomes wealthy an application could be made to the court to authorise a change in the terms creating absolute interests for Rocky and Sasha requiring Damien to release his life interest.

(g) What is meant by benefit?

The Variation of Trusts Act is based on the principle that a variation must be of benefit to the person on whose behalf the court is consenting. Benefits can be split between financial and non-financial benefits.

Financial benefits mainly cover a reduction in tax liability such as those contemplated in *Chapman* v. *Chapman*. It also covers other benefits: 'the word benefit ... is ... not confined to financial benefit, but may extend to moral or social benefit'.

The problem is trying to measure what is benefit and the amount of benefit. There is often an overlap between the two and the courts may try to offset a financial advantage against other disadvantages. An example of this lies in *Re Weston's Settlement*.

(i) Financial benefit

Re Seale's Marriage Settlement [1961] 3 All ER 136

This case concerned a trust created in England for the benefit of a husband, his wife and their children. A short time after the children were born the family emigrated to Canada. An application was made some years after they had emigrated to transfer the trust to Canada and to appoint Canadian trustees which would bring some tax advantages and would benefit the children. The court approved the scheme on the basis that the family had not left England in order to avoid tax but to resettle in Canada.

A different view was taken in the following case.

Re Weston's Settlement [1969] 1 Ch 223

An application to vary a trust where the family had left England to live in Jersey was refused. Two settlements had been created by Mr Weston in favour of his two sons and their children. He was a highly successful businessman and had placed large shareholdings in both trusts. As a result of a statutory change the shareholdings would now attract capital gains tax. In order to avoid the tax liability the settlor sought to vary the terms of the trusts by transferring them to Jersey. In order to do so the sons would have to take up residence in Jersey with their families. The court was asked to sanction the variation on behalf of the children and any future unborn children. The Court of Appeal refused holding that the transfer would not be of benefit to the children because although it was of financial benefit this was outweighed by the fact that it was not of social and other benefit to the beneficiaries. The court was also persuaded by the fact that the primary purpose of the application was to avoid tax.

This case suggests that a court may place greater weight on non-financial benefit than a financial benefit to the trust:

There are many things in life worth more than money ... I do not think it will be for the benefit of the children to be uprooted from England and transported to another country simply to avoid tax.

(Lord Denning MR)

This case is unusual and most cases involving a financial benefit to the beneficiaries will be authorised even where it involves some potential risk.

The court authorised a variation in *Ridgwell* v. *Ridgwell* [2007] EWHC 2666 which was primarily to avoid the payment of inheritance tax and capital gains tax and the court were prepared to uphold this on their behalf.

(ii) Non-financial benefit

Re Remnant's Settlement Trusts [1970] Ch 560

The court deleted a forfeiture clause in a settlement that would apply if the beneficiaries who were the daughters of the settlor either married a Roman Catholic or someone who practised Roman Catholicism. The husband and children of one of the daughters were Roman Catholics. Both the sisters applied to the court for authorisation to delete it because of the difficulties it could potentially bring to the families. The court approved this in spite of the fact that the children of the sister who had not married a Roman Catholic would lose financially. The court justified this by suggesting that there were benefits to all the children because the forfeiture clause could affect the choice of a future spouse.

(iii) Are the settlor's intentions relevant?

The court does not refuse approval under the Act where evidence is brought that the variation would be contrary to the intentions of the settlor. This Act concentrates far more on what benefit is derived from the variation for the beneficiaries under the trust.

At first decisions placed some weight on the settlor's intentions but later cases now view such intentions as far less important.

Compare these two cases.

Re Steed's Will Trusts [1960] Ch 407

Trust property, including a farm, had been left by the testator on protective trusts for the claimant for her life and on her death for whomever she had appointed. The testator wanted the claimant, who had been the testator's housekeeper during his lifetime, to be well provided for after his death. However he did not want her to have an absolute interest in the trust property because he did not trust her brother. The trustees were given power to appoint capital payments to the claimant and they could do so by selling the farm. The claimant applied for a variation of the terms of the trust which would remove the protective trusts and would then allow her to appoint to herself the farm. The variation would then make her absolute owner of the property. The court refused to authorise this. It was influenced by the settlor's wish to prevent the claimant from having access to the capital of the estate.

Goulding v. *James* [1997] 2 All ER 239

This case illustrates very well how comparatively little weight is now given to the wishes and intentions of the settlor. The testatrix had left her residuary estate on trust for her daughter June for life, with remainder for her grandson Marcus if he attained the age of 40. There was a further provision that if he died before his mother or before he reached the stipulated age any children that he had at his death would be able to share the capital absolutely. The testatrix died and at her death June and Marcus applied to the court for approval of an arrangement varying their interests under the trust. June was to take 45 per cent and Marcus was also to take 45 per cent and the remaining 10 per cent would be held for any unborn children of Marcus. There was evidence that the testatrix had not wanted her daughter June to be entitled to the capital because she was concerned about her son-in-law and his influence over her daughter. The testatrix had also wanted to delay her grandson's interest because of his lifestyle and she wanted him to become more mature before he received the capital. An application had to be made on behalf of the unborn children of Marcus.

The Court of Appeal was prepared to approve of the variation because the application satisfied the key criteria which was that it was for the benefit of any unborn children of Marcus.

EXAMPLE

Hans wishes to leave his estate to his daughter Juno and his two grandchildren Klaus and Lara who are both over 18 but he is concerned about his son-in-law Olaf who is often unemployed and spends money very lavishly. He draws up a trust whereby his daughter will receive income from the trust for her life and on her death the estate would be transferred to the children once they attained the age of 30. The trust also provided that if any of the children should die before reaching the age of 30 any of their children living at the date of their death should be able to take the capital. On Hans' death Juno applies to the court for a variation in the terms of the trust allowing two-thirds of the fund to be divided between herself and the two children and the remaining one-third to be held on trust for the children of Klaus and Lara.

Will the court be bound by the wishes of Hans?

It is unlikely that the court will follow *Re Steed's Will Trust* [1960] Ch 407 because there is a benefit for the unborn children of Klaus and Lara as they will now receive a fixed share whereas before they were not entitled to any part of the estate unless one or both of the children died before their thirtieth birthday.

(h) There must be variation and not a complete resettlement

In making any variation the court is anxious to avoid authorising a complete resettlement. However the courts have had difficulties in distinguishing between the two.

Megarry J. described the difference between a variation and a resettlement in *Re Ball's Settlement* [1968] 1 WLR 899: 'if an arrangement changes the whole substratum of the trust, then it may well be that it cannot be regarded merely as varying that trust'.

He continued by distinguishing when the court can intervene:

but if an arrangement, while leaving the substratum, effectuates the purpose of the original trust by other means, it may still be possible to regard that arrangement as merely varying the original trusts, even though the means as employed are wholly different and even though the form is completely changed.

(i) A variation and not a resettlement: authorisation granted by the courts

Re Holt's Settlement Trusts [1969] 1 Ch 100

The terms of a settlement were that the property was to be held for a mother for her life and then for any of her children who attained the age of 21. The scheme proposed to the court would allow her to transfer half the income from the trust to the children but their right to capital would be postponed until they reached the age of 30. This was authorised by the court because it was a genuine variation of the original terms of the trust.

(j) A resettlement of the original trust: authorisation refused by the courts

Re T's Settlement Trusts [1964] Ch 158

A settlement gave a minor the right to 25 per cent of the income from the trust once she attained her majority. The minor's mother applied to the court for the share of the income to be held on protective trusts for her daughter for her life and remainder to her children. The court viewed this as a complete resettlement of the trust and the application was refused.

Wyndham v. Egremont [2009] WTLR 1473

The issue of resettlement was considered recently in this case where the court was asked to approve a variation of a settlement concerning property in the Petworth estate in West Sussex. The purpose of the new arrangement had two aims: (a) to ensure the line of succession of the estate was attached to the two baronies and to devolve down the male line; (b) to ensure that tax liability was deferred by extending the applicable trust period.

Blackburne J. concluded that although this made considerable changes to the trust this was not a resettlement but a variation of the terms of a trust. He concluded:

> I have no doubt that the alterations to the pre-arrangement trusts contained in the arrangement which I have approved constitute a variation of those trusts and not a resettlement. The trustees remain the same, the subsisting trusts remain largely unaltered and the administrative provisions affecting them are wholly unaltered and the administrative provisions affecting them are wholly unchanged.

SUMMARY

This chapter examines the power of the court to intervene and vary a trust. Once a trust is fully constituted the terms cannot generally be varied and the wishes of a settlor will be carried out by the trustees. However the court has always had some limited powers to vary the terms of a trust in a genuine emergency and compromise. It also held power to vary a trust under a number of statutory provisions. Each of these had limitations and in many cases the court found it was unable to act. The limitations on the court's power to intervene became more pronounced after the case of *Chapman* v. *Chapman*. In this case the House of Lords held that the court could only intervene where there was a genuine dispute about the rights of the beneficiaries rather than unanimous agreement between the trustees that a trust should be varied. The rule in *Saunders* v. *Vautier* allows beneficiaries some control over variation of a trust but it can only be invoked where all the beneficiaries are of full age and are in agreement and are as a group entitled to the property. This rule has limitations as it cannot apply where the beneficiaries disagree or are not of full age and not fully entitled to the trust property. The Variation of Trusts Act has given the court very wide powers to authorise a variation in the terms of a trust if it is for the benefit of a beneficiary. Benefit has been widely defined and usually means financial benefit although it can include non-financial benefit as in *Re Remnant's Settlement Trusts* where the court deleted a forfeiture clause preventing the beneficiaries from benefiting under the trust if they married a Roman Catholic or practised Roman Catholicism. The court can act for a range of beneficiaries but only where they are unable to give consent to a variation themselves. The court cannot act on behalf of a beneficiary who could give consent personally. The courts cannot intervene where the terms proposed are not a variation but a complete resettlement of the trust as shown in *Re T's Settlement Trusts*.

17 Fiduciary duties and breach of fiduciary duties

KEY POINTS

- a fiduciary is someone who has agreed to act on behalf of another and owes particular duties;
- fiduciary duties include loyalty, good faith, not to profit from his position;
- a fiduciary relationship is automatically imposed in some relationships such as trustee–beneficiary, solicitor–client and director–board of directors; these relationships are fiduciary per se;
- some relationships are not automatically fiduciary but may become fiduciary in certain circumstances;
- examples of when a relationship may become fiduciary include where two people enter a joint venture or where an employee receives confidential information from his employer;
- fiduciary duties are applied strictly and it does not make any difference whether the fiduciary acted in good faith;
- the remedy for breach of fiduciary duties is restitution by the fiduciary which could take effect as a personal or proprietary remedy;
- under a personal remedy a trustee must account for any unauthorised profits to the trust;
- a fiduciary may hold unauthorised profits on constructive trust for his/her principal which would take effect as a proprietary remedy; and
- in limited circumstances a fiduciary may retain profits received through his/her position but generally only where permission has been granted by the principal or beneficiaries or from the court or the trust instrument.

1 THE NATURE OF A FIDUCIARY RELATIONSHIP

The fiduciary relationship is notoriously difficult to define. Fiduciary duties arise in a number of relationships and include core duties of good faith, loyalty and trust and a duty on behalf of the fiduciary not to put himself into a position where his personal interests conflict with his duties to his principal. Fiduciary duties are applied strictly and the court does not consider whether the fiduciary was acting in good faith when considering whether there has been a breach.

In *Bristol and West Building Society* v. *Mothew* [1998] Ch 1 Millett LJ described a fiduciary in the following terms: 'a fiduciary is someone who has undertaken to act for or on behalf of another in a particular manner in circumstances which give rise to a relationship of trust and confidence. The distinguishing obligation of a fiduciary is the obligation of loyalty.'

The reason for such strict enforcement is based on public policy reasons. The law is anxious to ensure that no fiduciary ever considers putting himself in a position where his personal interests and his duty to his principal conflict.

EXAMPLE

Leonard was appointed last year as trustee to a family trust set up by an old friend, Mehmet. The trust has a number of assets including shares in a private company called Cars for All Occasions owned by his friend. At a meeting of trustees he hears that the company has accepted an offer by another firm and it is likely that the shares will double in value. Leonard would like to purchase shares for himself before they increase in value. If he does so and makes a profit he will have to account to the trust for the shares. He has used the information that he has received for his own personal profit and the court will hold that he is in breach of the fiduciary duty that he owes to the beneficiaries of the trust.

Fiduciary relationships can be split into fiduciary relationships per se and fiduciary relationships arising within a particular context.

(a) Fiduciary relationships per se

Certain relationships automatically give rise to fiduciary duties. These include trustee–beneficiary, principal–agent, solicitor–client, mortgagees–mortgagors, company directors–the company and partners within a partnership.

The main feature of all these relationships is that in each one party is acting on behalf of another. This gives rise to scope for abuse of his/her position.

If a company director uses information that he finds out through his position, he cannot use that information for his own personal gain.

EXAMPLE

Peter sits on the board of a company carrying out exploratory work in the North Sea for gas fields. The company has found a potential field some distance from the east coast and a decision is taken by the board that the company will not pursue this on the grounds of cost. Peter decides to continue with the exploration himself and engages a firm of mining engineers to carry out the work. They find an extensive oilfield and Peter makes a huge personal profit for himself. This would be viewed as a breach of the fiduciary duty he owes to the company which arises automatically and although it did not want to continue to explore the mining potential of the area itself Peter has used the information for personal gain.

(b) Fiduciary relationships arising within a particular context

Some relationships do not automatically give rise to fiduciary duties but the courts could always find a fiduciary relationship where certain circumstances arise. An example would be the relationship of employer–employee. This relationship is not fiduciary per se. In many employment relationships fiduciary duties are not owed automatically but may arise in the context of the particular job because of the information that you receive through your employment.

Cobbetts v. *Hodge* [2009] EWHC 786 Ch

This case concerned a solicitor who had acquired shares in a company who were clients of his employers. It was held that he had to account for the shares to his employers as the opportunity to purchase them had come to him while he was in the firm's employment. In this case the solicitor was responsible for introducing business to his employers and he was paid a commission to do this and in this relationship he owed a fiduciary duty to the firm and must not misuse his position.

Likewise in many commercial contexts no fiduciary duties are automatically owed. However fiduciary duties may arise in the course of negotiations when information may be acquired within the commercial context and if that information is used for a personal gain the courts may decide that a fiduciary relationship has arisen.

2 THE ROLE OF FIDUCIARY RELATIONSHIPS IN ENGLISH LAW

A fiduciary will not be liable for all aspects of a fiduciary relationship. The law holds that not all fiduciary duties owed by a fiduciary carry the same liability.

An example would be a solicitor–client relationship. The relationship between the two is fiduciary per se and if at any time the solicitor put his own position before that of the client and made a personal gain through his position he would be accountable.

However where in the relationship he undertakes an ordinary duty expected of a solicitor, e.g. acting in a transaction on behalf of the client then the duty owed by the solicitor is confined to the professional relationship.

If the solicitor gives negligent advice in his professional capacity, the solicitor is not in breach of his fiduciary duty, but in breach of his duty of care.

It is also possible for fiduciary duties to no longer apply after the relationship has lapsed.

Attorney–General v. *Blake* [1998] Ch 1

This case shows that the fiduciary relationship can last after someone has left employment but it will not last indefinitely. Blake was a member of the Crown Secret Intelligence Service for nearly thirty years. He became an agent for the former Soviet Union and worked for them for ten years. For this he was eventually arrested and convicted of offences under the Official Secrets Act 1911 and was sent to prison for forty-two years. He escaped to the Soviet Union and wrote a book concerning his life as an agent. He had not sought permission from his previous employers, the Crown. The Attorney-General acting on behalf of the Crown tried to recover the profits he made on the sales of his book. As he had left employment in 1961 nearly thirty years before he published his book he argued that he no longer owed fiduciary duties to the Crown.

The Court of Appeal held that while he was employed by the Crown he owed fiduciary duties but once he left those duties ceased and the publication of the book was not a breach of fiduciary duty. However, he was held to be in breach of contract.

3 PURCHASE OF TRUST PROPERTY

The purchase of trust property by a trustee is strictly controlled. There is scope for the trustee to make a personal profit out of the transaction by purchasing the property at undervalue. A trustee cannot grant or sell trust property to himself under the self-dealing rule and if he does so it will be voidable at the instance of the beneficiaries. Where he purchases trust property from a beneficiary under the fair-dealing rule he must prove that the transaction was fair.

(a) What is the self-dealing rule?

The self-dealing rule prevents a trustee from purchasing trust property from the trust. In effect the trustee would be purchasing the property from himself because he holds the legal title to the property in his name.

The nature of the rule was described by Megarry VC in *Tito* v. *Waddell* (*No. 2*) [1977] Ch 106:

the self-dealing rule is ... that if a trustee sells trust property to himself, the sale is voidable by any beneficiary ... however fair the transaction.

EXAMPLE

Tony is trustee of a trust fund which includes 'Sailors Rest', a house by the sea near Whitby. The beneficiaries Sam, Rory and Phil are all over 18 years old and are the three children of the settlor, Don. After Don's death Tony decides to purchase the house for himself. He pays the market value of the property. Can Tony keep the house?

In purchasing trust property Tony is self-dealing. The transaction is voidable by any or all of the beneficiaries.

The beneficiaries are able to set the transaction aside or they can decide to adopt it. Once they have all adopted it, the court will uphold the trustee's purchase.

In this case if Sam, Rory and Phil all agree to the sale, then it cannot later be challenged unless they were not fully informed about certain details for instance development potential of the property known only to Tony.

(b) The self-dealing rule applied in practice

Kane v. *Radley–Kane* [1999] Ch 274

An example of circumstances when the self-dealing rule has been applied occurred in this case. The administrator of the estate of an intestate person purchased property for herself. She was the wife of the deceased and was also stepmother to his children. She transferred some shares from the estate into her own name which were worth £50,000 at the date of his death. Within a few years the value of the shares had increased to over £1.1 million. One of the stepchildren challenged the sale on the basis of the self-dealing rule.

The stepmother argued that as she could claim a statutory legacy under the intestacy rules worth £125,000 she was justified in claiming the shares. The court set aside the transaction. She had allowed her personal interest to conflict with her duty as administrator of the estate and the transaction could be rendered void by the beneficiaries.

Scott VC commented: 'in taking the Shiredean shares in satisfaction of her £125,000 statutory legacy she was entering into a transaction in which her duty and interest conflicted'.

Examples of when the self-dealing rule will not apply

The self-dealing rule can continue to apply to a trustee after he has retired if the object of retirement was to purchase trust property. Once some time has elapsed then the rule no longer applies to a trustee.

In *Re Boles and British Land Co.'s Contract* [1902] 244 a trustee purchased trust property twelve years after he had retired. It was held that the rule no longer applied to him.

Holder v. *Holder* [1968] Ch 353

The courts also adopted a less strict approach in this case. The testator died leaving his younger son, one of his daughters and his wife to act as executors. The property included two farms. The son renounced his executorship very soon after appointment having only carried out a few administrative functions and he then purchased one of the farms in the estate at a public auction. Another son sought to dispute the sale and have it set aside on the basis of the self-dealing rule. The Court of Appeal held that as he had only carried out administrative functions he had never strictly acted as executor and so the self-dealing rule could not be invoked against him. He had not been involved in the auction nor had he instructed the auctioneer.

The rule will also only apply once the trustee has been appointed and cannot be applied to transactions entered into before appointment.

Exceptions to the self-dealing rule:

1 consent from the beneficiaries;
2 authorisation from the court;
3 the trust instrument grants permission to the trustee to purchase the trust property;
4 the beneficiaries delay in objecting to the transaction. If the beneficiaries object to the transaction, they must do so within a reasonable time.

(c) What is the fair-dealing rule?

This rule is less strict than the self-dealing rule. Here the trustee purchases property from the beneficiary. The law is less stringent in these cases because the trustee is not purchasing from himself but from a beneficiary. However although such a sale carries less risk of a conflict of interest the onus will be on the trustee to show that the transaction was fair.

The trustee must show that it was at arm's length and the beneficiary was fully aware of all the material facts.

(d) Other property transactions

Renewal of a lease

If a trustee seeks to renew a lease for himself, then this also would be considered a personal profit and renewal would be refused. The best illustration of this rule can be found in the following case.

Keech v. Sandford (1726) Sel Cas Ch 61

This case shows how strictly fiduciary duties are applied. Property in a trust created in favour of a minor consisted of the profits of Romford market which was held under a lease. When the lease expired the trustee tried to renew the lease first on behalf of the beneficiary but this was refused although the landlord was prepared to renew in favour of the trustee but only in his personal capacity not as trustee. After this was done the trustee's actions were challenged on behalf of the beneficiaries. The court held that the trustee held the lease on constructive trust for the beneficiaries and must account for any profits he received although it was accepted that the trustee had acted in good faith throughout. The danger was that if the trustee were to be allowed to keep the lease for himself there would be an incentive not to press for renewal. See also Chapter 10 on constructive trusts.

Lord King VC:

it may seem hard that the trustee is the only person of all mankind who might not have the benefit of the lease; but it is very proper that the rule should be strictly pursued and not in the least relaxed; for it is very obvious what would be the consequences of letting the trustees have the lease.

4 TRUSTEES WHO MAKE UNAUTHORISED PROFITS FROM THEIR POSITION

The fiduciary has a duty to account for any unauthorised profits which he makes from his position. This is strictly applied and the courts do not distinguish between cases where the fiduciary acts in good faith with cases where the fiduciary acts dishonestly or fraudulently.

The general rule is that any profit received by someone in his capacity as trustee or fiduciary must account for that profit and it cannot be retained.

The rule is laid down in *Bray* v. *Ford* [1896] AC 44 by Lord Herschell:

It is an inflexible rule of the court of equity that a person in a fiduciary position, such as the respondent, is not, unless otherwise expressly provided, entitled to make a profit: he is not allowed to put himself in a position where his interest and his duty conflict.

The inflexibility of the rule is illustrated by the following case.

Boardman v. Phipps [1967] 2 AC 46

This case shows that even where the fiduciary has acted in the best interests of the trust any profit made must be accounted to the principal. A trust had been created for the settlor's family. The solicitor to the trust Mr Boardman was concerned about one of the investments which was a private company. He decided that the only solution would be for the trust to take control of the company so new management could be appointed which he anticipated would result in the company becoming profitable. He suggested to the trustees that they purchase more shares but they did not support this so instead he purchased the shares personally with one of the trustees. As a result of his actions the company became profitable. Both the trust and Mr Boardman made a profit. One of the beneficiaries claimed that Mr Boardman should transfer any profit to the trust because he had allowed his fiduciary duty and his personal interest to conflict.

The House of Lords held that he must return any profit made to the beneficiaries. Exceptionally in this case the court ordered a sum of money to be paid to him as compensation for his contribution towards the profitability of the trust.

It is possible to criticise the strict application of the rule here. If Mr Boardman had not intervened in the way that he did, the trust would have been far less profitable and the beneficiaries would have been far worse off.

Regal Hastings v. Gulliver [1942] 1 All ER

This case is another example of the strictness of the rule against even a bona fide fiduciary. The claimant company Regal purchased two cinemas. The company already owned a cinema and the company intended to sell the three cinemas together. The company formed a subsidiary company to pay for the purchase but it could not raise sufficient cash to pay. Four of the directors of the company purchased the shares for themselves personally and then later sold the shares for a profit. At all times the directors had acted in good faith but the company successfully claimed the profit made on the sale of the shares.

The rule of equity which insists on those, who by use of a fiduciary position make a profit, being liable to account for that profit, in no way depends on fraud, or absence of *bona fides*.

(Lord Russell)

(a) Should the rule against the receipt of unauthorised profits obtained by fiduciaries be reviewed?

The strictness of the rule has been criticised in more recent cases.

Murad v. Al-Saraji [2005] EWCA Civ 959

In this case the Court of Appeal unanimously criticised the strict rule which forces fiduciaries to account for any gain received from their position even where they have acted in good faith. A hotel was purchased for £4.1 million as a joint venture by two sisters who contributed £1 million and Mr Al-Saraji £500,000. The price was in fact £3.6 million and Mr Al-Saraji contributed nothing towards the sale. The sisters claimed that Mr Al-Saraji should be accountable for the discrepancy in the price and it should be paid to them on the basis that he owed them a fiduciary duty. He was in breach when he did not disclose the fact that the price had been reduced and he was not paying any money towards the purchase because the vendor owed him money. Reluctantly the Court of Appeal held that Mr Al-Saraji had to account for the discrepancy in the payment even though the sisters would have pursued the deal in any event.

Consider the following comments from Arden LJ:

It may be that the time has come when the court should revisit the operation of the often inflexible rule of equity in harsh circumstances, as where the trustee has acted in perfect good faith and without deception or concealment, and in belief he was acting in the best interests of the beneficiary ... It would not be impossible for a modern court to conclude as a matter of policy that, without losing any of the deterrent effect of the rule, the harshness of it should be tempered in some circumstances.

Unauthorised profits can arise in other contexts.

(i) A director's fees

It may be necessary to hold shares in a company in order to qualify as a director. Where a trustee uses the trust shareholding to become a director of a company the trustee cannot keep the remuneration payable to him as a director for himself.

In *Re Macadam* [1946] Ch 73 trustees who had appointed themselves as directors through provisions in the will and then received payment had to account for this to the trust. They could not keep it for themselves.

The judge in the case summed up the position as follows:

Did he acquire the position in respect of which he drew the remuneration by virtue of his position as trustee? In the present case there can be no doubt that the only way in which the plaintiffs became directors was by the exercise of the powers vested in the trustees of the will under article 68 of the articles of association of the company.

(Cohen J.)

Where the appointment as director is not directly linked to the trust then the trustee is entitled to retain any remuneration paid even if the trust has a shareholding in the company.

The trustee may also retain the director's remuneration if this is expressly authorised under the trust instrument.

In *Re Llewellin's Will Trust* [1949] 1 Ch 225 the trust instrument expressly allowed the trustees to appoint themselves as directors and it was accepted that as an appointment as a director would also allow them to award themselves remuneration they should be able to keep this for themselves.

(ii) Commission

A trustee must also account for any commission that he receives directly as a result of his position.

In *Williams* v. *Barton* [1927] 2 Ch 9 a trustee who was also a stockbroker's clerk received a sum in commission for himself having introduced the trust to the firm of stockbrokers. A second trustee successfully claimed that the sum should be held for the trust because the trustee had received the commission directly through his role as trustee.

(iii) Profits received in competition with the trust

Where the trust assets include a business the trustee must not set up in competition with the trust. Competition will depend on the facts.

In *Re Thomson* [1930] the court held there was breach of the trustee's fiduciary duty where he set up as a yacht broker which was in direct competition with the yacht-broking business which was one of the principal assets of the trust.

When a trustee or fiduciary ceases his duties then competition is permissible.

5 BRIBES

If a trustee or fiduciary receives a bribe which arises because of his position, the bribe must be accounted to his principal or the trust and must be returned to the principal together with any profit made as a result of the bribe. The law can either hold that the sum received is held on constructive trust or that the fiduciary is personally liable to return the bribe.

Originally it was held that only the sum of the bribe must be returned and any profit made could be retained by the fiduciary.

Lister & Co. v. *Stubbs* (1890) 45 Ch D 1

An agent Stubbs who was responsible for engaging suppliers for his principal received bribes from another company to ensure that the work was given to it. Stubbs invested the bribes and made a further sum of money. The Court of Appeal held that the bribe must be returned but not the increase in value. The relationship was not one of constructive trust but a debtor–creditor relationship arising in contract where Stubbs was regarded as the debtor of Lister & Co.

This approach although subject to considerable criticism was left unchanged for almost one hundred years until the Privy Council decision in *Attorney-General for Hong Kong* v. *Reid* (1994) (below). Although a decision of the Privy Council is not strictly binding on English courts, it was followed in other decisions in the UK courts.

Attorney–General for Hong Kong v. Reid [1994] 1 All ER 1

This case concerned a public prosecutor for the Hong Kong government. During the course of his work he received a number of bribes from defendants. He used the money to purchase three houses in New Zealand which had increased in value. The Privy Council held that the Crown was entitled to claim the houses which included the increase in value.

The Privy Council applied the maxim of equity that 'equity sees that as done which ought to be done'. It meant that the law regarded the bribes as the property of the Crown as soon as it was received by Reid.

According to Lord Templeman:

As soon as the bribe was received it should have been paid or transferred ... to the person who suffered from the breach of duty. Equity considered as done that which ought to be done. As soon as the bribe was received ... the false fiduciary held the bribe on a constructive trust for the person injured.

Daraydan Holding Ltd v. Solland International Ltd [2005] Ch 119

Attorney-General for Hong Kong v. *Reid* was subsequently followed in this case which concerned the receipt of bribes by Mr Khalid a fiduciary who acted for a property company which was engaged in developing properties. Mr Khalid was responsible as the company's agent for obtaining quotations for work to be carried out on the properties and he received a personal profit from one company and it was held that following *Attorney-General for Hong Kong* v. *Reid* this must be accounted for to the developers.

EXAMPLE

Shane works for a large garden centre called West Country Gardens in their advice department. Shane is often asked to recommend garden designers and planners. He is approached by SmartGardens Ltd who design gardens. Martin who is their managing director offers Shane £750 for every customer of West Country Gardens who uses SmartGardens Ltd. He asks Shane to give them the work rather than anyone else. Over two years Shane receives over £50,000 which he invests in shares in Garden Products. The shares double in value due to a successful promotion. Can Shane keep the shares?

Shane cannot keep the shares because he purchased them with the money received from Martin. According to Lord Templeman in *Attorney-General for Hong-Kong* v. *Reid* as soon as Shane received the money it should have been transferred to the person suffering the breach of duty in this case, his employers West Country Gardens. The money is held on constructive trust and where it is applied to purchase property the person suffering the breach of duty can claim the property rather than just the bribe itself.

Attorney-General for Hong Kong v. *Reid* has now been doubted by *Sinclair Investments* v. *Versailles Trade Finance* [2011] EWCA Civ 34 discussed below.

6 USE OF CONFIDENTIAL INFORMATION AND OPPORTUNITIES

Where someone such as a director of a company receives information concerning an opportunity through his/her company and uses that information for personal gain they are liable to account for any profits they receive through exploitation of that opportunity. The law has been very strict in this area.

An example arose in the following case.

IDC v. *Cooley* [1972] 1 WLR 443

The managing director of IDC, Mr Cooley was offered a contract personally by the Eastern Gas Board to build new gas depots. He was responsible for negotiating such contracts on behalf of IDC but the Gas Board had refused to negotiate with his company. Although he was taking an opportunity which would never have been available to IDC he was still held liable to account for any profit he had received. The court was influenced by the fact that he had been released from his role as managing director by falsely claiming that he was ill.

Confidential information is regarded as property belonging to a fiduciary's principal so if it is exploited the profits can be claimed by the principal. This goes to the heart of the fiduciary relationship. It is a relationship that is based on loyalty to the principal and also trust and confidence.

(a) What does confidential information mean?

If through one's position either as an employee or as a company director someone hears of a business opportunity which is not in the public domain that information is regarded as confidential.

EXAMPLE

Sayeed owns a company Crystal Clear Drinks which produces mineral water which sells at a premium price. He is negotiating with Rashid who has a soft drinks firm to amalgamate their businesses. They enter into negotiations to purchase land in Derbyshire and through the negotiations they hear that there are possible springs located on some land (Plot One) which can be used to source mineral water. They also hear that this extends to neighbouring land (Plot Two) they jointly buy Plot One but Sayeed puts in a private bid to buy Plot Two for himself and he successfully purchases the land. He develops the land and makes a profit for himself.

Rashid claims the profit and the law is likely to uphold his claim. It would not matter that Rashid had no intention of pursuing the opportunity himself. It is the fact that the information about the possibility of further sources of mineral water was received in the course of negotiations that matters in this case.

(b) When will use of confidential information be regarded as breach of a fiduciary duty?

LAC Minerals Ltd v. International Corona Resources Ltd (1989) 61 DLR (4th) 14

This case concerned two companies who were negotiating at arm's length about a possible joint venture between them to exploit minerals. The claimants owned the land where the minerals were located but through investigation it became apparent to both parties that there was a chance that there were minerals in neighbouring land. The land was put up for sale and the defendants purchased it in spite of a competing offer from the claimants. The defendants then developed the mine for themselves without the consent of the claimants. The court held that a fiduciary relationship had arisen as soon as the negotiations had been entered into and all confidential information received during those negotiations would be held for them both jointly. If one party used that information for himself, it would be a breach of the duty owed.

Sinclair Investment Holding SA v. Versailles Trade Finance Ltd

In this case the court revisited the issues arising from the use of confidential information by a fiduciary. (This case is also relevant to issues arising concerning the liability of a stranger for breach of trust, the topic of Chapter 19.)

The Versailles Group was a large company in which a number of smaller companies had interests including Marrlist Ltd owned by Mr Cushnie who also had a direct interest in the Versailles Group and was a director. The group was involved in a scheme where goods were purchased at a low discounted price and sold on at full price thereby making a large profit. Sinclair Investment Holdings funded purchases of these goods to the value of £2.35 million. A term was inserted into the agreement between Sinclair and Versailles that any money lent that was not used for buying and selling goods would be held on trust. In fact Versailles did not use the money in the way agreed but instead used it for the company's own purposes to improve its overall trading position. Mr Cushnie made a personal gain because his shareholding in Versailles increased in value as a result of the improvement to Versailles's trading position. He used the money he received to pay off a mortgage on a property he owned. Sinclair Investment Holdings argued that Mr Cushnie was in a fiduciary relationship with them and they argued that the £2.35 million was held on constructive trust for them.

Was Mr Cushnie in a fiduciary relationship with Sinclair Holdings?

Normally there would be no question that a company director would owe fiduciary duties to another company investing in the company although he would owe duties to the board of directors but it is clear that a fiduciary relationship can arise outside the usual relationships in certain circumstances.

This was outlined by Arden LJ in her judgment: 'If it is alleged that a person who does not fall within the usual categories of a fiduciary relationship, such as trustee and director, made manifest his intention to enter into a fiduciary relationship – that is, to undertake to the other a duty of loyalty – there would be sufficient pleading of fiduciary relationship.'

It was held that the claimant S Ltd was not entitled to a proprietary claim to the proceeds of sale of shares even though they had been obtained in breach of fiduciary duties owed by the defendant Mr Cushnie. Any claim against him would be personal only.

Crown Dilmun Ltd v. Sutton and Another
[2004] EWHC 52 (Ch)

This case provides another example of the extent of the liability of a fiduciary where the claimant company successfully claimed that a fiduciary had exploited opportunities that he had gained through his position as a managing director of a company. Mr Sutton was a director of a property development company. He was employed by the company and his contract contained restraint-of-trade clauses which held that after he left the company he had to keep confidential information that he had received while employed confidential and not to use this information for his own purposes. Mr Sutton became aware of an opportunity to develop Fulham Football stadium at Craven Cottage which he decided to exploit for his own personal profit, having left the employment of the company. The court held that he had not made full disclosure to the company and he was bound by the restraint of clauses so he was liable to account to the company for any profit that he had made from this opportunity.

(c) In what circumstances could a fiduciary retain a profit made from an opportunity or confidential information obtained from the fiduciary relationship?

There are several circumstances when a profit can be retained by a fiduciary.

(i) Authorisation by the principal, the court, the beneficiaries or the trust instrument allowing the fiduciary to exploit an opportunity

Queensland Mines v. *Hudson* (1978) 18 ALR 1

Mr Hudson had exploited an opportunity which he had obtained in his position as managing director of Queensland Mines and had made a personal profit. The company was involved in exploration of mining operations in Tasmania. Although the company was granted licences to start mining operations, it lacked the finance to pursue this. Mr Hudson resigned as managing director and several years later used the licences himself and eventually sold them to another company. The board of directors of Queensland Mines claimed the profits from Mr Hudson arguing that he was in breach of his fiduciary duties to the company. The Privy Council held that he could retain these profits because they had been authorised by Queensland Mines. There had been full disclosure by Mr Hudson at the time when the licences were received that he intended to use the opportunity for himself and they had agreed. It may be argued that the Privy Council had wrongly assumed that consent could be acquired from the other directors but today under the Companies Act 2006 it is provided that directors owe their duties to the company and under s.175 Companies Act 2006 the shareholders must give their consent to the director to pursue an opportunity derived from information received through the company.

In *Boardman* v. *Phipps* (discussed above) there could never have been authorisation from the trustees because in practical terms it was not possible. One of the trustees was too elderly and infirm to give consent. There was also no evidence that Mr Boardman had explained to the beneficiaries the reasons why he was purchasing the shares in the company so he could not rely on this as a defence.

(ii) Where the information or opportunity is no longer confidential but is in the public domain

> **EXAMPLE**
>
> Rosie is a trustee. The trust owns land under which lie extensive mineral deposits. During a trustees' meeting she finds out from surveyors advising the trustees that there is a strong possibility that the neighbouring land also has valuable mineral deposits. If Rosie now buys the land for herself at auction, she will be in breach of her fiduciary duty if the possibility of mineral deposits is not disclosed publicly at the auction. She will hold the land as constructive trustee for the trust.
>
> If she buys the land at auction and the particulars of sale outline the information from the surveyor that mineral deposits are likely to be found on the land, then the information is in the public domain and she will not be using information privy to her purely through her position as trustee.
>
> In *Attorney-General* v. *Blake* (discussed above) the information about Blake's activities as a spy was no longer confidential but in the public domain when he published his book and so could not be said to be in breach of a fiduciary relationship.

(iii) Where the fiduciary has retired from the relationship and sufficient time has elapsed

Island Export Finance Ltd v. *Umunna* [1986] BCC 460

This case shows that there must be a genuine lapse of time in order for the fiduciary to be able to retain any profit. Island Export Finance had a contract with the government of Cameroon to supply post boxes to it. Mr Umunna resigned from his position within the company after the contract had expired and then entered into a similar contract to supply the same post boxes to the government. While working for Island Export Finance, Mr Umunna had acquired expertise in this field which he was able to use in his new role. The company sued him for the personal profit he had received under his contract with the government. It was material to this case that the company had no wish to pursue the business once its contract to supply the government had ceased.

Compare this case.

CMS Dolphin v. Simonet [2001] 2 BCLC 704

The court held that the co-founder of an advertising agency, Mr Simonet must account for the profits that he made after leaving the advertising agency and setting up on his own to his former partner. The circumstances were that he had disagreed with the co-founder of the agency and he left taking with him a number of clients of the agency. The co-founder successfully argued that Mr Simonet had been in breach of his fiduciary duty as director of the agency in diverting work away from their advertising agency to his new agency and so he was liable to account for any profits made as constructive trustee.

7 JOINT VENTURES

Where two people agree to purchase property for the benefit of them both and one person then exploits the opportunity for personal gain the court holds that the property is held on constructive trust for them both. This is a principle from the following case.

Pallant v. Morgan [1953] Ch 43

The facts of the case concern an agreement between two people that neither would bid against the other at an auction and if one was successful in purchasing the property he would hold it on behalf of the other. It was then agreed that the defendant's agent would try to bid for the property which he successfully did. The claimant sought his share from the defendant based on their agreement.

It was held that although the terms of the agreement were not clear because they had not agreed in what shares the property was to be held nevertheless the claimant was entitled to a share.

Approval for the Pallant v. Morgan principle

The principle has been approved in later cases, in particular *Banner Homes* v. *Luff* [2000] 2 WLR 772. However the *Pallant* v. *Morgan* equity can only be raised where there is evidence of a joint venture.

8 NATURE OF THE REMEDIES FOR BREACH OF FIDUCIARY DUTY

Where a fiduciary makes an unauthorised profit he must make restitution to his principal. The fiduciary will hold the property as a constructive trustee and he may be expected to return the property or he may be expected to account personally for the profits received. The remedies are alternative and cannot both be claimed against the fiduciary.

(a) The nature of a personal remedy

In *Lister & Co.* v. *Stubbs* (discussed above) the court held that the remedy was personal only. When Mr Stubbs received the bribe when looking for tenders on behalf of his employer there was no question that of course he must return it to his employer but should he return the amount he had received having invested it in shares and receiving a profit? The court held that he had a contractual debtor–creditor relationship with Lister & Co and therefore all he owed to his employer was the money received from the bribe and not the profit. The court awarded a personal remedy.

Personal remedies include an account of profits which would usually mean that the claimant actually receives the same amount back as he would if the remedy were to be proprietary.

In *Boardman* v. *Phipps* the beneficiary claimed: (a) a declaration that the shares purchased by Boardman should be held on constructive trust for him; (b) an account of the profits received by Boardman; and (c) an order requesting that the shares be transferred to him. The House of Lords imposed a personal remedy on Boardman. This resulted in the profit on the shares being returned to them. They did not address the important question of whether Boardman held the shares on constructive trust although it was raised and accepted that where someone uses his position to get information and that information is used for personal gain it can generate a constructive trust of the property which would be proprietary in nature. If Boardman had been insolvent, then this would have been very significant as the personal remedy of an account for profits would have merely put the beneficiaries into the queue along with other creditors. The beneficiaries were able to recover the same amount as would have been recovered had he been awarded a proprietary remedy.

(b) The nature of a proprietary remedy

A proprietary remedy allows the claimant to recover any increase in value of the asset. This increase can be justified because in awarding a proprietary remedy the court is holding that the claimant owns the asset from the moment that the unauthorised profit has been made and so any increase will automatically pass with the recovery of the asset. The asset is said to be held on constructive trust for the claimant.

In *Attorney-General for Hong Kong* v. *Reid* the Privy Council considered the question of whether property purchased through bribes obtained from defendants by a prosecutor for the Crown were held on constructive trust or whether the Crown had to be satisfied with the value of the bribes themselves. Lord Templeman held that the bribes and any property purchased with the bribes were held on constructive trust for the government:

> As soon as the bribe was received it should have been paid or transferred instanter to the person who suffered from the breach of duty. Equity considers that which ought to have been done. As soon as the bribe was received, whether in cash or in kind, the false fiduciary held the bribe on a constructive trust for the person injured.

The difference between remedial and constructive trusts was discussed in Chapter 10. In *Attorney-General for Hong-Kong* v. *Reid* the institutional constructive trust was imposed automatically at the point when the profit was received. As discussed earlier the remedial constructive trust has not been used in the UK courts.

However it has been used in other jurisdictions and a remedial constructive trust was imposed in *LAC Minerals Ltd* v. *International Corona Resources Ltd* (1989) (discussed above). The difference lies in the intervention of the courts. If circumstances give rise to a constructive trust such as where a bribe has been received, then it will arise as soon as the bribe has been received without the intervention of the courts. The court cannot intervene and decide whether or not to impose the trust. If the court can impose a remedial constructive trust, it is imposing a remedy so the court can take into account such matters as the needs of creditors and whether the constructive trust is appropriate in the circumstances of the case. In the light of *Sinclair Investments* a constructive trust would not be imposed where a bribe of secret profit has been received.

(c) When does it make a difference whether the remedy is personal or proprietary?

(i) When the defendant is insolvent

The main effect of the difference in remedy arises when the defendant is insolvent. Where a personal remedy has been awarded and the defendant becomes insolvent the claimant will only rank as a creditor which means he has little hope of fully recovering the full loss. If a proprietary remedy has been awarded, the claimant is held to have an equitable interest in the property and so because his/her claim is based on ownership of the property his/her claim will rank outside the queue of creditors and the claimant will leap to the front of that queue. The claimant can recover the property in its entirety.

Recent judicial comment in *Daraydan Holdings* v. *Solland International Ltd* [2004] EWHC 622 suggests that the imposition of a constructive trust and the distortion of the queue of creditors should not be regarded as creating a problem because the property could not be regarded as rightly belonging to the fiduciary and so could never be used as part of his/her estate towards the payment of debts.

There are powerful policy reasons for ensuring that a fiduciary does not retain gains acquired in violation of fiduciary duty, and I do not consider that it should make any difference whether the fiduciary is insolvent. There is no injustice to the creditors in their not sharing in an asset for which the fiduciary has not given value, and which the fiduciary should not have had.

(Lawrence Collins J.)

EXAMPLE

Kerry and Jack are two trustees of a family trust. The trust property includes a property development firm. At a meeting of the trustees Kerry discovers that property in a certain area is about to rise in value because of a proposed merger with another firm of property developers who build very keenly sought-after high-quality houses and flats. Kerry purchases two houses in the area each for £300,000 before the merger takes place. Within two years both houses rise in value by 50 per cent so each is now worth over £450,000. The beneficiaries find out that Kerry purchased the houses because he was privy to this information through the trust and they claim that the profit on each of the houses should be transferred to them.

As Kerry is solvent the value of the increase in value must be returned to the trust. If however Kerry becomes insolvent, the beneficiaries would lose if they claimed a personal remedy. The beneficiaries would be able to claim for the profits made by Kerry but only as creditors and their claim would rank alongside all the other creditors of Kerry. It is unlikely that they could recover the full £300,000.

(ii) When the value of the asset has fallen

The other main difference between a personal and proprietary remedy arises when the value of the asset has fallen. If the asset retains its value or makes a profit, then under the personal remedy of account for profits against a solvent fiduciary the principal will receive the profit back. If the claim is a personal remedy, the fall in the value of the asset is irrelevant as the fiduciary owes the value of the asset taken at the time the fiduciary makes a profit. However by way of comparison if the asset has fallen in value, then under a proprietary remedy the claimant stands to make a loss because the claimant claims the asset as his own.

EXAMPLE

Sunil and Aaronjit are both trustees of a family trust. The trust has a large shareholding in a private company. They discover that the company is about to be publicly floated on the stock market and the value of the shares is predicted to treble. Sunil decides to purchase a number of shares for himself personally. The shares rise in value. When the beneficiaries discover that Sunil has purchased the shares for himself and made a profit they claim the profit for the trust. If it could be argued that Sunil used confidential information for personal gain, he must return any profit to the beneficiaries. However if the shares later fall in value and a personal remedy is granted, Sunil will have to return the full value of the shares at the time their value increased and he used confidential information for his own benefit whereas under a proprietary remedy the increase in value will be lost as the beneficiaries claim that the shares belong to them.

SUMMARY

This chapter examines the nature of fiduciary duties. Fiduciary duties are difficult to define. They include loyalty, to act in good faith and not to let personal interests conflict with those of the trust. Fiduciary relationships usually arise where one person has undertaken to act for another. A fiduciary relationship is presumed in certain circumstances such as between trustee–beneficiary, solicitor–client and company director–board of directors. It also arises in certain circumstances where it is not presumed but a relationship develops where the law will impose the relationship upon the parties. Not all duties owed by a fiduciary will be fiduciary in nature. A solicitor will owe a duty of care to a client which if broken will not be regarded as a breach of a fiduciary duty. Fiduciaries cannot make a profit from their position which is very strictly applied. This is illustrated by the case of *Boardman* v. *Phipps* where the court recovered profits made by a solicitor advising a trust where the trust had benefited from the fiduciary's actions. A trustee cannot purchase the trust property as it would involve a purchase from himself unless it is expressly authorised by the court or beneficiaries. This is referred to as the self-dealing rule. By contrast under the fair-dealing rule a trustee may purchase the share of a beneficiary if the transaction is shown to be at arm's length and the beneficiary is fully aware of the material facts. Any profit which is derived from his position as a fiduciary must be disgorged to the principal for instance director's fees if the directorship is directly attributable to his position such a vote from shares held by a trust as shown in *Re Macadam*. The law does not differentiate between profits made in good faith and those which are obtained fraudulently. Where a fiduciary receives a bribe this sum will be held on constructive trust for the principal as shown in *Attorney-General* v. *Reid*. This reversed the position under *Lister* v. *Stubbs* where it was held that the bribe was held only as a debtor and not on trust. Recently the *Lister* v. *Stubbs* decision has been reinstated in *Sinclair Investments* v. *Versailles Trade Finance Ltd*. Property can include confidential information received in the position as fiduciary and if this is used to make a personal profit the profit cannot be retained by the fiduciary as illustrated in *IDC* v. *Cooley*. Where the fiduciary has authorisation from the trust instrument or his principal or from the court profits may be retained. In limited cases the fiduciary can retain a profit made from an opportunity or through confidential information such as where it has been authorised by the court, the beneficiaries or under the trust instrument. A profit can also be retained where it is no longer confidential but in the public domain as shown in *Attorney-General* v. *Blake*. The fiduciary can also retain a profit where he has retired from the trust and sufficient time has elapsed since his retirement. The remedy against a fiduciary is usually proprietary which means that increases in value can be recovered and in the event of the fiduciaries' insolvency the principal's claim will be ahead of those of the creditors.

18 Breach of trust and defences to breach of trust

KEY POINTS

- a trustee can commit a breach of trust by omission as well as commission;
- the duties owed by a trustee are found in the trust instrument, statute and common law;
- a trustee is personally liable for any breach of trust;
- trustees are jointly and severally liable for breaches of trust;
- a trustee will only be liable to compensate the trust fund where there is a causal link between his own breach and the loss;
- a trustee may be entitled to an indemnity from a co-trustee;
- a trustee can seek to limit or exclude his liability for any breach of trust by relying on an exclusion clause;
- trustees can rely on a number of defences including:
  - consent from the beneficiaries;
  - a statutory defence under s.61 Trustee Act; and
  - the Limitation Act.

1 INTRODUCTION

A trustee undertakes a number of duties when taking on the role of trustee. Breach of these duties will give rise to a possible action for breach of trust by the beneficiaries. Breach can arise either by omission (omitting to carry out an act which he ought to carry out) or by commission (carrying out an act which he ought not to do).

Millett LJ described the various ways a trustee can commit a breach of trust as follows:

> Breaches of trust are of many different kinds. A breach of trust may be deliberate or inadvertent; it may consist of an actual misappropriation or misapplication of the trust property or merely an investment or other dealing which is outside the trustees' powers; it may consist of a failure to carry out a positive obligation of the trustees or merely of a want of skill and care on their part in the management of the trust property.
>
> (*Armitage* v. *Nurse* [1997] 3 WLR 1046)

The duties of a trustee can arise expressly from the trust instrument or generally from common law or under statute. Consider the following examples of how such duties arise.

(a) Duties under the trust instrument

If the trust is a fixed trust, the trust instrument will name the beneficiaries to benefit and the amount each is to receive. In this case it will be a breach of trust if the trustee distributes either to the wrong beneficiary or distributes the incorrect amount to one or more of the beneficiaries.

(b) Duties under common law

The Trustee Act 2000 and the Trustee Act 1925 and other recent legislation have together made many of the duties of a trustee statutory duties but where there are gaps in the legislation the trustee's duties will arise from common law. An example would be the duty of the trustees to provide the beneficiaries with trust accounts. Failure to provide a beneficiary with a copy of the trust accounts would be a breach of trust.

(c) Duties under statute

The Trustee Act 2000 includes detailed description of some of the duties of trustees in particular the duties owed by trustees when investing the trust property.

Section 4 describes a trustee's duty to have regard to the standard investment criteria which means that a trustee must from time to time review the investments of the trust and consider whether they are suitable and also sufficiently diversified. Failure to review the investments and to check on their suitability in relation to the specific trust could constitute a breach of trust.

2 WHAT IS A BREACH OF TRUST?

A trustee is liable for any breach of trust that causes a loss to the beneficiaries. The trustee must restore to the trust fund the property taken in breach of trust or the equivalent value.

(a) Personal liability of the trustee

Trustees are personally liable for a breach of trust to compensate the trust fund. Their liability is personal and not proprietary except where the trustee has misappropriated trust property for himself and he/she then has a duty to restore the property to the beneficiaries.

A trustee will not normally be liable for a breach of trust that occurred before he was appointed. One of the duties of a trustee is to make himself fully aware of the trust documents and he may be liable for a breach if he does not make inquiries on appointment.

A trustee will not be liable for breaches that occur after appointment unless the trustee has retired in order to facilitate a breach of trust.

Where a breach has been proved against a trustee a claim will lie against his/her estate even after he/she has died.

(b) The liability of a trustee for a breach of trust is strict

Traditionally a trustee was liable to the beneficiaries whenever a breach of trust could be identified. This was in effect strict liability. The trustee could not bring to his/her defence an argument that the breach had not caused the loss to the trust. All the beneficiary needed to do would be to point to a breach and claim back any loss that had occurred to the trust fund at the time of the breach. It was not necessary to specifically link the breach with the loss.

EXAMPLE

Sandra and David are trustees of a trust fund set up for the three children of the settlor, Chris, Dana and Eddie who are all over 18 years old. The trust instrument expressly forbids the trustees from investing in any company that is involved in the sale of tobacco and tobacco-related products. Sandra and David jointly decide to invest some of the trust funds in International Foods UK. Unknown to them the company has a subsidiary firm which sells cigars internationally. The following year all the investments fall in value and the trust fund loses 20 per cent of its value. Under the traditional approach the fact that Sandra and David have committed a breach of trust by breaching the terms of the trust instrument they would be liable for any loss that arises irrespective of whether the breach actually caused the loss to the trust. This would seem to be unfair where the value has fallen because of a general fall in the value of shares.

A fairer approach was introduced in *Target Holdings* v. *Redferns* (see below) which lays down the current test for liability of trustees for breach of trust.

(c) A trustee will only be liable for a breach which caused the loss to the trust

Target Holdings v. *Redferns* [1996] 1 AC 421

The principle laid down in this case is that a trustee will only be liable for any breach if it can be shown that the *breach of trust caused the loss to the trust*.

The facts of *Target Holdings* v. *Redferns* concern the purchase of property by a company called Crowngate with the aid of a loan of £1.5 million from Target Holdings (the mortgagees) secured against the property which was believed to be worth £2 million. The valuation of the property had been fraudulent and the property was in fact worth much less. The sum to be lent was forwarded to the solicitors Redferns, who were acting for both the purchasers and the mortgagees. The terms of the loan were that the money was not to be released by Redferns until a legal charge had been executed over the property. This was important to the mortgagees because it would ensure that they had enforceable rights in the property should Crowngate default on the mortgage. In breach of the trust, the money was advanced to Crowngate before the charge was executed and the sale completed although the charge was executed a few days later. Crowngate then defaulted on the repayments of the loan and Target Holdings repossessed and sold the property but the sum realised was £500,000 which was far less than the value of the loan. The claimants, Target Holdings sued both the valuers and the solicitors Redferns for the outstanding amount £1 million. They sued the valuers for their negligent valuation but as they were now in liquidation it was pointless to pursue them. They sued Redferns for breach of trust and claimed that they should compensate them for their loss, which was £1 million. Redferns had to concede that they had committed a breach of trust.

They received the money from Target Holdings on trust to hold it until they were given instructions to advance the money to Crowngate and they had forwarded the money before the sale was complete and before Target Holdings had instructed them to do so. However the sale was completed a few days later. Nevertheless Target Holdings sued Redferns for the breach of trust and the key issue was whether the loss suffered by Target Holdings was attributable to them.

(i) Why did Target Holdings suffer a loss?

1 the fraudulent valuation from the valuers;
2 a dramatic fall in property prices due to a recession at the time of the sale of the property.

The real reason for the loss was not the failure by Redferns to secure the charge, the charge had been secured albeit after the money had been advanced and Target Holdings had been able to repossess the property and sell it.

(ii) The decision in the Court of Appeal

The Court of Appeal upheld Target Holdings' claim and held that the liability of a trustee was strict and where a breach of trust by the trustee could be proved the trustee was liable to restore any loss to the trust fund suffered at the time irrespective of whether that loss and the breach were connected.

(iii) The decision in the House of Lords

The House of Lords reversed the decision of the Court of Appeal on the basis that Redferns could only be liable if the loss suffered by Target Holdings was attributable to the breach committed by them.

In considering the case the House of Lords was conscious that the facts of this case differed from the facts of the traditional family trust and the House thought it was inappropriate to transfer the rules from these trusts to a trust imposed in a commercial relationship.

Lord Browne-Wilkinson described the traditional trust in this way:

In relation to a traditional trust where the trust fund is held in trust for a number of beneficiaries having different, usually successive equitable interests (e.g. to A for life with remainder to B), the right of each beneficiary is to have the whole trust fund vested in the trustees so as to be available to satisfy his equitable interest when, and if, it falls into possession. Accordingly, in the case of breach of such a trust involving the wrongful paying away of trust assets, the liability of the trustee is to restore to the trust fund, often called 'the trust estate' what ought to have been there.

Lord Browne-Wilkinson then explained that the trust was now often used in a different context:

In the modern world the trust has become a valuable device in commercial and financial dealings. The fundamental principles of equity apply as much to such trusts as they do to the traditional trusts in relation to which those principles were originally formulated.

He continued by pointing out that it was important that the principles of commercial trusts and the more traditional family trust should be distinguished. The important feature of the trust in this case was that Redferns held the funds of Target Holdings on bare trust.

He accepted that the rules concerning breach of trust and the restoration of the trust fund had largely been developed on the basis of the traditional trust rather than in the commercial context:

The equitable rules of compensation for breach of trust have been largely developed in relation to such traditional trusts, where the only way in which all the beneficiaries' rights can be protected is to restore to the trust fund what ought to be there. In such a case the basic rule is that a trustee in breach of trust must restore or pay to the trust estate either the assets that have been lost to the estate by reason of the breach or compensation for such loss.

(iv) Establishing a causal link

Lord Browne-Wilkinson accepted that the common law rules of remoteness of damage and causation would not apply in cases of breach of trust but he did consider that there must be some connection between the breach of trust and the loss suffered by the trust: 'There must be some causal connection between the breach of trust and the loss to the trust estate for which compensation is recoverable, viz. the fact that the loss would not have occurred but for the breach.'

The House of Lords accepted that there had been a breach by Redferns but Target Holdings would also have to show that there was a causal connection between the breach committed and the loss suffered by Target Holdings. Lord Browne-Wilkinson and the other members of the House of Lords set aside the decision of the Court of Appeal and did not hold Redferns liable for the loss suffered by Target Holdings.

EXAMPLE

UpMarket Loans agrees to lend £1 million to Camden Housing Developments (CHD), a property development company that purchases rundown houses in North London in order to develop them and to sell them at highly inflated prices. CHD wishes to purchase two large terraced houses. UpMarket Loans has not dealt with CHD before and is concerned that the money lent is held by its solicitors until the sale has been completed. UpMarket Loans writes to Goode, Simple and Smith (GSS), a firm of solicitors acting for CHD, and state that GSS is not to forward the money to CHD until the sale has been executed. In fact CHD is involved with a complex mortgage fraud and have been borrowing large sums of money for the past year from various mortgagees. GSS is busy one Monday morning and in response to a call from CHD the money is forwarded to CHD before the sale is complete. The sale is completed two weeks later and UpMarket Loans is granted a charge over both properties. Six months later CHD fails to repay a mortgage instalment and when UpMarket Loans tries to contact CHD it learns that the company has disappeared. UpMarket Loans repossesses the properties but property prices in London are at their lowest for ten years and it only recovers £400,000. This is partly because the houses are in a much worse state of repair than the surveyor had reported. UpMarket Loans brings an action against GSS to recover the outstanding loss. They cannot sue the surveyors because they are now in liquidation.

UpMarket Loans will be successful if it can link the breach of trust committed by GSS with the loss suffered by it. According to Lord Browne-Wilkinson it must be possible to link the breach with the loss suffered. He laid down the need to find a causal link between the breach and loss. In this case the real reasons for the loss were partly the fall in property prices and partly the negligent surveyor's report on the state of repair of the properties.

(d) Cases decided after *Target Holdings*

Swindle v. *Harrison* [1997] 4 All ER 705

This case concerned a claim by a purchaser of property Mrs Harrison against a solicitor Mr Swindle who lent a client some money for the purchase of a hotel. The solicitor was going to make a hidden profit from the transaction and was also aware of the poor commercial history of the hotel. The purchaser mortgaged her own home to raise the money but she needed extra financial support in order to complete the purchase. The extra amount was lent personally by the solicitor but later the purchaser defaulted on the repayments of both loans because the purchase proved to be a financial disaster. The solicitor claimed the outstanding money from her and she counterclaimed by bringing an action against him for failing to disclose the information about the hotel's poor financial history. She argued that if she had known this she would not have proceeded with the purchase. The court held that in order to be successful she would have to show that she would not have proceeded with the transaction if she had known the full facts. The Court of Appeal found that she would still have gone ahead with the loan from the solicitor in order to finance her business and it was not his breach which caused her loss but rather the failure of the business.

A comment by Evans LJ explains the role of Mr Swindle the solicitor in this case saying that his failure to disclose:

cannot be said to have led to the making of the loan, even on a but-for-basis, precisely because disclosure of the true facts would not have affected her decision to accept it. Since she would not have accepted the loan and completed the purchase, even if full disclosure had been made to her, she would have lost the value of her equity in her home in any event.

Bristol & West Building Society v. *Mothew* [1998] Ch 1

This case also concerned a claim against a solicitor who was acting both for a lender and a borrower for incorrect advice given to the lender. The advice concerned the creditworthiness of the borrower. The lender sought compensation from the solicitor who had paid over the money to the borrower. The court had to consider the equitable liability of the solicitor who was in breach of his duty to act with due skill and care.

Millett distinguished these cases from situations where a trustee is in breach and concluded that where a fiduciary is in breach of certain duties then the common law principles will apply; whereas a trustee in breach of trust cannot plead rules of remoteness to reduce his liability once the causal connection between the breach and the loss has been found.

Equitable compensation for breach of duty of skill and care resembles common law damages in that it is awarded by way of compensation to the plaintiff of his loss. There is no reason in principle why the common law rules of causation, remoteness of damage and measure of damages should not be applied by analogy in such a case.

EXAMPLE

Tolly and Tolly (T&T) are solicitors acting for Kingsgate a property development company and Ace Lenders in the same transaction. Kingsgate are borrowing £1 million to fund a purchase of properties in an area near Surbiton, Surrey. One of the terms of the finance arrangement is that the money is not to be forwarded to Kingsgate until the charge has been finalised on the property. T&T hear informally that Kingsgate have had difficulties raising finance and have had some issues with repayments in the past but they do not disclose this to their clients Ace Lenders. In breach of this arrangement T&T forward the money to Kingsgate two weeks before the transaction is finalised. T&T later default on the loan and when Ace Lenders repossess the property it only realises half the value due to the recent rapid decline of property prices.

Can Ace Lenders recover their loss (£500,000) from T&T?

1 Breach of trust. First, they must establish a causal link between the loss and the breach by T&T according to *Target Holdings* v. *Redferns*. The real reason why the lenders did not recover their money was not the breach of trust in advancing the money before the charge had been finalised but because the property prices had fallen. If however a link had been found between the two because perhaps the charge had been improperly created and so limiting the extent of interest in the property for Ace Lenders, then other issues such as the fall in property prices would have been irrelevant and T&T would have had to carry *all* the losses suffered by the trust fund.

2 Breach of duty and care and skill. Second, Ace Lenders may rely on T&T's failure to tell them about the creditworthiness of Kingsgate. This issue is one related to the solicitor's duty of care and skill and is much closer to a breach of duty of care under negligence than a breach of trust. If Ace Lenders could show that it would not have lent money if it had been alerted to the facts known to T&T about Kingsgate, then T&T can rely on the ordinary rules of remoteness and argue that it should not carry all the losses particularly those suffered as a result of the fall in property prices.

3 JOINT LIABILITY, CONTRIBUTION AND INDEMNITY

The trustees' liability is said to be joint and several. This means that they are all liable for a breach if the beneficiaries can show that they have all committed a breach of trust. The trustee who fails to check a fellow trustee is equally in breach of trust as the trustee who wrongfully meddles in the trust property. However, where a breach of trust has occurred, the beneficiaries are entitled to choose to sue just one of them because for example the others have no money and the beneficiaries consider it to be a waste of resources to pursue them.

(a) Trustees are only liable for their own breaches of trust

Where a trustee has acted properly and has carried out his duties he will not be liable for a breach of trust by a co-trustee. Where he has failed to keep a proper check on a co-trustee his failure to act will constitute a breach of trust.

Bishopsgate Investment Management Ltd v. *Maxwell* (*No. 2*) [1994] 1 All ER 261

This case illustrates the rule about joint liability of trustees. In this case two trustees Ian and Kevin Maxwell had allowed money from a pension fund to be wrongly transferred.

One of the trustees Ian had signed blank transfer forms and he had not inquired about the transactions. He claimed that he was not liable for the losses because his brother could not prove that his omission to make inquiry led to the loss. The Court of Appeal held that this was not a case of omission but a case of commission of a breach of trust because the funds had been wrongly transferred and the second trustee (Ian) was liable for this.

EXAMPLE

Horace, Iris and Myrtle are three trustees of a fixed trust. A breach of trust has been committed by Horace who has misappropriated trust property for himself. However it is clear that Iris and Myrtle did not exercise sufficient control over Horace and so are liable themselves for a breach arising from omission to act. Iris lives on her own on a fixed income and Horace has been declared bankrupt but Myrtle has considerable assets of her own. In these circumstances the beneficiaries may choose to sue Myrtle alone.

The fact that the law will regard trustees as liable for a breach where they have omitted to act as well as where they have committed a breach may seem unfair and it may seem fairer if the trustee who actively commits a breach of trust carries a greater penalty.

EXAMPLE

Where one trustee is successfully sued by the beneficiaries he/she has the right of contribution against the other trustees. This means that in the example above where Myrtle is successfully sued by the beneficiaries she has the right to pursue the other trustees Iris and Horace. She may decide it is not worth pursuing them but if Iris were to become wealthy through an unexpected gift or lottery win she must repay Myrtle.

The apparent unfairness of the strict application of the rule that trustees are always jointly liable for a breach of trust has been addressed in s.2(1) Civil Liability (Contribution) Act 1978. The Act allows the court some discretion in apportioning liability among the trustees. Under s.2(1) contribution between the trustees will be 'such as may be found by the court to be just and equitable having regard to the extent of that person's responsibility for the damage in question'.

Further, the court has the power to grant a full or partial indemnity to any person it considers to be an innocent party in the committal of the breach.

(b) What is an indemnity?

This means that one trustee who is liable for a breach of trust could be given an exemption from liability in certain circumstances. The right to be indemnified arises from common law and can apply in a range of different situations.

(c) Where a trustee has committed a breach of trust fraudulently

If a co-trustee has acted fraudulently, then the other trustees are entitled to an indemnity from that trustee.

(d) Where one trustee alone has benefited from the breach

Bahin v. *Hughes* (1886) 31 Ch D 390

A testator had left part of his estate to his three daughters on trust. One of the daughters carried out all the duties involved in administration including making decision on investments. One daughter Mrs Edwards who later died did not give her consent to the investments made. Later it was discovered that part of the fund had been invested in unauthorised investments and had made a loss and the beneficiaries successfully sued the trustees for breach of trust. Mr Edwards (widower of Mrs Edwards) claimed that the active trustee should indemnify him against the loss to his late wife's estate. The court refused to grant an indemnity holding that the trustees were all jointly and severally liable for the losses made.

(e) Where the trustee is a solicitor and the co-trustees have relied on his advice

In *Re Partington* (1887) 57 LT 654 a solicitor was one of two trustees. He gave advice to his co-trustee about an investment in a mortgage. This type of investment was not appropriate for the trust and a loss was suffered. It was held that the solicitor trustee had to indemnify his co-trustee because he had relied on the solicitor's opinion as a professional person.

Compare the following case.

Head v. *Gould* [1898] 2 Ch 250: a lay trustee could not claim to be indemnified by a co-trustee who was a solicitor because the lay trustee had actively encouraged the co-trustee to act in breach of trust.

(f) Where a trustee is also a beneficiary

Under the rule in *Chillingworth* v. *Chambers* [1896] 1 Ch 685 where a trustee is also a beneficiary he is under a duty to indemnify his co-trustee to the extent of his beneficial interest. Where the loss is greater than his beneficial interest then that loss will be shared between the other trustees.

EXAMPLE

Dan, Fred and Robin are trustees of a large fund of £2 million. Dan has a fixed interest under the fund valued at £200,000. The three trustees take the decision to invest in unauthorised investments and the fund makes a loss of £500,000. Dan must indemnify his co-trustees to the value of £200,000 irrespective of whether he has received anything from the fund to date.

4 REMEDIES FOR BREACH OF TRUST

The nature of the remedy for breach of trust is compensatory. This means that the trustee must compensate the trust fund for any loss that it suffers as a result of the breach of trust. Therefore the basis of the claim is not to recover any profit made but to restore losses to the fund. However as seen above the liability of a trustee is now based on whether a causal link can be established between the loss to the fund and the breach of trust.

5 SPECIAL ISSUES ARISING IN BREACH OF TRUST

(a) Investment

One of the key duties of a trustee is the duty to safeguard the trust property which includes investing the fund. A number of rules have developed regarding losses that arise as a result of improper investments.

Before the Trustee Investment Act 1961 and the Trustee Act 2000 the range of investments that a trustee could make was much more narrow and so the trustee was much more at risk of making an unauthorised investment. Today the risk is greatly reduced.

(b) Purchase of unauthorised investment

Where a trustee has purchased an improper investment he will be liable for any loss which is incurred to the trust on sale of the assets.

Knott v. *Cottee* (1852) 16 Beav 77

This case concerned the purchase of foreign stock and Exchequer bills contrary to the express terms of the trust instrument which held that the trustees could only invest in government stock. The investments were sold at a loss and the trustees were liable to compensate the trust fund for that amount. Evidence from the trustees that the foreign stock would have increased in value if it had been retained and so make a profit for the trust did not reduce their liability.

(c) Improperly retaining an investment

Where a trustee improperly retains an investment and fails to sell it as instructed the trustee will be liable for the loss suffered being the difference between the value of the asset at the time he should have sold it and the actual value realised.

Fry v. Fry (1859) 28 LJ Ch 591

A testator had directed his trustees to sell some property as soon after his death as possible. The trustees advertised the property in 1836 for £1,000. The following year 1837 they received an offer of £900 which they refused. In 1843 a railway was built near the property which reduced its value considerably and the property was still unsold in 1856 when the last of the two trustees died. It was held that their estates must make good the loss to the estate of the difference between the offer received in 1837 and the actual value of the property in 1856.

(d) Improper sale of investments

Where the trustees sell authorised investments and invest in unauthorised investments they will be liable for any loss caused and in particular will be liable to reinvest in the authorised investments. This rule can appear quite harsh when put into effect as seen in the following case.

Re Massingberd's Settlement (1890) 63 LT 296

Trustees had power to invest in government stock. They decided to sell some government stock and invest in mortgages which were not authorised. No loss was suffered from the unauthorised investment but the trustees were ordered to repurchase equivalent authorised stock. The cost of the authorised investments had risen in value and the trustees had to personally fund the difference.

(e) Offsetting losses and gains

A trustee who loses on one transaction but makes a gain on another both of which were unauthorised would be tempted to argue that there is no actual loss to the trust fund. However there is an important principle that each breach of trust is to be treated independently of the other. So a loss on one breach of trust cannot be offset by a gain in another transaction.

Where a trustee is liable in respect of distinct breaches of trust, one of which resulted in a loss and the other in a gain, he is not entitled to set the gain against the loss, unless they arise in the same transaction.

(Brightman J. in *Bartlett* v. *Barclays Bank Trust Co. Ltd*
(No. 2) – discussed below)

Where the profit and loss constitute one transaction then the court will allow the losses to be offset by the gains.

Bartlett v. *Barclays Bank Trust Co. Ltd (No. 2)* [1980] Ch 515

Trustees decided to restructure investments in a fund and the investments were split into two land funds called the 'Guildford' project and the 'Old Bailey' project. The 'Guildford' project made a profit of over £271,000 while the 'Old Bailey' project made a loss of £585,000. The trustees successfully argued that the two funds were linked as the investments had been entered into at the same time. This can be seen as a fairly liberal application of the rule since the transactions could not strictly be said to be one transaction.

(f) Interest

As a general rule the beneficiaries are entitled to claim interest from the trustees as well as compensation to the fund. The rate of interest was once a set rate of 4 per cent with an increase where fraud was involved. This was inappropriate in times when interest rates were high and in more recent cases the rate has been linked to bank lending rate. The rate of interest is at the discretion of the court.

Traditionally only simple interest has been paid which is appropriate in personal actions. This was at issue in *Westdeutsche Landesbank Gironzentrale* v. *Islington LBC* [1996] 2 WLR 802 where Westdeutsche sought to recover compound interest on money lent to Islington Borough Council. They could only recover compound interest if they could establish that the money was received by the Council under trust rather than under contract. Since no trust could be proved only simple interest could be claimed.

More recently the House of Lords has revisited the issue of whether compound interest could be payable in some circumstances in *Sempra Metals Ltd* v. *HM Commissioners of Inland Revenue* [2008] 1 AC 561. By a majority decision it was held that the court has jurisdiction to award compound interest in a common law case of restitution. The circumstances were exceptional and it was felt that the award of compound interest was the only way that the courts could do justice to the claimants.

6 DEFENCES TO AN ACTION FOR BREACH OF TRUST

Although the trustee may be found to have committed a breach of trust which causes loss a trustee may escape liability to pay compensation if he can successfully raise one of a number of defences.

(a) Trustee exemption clauses

Increasingly trustees try to limit their liability by insisting that a clause be placed in the trust instrument exempting them from or limiting their liability for loss.

The extent of the trustee's rights to exclude themselves from actions for breach of trust were examined in *Armitage* v. *Nurse* [1997] 2 All ER 705 where a beneficiary brought an action for breach of trust against the trustees of a marriage settlement drawn up over property for the benefit of the mother of the beneficiary and herself. The land held for the beneficiary had been managed poorly and had fallen in value.

The trustee exemption clause in *Armitage* v. *Nurse*

The trustees relied on a clause which was phrased as follows 'no trustee shall be liable for any loss or damage which may happen to Paula's fund or any part thereof or the income thereof at any time or from any other cause whatsoever unless such loss or damage shall be caused by his own actual fraud'.

Millett LJ considered how far such a clause extended. He concluded that an exemption clause can exclude liability for breach of trust other than those breaches which occur as a result of actual fraud on the part of the trustee. Therefore the exemption clause can cover breaches which arise as a result of negligence of lack of care and skill.

I accept ... that there is an irreducible core of obligations owed by the trustees to the beneficiaries and enforceable by them which is fundamental to the trust. If the beneficiaries have no rights enforceable against the trustees, there are no trusts. But I do not accept the further submission that these core obligations include the duties of care and skill, prudence and diligence.

Dishonesty was further considered in this more recent case.

Walker v. *Stones* [2001] QB 902

In this case the court considered whether a solicitor who had honestly believed he was acting in the beneficiaries' best interests could be held to be dishonest by applying objective standards. The Court of Appeal adopted a combined approach as stated by Sir Christopher Slade: 'that clause in my judgment would not exempt the trustees from liability for breaches of trust, even if committed in the genuine belief that the course taken was in the best interests of the beneficiaries if such belief was so unreasonable that no solicitor-trustee could have held that belief'.

(b) Why do exemption clauses attract criticism?

Beneficiaries are volunteers and therefore have no recourse against a trustee who acts in breach of his duties; beneficiaries are not party to the original trust instrument and so have no input into the terms of the trust; professional trustees are paid for their services and it would be wrong to allow them to escape liability for negligence by relying on an exemption clause.

In 2006 the Law Commission published a consultation paper which recommended that such clauses should still be permitted in the case of professional trustees but that instead there was an obligation on the professional trustee to ensure that the settlor is made aware of the effect of an exemption clause in the trust instrument. The Law Commission was reluctant to suggest legislation in this area.

(c) Consent from the beneficiaries

Where a beneficiary gives consent to a trustee to carry out a certain act or the beneficiary instigates an action by the trustee this can be a complete defence in certain circumstances.

(d) Conditions for consent to be a defence for a trustee

The beneficiary giving consent:

1 must be of full age;
2 must be of sound mind; and
3 must have full knowledge of all the facts.

In *Re Pauling* (below) the courts held that a mental illness may not affect consent. So where a beneficiary was found to be schizophrenic his ability to consent to the trustees' actions would not be affected. It is also important that consent must not be given by a beneficiary while undue influence was exerted over him. If consent is given by a beneficiary immediately after he/she reaches the age of majority, then it may not be freely given but the courts held in *Re Pauling* that soon after the beneficiary reaches the age of majority it is presumed they are no longer under the influence of their parents.

Re Pauling's Settlement Trust [1964] Ch 303

Trustees were holding a fund for Miss Pauling for her life and then for her children. She married and led a lifestyle well beyond her means. On her instigation her children sought advances of income which were really for their mother's benefit. Later they brought actions against the trustees arguing that the advances had been made in breach of trust. The trustees argued that the advances had been made with the acquiescence of the beneficiaries and having given their consent they were prevented from then bringing an action for breach of trust. It was accepted that although the beneficiaries may have been under the influence of their mother while under age there was no presumption of undue influence after they reached the age of majority.

The key issue here is that the beneficiary is aware of what he/she is concurring in although it is not necessary that the beneficiary should know the action will be a breach of trust. The trustee need only show that the beneficiary is fully aware of all the facts at the time he/she consents to the trustee.

The key feature in *Re Pauling* was the fact that the beneficiaries were aware that they were consenting to an advance which was to be used towards their mother's debts rather than for their own financial needs.

The judgment of Wilberforce J. at first instance indicates when the defence might be effective:

the court has to consider all the circumstances in which the concurrence of the *cestui que trust* [beneficiary] was given with a view to seeing whether it was fair and equitable that, having his concurrence, he should afterwards turn around and sue the trustees: that, subject to this, it is not necessary that he should know that what he is concurring in is a breach of trust, provided that he fully understands what he is concurring in, and that it is not necessary that he should himself have directly benefited by the breach of trust.

EXAMPLE

Flora, Gwen, Homer and Ian are all beneficiaries under a fixed trust created by their father. Each is to receive their share when they reach the age of 30. The trust includes an express term that the trustees must not invest in publicly quoted firms on the stock market. Flora is aged 16 and lives at home with her widowed mother. Gwen, aged 20, suffers from depression and lives in sheltered housing but has a job at a local branch of the NSPCA. Homer is aged 19 and is at university and Ian is aged 22 and has a job in a local bank. Ian is appalled at the investment terms of the trust and urges the trustees to invest more widely seeing an opportunity to make substantial amounts of money. His brother Homer is suspicious of this course of action but Ian forces him to agree. His sisters both fully support him. The stock market suffers a dramatic fall and half the value of the fund is wiped out. Homer wishes to sue for breach of trust. The trustees argue that they acted with the full consent of all the beneficiaries.

The trustees were in breach of an express term of the trust. They may argue that the beneficiaries had given their consent. In this case not all the beneficiaries were capable of giving consent as Flora is under age and only the court can give consent on her behalf. Homer may not have given his consent freely. It will depend on whether he was fully aware of what he was agreeing to. Although Gwen is suffering from a mental condition this may not affect her ability to consent to the action by the trustees.

(e) Impounding the beneficiaries' share

A trustee may be entitled to be indemnified by a beneficiary who has consented to or instigated a breach of trust. Where one beneficiary has consented to the breach and the other beneficiaries successfully sue the trustee the trustee may be able to impound that beneficiary's share.

The court may order this under its inherent jurisdiction but it is strictly limited to cases where the beneficiary was fully informed of the facts at the time the breach was committed and usually only where the beneficiary instigated the breach. If the beneficiary has merely given consent to the breach, then the court will only impound his/her share if consent was given in writing and the beneficiary gained a personal benefit from the breach.

The court also has statutory powers to impound the beneficiary's interest under s.62 Trustee Act 1925 on proof that the beneficiary instigated, requested or consented to a breach.

(f) Section 61 Trustee Act 1925

Under this section the court is able to relieve a trustee of some or all of his/her liability for a breach of trust under certain conditions:

if it appears to the court that a trustee, whether personally appointed by the court or otherwise, is or may be personally liable for any breach of trust ... but has acted honestly and reasonably, and ought fairly to be excused for the breach of trust and for omitting to obtain the direction of the court in the matter in which he committed such breach, then the court may relieve him either wholly or in part from personal liability for the same.

There are three aspects to this defence: the trustee must have acted honestly, reasonably and ought fairly to be excused. The trustee must satisfy all three before the defence will be applied in his/her favour. This is a discretionary section and the court may exercise its discretion in granting relief. To prove that one comes within the section is merely a first step towards relief.

Acting honestly requires the trustee to show that he/she acted in good faith. Honesty is at the core of the trustee's role so this aspect has rarely been considered before the courts.

Perrins v. *Bellamy* [1899] 1 Ch 797

This case concerned trustees who had received advice from solicitors that they had the power to sell property. This advice was incorrect and the trustees were sued for breach of trust when they sold certain property which affected the interest of one of the beneficiaries. They relied on s.61 Trustee Act in their defence. The judge pointed out that the real issue in most case brought under this section was whether the trustee had acted reasonably:

the legislation has made the absence of all dishonesty a condition precedent to the relief of the trustee from all liability. But that is not the grit of the section. The grit is in the words 'reasonably and ought fairly to be excused for the breach of trust'.

(Kekewich J.)

Reasonably is far more contentious. To act reasonably as a trustee means that you have acted according to the standard of care expected of a trustee. Comments made by Byrne J. in *Re Turner* [1897] 1 Ch 536 suggest that it is difficult to set out any strict rules on what is considered reasonable. He said he thought it would be 'impossible to lay down any general rules or principles to be acted on in carrying out the provisions of the section, and I think each case must depend on its own circumstances'.

He continued reflecting on the section saying that the provisions of the section 'were intended to enable the court to excuse breaches of trust where the circumstances of the particular case showed reasonable conduct, but it was never meant to be used as a sort of general indemnity clause for honest men who neglect their duty'.

(g) When has the trustee acted reasonably?

In *Perrins* v. *Bellamy* (above) it was thought to be reasonable for the trustees to rely on the advice of the solicitor on whether the trustees had a power of sale.

Re Evans [1999] 2 All ER 777

In this case relief was granted to the administratrix of her father's estate. Her father had died intestate and the only two beneficiaries were herself and her brother who had been missing for over thirty years. She took out insurance before distributing the estate to herself as the sole recipient. She honestly believed her brother to be dead. He returned unexpectedly and it was found that her insurance only covered the capital due to him and not the interest payments. He sued her for her failure to take out adequate insurance. The court was sympathetic to her position particularly because she was a lay trustee of a small estate and found in her favour allowing her to rely on s.61 in her defence.

The court has taken a different approach to professional trustees and is less likely to allow a professional trustee to rely on this section.

(h) When have the courts found the trustee to act unreasonably?

Ward-Smith v. Jebb [1964] 108 Sol Jo 919

Payments were made by two trustees to a beneficiary who they believed to be entitled to such. One trustee was a solicitor and he had misinterpreted the effect of the Adoption Act 1949. The court did not relieve either him or his co-trustee of liability because it was held that it was their duty to ensure that they fully understood the effect of the law and if they did not they should seek legal advice to assist them.

Re Stuart [1897] 2 Ch 583

A trustee who had invested money by way of an equitable mortgage could not rely on s.61 because although the trustee was authorised to invest by way of mortgage the security taken was not sufficient. In this case the judge considered that the trustee had acted in a way that he would not have done if the money had been his own.

(i) Ought fairly to be relieved

Where the trustee is found to have acted fairly and honestly in most case the court will award relief to the trustee. As pointed out by Kekewich J. in *Perrins* v. *Bellamy*: 'in the absence of special circumstances, a trustee who has acted "reasonably" ought to be relieved, and it is not incumbent on the Court to consider whether he ought "fairly" to be excused, unless there is evidence of a special character showing that the provisions of the section ought not to have be applied in his favour'.

Marsden v. Regan [1954] 1 WLR 423

The defendant was the executrix of the deceased who had died with considerable debts. She had paid off all the business creditors of the deceased with the exception of the claimant who had been the landlord of the deceased's business premises. The court at first instance had found in favour of the defendant who claimed that she had acted honestly and reasonably but this was later doubted in the Court of Appeal. However the Court of Appeal held that it was for the judge to decide whether the defendant had acted reasonably and the court was unwilling to interfere with the finding at first instance.

EXAMPLE

Terry and Rupert are trustees of a trust. Terry is a solicitor and Rupert is a lay trustee. Under the terms of the trust £200,000 has been left to the Friends of Socialist Thought which appeared to be an educational charity but was in fact a front for a left-wing political organisation and was later found not to be charitable. Terry and Rupert had already distributed the funds to it before its status was challenged by the Charity Commission and when they tried to recover the money it had already been spent by them. The beneficiaries tried to recover the money from Terry and Rupert who relied on s.61 Trustee Act 1925 in their defence. The problem in this case is that Terry is a solicitor and he should have checked on the charitable status of the group. The court might be more sympathetic to a lay trustee.

(j) The Limitation Act 1980

Under s.21(3) Limitation Act 1980:

subject to the preceding provisions of this section, an action by a beneficiary to recover trust property or in respect of any breach of trust, not being an action for which a period of limitation is prescribed by any other provision of this Act shall not be brought after the expiration of six years from the date on which the right of action accrued.

The effect of this section is that a beneficiary cannot bring an action against a trustee after six years have passed.

The section refers to trustees and includes personal representatives, constructive trustees as well as express trustees.

This relief is only available for a breach of trust and not for breach of fiduciary duty. This is not covered by the statute but the common law doctrine of laches (see below) will apply.

A beneficiary under a disability is an exception although where he/she ceases to be under that disability time will begin to run again. The reason for this exception is that the beneficiary would have no means of finding out about the breach of trust.

The section expressly mentions that the right of action will not apply until the interest has accrued. In practical terms it means that for the remainderman the interest must have fallen into possession.

EXAMPLE

Venus leaves her estate for her husband Samson for his life and for her three children on his death. The trustees are Ed and Nick. They wrongly apply capital to Samson which is in breach of the trust provisions. They took advice from a solicitor who interprets the trust provisions incorrectly. They also purchase some of the assets of the estate at undervalue. None of this comes to light until after Samson's death. The application of capital to Samson is a breach of trust but the beneficiaries have only six years after their interests take effect to bring an action against them. The purchase of trust assets at undervalue by the trustees would constitute a breach of a fiduciary duty and there is no time limit for the beneficiaries to bring an action.

Section 21 Limitation Act 1980 will not apply in cases of fraud or a fraudulent breach of trust to which the trustee was a party or privy.

Thorne v. *Heard* [1894] 1 Ch 599

A solicitor was allowed to retain the proceeds of sale of trust property by the trustees which he used for his own purposes. This was a fraudulent use of the money which the trustees were unaware of. The beneficiaries brought an action outside the limitation period but the court did not apply the exception for fraud because the fraud in this case was that of the solicitor and not that of the trustee.

It will not apply to recovery of trust property from the trustee or the proceeds of sale of trust property.

Re Howlett [1949] Ch 767

This case concerned a claim by a daughter against her father who was a trustee and had retained trust property for his own benefit but had failed to pay any rent to the estate. The daughter successfully brought an action although the limitation period had already ended because the case fell within one of the exceptions within s.21(1)(b) Limitation Act 1980, namely that the trustee had retained trust property in his hands.

It is important to distinguish between claims which come within the section and those that fall outside because of the limitation period that will apply.

(k) The doctrine of laches

What is the doctrine of laches?

The doctrine of laches is an equitable doctrine which prevents an action being brought against a trustee where the claimant has unduly delayed in bringing the action because the court considers it inequitable to do so.

In most cases there is a statutory period within which an action must be brought under the Limitation Act 1980. There has been considerable debate as to whether the doctrine will apply where the statutory limitation period applies.

The doctrine is applied at the discretion of the court. Laddie J. identified a number of matters that will be relevant when deciding whether or not laches should apply:

the courts have indicated over the years some of the factors which must be taken into consideration in deciding whether the defence runs. Those factors include the period of the delay, the extent to which the defendant's position has been prejudiced by the delay, and the extent to which the prejudice was caused by the actions of the plaintiff.

(*Nelson* v. *Rye* [1996] 2 All ER 186)

In more recent cases the courts have applied the test of unconscionability. In *Patel* v. *Shah* [2005] EWCA Civ 157 the Court of Appeal prevented the claimants from asserting their property rights in property which had for many years been running at a loss but had recently risen in value. The defendants claimed that the claimants had unduly delayed in bringing an action against them.

However in *Fisher* v. *Brooker and Others* [2009] 1 WLR 1764 a claim brought after thirty years by a composer of a popular song Procul Harum's 'Whiter Shade of Pale' was not barred under the doctrine of laches. The defendants in this case had not been prejudiced by the delay, indeed they had continued to receive royalties which were due to the song's writer.

SUMMARY

This chapter examines the liability of a trustee for breach of trust. A trustee is liable for breach of trust where he fails to perform his duties under the trust instrument or common law or under statute. A trustee is liable for any breach of trust that causes loss to the beneficiaries. A breach of trust can include an omission to act such as supervising a co-trustee as well as a commission of a breach of trust. A trustee will only be liable for his own breach of trust but where a breach has been committed by the trustees as a group they are jointly and severally liable for the breach. The liability of a trustee is strict but the beneficiary must first prove that there is a causal link between the breach and the loss suffered to the trust as held in *Target Holdings* v. *Redferns*. Once a causal link has been established the rules of remoteness do not apply to trustees in cases of breach of trust. The court can apportion liability between the trustees in any way it thinks just applying the Civil Liability (Contribution) Act 1978. A trustee is entitled to be indemnified by a co-trustee in certain circumstances including where the co-trustee has acted fraudulently. Where a solicitor gives advice to his co-trustees and they rely on his advice they are entitled to be indemnified for any loss arising from his advice. Special rules apply to breaches of trust by trustees in relation to investment decisions such as the improper retention of an investment or the improper sale of an investment. The trustee is entitled to rely on a trustee exemption clause which will allow him to exempt liability for any act except where it involves dishonesty and fraud. There are a number of defences available to a trustee including a statutory defence under s.61 Trustee Act 1925 which allows them to be relieved of his/her liability if he/she acted honestly, fairly and ought fairly to be excused. Trustees can also rely on a time bar under the Limitation Act 1980 and consent given by the beneficiaries to the breach of trust. When a beneficiary gives consent he must be of full age, must give consent freely and must be fully aware of the facts.

19 Remedies against strangers to a trust

KEY POINTS

- in some circumstances a stranger to a trust may be held liable as a constructive trustee;
- a stranger may be liable if he has received trust property knowingly;
- a stranger may be liable if he has assisted in a breach of trust dishonestly;
- a stranger may be liable if he has become a trustee *de son tort*;
- the test for dishonesty is an objective test although the court can look at the state of mind of the defendant;
- traditionally knowing receipt depended on proof of a requisite level of *Baden* knowledge;
- today knowing receipt depends on proof of unconscionability;
- a stranger is liable for knowing assistance if he satisfies the test for dishonesty; and
- a trustee *de son tort* is someone who holds trust property not as a trustee but behaves as a trustee in relation to that property.

key points

1 INTRODUCTION

In some circumstances a person may be liable as if he is a trustee when he becomes involved in some way with a trust. The court can then make that person personally liable for breach of trust. The stranger will be liable to compensate the trust fund for any losses suffered. This will be particularly important where the trustees cannot be found or the trustee is bankrupt and therefore has no funds with which to compensate the trust fund.

Generally people involved with a trust other than as a trustee will not automatically become liable to compensate the trust if a loss is suffered. For example if someone gives negligent advice to the trust or acts in a negligent manner as agent to the trust his liability will lie in tort or contract.

A person involved in a trust as a 'stranger' will be liable as a trustee when evidence can be shown that he/she intermeddled in trust property either by knowing receipt of trust property or by dishonest assistance in a breach of trust or by becoming a trustee *de son tort*.

In these cases the 'stranger' becomes a constructive trustee because the courts are imposing trusteeship.

The circumstances where the court will impose trusteeship are described by Lord Selbourne in *Barnes* v. *Addy* (1874) 9 Ch App 244:

> those who create a trust clothe the trustee with a legal power and control over the trust property, imposing on him a corresponding responsibility. That responsibility, may ... be extended in equity to others who are not properly trustees, if they are found either making themselves trustees *de son tort*, or actually participating in any fraudulent conduct of the trustee ... but on the other hand, strangers are not to be made constructive trustees merely because they act as agents of trustees in transactions within their legal powers ... unless those agents receive and become chargeable with some part of the trust property, or unless they assist with knowledge in a dishonest and fraudulent design on the part of the trustees.

2 DIFFERENT TYPES OF LIABILITY AS A STRANGER TO A TRUST

(a) Knowing receipt of trust property

A person will be liable as a constructive trustee if he/she knowingly receives trust property. Liability rests on proof of knowledge which is sufficient to fix the recipient with liability, and of receipt of the trust property.

The level of knowledge required has been uncertain over the past thirty years. This is discussed later in the chapter.

EXAMPLE

Albert is trustee to a family trust. He dishonestly takes trust assets from the trust including two valuable paintings and gives one to his Uncle Bernie and one to his Uncle Carl. Uncle Bernie is suspicious of the painting and believes that the painting has come from the trust which he knows about. Uncle Carl is not suspicious, he knows nothing of the trust and thinks Albert is being kind and generous as he has made frequent unexpected gifts to him before. In both cases the paintings are later stolen. Albert is primarily liable for the loss of the paintings but if he is bankrupt the beneficiaries will look to the recipients of the property for compensation. Uncle Bernie will have to compensate the trust for its loss as he will be held to have received the trust property knowingly. Uncle Carl will not be held to be a constructive trustee because he received the trust property without the relevant knowledge. If he still had the painting, he would have to return it but now it has been stolen he is not liable to make good the loss because he is an innocent third party.

(b) Dishonest assistance in a breach of trust

A person will be liable as a constructive trustee if he/she assists in a breach of trust dishonestly. The breach of trust by the trustee need not be dishonest and could include an innocent breach of trust. In this case the stranger never receives trust property into his/her hands.

EXAMPLE

David is a trustee of a family trust. He is also running a restaurant. He wants to expand the business and he needs some cash immediately. He transfers £300,000 of the trust money into his business. His finance director Egan is aware of the source of the money. The restaurant runs into financial difficulties and David is declared bankrupt. The beneficiaries may be able to recover the lost cash from Egan on the basis that he dishonestly assisted in a breach of trust. Egan may be found liable as a constructive trustee and personally liable to compensate the trust fund for its loss.

(c) Trustee *de son tort*

Anyone who takes it upon himself to act as trustee for the benefit of beneficiaries under a trust will be liable as if he/she were a trustee. In this case the stranger will receive trust property into his/her hands but on behalf of others. This compares with knowing receipt of trust property where the stranger receives the trust property for himself and does not purport to act on behalf of others.

EXAMPLE

Fergus is a bank manager and Gregory has various deposits at the bank. Gregory is a lay trustee and he transfers all the trust funds into his bank in a separate account. Fergus sees an investment opportunity for the trust and acting without consulting Gregory, Fergus invests half the funds in the investment. It proves to be disastrous and the trust fund loses one-quarter of its value. Fergus may be liable in this situation as a trustee *de son tort*. He acted on behalf of the beneficiaries as if he were a trustee and in that situation the law would regard him as personally liable for any breach of trust.

3 PERSONAL AND PROPRIETARY REMEDIES AGAINST STRANGERS TO THE TRUST

(a) Personal liability

The liability of a trustee is personal and also strict. If the court finds a stranger to be liable as if he/she is a trustee, then his/her liability will also be personal and strict. This means that any loss to the fund must be made good from the personal funds of the stranger. As liability in this situation is personal it would cease if the stranger became bankrupt just in the same way that it ceases where a trustee becomes bankrupt.

(b) Proprietary liability

Liability may be proprietary where a stranger has trust property in his hands. If a third party who is not a beneficiary under the trust receives trust property gratuitously, he/she cannot claim it for himself and the property must be returned even where the receipt of the property is innocent. The claim of the beneficiaries to the property where it is still in the hands of the trustee will take priority where a trustee becomes bankrupt. However where the property is lost, dissipated or transferred to another then the stranger will not be liable for the loss to the trust fund. If the stranger no longer has trust property in his hands, the beneficiaries have no right of action against him/her. Proprietary remedies will be replaced by personal liability of the stranger if he/she can be said to have knowingly received trust property.

4 KNOWING RECEIPT OF TRUST PROPERTY

The trustee is strictly liable for any losses that arise to the trust fund through his breach of trust. If the trustee takes property in breach and transfers it to a third party, the trustee will be liable to restore that property or make good the loss to the trust fund. In most cases the beneficiaries will be able to recover any losses from the trustee once they have established a breach and a causal link between the breach and the loss.

(a) What if the trustee has no money or has just been declared bankrupt?

Where the trustee has been declared bankrupt an action for breach of trust will not result in the restoration of the loss to the trust fund.

If someone else received the trust property as a volunteer, the beneficiaries can recover the property from them regardless of whether they knew it was trust property or not.

EXAMPLE

Joy is a trustee of a trust fund comprising valuable jewellery. Lucy and Mary are the beneficiaries. Joy takes a diamond brooch from the trust fund in breach of trust and gives it to her niece Kay. Kay believes it is a present in anticipation of her marriage in a few months' time. Lucy and Mary can recover the brooch from Kay as they have the equitable title to the trust property. If Kay sells the brooch and dissipates the proceeds, Lucy and Mary cannot force Kay to make good the loss as she would not be held to be a constructive trustee.

Further, if the beneficiaries can prove that the stranger has knowingly received the property but has now disposed of it, then the beneficiaries may be able to enforce their rights against the stranger as constructive trustee and the stranger will have to compensate the trust for the loss.

EXAMPLE

Joy is trustee of a trust fund comprising valuable jewellery. Lucy and Mary are the beneficiaries. Joy takes an emerald necklace from the trust fund in breach of trust and gives it to her goddaughter Norma. Norma is aware that it could be from the trust because Joy told her about the fabulous pieces of jewellery in the fund last year. Norma sells the necklace and spends the proceeds on a luxury holiday for herself and her new husband. Lucy and Mary could enforce their rights against Norma as constructive trustee and she would be forced to compensate the trust fund for the value of the emerald necklace.

(b) Where property is received by a stranger in exchange for valuable consideration the beneficiaries cannot pursue their claim against the purchaser unless he was aware of the trust at the time of receipt

He can plead the defence of bona fide purchaser for value without notice.
The action relies on proof of the following elements:

1 a disposal of assets in breach of trust or in breach of fiduciary duty;
2 receipt of the trust property by the stranger; and
3 the requisite standard of knowledge.

(i) Disposal of assets in breach of trust or in breach of fiduciary duty

The first requirement for the claimant must be to establish that the assets have been disposed of in breach of trust or breach of fiduciary duty. This is not just confined to breaches of trust by a trustee. It could include a range of different situations including the transfer of assets by a company director in breach of his fiduciary duty.

(ii) Receipt of trust property

The beneficiaries can only pursue a stranger who has received the property for his own benefit. If someone merely 'holds' the trust property in their name, then he cannot be liable as a stranger: 'the recipient must have received the trust property for his own use and benefit' (Millett J. in *Agip (Africa) Ltd* v. *Jackson* [1990] Ch 265). So where someone receives trust property in what can be termed 'ministerial capacity' rather than 'beneficial capacity' he/she will not become a constructive trustee. In this case the defendants were not held liable because they had received money as agents rather than beneficially.

The property received must be in an identifiable form. This is fairly straightforward where trustees takes trust assets from the trust fund and transfer them to another individual. In commercial transactions where assets are taken in breach of fiduciary duty and then passed through several different people it may be more difficult to prove actual receipt of the trust property.

El Anjou v. *Dollar Land Holdings* [1993] 3 All ER 717

An agent of a wealthy investor was persuaded to invest in a number of companies which were simply nominal companies set up for fraudulent trading in shares.

The investment was made and the monies passed through several different hands and through different jurisdictions eventually being invested in England in a property development company called Dollar Land Holdings Ltd. The claimant brought an action against Dollar Land Holdings Ltd on the basis that it had knowingly received trust property. Although at first instance Millett J. was not convinced that the company had sufficient knowledge to establish liability he was prepared to hold that there had been receipt of the property by Dollar Land Holdings Ltd. This aspect of Millett's judgment was upheld by the Court of Appeal.

(iii) Knowledge

The degree of knowledge necessary before a stranger becomes liable has been subject to some debate. Indeed it has been suggested that liability for knowing receipt should be strict and the receipt of trust property should be all that is necessary for the claimant to prove.

In spite of this, liability for knowing receipt of trust property is still fault based so the beneficiaries must prove some degree of knowledge before the stranger will be liable.

Knowledge need not be fraudulent or dishonest and ignoring the obvious may give rise to liability.

Vinelott J. made it clear in *Eagle Trust plc* v. *SBC Securities Ltd* [1992] 4 All ER 488 that it was not necessary to show that there had been dishonesty, merely that there had been 'knowledge':

in a 'knowing receipt' case it is only necessary to show that the defendant knew that the money paid to him were trust moneys and of circumstances which made the payment a misapplication of them. Unlike a 'knowing assistance' case it is not necessary to show that the defendant was in any sense a participator in the fraud.

Although it is not necessary to prove dishonesty or fraud the claimant must show that the defendant 'received' the trust property with relevant knowledge.

Belmont Finance Corp v. *Williams Furniture Ltd (No. 2)* [1980] 1 All ER 393

A number of company directors, who were all aware that a scheme for the unlawful purchase of shares was an improper use of funds were held liable for knowing receipt of funds even though they had not acted fraudulently.

The Court of Appeal held that it was not necessary to prove fraud merely that they had knowledge or ought to have known that the money that each received from the sale of the shares was money impressed with the trust.

(c) The *Baden* test for knowledge

The courts have traditionally approached the issue of what constitutes sufficient knowledge by trying to categorise the various types of knowledge into different levels.

In *Baden Delvaux and Lecuit* v. *Société Générale* [1983] BCLC 325, HC; [1993] 1 WLR 509 Peter Gibson J. set out a scale of knowledge that a stranger may hold when receiving trust property (the *Baden* levels of knowledge):

1 actual knowledge;
2 wilfully shutting one's eyes to the obvious (sometimes known as Nelsonian blindness);
3 wilfully and recklessly failing to make such inquiries as an honest and reasonable man would make;
4 knowledge of circumstances which would indicate the facts to an honest and reasonable man; and
5 knowledge of circumstances which would put an honest and reasonable man on inquiry.

The different levels can be split into two groups. The first three levels involve subjective elements and the last two levels involve an objective assessment. The last two categories are also categories based on negligence rather than deliberate wrongdoing. The categories suggest that the recipient of the property has failed to make inquiries negligently rather than dishonestly.

EXAMPLE

Selina is given a present of a valuable picture by her boyfriend Tito. She knows he has no money and is surprised by his generosity. She is unaware that he is a trustee and she fails to ask any questions about the source of the gift.

If Selina is aware that Tito has recently been made a trustee and that coincides with the receipt of the gift, then she has wilfully and recklessly failed to make inquiries that an honest man would make. It is the fact that she is aware that he is trustee that would take her from categories 4 and 5 into category 3.

Re Montagu's Settlement Trusts [1987] Ch 264

This case concerned property held in trust for successive generations of Dukes of Manchester. The tenth Duke of Manchester had agreed to draw up an inventory of chattels in the estate while the ninth Duke was still alive. He failed to do this and when the ninth Duke died the tenth Duke inherited all the chattels but without an inventory of them all. Some were left to him personally and the rest formed part of the trust. The tenth Duke sold a substantial number of the chattels and on his death the eleventh Duke claimed that many of these were chattels that belonged to the trust. He brought an action against the tenth Duke's estate for knowing receipt of trust property and claimed that it should either return the missing chattels or compensate the trust for their value.

The court held that although he had received trust property he had not received it with 'knowledge' not whether he had 'notice' of prior interests in the trust property. Megarry VC stated that in order to be liable the conscience of the defendant must be affected which required 'want of probity'. He found that only the first three levels of *Baden* knowledge would establish 'want of probity' and not the knowledge of circumstances which would indicate the facts to an honest and reasonable man.

Megarry's view of what is necessary in order to establish 'knowing receipt' has received judicial support and subsequent cases have tended to look more closely at the 'conscience' of the defendant.

(d) An alternative test for knowledge in knowing receipt cases: has the conscience of the defendant been affected?

The following cases have followed Megarry's view of the test for knowing receipt.

Hillsdown Holdings plc v. *Pensions Ombudsman* [1997] 1 All ER 862

This case concerned a company which had persuaded the trustees to transfer funds from the pension fund to itself. The company was held liable for 'knowing receipt':

in considering whether a constructive trust has arisen in a case of the knowing receipt of trust property, the basic question is whether the conscience of the recipient is sufficiently affected to justify the imposition of such a trust.

BCCI v. *Akindele* [2001] Ch 437

A entered into an artificial loan agreement with BCCI with the intention of giving an impression of liquidity to the outside world which was false. The arrangement was that A would pay money to the company in order to purchase shares for himself but the shares would be repurchased by the company at a higher price which would always give a fixed return to A of 15 per cent. When the company became insolvent the liquidator sought to recover the loss from A arguing that he had sufficient knowledge of the moneys received to make him liable for knowing receipt of trust money.

The court decided that when the defendant paid the money to the company before he received the shares there was nothing to suggest that it was operating a fraudulent scheme and A was unaware of any fraudulent activity.

Nourse LJ considered the various tests for knowing receipt and concluded:

I have come to the view that, just as there is now a single test of dishonesty for knowing assistance, so ought there to be a single test of knowledge for knowing receipt. The recipient's state of knowledge must be such as to make it unconscionable for him to retain the benefit of the receipt. A test in that form, though it cannot, any more than any other, avoid difficulties of application, ought to avoid those of definition and allocation to which previous categorisations, have led.

The view of Nourse LJ appears to be the test to apply in cases of knowing receipt rather than the *Baden* levels of knowledge which have difficulties in application. However to suggest that liability arises from unconscionability is not without difficulties because it is not clear what behaviour is unconscionable.

5 DISHONEST ASSISTANCE IN A BREACH OF TRUST

A third party or accessory may be liable to make good the loss to the trust fund without ever holding the trust property beneficially and without ever purporting to act as trustee. The accessory merely 'assists' in a breach of trust. However in order to be liable his behaviour must be dishonest.

The case of *Royal Brunei Airlines* v. *Tan* (below) [1995] 2 AC 378 sets out the modern law in this area following principles laid down earlier in *Baden Delvaux*. It laid down that four requirements must first be proved for a successful claim against a stranger for assistance in a breach of trust:

1 there must be a trust;
2 there must be breach of trust – this could be an innocent breach as well as a fraudulent breach;
3 there must be assistance in the breach of trust. Assistance is construed as conduct which actively assists in the breach of trust. In *Brinks Ltd* v. *Abu-Saleh and Others* (*No. 3*) The Times 23 Oct 1995 the wife of a bank robber who took large amounts of gold bullion to Switzerland could not be held to assist in a breach of trust where she was unaware of the purpose of the visits. She had simply accompanied her husband on their trips abroad and she could not be found to be an accessory to the breach. Her behaviour was at most acquiescence in the breach which could not be sufficient to found liability;
4 the stranger must be dishonest.

Royal Brunei Airlines v. *Tan* [1995] 2 AC 378

The case concerned a travel agent who was appointed as agent for an airline. It was to receive payments for ticket sales to be held on trust until they were forwarded to the airline. Instead of keeping the sums separate the travel agent paid money received from ticket sales into its own current account using the money for its own purposes.

The airline terminated the contract when the agency fell into arrears with the payments. The agency then became insolvent. As a result the airline sought to recover the sums from the agency's managing director and principal shareholder Mr Tan.

The case was eventually heard by the Privy Council and two issues were considered by the court:

1 in cases of dishonest assistance must the claimant show that the trustee had acted dishonestly or fraudulently as well as the accessory:
2 what was the test for dishonesty for the accessory?

(a) Dishonesty on the part of the trustee (the travel agent)

In cases of dishonest assistance prior to *Tan* the claimant had to show that both the trustee and the stranger had been dishonest. If the trustee had committed a breach of trust but it was a technical and/or innocent breach of trust, the stranger would escape liability.

In this case the agency had not been fraudulent but it had committed a breach of trust in paying the money received from customers into its own account rather than keeping the sums separate.

Lord Nicholls reviewed the previous authorities and held that liability for an accessory was no longer dependent on a finding that the trustee was also acting dishonestly or fraudulently. The key issue was whether the accessory was acting dishonestly:

dishonesty on the part of the third party would seem to be sufficient basis for his liability, irrespective of the state of mind of the trustee who is in breach of trust. It is difficult to see why, if the third party dishonestly assisted in a breach, there should be a further prerequisite to his liability, namely that the trustee also must have been acting dishonestly.

(b) The test for dishonesty for the accessory (Mr Tan)

Although the travel agency had not acted fraudulently Mr Tan had acted dishonestly. Lord Nicholls considered the second question of what constitutes dishonesty for an accessory to a breach of trust.

The Privy Council rejected the categories of knowledge set out in *Baden* for cases of accessory liability:

'knowingly' is better avoided as a defining ingredient of the principle, and in the context of this principle the *Baden* ... scale of knowledge is best forgotten.

(Lord Nicholls)

The Privy Council preferred instead to use 'dishonesty' as a basis of liability of an accessory. Lord Nicholls described how the courts would assess dishonesty:

honesty has a connotation of subjectivity, as distinct from the objectivity of negligence. Honesty, indeed, does have a strong subjective element in that it is a description of a type of conduct assessed in the light of what a person actually knew at the time, as distinct from what a reasonable person would have known or appreciated.

He continued:

for the most part dishonesty is to be equated with conscious impropriety. However, these subjective characteristics of honesty do not mean that individuals are free to set their own standards of honesty in particular circumstances. The standard of what constitutes honest conduct is not subjective. Honesty is not an optional scale, with higher or lower values according to the moral standards of each individual.

He concluded that a purely subjective test could not be used: 'If a person knowingly appropriates another's property, he will not escape a finding of dishonesty simply because he sees nothing wrong in such behaviour.'

The Privy Council took an objective view of what constituted 'dishonesty' in *Tan*.

The courts have grappled with the problem of the test for dishonesty. The issue for the courts is which of the following tests should be applied:

1 A purely subjective test: this is sometimes referred to as the 'Robin Hood test' whereby the defendant can escape liability by arguing that according to his standards his behaviour was not dishonest. The subjective standard was rejected by the court in *Tan* and also in subsequent cases.

2 A purely objective test: this test applies an objective standard of dishonesty whereby the same test is applied to every defendant and his/her understanding of dishonest conduct is ignored.

3 A combined test: under this test the conduct is assessed by the ordinary standards but it must be shown that the defendant realised that by this standard his conduct was dishonest. This combines the objective test with the subjective elements taking into account what the defendant actually believed. This draws on the test used in criminal law under *R* v. *Ghosh* [1982] QB 901 where the court considers whether the defendant would have known that what he was doing would be regarded as dishonest by honest people.

The test laid down by Lord Nicholls in *Royal Brunei Airlines* v. *Tan* (above) has been reviewed in a number of subsequent cases which are considered below.

Twinsectra Ltd v. Yardley [2002] 2 All ER 377

This case concerned a solicitor Mr Leach who had transferred money in breach of trust to a borrower, Mr Yardley. The money had been held in trust for the lender, Twinsectra Ltd by another firm of solicitors Roper and Sims who were trustees on its behalf. The money was transferred to Roper and Sims on the explicit instructions that the money should only be used by Mr Yardley for specific property acquisitions and not generally for other purposes. Mr Leach advanced the money without ensuring that the specific instructions were followed. The money was used for other purposes and Mr Yardley defaulted on the repayments. The instructions concerning use of the funds had been explained by Mr Sims to Mr Leach at the time of the transfer of the funds to him.

Although the Court of Appeal held that Mr Leach was liable for dishonest assistance the House of Lords rejected the claim of Twinsectra because although Mr Leach had been negligent it held that he had not been dishonest. The House applied a 'combined' test for dishonesty.

(c) The test for dishonesty in *Twinsectra* v. *Yardley*

(i) Lord Hutton

The key judgment in the case was given by Lord Hutton. He considered that the test for dishonesty should revolve around:

1 first, looking at what reasonable and honest men consider to be dishonest; and
2 second, looking at whether the defendant considered what he had done was dishonest by the standards of honest and reasonable men.

In the case of Mr Leach the court had to consider whether his actions could be dishonest according to the standards of reasonable and honest men and second whether Mr Leach believed that what he was doing was dishonest by the standards of reasonable and honest men. In this case the court would consider solicitors acting in the same transaction as Mr Leach.

I think that it would be less than just for the law to permit a finding that a defendant had been 'dishonest' in assisting in a breach of trust where he knew of the facts which created the trust and its breach but had not been aware that what he was doing would be regarded by honest men as being dishonest.

Mr Leach was not liable because he did not think that what he did was dishonest by the standards of reasonable and honest solicitors. It would be possible to argue that this test allows the defendant a chance to escape liability by pleading ignorance of the standards of ordinary and honest people albeit similar to himself.

(ii) Lord Millett

Lord Millett gave a dissenting judgment in which he argued that the test should be an objective test which had an element of subjectivity such as the expertise of this particular defendant. He preferred the objective test adopted by Lord Nicholls in *Tan*.

In my opinion Lord Nicholls was adopting an objective standard of dishonesty by which the defendant is expected to attain the standard which would be observed by an honest person placed in similar circumstances. Account must be taken of subjective considerations such as the defendant's experience and intelligence and his actual state of knowledge at the relevant time. But it is not necessary that he should actually have appreciated that he was acting dishonestly; it is sufficient that he was.

The 'combined test' laid down in this case has been subject to considerable criticism because of its subjective element. It has been revisited and redefined in subsequent cases.

Barlow Clowes International Ltd (in liquidation) v. *Eurotrust International Ltd* [2006] 1 WLR 1476

A defendant, Mr Henwood, sought to escape liability by pleading that he could only be dishonest if he was aware that he was dishonest by ordinary standards of honest and reasonable men. He was a director of a company, Eurotrust in the Isle of Man which ran offshore financial services. It had received money from Barlow Clowes and an associated company which had been founded to run a fraudulent investment business. His company had been receiving exceptionally large sums of money and it was argued that he should have been aware that the money he received belonged to investors. Barlow Clowes went into liquidation and the receiver sought to recover losses suffered by the investors from Eurotrust.

There were some clear differences in the facts in this case. Mr Henwood the defendant was very different from Mr Leach in *Twinsectra* v. *Yardley*. He must have had suspicions at the time when the large sums of money passed into his company that the money belonged to the general public. He was shown to be aware of the dishonesty of the parties he was dealing with.

Although the Court of Appeal found he was not dishonest because he could not be shown to be dishonest by subjective standards he was found to be dishonest by the Privy Council who revisited the combined test laid down in *Twinsectra* v. *Yardley*. It reviewed the subjective element of the test and the reasoning in the House of Lords. The court had to account for the earlier approach taken by the House of Lords and it did so by reinterpreting the way the House of Lords had come to its conclusions.

(iii) Lord Hoffmann

The reference to 'what he knows would offend normally accepted standards of honest conduct' meant only that his knowledge of the transaction had to be such as to render his participation contrary to normally acceptable standards of honest conduct. It did not require that he should have had reflections about what those normally acceptable standards were.

He continued with a comment on his own speech in *Twinsectra*:

similarly in the speech of Lord Hoffmann, the statement that a dishonest state of mind meant 'consciousness that one is transgressing ordinary standards of behaviour' was in their Lordships' view intended to require consciousness of those elements of the transaction which makes participation transgress ordinary standards of honest behaviour. It does not require him to have thought about what those standards were.

The test for dishonesty under *Barlow Clowes* v. *Eurotrust* is a test which allows the court to consider whether the actions of the defendant were dishonest by the normally acceptable standards of honest conduct. It did not require the defendant to have thought what the normally acceptable standards might be.

The test for dishonesty has been revisited by both the Court of Appeal and High Court since *Barlow Clowes* v. *Eurotrust* but not by the Supreme Court.

Abou-Rahmah v. Abacha [2007] 1 Lloyd's Rep 115

This case concerned a claim by a lawyer practising in Kuwait and a Kuwaiti trading company against a Nigerian bank, City Express Bank. They were victims of a fraud which had been perpetrated by the defendants who had persuaded them to invest large sums of money in a trust. The claimants paid the money into a bank account held at the bank. The defendants disappeared and the claimants never received the investments. The claimants sought to recover their loss from the bank arguing that it had dishonestly assisted in the breach of trust.

Applying the test from *Barlow Clowes* v. *Eurotrust* the Court of Appeal held that the bank was not liable. The claimants would have to show that when the bank received the money from the defendants it suspected that they were involved in a fraud. The court found that a general suspicion would not be enough.

EXAMPLE

Standard Investment Bankers International is an international bank situated in Switzerland. The turnover in a single week can amount to the equivalent of £3 million. A customer arouses suspicions when deposits in a single week amount to £300,000 when previously activity on the account never amounted to more than £100,000. When asked about the increase in activity in the account the customer explains that he has had an unusually successful period as a private investor. The large deposits continue intermittently for several months.

It is discovered that the customer has been taking investment monies from clients and depositing them in his own account. He has absconded with the money which he withdrew last week from the bank. Can the bank be found liable as an accessory?

The bank can only be liable if it has behaved in a way that is dishonest according to the ordinary standards of reasonable and honest men. The court in *Abou-Rahmah* v. *Abacha* was at pains to point out that any general suspicion that the bank may have about the behaviour of a customer can only give rise to liability if the bank's suspicions about a customer were specific rather than general.

Attorney-General of Zambia v. *Meer Care & Desai* [2008] EWCA Civ 1007

The issues were again revisited in this case where the various tests were reviewed by the Court of Appeal. The case involved a claim against a solicitor who had received funds into his client account which were the proceeds of a complex fraud. The question was whether he had behaved dishonestly.

The judge at first instance held that dishonesty in these cases depended on a question of fact whereby the state of mind of the defendant had to be judged not in the light of his subjective knowledge but by reference to an objective standard of honesty.

Smith J. held that:

the test is clearly an objective test but the breach involves a subjective assessment of the person in question in the light of what he knew at the time as distinct from what a reasonable person would have known or appreciated ... merely because a person says he did not believe what he did was dishonest does not mean the court has to accept that. If the court is of the opinion that with his knowledge he consciously departed from the objective standards of propriety he is dishonest.

The judge at first instance had found that the solicitor had been dishonest but the Court of Appeal disagreed. It considered that the judge at first instance had applied the test for dishonesty incompetently because the judge had assumed that the solicitor was competent. The court seems to suggest that the court can objectively evaluate the competency of the defendant. It is possible to find that a solicitor is not dishonest even though a competent solicitor would have recognised that what he was doing was dishonest.

(d) Conclusions of the test for dishonesty in dishonest assistance

The test for dishonesty continues to involve a subjective element but it has reverted to an objective test. The main difference in the test after *Barlow Clowes* v. *Eurotrust* is that it is no longer possible for the defendant to set his own standards of what he perceived as dishonest. However it is possible for the courts to apply a subjective standard by evaluating the defendant's conduct against the standards of similar people.

6 TRUSTEE *DE SON TORT*

Where a person who has not been appointed trustee intermeddles with the trust and takes it upon himself to act as if he were trustee he will be held liable as if he were in fact a properly appointed trustee.

Those who, though not appointed trustees, take on themselves to act as such and to possess and administer trust property for the beneficiary, become trustees *de son tort*.

(Ungoed-Thomas J. in *Selangor United Rubber Estates Ltd* v. *Cradock (No. 3)* [1968] 2 All ER 1073)

Blyth v. *Fladgate* [1891] 1 Ch 337

A firm of solicitors held assets of a marriage settlement after all the trustees had died and at the request of the husband the assets were lent on mortgage. As there were no active trustees the firm appeared to step into the role of trustees itself. Later there was a shortfall after the security had been sold and the claimants sought to recover the loss from the solicitors' firm because it had acted as if it were a trustee.

The firm was held liable to compensate the settlement for the loss that it had suffered.

In these cases there can be no claim against the stranger unless it can be shown that the trust property or its equivalent was transferred into his/her hands. While it remains in the trustee *de son tort*'s hands the property can be recovered by the beneficiaries who will have proprietary rights and their claim will take priority above any creditors should the trustee *de son tort* later become bankrupt.

SUMMARY

This chapter considers the liability of strangers who become involved in a trust and whether a third party who has not been appointed as a trustee can be held to be a constructive trustee. There are three separate circumstances when a stranger can be liable as a constructive trustee: when he is a trustee *de son tort*; when he knowingly receives trust property for his own benefit or he dishonestly assists in a breach of trust. A stranger will be held to be a trustee *de son tort* where he has acted as if he were a trustee but had not been expressly appointed. A stranger will be liable for the receipt of trust property if he has received trust property beneficially and it is unconscionable for him to retain it as held in *BCCI* v. *Akindele*. This test replaces the former test which laid down that liability rested on different levels of knowledge which were referred to as the *Baden* levels of knowledge. The third situation when a stranger may be liable as a constructive trustee is where a third party dishonestly assists in a breach of trust. In order to find a stranger liable as a constructive trustee in these circumstances the claimant must prove there is a breach of trust and the stranger has assisted in that breach dishonestly. The test for dishonesty has been considered in a number of recent cases. The House of Lords introduced a combined test in *Twinsectra* v. *Yardley* combining a subjective and objective test but this has been revisited in *Barlow Clowes* v. *Eurotrust* by the Privy Council who held that the test for dishonesty should be an objective test but it incorporates a subjective level by allowing a court to consider the competency of a particular defendant but not allowing a defendant to set his own standards of honesty.

20 Tracing

KEY POINTS

- tracing is neither a claim nor a remedy but a process;
- tracing is a proprietary claim and gives the claimant priority over creditors in bankruptcy and also allows any increases in value to be claimed;
- tracing allows the claimant to claim a substitute asset for his own;
- tracing should be distinguished from following which allows the claimant to recover his asset as it moves through the hands of different people;
- tracing at common law is based on legal ownership of property;
- tracing at common law ceases where funds become mixed unless the asset can be separated from the whole;
- tracing in equity allows tracing into mixed funds;
- in order to trace in equity the claimant must prove a fiduciary relationship and an equitable interest in the property;
- where a trustee mixes trust funds with his own funds in a bank account the rules always presume that the trustee withdraws his own funds first;
- where funds in a bank account of a trustee are dissipated a beneficiary can claim against any asset purchased by the trustee with the funds;
- where funds of two innocent volunteers are mixed the court traditionally could choose either to apply *Clayton*'s *Case* or distribute the funds *pari passu*, which is today the preferred method; and
- the right to trace ceases when the assets have been dissipated or when the property is in the hands of a bona fide purchaser for value or when it is inequitable to trace.

1 INTRODUCTION: WHAT IS TRACING?

Tracing is a process or mechanism which involves the owner of property identifying an asset in the hands of a third party. Tracing is not a remedy nor is it a claim.

Lord Millett described tracing as follows:

it ... is neither a claim nor a remedy. It is merely the process by which a claimant demonstrates what has happened to his property, identifies its proceeds and the persons who have handled or received them, and justifies his claim that the proceeds can properly be regarded as representing his property.

(*Foskett* v. *McKeown* [2001] 1 AC 102)

EXAMPLE

A trustee Mike takes a valuable antique table which belongs to the trust and gives it to his cousin Nerys who sells it to her friend Olive.

The beneficiaries have proprietary rights in the table and can claim it back from Nerys. When Nerys sells the table to Olive the beneficiaries have rights to trace into the money which represents the proceeds of sale of the asset.

Tracing is a proprietary claim giving the claimant all the advantages of claiming rights in property as opposed to personal rights against an individual. This has two clear advantages:

1 it allows the claimant's rights to take priority over others in bankruptcy in particular ordinary creditors (anyone who is owed money by the bankrupt but who does not have special priority);
2 it also allows the claimant to claim any increase in value of the property.

One contentious issue concerning tracing is whether there should be one single right to trace or should there be a separate right to trace at common law and a separate right to trace in equity. Lord Millett has been one of the fiercest critics of retaining the two distinct claims: 'given its nature there is nothing inherently legal or equitable about the tracing exercise. There is no sense in maintaining different rules for tracing at law and in equity.'

In spite of his criticism and call for a uniform set of rules to apply, the two separate rights to trace remain.

2 TRACING AND FOLLOWING

Following is another way of locating assets but it is distinct from tracing. Lord Millett described the difference as follows:

> following is the process of following the same asset as it moves from hand to hand. Tracing is the process of identifying a new asset as the substitute for the original asset into the hands of the new owner or to trace its value into the new asset in the hands of the same owner.
>
> *(Foskett v. McKeown)*

Following can allow the claimant to claim assets where they have become mixed with others but the right will cease where the assets are destroyed. It is based on identification of the asset so when an asset is mixed it may still be able to identify a part of the whole.

EXAMPLE

Jeffrey is a farmer. Some of his grain is stolen by Crook. Crook mixes it in a silo with some of his own grain. The silo then holds grain part of which can be claimed by Jeffrey and part belongs to Crook. It is perfectly possible for Jeffrey to claim a share of the wheat in the silo. However if all the wheat is sold by Crook then Jeffrey would cease to be able to follow the asset but there may be a right to trace into the substitute asset, i.e. the proceeds from the sale.

3 TRACING AND CLAIMING AT COMMON LAW

Common law recognises the right of a claimant to trace his own property provided the property has not been mixed. It is based on legal ownership of the property.

(a) Common law tracing through clean substitutions

The right to trace at common law can subsist through clean substitutions of one type of property for another as illustrated by the following case.

Taylor v. Plumer (1815) 3 M & S 562

Sir Thomas Plumer gave his stockbroker Walsh a bank draft with instructions to invest in Exchequer bills. Walsh who was in financial difficulties ignored the instructions and invested partly in bullion and partly in American securities. He tried to abscond but was caught. He was bankrupt and his trustee in bankruptcy claimed the bullion and securities. It was held that Sir Thomas Plumer had a good claim at law as he could trace through the money given to Walsh into the substitute property.

The important point here is that the substituted property in the above case American securities and bullion for the bank draft retains a form that can easily be identified. The actual form of the property can undergo any number of changes so long as there is always an identifiable substitute after each change.

Banque Belge pour L'Etranger v. *Hambrouck* [1921] 1 KB 321

Similar facts arose in this case where Hambrouck a cashier at a bank had forged cheques taken from his employers and then paid them into his account. Later he took money from his account and transferred it to his mistress who paid the money into her account. The court held that it was possible for the bank to trace into her account and recover the money. It was important that neither Hambrouck nor she had mixed the money with any money of their own.

Jones & Sons (a firm) v. *Jones* [1996] 3 WLR 703

In this case it was held that money could be traced at common law through clean substitutions and it was also possible to recover an increase in the value of the substitute property. A firm of potato growers got into financial difficulties. Just before it was adjudicated bankrupt one of the partners gave a cheque to his wife for £11,700 from the partnership funds. The timing of this was such that the court regarded it as an act of bankruptcy. The wife used this sum to invest in potato futures and received £50,760 which was paid into a deposit account which had no previous funds in it. The trustee in bankruptcy claimed the sum in the deposit account. He argued successfully that once the cheque had been taken from the partnership it belonged to the trustee in bankruptcy because it had been taken immediately before the partnership was declared bankrupt and so the wife could never have title to it. As a result, title to the money already vested in the trustee in bankruptcy when the wife received it and any profit made with the money would vest in the trustee in bankruptcy and could not be claimed by the wife.

Lipkin Gorman v. *Karpnale* [1991] 2 AC 548

Common law tracing was considered by the House of Lords in this case where a firm of solicitors sought to recover money that had been paid to the Playboy Club by one of their partners, Cass. He had taken the money from the firm's account and spent it gambling at the club. The House of Lords concluded that although the firm had no proprietary right in the money drawn from it by Cass, it could claim that the bank's debt was a 'chose in action' (meaning giving a right to recover a sum of money) which was the legal property of the claimant firm. Cass had withdrawn the money from the firm and that created a debt in favour of the firm, the debt was transferred to the club and as the money was paid under an illegal contract (a gambling contract) they could not claim to be bona fide purchasers for value so the right to trace was not lost. The firm were entitled to recover their money at common law for money 'had and received'. In this case it is important to consider the debt as property owned by the firm and capable of recovery.

(b) Common law tracing through mixed funds

An important feature of all the above cases was that at no time was the money received mixed with other funds. The right to trace would be lost as soon as the money was mixed with other funds as pointed out by Lord Ellenborough in *Taylor* v. *Plumer* (above):

for the product of or substitute for the original thing still follows the nature of the thing itself, as long as it can be ascertained as such, and the right only ceases when the means of ascertainment fail, which is the case when the subject is turned into money, and mixed and confounded in a general mass of the same description.

Where funds are traced through intangible goods such as money a problem arises where the money has passed through several different bank accounts because of the risk that the money will become mixed with other monies through the clearing process.

This is illustrated by the complex facts of the following case.

Agip (Africa) Ltd v. *Jackson* [1990] 1 Ch 265

The claimant firm (Agip) was defrauded by its own accountant, who had fraudulently substituted the names of the defendants on a number of payment orders signed on behalf of Agip. The monies were taken from an account in a bank in Tunisia and telexed through the New York clearing system through to a branch of Lloyds Bank in London with an order to take monies from Agip's account. The name on one of the payment orders was a dummy company called Baker Oil Services Ltd who had the account at Lloyds bank. Instructions were then given by a New York bank that the London bank should be reimbursed through the New York clearing system. Unfortunately this never happened because by the time the instruction was received the money in the Lloyds account had been paid. Later Lloyds Bank discovered the fraud and tried to recover what monies remained in the account. The defendants claimed they had been acting innocently throughout. Most of the money had been extracted from the account but what remained was claimed by the claimant company who argued that it had the right to trace at common law.

The right to trace at common law was refused both at first instance and on appeal. The right to trace in equity was upheld (this is discussed below). There was no right to trace at common law because it was impossible to identify the money paid into the defendant's account as money belonging to the claimant company. All that had happened was that instructions were given by Agip and in the words of Millett J.: 'nothing passed between Tunisia and London but a stream of electrons'. This view is a less convincing reason than looking at the source of the money which was from the New York banking system where the money had inevitably become mixed with other sources of money and so could not be properly traced at common law. This was a mixed substitution of intangible goods.

Although intangible goods, in particular money, cannot be traced into a mixed fund it is possible to trace into a mixed bulk of tangible property such as grain or oil or even shares. The important point in these cases is that the bulk remains complete.

Indian Oil Corporation Ltd v. Greenstone Shipping Co. SA (Panama) (The Ypatianna) [1988] QB 345

This issue was discussed in this case. Staughton J. explained how the court may resolve the problem:

where B wrongfully mixes goods of A with goods of his own, which are substantially of the same nature and quality, and they cannot in practice be separated, the mixture is held in common and A is entitled to receive out of it a quantity equal to that of his goods which went into the mixture, any doubt as to that quantity being resolved in favour of A.

This principle was followed in further cases. In *Glencore International AG* v. *Metro Trading International Inc.* (*No. 2*) [2001] 1 Lloyd's Rep 284 tracing at common law was allowed where the product, in this case oil, was treated in such a way that it produced a new product. The claimant company could still trace into the whole and claim a proportion for itself.

EXAMPLE

If crude oil is stolen from Oil Products UK and is then mixed fraudulently with crude oil from Dodgy Oil International, it is possible to trace into the mixture. Although the oil is from two different sources it is possible to calculate the proportions of the whole by simply working out the proportions when they were mixed together.

4 TRACING IN EQUITY

The rules of tracing in equity are far more flexible than those of common law. This allows tracing through mixed funds and the rules of tracing in equity have been particularly useful when seeking to trace through a bank account which contains mixed funds.

(a) The right to trace in equity

The claim to trace in equity is based on proof of two requirements:

- proof of an initial fiduciary relationship; and
- the claimant has an equitable title or beneficial interest and not the legal title of the property.

(i) Proof of an initial fiduciary relationship

The right to trace in equity can only arise where it can be proved that there was an initial fiduciary relationship between the claimant and the person who has misappropriated the funds.

This requirement has been repeated over many years in cases concerned with the right to trace in equity.

In *Sinclair* v. *Brougham* [1914] AC 398 the House of Lords had commented that a right to property recognised by equity 'depends upon there having existed at some stage a fiduciary relationship of some kind ... sufficient to give rise to the equitable right of property'.

This recognition of the need for a fiduciary relationship was repeated some years later by Lord Greene MR in *Re Diplock* (below) who said:

equity may operate on the conscience not merely of those who acquire a legal title in breach of some trust, express or constructive, or some other fiduciary obligation, but of volunteers provided that as a result of what has gone before some equitable proprietary interest has been created and attaches to the property in the hands of the volunteer.

Re Diplock [1948] Ch 465

This case concerned a number of distributions to various charities which were successfully challenged by the next of kin on the basis that they failed as charitable gifts. The wording of the gifts had allowed the possibility that the gifts could be made for purposes which were not exclusively charitable. The next of kin then sought to trace into the accounts of the charities in order to recover the money. They could do so because there had been a fiduciary relationship between the executors and those benefiting under the estate.

(a) Example where no fiduciary relationship existed

In *Jones (FC) & Sons (a firm)* v. *Jones* (above) there would have been no right to trace for the trustee in bankruptcy if Mrs Jones had mixed the money from the partnership with other money in the account. First, the right to trace at common law would have been lost because the funds would have been mixed; second, the right to trace in equity could not have arisen because Mrs Jones did not owe any fiduciary duties when she received the money and so there was no initial fiduciary relationship.

(b) Example where a fiduciary relationship has been found to exist after the misappropriation of the funds

The need to show first that a fiduciary relationship existed may give rise to difficulties so sometimes the court has been prepared to find a fiduciary relationship on which to found a right to trace in equity. This search for such a relationship can seem to be artificial and seems to undermine the requirement.

This can be illustrated by the following case.

Chase Manhattan Bank NA v. *Israeli–British Bank (London) Ltd* [1981] Ch 105

By accident the Chase Manhattan Bank paid $1 million to the Israeli-British Bank twice in the same day. It was purely a clerical error. The Israeli-British Bank was already financially insecure and became bankrupt almost immediately and Chase Manhattan wanted to recover the second payment by tracing in equity. If they could trace in equity, the claim would be proprietary and would rank above other creditors.

There was no fiduciary relationship between the two banks in their ordinary trading relationship. The money was part of a commercial transaction and was not subject to a trust. However it was possible to find a fiduciary relationship when the second payment was made because that was paid under a mistake and that would immediately give rise to a fiduciary relationship:

a person who pays money to another under a factual mistake retains an equitable property in it and the conscience of that other is subjected to a fiduciary duty to respect his proprietary right.

(Goulding J.)

(ii) The claimant has an equitable title or beneficial interest and not the legal title of the property

Tracing in equity is based on showing that the claimant has an equitable interest in the property. Once the claimant can show a fiduciary relationship, an equitable interest in the property automatically arises because it is now subject to a trust.

These are some situations where such a relationship exists allowing the right to trace in equity as set out in the following several situations and examples.

Trustee and beneficiary

The obvious example is the right of a beneficiary to trace in equity against the trustee who has misappropriated trust funds.

An example arose in which one of the key cases on the basis of the right to trace in equity is the following case.

Foskett v. McKeown [2001] AC 102

This case concerned a trustee Mr Murphy who had received money from various investors who wished to invest in a land development project in Portugal. In 1986 Mr Murphy took out a life assurance policy on his own life which on his death would pay out £1 million to his dependants. The policy required five payments each of approximately £10,000. Three of the premiums were paid out of his personal funds but he used the money he held on trust for the investors for two of the premiums. Mr Murphy committed suicide in 1991 and the claimant beneficiaries (the investors) claimed a share of the £1 million paid out on his death as opposed to merely the amount taken from the fund approximately £20,000.

The House of Lords held that the investors and the beneficiaries of the property held on trust by Mr Murphy, were entitled to a pro rata share of the proceeds of the amount paid out by the insurers which amounted to £400,000. The basis of their claim was their proprietary interest in the money paid over to Mr Murphy which was held on trust for them. This money could then be traced into the insurance policy and as they had a proprietary right they were entitled to any increase in the value of the policy.

Lord Millett explained the process as follows: 'It is, however of crucial importance in the present case to appreciate that the purchasers do not trace the premiums directly into the insurance money. They trace them into the policy and thence into the proceeds of the policy.'

Profits received by a fiduciary in breach of duty

In Chapter 17 it was concluded that profits received in the form of bribes by a fiduciary in breach of his relationship may be held under constructive trust. This was a reversal in the law arising in *Attorney-General for Hong Kong* v. *Reid* [1994] 1 All ER 1 from a rule laid down in *Lister & Co.* v. *Stubbs* (1890) 45 Ch D 1. In *Reid*, it was possible to trace into the fund received by Reid in breach of his fiduciary duty which he had used to purchase property in New Zealand. It was possible to trace directly into the properties in that case.

Stolen funds

The issue of whether it is possible to trace in equity against a thief has been considered in several cases.

In *Westdeutsche Landesbank Girozentrale* v. *Islington Borough Council* [1996] AC 669 Lord Browne-Wilkinson commented: 'I agree that the stolen moneys are traceable in equity. But the proprietary interest which equity is enforcing in such circumstances arises under a constructive, not a resulting trust ... money stolen from a bank account can be traced in equity.'

The suggestion here is that the right to trace arises from the fact that the thief cannot gain title to the property, it remains with the owner and the fraudulent nature of his action will give rise to a constructive trust.

(b) Tracing in equity through a mixed fund

Tracing through a mixed fund is allowed in equity as long as the property remains identifiable. Unlike common law it is possible to claim into assets, which have been mixed with assets belonging to the fiduciary, or trustee. The law has long been based on a presumption against the trustee. The claimant will always be able to claim that he/she has the first claim over any property and any increase in value can be claimed by the beneficiary as seen above in *Foskett* v. *McKeown*.

(i) Tracing in equity through the banking system

The majority of cases of tracing in equity will concern funds in a bank account. A number of rules and presumptions have emerged over the years which guide the court when deciding how a limited fund is to be split between the various claimants in particular between the trustee and the beneficiaries.

(ii) Trustee mixes own funds with those of beneficiaries

(a) The rule in *Re Hallett's Estate*

This rule lays down that where a trustee withdraws money from a bank account containing a mixture of trust money and money of his own, the trustee is deemed to be withdrawing his own money first. This is sometimes called the presumption of the honest trustee.

Re Hallett's Estate (1879) 13 Ch D 696

The case concerned a solicitor who had taken money from a trust account and mixed it in his own bank account. He later took various payments out from the account and although there was enough money to pay the trust fund back in total there was not enough in the account to pay all the debts of the solicitor.

The rule was applied allowing the beneficiaries to claim that the money taken out was deemed to be that of the solicitor. This allows the beneficiaries to claim any money left in the account for themselves.

(b) The rule in *Re Oatway*

This rule reverses the presumption of the honest trustee in *Re Hallett's Estate* and lays down that where a trustee uses money from a mixed account to purchase an asset, the trustee is assumed to have used trust monies to buy the asset. This allows the beneficiaries to claim rights in an asset where the bank account does not have sufficient funds to satisfy their claims.

Re Oatway [1903] 2 Ch 356

A solicitor had misappropriated trust funds over a period of time and had gradually spent the funds so that there was nothing left in the account. The beneficiaries claimed a right over assets which had been purchased with the money namely some shares which had increased in value. The court held that the beneficiaries had a good claim for the shares.

However it should be noted that the beneficiaries do not have the right to claim an asset where there are sufficient funds in the bank account to pay the claim of the beneficiaries. They may prefer to claim an asset because it may have risen in value rather than the money in the bank account.

(c) The rule in *Roscoe* v. *Winder*

This rule limits the claim of a beneficiary in a bank account to a sum equivalent to the lowest intermediate balance. This means that the claim is limited to what is in the bank account at the time of the appropriation. If the trustee pays in money after the trust funds have been deposited, then that money is clearly not money that can be claimed by the beneficiaries.

Roscoe v. *Winder* [1915] 1 Ch 62

This case concerned a fiduciary Mr Wigham who as part of a sale of a company agreed to collect all the debts of the company and to pay them over to the seller. He did collect the debts but he withdrew them for his own purposes and only £25 was left in the account. He then paid in substantial amounts from his own funds and then later died. The sellers of the company wanted to claim the debts owed to them from the account but the court held that the most they could claim was £25 as that was the lowest sum in the account after he had withdrawn various amounts.

> **EXAMPLE**
>
> Ben is trustee of the Campion Family Trust (CFT) and he takes various sums from the trust over a period of six months, mixing the money with funds in his own account. In January he has £1,000 in his account and he takes £4,000 from the CFT and deposits it into his bank account. In February, he takes a further £3,000 from CFT and deposits it in the account. In April, he withdraws £6,000 to pay for a luxury cruise. In June he wins a considerable sum gambling and deposits £4,000. In July, he falls seriously ill and dies. The beneficiaries claim the remaining money in his account. However under the rule in *Roscoe* v. *Winder* the beneficiaries are limited to the lowest sum before he made the deposits of money in June. In April, the funds stood at £8,000 and then he withdrew £6,000 to pay for the cruise so the most the beneficiaries can claim through tracing is £2,000.

(c) Where the funds of two innocent volunteers are mixed the first monies deposited are presumed to be the first monies taken out under the rule in *Clayton's Case* unless this produces an unfair result and then *pari passu* is applied

If the trustee or fiduciary has misappropriated funds from two different trust funds and deposited them in his own account but not mixed them with his own money, the problem for the court is to decide how to act fairly to two innocent claimants. Two rules have emerged to be applied in these situations.

(i) *Clayton's Case* (1816) 1 Mer 572

This rule holds that where funds are deposited which belong to an innocent volunteer and are followed by funds of a second innocent volunteer any withdrawals will always fall against the first deposit and so if any money remains in the account the second claimant has a better claim than the first.

> **EXAMPLE**
>
> Vivien is trustee of the Baker Trust (BT) and the Cobra Trust (CT) and the Delta Trust (DT). In January she takes £5,000 from BT and deposits it in her account. In February she takes £4,000 from CT and then in March she takes £6,000 from DT.

She decides to spend some of the money on her daughter's wedding in June and takes out £8,000. The breach of trust is discovered in July and Vivien is declared bankrupt. All three trusts wish to claim a share of the money that remains in her bank account.

Under the rule in *Clayton's Case* BT loses everything and CT can only claim £1,000. However DT can claim the whole of the remaining £6,000. This can seem a very unfair rule as it is purely fortuitous that the money was taken from BT first and DT last.

(ii) *Pari passu*

It often seems very unfair that one trust fund or one innocent volunteer can recover all the funds that have been taken whereas the other fund loses everything. A fairer way is to divide the funds in the account proportionately between the claimants according to how much has been taken.

EXAMPLE

Kathryn is a solicitor acting for a number of clients. Over a period of a year she extracts funds from three clients' accounts and deposits them in a new bank account in her own name. In January she takes £5,000 from Mr Willing and in July she takes £5,000 from Mrs Trusting and in November she takes £10,000 from Miss Innocent. In December she takes out £10,000 to throw a Christmas party for all her friends. In January her misdoings are discovered. The three clients all want their money back but she is declared bankrupt. If *Clayton's Case* were applied, Mr W would get back nothing nor would Mrs T but Miss I could claim back everything. Under *pari passu* the funds in the account would be added up and then divided proportionately between them. One-quarter to Mr W one-quarter to Mrs T and one-half to Miss I. There remains £10,000 in the account. So Mr W would get £2,500 as would Mrs T but Miss I would get £5,000. Under this rule Miss I gets considerably less but applying *pari passu* does appear to be fairer to the parties taken together as a group.

The rule in *Clayton's Case* will not be applied where it would produce an unjust or inequitable result. This can be illustrated by *Barlow Clowes International Ltd (in liquidation) v. Vaughan* [1992] 4 All ER 22. Money in an investment scheme had been dissipated and the company was now in liquidation. A large number of investors had lost their money and the issue was how their claims could be satisfied. At first instance the court applied the rule in *Clayton's Case* and held that the funds should be distributed on a 'first in first out' basis. The Court of Appeal reversed this decision. Woolf LJ commented that 'because of their shared misfortune the investors will be presumed to have intended the rule not to apply'. *Pari passu* applied to the distribution of the funds instead.

(iii) The North American method

There is a third possible approach to sharing limited funds in an account between a number of innocent claimants. This is the 'North American method' where the loss is distributed among the parties at each withdrawal from the fund. This is a much more subtle method than *pari passu* but it is also much more complicated and has been rejected by the courts in England. Lawrence Collins J. commented in *Commerzbank Aktiengesellschaft* v. *IMB Morgan plc* [2004] EWHC 2771 that the method was 'impracticable and unjust' and it remains to be seen whether UK courts will ever embrace it.

(d) Limits of equitable tracing

There are limitations on the right to trace in equity in spite of the ability to trace into mixed funds.

(i) Where the funds are in the hands of the bona fide purchaser for value without notice of the equitable interests

Where trust property is purchased by a bona fide purchaser for value, he will take the property free of the beneficiaries' interests provided that he does not have notice of their rights. The key issues are:

1 Whether consideration had been provided; whether the purchase has taken place in good faith; whether the purchaser has notice of the rights.
2 If the property is transferred to a volunteer, then the property can be traced. It is only where the property is purchased that the right to trace will cease.

EXAMPLE

Connie receives a valuable vase from her friend Dave. She does not know that Dave has taken it from a trust fund in breach of trust. When the beneficiaries discover the breach they have the right to recover the vase from Connie. In this case Connie is a volunteer.

Compare these facts:

Dave sells Connie a valuable vase for a reasonable price. Connie is aware that she is getting a good bargain and agrees the price. It is later discovered that Dave has taken the vase in breach of trust. In this case Connie could argue that she is a bona fide purchaser for value and the beneficiaries would have to pursue Dave for the value of the vase.

(ii) Where the funds have been dissipated

The right to trace will be lost where the funds are dissipated or destroyed. The reason for this is that there is no longer any specific property into which the parties can trace.

Examples included spending the funds on a holiday or a meal in a restaurant. It also includes attempting to trace into overdrawn bank accounts.

In *Bishopsgate Investment Management Ltd* v. *Homan* [1995] Ch 211 it was held that it was not possible to trace into an overdrawn account and money paid into an account by a trustee to reduce his overdraft could not be traceable.

Where the money from the trust is used to discharge a secured debt, e.g. payment under a mortgage it is possible for the rights of the beneficiaries to be subrogated to the position of the secured creditor. This means the beneficiaries will take the position of the mortgagees. This was applied in *Boscawen* v. *Bajwa* [1995] 4 All ER 769 where money had been lent on mortgage by a bank to a purchaser. The seller also had a mortgage. The bank forwarded the money on behalf of the seller's solicitors who used it to discharge the seller's mortgage. The seller subsequently went bankrupt and the sale never went through. Under subrogation the rights of the bank were transferred to the rights of the original lenders and could now take effect as a charge on the property. The importance of this was that the bank's interest now took priority over the interests of other creditors.

(iii) Where it is inequitable to trace

It would be inequitable to trace where the recipient's position has changed significantly since the receipt of the property.

This is illustrated in *Re Diplock* (discussed above). A number of charities had spent the money in order to improve property. Technically the claimants could trace into the properties and place a charge over the property. The charge would allow the claimants to force a sale. The courts viewed this as inequitable particularly in view of the fact that in each case it was a charity that owned the property. It is also possible to argue that it would be difficult to place a value on the improvements made to the properties and so it would be difficult to quantify the interest that the claimants would hold in each property.

SUMMARY

This chapter considers tracing both at common law and in equity. It shows that tracing is neither a remedy nor a cause of action but a process allowing recovery of property. Tracing gives proprietary rights which carry with them priority over creditors in bankruptcy and also the right to claim any increase in value of the assets claimed. However, common law tracing has a serious limitation because it ceases where property becomes mixed and ceases to be readily identifiable. It is this limitation that prevents common law tracing in many cases. The right to trace in equity does not cease where property is mixed but it does cease where property is dissipated or sold to a bona fide purchaser for value without notice of the rights or it is inequitable to trace as shown in *Re Diplock*. Tracing in equity is dependent on proof of two requirements: a fiduciary relationship and an equitable interest in the property. The courts have been prepared to find a fiduciary relationship in circumstances where it would not necessarily arise. An example is shown in the case of *Chase Manhattan Bank NA* v. *Israeli-British Bank (London) Ltd*. A number of rules have developed in connection with how the courts should approach mixed funds in a bank account. The rules in *Re Hallett* and *Re Oatway* show us that the courts lean against the trustee when he has mixed his own funds with those of the beneficiaries. However in cases where funds of two or more innocent volunteers have been mixed in one account by a trustee and are insufficient to satisfy all the claims the courts try to act fairly towards all the parties. The rule in *Clayton's Case* is applied where assets of two or more innocent volunteers are mixed together in one bank account and the court holds that 'the first money in will be deemed the first money out'. This rule does not always produce a fair result because it may be a matter of chance when money was first deposited by the trustee in breach of trust. Today *pari passu* is often applied allowing the apportionment of the remaining funds between all the innocent claimants.

INDEX